# HELPING MEN Change

To my husband, Bill Ress,
whose unwavering support, clarity of perspective, and
belief in the importance of this project
were essential to both the process and product
of this book

# HELPING MEN *Change*

## THE ROLE OF THE FEMALE THERAPIST

## BETH M. ERICKSON

**SAGE** Publications
*International Educational and Professional Publisher*
Newbury Park   London   New Delhi

*For information address*:

 SAGE Publications, Inc.
2455 Teller Road
Newbury Park, California 91320

SAGE Publications Ltd.
6 Bonhill Street
London EC2A 4PU
United Kingdom

SAGE Publications India Pvt. Ltd.
M-32 Market
Greater Kailash I
New Delhi 110 048 India

Printed in the United States of America

**Library of Congress Cataloging-in-Publication Data**

Erickson, Beth M.
    Helping men change : the role of the female therapist / Beth M. Erickson.
        p. cm.
    Includes bibliographical references and index.
    ISBN 0-8039-4545-0 (cl)
    1. Men—Mental health. 2. Women psychotherapists.
3. Psychotherapy. 4. Psychotherapist and patient. I. Title.
    [DNLM: 1. Psychotherapy. 2. Role. 3. Physician—Patient
Relations.  WM 420 E675h 1993]
RC451.4.M45E75  1993                                    93-2675
155.6'32—dc20                                              CIP

93  94  95  96  10  9  8  7  6  5  4  3  2  1

Sage Production Editor:  Judith L. Hunter

# Contents

# Foreword

The usefulness of Beth Erickson's book is readily apparent. However, the importance of Erickson's contribution can be appreciated only through an understanding of the monumental current crisis in society, gender, family, and psychotherapy. Family therapy has developed at a time when family life is undergoing the most wrenching change in history: the decline and fall of patriarchy.

For the past two hundred years, each generation of men has had less power and each generation of women has had more options than the last. It is all happening with dazzling speed. Any expectation of marriage and family will be inappropriate. The structure of family life has changed so rapidly that each generation seems stuck with a useless, inapplicable model from the last generation. Few children grow up in families they would be able to re-create, much less want to re-create. Each generation—in fact each couple—has the challenge of having to create some workable model of postpatriarchal family life.

Furthermore, everything a child learns about his or her own gender or about the gender of his or her eventual partner will be outdated before it can be put into effect.

And the bulwark against confusion and despair, the beacon of hope and wisdom amidst all this chaos, is family systems theory and therapy, which has influenced essentially all of the psychotherapies. Family therapy has the charge of clearing a path through the rubble, providing wisdom and foresight, even when the changes happen so rapidly they spin the heads of professionals at the change.

Even the family therapists have been floating in the cultural soup. Our notions of the paths to mental health and happiness have been products of our times. And the times of collapsing patriarchy have been disorienting.

In the '40s, family therapy, or the antecedent of family therapy, centered on preaching and teaching the principles of patriarchal family life, as if the patriarchal, sex-hating, woman-fearing male God of war demanded the gender arrangements then in style, and would inflict mental illness on anyone who wavered.

In the '50s, family therapy feared the weakening of patriarchy and organized a big mother bash, a Freudian witch-hunt, in which the evil mothers no longer put hexes on their children, but loved them into insanity. Mothers were sent back to the kitchen, while therapists tried desperately to strengthen fathers by bowing and scraping before them. Men were considered too delicate to change, so therapy consisted of letting them watch while therapists bashed the womenfolk in the family.

In the revolutionary '60s, family therapy recoiled from patriarchy and militarism. Therapists glorified adolescents instead, and blamed everything on parents in general. We thought changing the world meant traveling in earth shoes and love beads, helping people to escape society and family life. Family therapy began to see family as the illness, not the cure. One thing all family therapists had in common back then was the firm conviction that families drive people crazy and that parents are the root cause of mental illness. The solution to most of life's problems was to leave home.

In the narcissistic, postrevolutionary '70s, no one dared display adult tendencies or have values. Ostensibly neutral family therapists, each armed with his or her own designer techniques, decided that wisdom was out and gimmicks were in. Family therapy of the '70s was perfect for a world in which people wanted the freedom to live well without the responsibility of growing up.

Every irresponsible thing the client did was his or her family's fault. When the patient screwed up, the patient didn't have to change, but the family did.

By the '80s, Rachel Hare-Mustin and others had noticed that there were two genders and they were not identical and inter-changeable. Family therapy suddenly became three dimensional! It was a liberating time for men, women, and their therapists.

But soon, all problems were considered to have been caused by society (i.e., straight white males) and only political solutions were thought to be workable. It began to seem politically incorrect for therapists to notice anything except gender power discrepancies and men's abuse of women.

Family therapy in the '80s bashed men the way family therapy in the '50s had bashed women. A popular wisecrack defined a "dysfunctional" family as "one with a man in it." The favorite therapeutic goal of the era was to free people from the tyranny of marriage. Divorce was considered not just normal but healthy. I fully expected some therapist to go on TV and announce that any child whose parents hadn't divorced lately was deprived.

At every decade there have been excuses, and we have found things that worked and things that didn't. We've been trying to help families find a way to reorganize as patriarchy collapsed. Directly or indirectly (we've got to get over the naive conceit that we can be neutral and that our values don't influence our clients) we've encouraged our clients and our society to bash women in the '50s, to run away from home in the '60s, to refuse to create families in the '70s, and to bash men in the '80s. We've tried everything except coming together as equals. Maybe we zigged when we should have zagged because we didn't see the problem clearly: Patriarchy was collapsing and it disoriented people about what they were to do with their genders. People didn't know how to make families anymore, and we were too neutral or too confused to tell them.

People are scared. The world is changing too fast and the family is not keeping up. At the moment, the divorce rate is so high, no child in America can expect to grow up in a stable family. Men and boys raised without fathers are getting increasingly and predictably violent in their efforts to approximate a model of masculinity when they have never known a grown man in domestication. Many women, understandably, have given up on men except as an intermittent diversion and something to complain about. More and more women and girls decide to eschew the impermanent sham of marriage, and try to raise their children alone, which will produce a generation of men who are even more confused than the last.

With the welcome but still disorienting collapse of patriarchy, we can set up families without men, but then we have to find something for the men to do other than to spread sperm and violence. It's a mess: not only the most rapaciously self-indulgent but also the most violent society the world has ever known, and getting worse. We have given our blessing to the destruction of the family and we have called it mental health, but as we stand here in this jungle, what do we do for an encore? Did we really have to destroy the family to repeal patriarchy? Are men really beyond change?

We haven't seen the last of patriarchy yet. But it is not too soon for us therapists to start preparing men for the postpatriarchal world. Perhaps the thrust of the '90s will be the discovery of the forgotten gender: men. Just in the last few years, a literature on men has emerged. Some of it calls for a return to patriarchy. Some of it realized there is no going back, yet decries men's dependency on women and need for female affirmation of masculine identity. Some of it applies a feminist consciousness to the experience of men. From this literature, men might be understood as fellow sufferers from patriarchy, as confused and fatherless boys who lack guides and mentors in developing from boyhood into manhood, as pitiful creatures drowning in shame because they don't have nearly as much power as women, other men, cultural mythology, and their own fathers expected them to have. But what men experience as men is clearly very different from the insensitive, power-grabbing, abusive monster women experienced in the feminist literature. Both are clearly right, but both are only part of the picture.

The current gender revolution has focused mostly on the benefits of women treating women and men treating men, both helping the members of their gender to appreciate the shared gender experience and to stop seeing themselves only through the eyes of the "opposite sex."

I used to say that everyone needed, at some point in life, a therapist of each gender. That is both patriarchal and silly, as it assumes that each therapist is a representative of his or her gender, and serves primarily as a gender object, if not a sex object, to his or her clients. Obviously, good therapists should be far enough past their own gender fear, gender anger, gender dependency, gender lust, to experience the experiences of people of both genders.

It does not always work out that way. Some female therapists are still so outraged by the abuses of patriarchy that they don't care much about the plight of men. Others shrink from these revelations because they fear getting sucked back in to the great mother role of sacrificing themselves as they take care of men. And there are male therapists who fear female criticism to such a degree that they recoil from all that is traditionally male and are first in line to bash men for being men. There are male therapists who resist the feminist critique, who ridicule the male sensitivity literature, and who bravely pretend that patriarchy is still in style and Henry VIII is still on the throne. I'm distrustful of any therapist, male or female, who does not fully resonate with the psychology and experience of both genders.

Rich Meth and Rob Pasick, in their 1990 groundbreaker *Men in Therapy: The Challenge of Change*, opened up men to therapeutic dissection. They presented men as we really are, away from the macho posturing, the patriarchal myths, and the feminist nightmares, and told therapists how men could be changed.

Beth Erickson's book is the next step in leading therapists out of the postpatriarchal rubble. Erickson's book is intended to help female therapists see how men suffer and how women can help. It does that beautifully, but it does much more. It is vigorously empowering both to female therapists and to male clients. Erickson is unafraid either of male power or of male pitifulness. She's not angry with men and she knows men can change. She clearly likes men, but is not seduced by male ploys. She comfortably understands all a solid therapist needs to know about boundaries, therapy, gender, families, and change, and then some. She doesn't need tricks, and she ignores the famous tricky therapists. Instead she cites solid, highly gender sensitive therapists such as Jan Kramer, Gus Napier, Meth and Pasick, Bepko and Krestan, Marilyn Mason, Lois Braverman, and Pearl Rosenberg.

I read *Helping Men Change* while on vacation in South Carolina, looking across the marshes Pat Conroy made famous in his novel *The Prince of Tides*. I kept making the inevitable comparison between Beth

Erickson and Barbra Streisand's Dr. Lowenstein, who treated Nick Nolte for his impotence and shame over his failure to rescue himself and, more importantly, his mother and sister from a brutal rape. Dr. Lowenstein did not seem to know how to do therapy with a man who looked so strong and felt so weak, so she seduced him, and not only had an affair with him, but put him up to bullying her nasty husband and teaching her son to play football. The therapy was patriarchal, with the female therapist going both helpless and seductive in order to make the man feel powerful. The therapy did work in a way, and Nolte was able to return to his wife and daughters and resume both working and loving, but each time he would drive across the marsh he would call out "Lowenstein, Lowenstein."

We don't know what Streisand's Dr. Lowenstein called out as she went to work, but if I were her supervisor, I would tell her she would do well to call out "Erickson, Erickson."

Beth Erickson, unlike Dr. Lowenstein, is both a postpatriarchal therapist and a highly sensible person. She has written a highly sensible book that teaches women to respect men and change them, rather than to nurture and protect them. And while it is directed toward the women who would treat men, it is an enlightening and steadying book for any therapist. I'm a better man and a better therapist for having read it.

Erickson! Erickson!

Frank Pittman, MD

# Preface and Acknowledgments

I began the long journey of writing this book about helping men change not because I believe that men need to do all the changing in the world or in relationships. They don't. Rather, I wrote it because I felt called to articulate what I had come to understand about relating to men through my own clinical and personal encounters.

I decided to write it with women as my primary audience because I wanted to talk with people who may realize that, after a lifetime of relating to men in one capacity or another, they likely still don't fathom fully the male experience. Heaven knows, many men do not! After all, as women, it is harder still for us to grasp fully the contradictions of men's lives. How is it, for instance, that men, who have been so privileged in the overt power arena, can also feel so impotent and incompetent in other spheres of their lives? What compels men to deny or to cover up their internal experience? Why do men have such confounding ways of manifesting their feelings, especially their fears? Perhaps it can help us all if both men and women can come to appreciate the harsh reality of many men's daily lives that Keen articulates (1991, p. 83).

[Men are] trapped within modern masculine madness and can't find
the exit; we live in the urgency of the moment, captive to quarterly
reports and the trends of the day, but desperately needing an opening
beyond the present to something that offers us more hope and dignity.

I also wrote this book to empower therapists—both women and
men—to act as men's shamans on their journey toward more hope
and dignity. Otherwise, we as a culture will be no further ahead,
despite all the apparent advances toward equality made over the
past four decades.

Rather than to join the chorus of women who appear to be
saying, to paraphrase the words of the song from *My Fair Lady*, "Why
can't a man be like a woman?" most of the time I do not wish that.
Instead, I wish to assist men in retaining and celebrating the best
parts of their manhood while they change the troublesome parts,
learning to better relate to women, and helping women begin to
comprehend and honor both women's and men's best ways of being
while we work together to change each sex's problematic practices.

So although this book is written about helping men change, it
is really about the interdependence of women and men. We ur-
gently need new visions of manhood *and* womanhood. I agree
with Satir when she said, (quoted in Leupnitz, 1988, p. 55) "I am
for *personhood*. I want to help women find their self-worth and take
their place in society. But not at the expense of men." As Keen said
in his inspiring book *Fire in the Belly: On Being a Man*, "The most
hopeful thing we can do to end the war between the sexes is
merely to witness to each other, tell our stories, and listen quietly"
(1991, p. 10).

This book is replete with opportunities for the reader to witness
men and women telling their stories. Laced throughout the book
are actual excerpts of sessions, so that the reader can hear women's
and men's voices articulating their own experience. In fact, it is
their statements that led me in the writing of the book. Rather than
for me to superimpose my thoughts onto their words, I began
writing each chapter by pouring over the mountains of session
transcripts I had, to see what their voices could teach me. So in a
very real and special way, my clients led me in the writing of this
book. To them I am extremely grateful.

When clients are quoted, they are their actual words that I later
got their permission to use. I have not doctored them up in any

way except with occasional bracketed phrases to improve the passage's readability. Of course, although their words are actual and verbatim, all identifying information is disguised. As I said in the letter I sent them requesting their permission to use their words for publication, "You may note in reading the piece [I wish to use] that you may have gained or lost years, siblings, parents, and/or children. All of this is in an effort to protect your rights to privacy." Each person whose words are used signed a written consent form allowing me to do so, agreeing that his or her privacy had been sufficiently protected.

Many people sent letters with the signed consent forms or discussed in the next session their responses to reading the excerpt(s) I wished to include. Many of these responses themselves are instructional. Samples of these are:

*T.J.:* "When I got your letter, I couldn't wait to read it. I stood in the kitchen and cried, remembering all we had been through."

*Heidi:* "I burst into tears when I read this. I don't recall saying the first sentence, but the rest is a painful memory. Perhaps the first sentence is so foreign because I no longer feel that that is a part of who I am now."

*Aaron:* "It was painful to read our excerpts, but when we finished, we felt closer."

*Laura:* "Reading the excerpts helped me remember that special time in our lives when we both realized how important we were to each other. Thank you for giving us a chance to relive it."

It is hoped that the above excerpts give a foretaste of the life that clients' words contribute to these pages. Further, these clients' responses point the way to the quality of healing they were able to find from the process detailed in the book.

Last spring in our local area, two young males each had their arms ripped off in separate accidents. Both men required many hours of very delicate microsurgery, and the local news media spent weeks detailing the intricacies of the surgery and of their recovery. One day during this time, a client of mine began a therapy session with the following insight that likened our work— and the approach articulated in this book—to microsurgery.

*Murray:* [Our therapy] is like doing microsurgery.
*Therapist:* How so?

*Murray:* It's so intricate, so interconnected! All the little capillaries, all the
   little nerve endings, everything has to be sewn together before the
   arm gets back on.
*Therapist:* How is what we are doing that intricate?
*Murray:* I've got to get shaken out of this depression and all of these
   inferior feelings. That's the goal. But it's not just that. It's me and my
   mom. It's me and my brothers. It's me and [my wife]. It's how we
   argue and how we don't argue. The microsurgery is tying all those
   pieces together. So many loose ends have to be tied together to get
   the arm back on or to get my head back, or to get a good head, for a
   change.
*Therapist:* That's a wonderful analogy! Which is why it's not time yet for
   us to work with [your wife], because we don't have enough pieces
   tied together yet.
*Murray:* I know.
*Therapist:* How do you feel about where you are in the process?
*Murray:* I'm making progress, but it still seems like so much—and I don't
   know if I can quite attain it.
*Therapist:* You can! You can!

Everything in one's life relates to and is tied up with everything
else. The wholeness of people, like the wholeness of an arm with
a body, depends on connecting each element, rather than on providing Band Aids and quick fixes. And when attention is not paid
to all parts of the soul and the psyche that need healing, those
parts will remain impaired and therefore will distract from that
individual's full functioning. Just as when the elements of an
injured arm do not heal properly they leave an impairment, failure
to address the layered aspects of an individual's life will leave
functional impairment as well.

   Intricacy of the concepts in this book is not its only complexity.
The process of writing this book involved a web of very important
contributors to the birth and development of my ideas. First, I
need to thank the prototype in my life of a strong and loving
woman, my now dead mother, Mildred Rask Erickson. I also wish
to thank my professional mother and mentor, Jan Kramer, for her
model that it is possible for a woman to be competent and caring.
The imprint of both of these women on my life is immeasurable.
Further, I am grateful to my friends and colleagues who helped by
encouragement, support, and reading a chapter or section of the
book while I was in the process of making sure it made sense. First,
I am grateful to my husband and best friend, Bill Ress, who read

every word of this manuscript, sometimes more than once. I also owe a debt of gratitude to Karen Gail Lewis, David Moultrup, Terry Trepper, Richard Meth, Frank Pittman, Holli Reitmulder, Pearl Rosenberg, Bill Dorn, Michele Gargan, Jo-Ann Krestan, and Nanine Ewing, who read segments of the book to help ensure that what I was writing was coherent and significant. Thanks also go to David Opsahl and Iris Cornelius, two colleagues and friends who were my sanity checks in a sometimes insane world. Perhaps the person who had the least enviable job was my typist, Marilyn Nelson, who took handwritten squiggles and muffled tapes and made them into usable transcripts. So she deserves many kudos.

There are three special people who have been guiding lights to me as a writer. First, I owe thanks to Tom Grady, now Editor at HarperSan Francisco, who first believed in me many years ago and saw that I was capable of bringing a book to life. And I need to thank my writing mentor, Terry Trepper, whose encouragement as a book series and journal editor was especially meaningful and whose backing was there to such an extent that I could bring him "dumb" questions. And I also owe a very fond thank you to my editor at Sage Publications, Inc., Marquita Flemming, for her vision that I could produce a finished book and for her encouragement and enthusiasm at every step along the way. But mostly, I would like the thank my clients who have taught me every bit as much as I have taught them. We have learned together, and their words scattered throughout this book reflect the ongoing didactic process in which we were engaged.

Beth M. Erickson, Ph.D.
Minneapolis, Minnesota
January 1993

# References

Keen, S. (1991). *Fire in the belly: On being a man.* New York: Bantam.
Leupnitz, D. (1988). *The family interpreted: Feminist theory in clinical practice.* New York: Basic Books.

# Introduction:
# The Threads That Connect

Driving home from the office, I do some of my best reflecting. Most days, I wish I lived farther away so that I had more time to ponder before the needs and demands of my life at home impinge. The following vignettes highlight my musings in a typical week. They exemplify different threads and layers that converge into one strand: people's need for and yet fears about each other. And they reveal the array of relationship problems that are common in the daily life of a family therapist. Looking at them through the lens of gender issues alters the vantage point, showing up men's and women's interdependence on each other and the painful and familiar struggle that ensues when people are unable to attain an adequate level of trust and comfort with and about each other, whether at work or at home.

## Highlights From a Week

**Monday**

Linda, homemaker and mother of two, requested an emergency appointment over the weekend. Early this morning, my week begins with her sharing about the storm I have seen brewing over the last few months. After sticking it out for 15 years in an arid marriage, she recently divorced and admits in retrospect realizing as she walked down the aisle that she was making a mistake. It took her all those years to face herself and that reality. Now the married man with whom she is having an affair catalyzes her despair when he confesses that he will not leave his wife, despite repeated promises to do so. She is bereft, suicidal. I am scared. Although she has confessed having self-destructive thoughts since her father died when she was 6, this time I fear she might carry them out. She reluctantly and angrily gives me the no-suicide contract I request, and I call a physician colleague to set the stage for hospitalization, should that be necessary.

Later that day, my women's group in which she participates insists on that promise as well. We all appear edgy about her desolation and sad that she would allow a man's actions to make her question her own worth to this degree. I suspect aloud that our periodic silence signals that each of us wonders about the extent to which we have permitted, even invited, men to define us. I struggle with my own fears and tears for her in group.

**Tuesday**

I am deeply moved when Barry, a very successful middle-aged physician, allows tears to stream down his face as he describes the shambles of his life and his humiliation at needing psychiatric hospitalization 11 years ago, during his last attempt to straighten up. The trigger for his breakdown was the end of an extramarital affair with a woman whom he believed at the time he loved. Now he vacillates between two extremes of stark terror. He knows that his beginning to explore himself and his relationship issues in earnest could mean the end of his marriage. And yet, he has only more desperate loneliness to which to look forward if he does not face himself and his wife and try to improve or end the relationship. What finally got him to my office was his facing the fact that deep loneliness will certainly haunt him if he does nothing. This is only the third session, and his willingness to show me his despair, rather than intellectualize about it, is very promising.

I capitalize on that moment to test the strength of our therapeutic alliance, as well as to learn more about his two previous therapies with male psychiatrists. I ask why he chose a woman for therapy this time. Without a moment's hesitation, he says, "I have never trusted women, which goes all the way back to my relationship with my mother. This time, I want a female therapist so that I can learn to trust them. And I believe I can trust you, even if I can't feel it yet." I feel a combination of awe and disquiet at glimpsing the extremely high stakes for him in our work.

### Wednesday

In my professional women's therapy group today, Sharon, who recently was named the first female chief executive officer in the country in her line of work, expresses her anxiety about being forced to supervise a rigidly stereotypic male. We identify with her as this extremely competent woman struggles to allow herself to experience and then to share her vulnerability and fear.

We smile as Sharon repeatedly expresses her relief that we offer a place where she can come and feel, without fear of judgment. We note with irony that there is a growing legion of women who now struggle to repress their feelings, who now, along with men, fear appearing weak when emotional. We help with the pain born of her internal battle with her socialization as a woman, which inclines her toward taking too much responsibility for difficulties and toward being a "good girl" in an attempt to make the relationship work. She quietly confesses her ulcer is screaming again. We urge her to learn to draw her boundaries, so she will not continue to sacrifice herself. None of us dares to speak the question I suspect we are all thinking. How much should she—or any one of us—have to sacrifice to be a pioneer? I feel a mixture of worry for her and pride in her.

### Thursday

Karen and Mel, young CPAs in the same firm, are in their first marriage. They are beginning to learn how they have used intellectualization and competition as defenses against intimacy. They report a major explosion just after the last session. Mel refused to directly express any of the emotion he was feeling afterward, although he acknowledges now he knew he needed to. So he picked a fight. I speculate aloud that this may be his way of changing the subject, so he needs neither to feel his feelings nor to share them with Karen. He smiles. She also acknowledges some confusing feelings about his beginning to make the changes she says she wants. So she fights to regain control and push him away.

Although we have made progress in many areas in the few months they have been in treatment, clearly we have more work to do. I am not surprised; nor am I particularly discouraged, though they are. I remind them that this, too, is part of the typical back-and-forth motion of change.

### Friday

Burt and Marilyn come in today for the 14th session since he requested marital therapy. The crux of their problem is fairly standard: failure to communicate, with the resulting lack of intimacy. The manifestations of this lack of trust also are fairly standard: constant conflict, workaholism, and an extramarital affair. My task, too, is standard: to help them find intimacy. The variables in this case, however, make the work not so standard. His occupation is one complication. He is second in command of a huge corporation with installations in 48 states. Because this milieu is bottom-line and results oriented, I am acutely aware that I have some extra considerations in establishing my credibility with him. This is partly due to my age and appearance, partly because psychotherapy is anything but precise and easily measurable, and partly because his $6 million annual income puts him in a different stratum from most therapists and certainly from me. Both 51 years old, they are college sweethearts in their first marriage. Other complications are the layer upon layer of scars and defenses in the wake of their 28 years of battling, which resulted in profound and chronic marital disappointments, multiple corporate moves and dislocations, and the eventual, almost inevitable, affair.

Because they had a very moving and productive session last time, I remind myself they probably will come back to therapy again polarized. The trouble is, I forget to predict it aloud for them.

After inching toward each other, they do indeed return to fighting. I feel frustrated by my own oversight and at still having trouble getting behind their fears, so well masked by accusations and threats. I remind myself to practice patience, so I can teach it to them.

## The Threads That Connect

What do all these vignettes have in common? Many threads connect both the concepts in this book and men's and women's experience. One thread is the interdependence of men and women. Another thread is the desire for that interdependence. A third thread is the universal human need to be understood and the pain and suffering that deprivation of this need brings. Woven throughout this book, these themes create a tapestry with many textures, layers, and colors.

Women and men experience a natural interdependence. Liberating only women will put them at a distinct disadvantage for being able to establish meaningful relationships of any kind with men. What good does it do women to liberate themselves, if men are still unfree—limited either by their own expectations or by society's decrees—to actualize their full emotional as well as intellectual potential as human beings?

For women who are certain they have no interest in interacting with men and who can eliminate virtually all contact with men, even extended family members, this dilemma seems of no consequence. However, for those who choose to or need to interact with men, there can be an ache that accompanies trying.

Time after time I have heard women express their anguish about their failed quest for emotionally available men. And although they may language it differently, more and more I am hearing the same ache for meaningful relationships and genuinely satisfying lives expressed by men. So the question becomes, how do we as therapists help clients, women and men, find what they seek?

## Current Cultural Milieu

We as therapists need to ask ourselves, has the liberation that has taken place in the last three decades genuinely been liberating

of either sex? Bepko and Krestan (1990) raise an interesting issue
when they state,

> It's true that since the women's movement began, more women have
> joined the work force and more men spend some of their time in
> child care. But not only are these changes more superficial than
> substantial; the truth is that what may seem like greater role flexi-
> bility may actually be more role strain. What appears to be true is
> that both women and men are freer to add new behavior to their
> existing roles, but they are not truly free to let go of any of the old
> behaviors that *define them as adequate men and women* [italics added].
> What looks like flexibility is really an increase in pressure for both
> men and women to be and do more. (p. 166)

Even when men and women both want desperately to loose the
chains that bind us, this clearly is easier said than done. And
beginning to drop some of those chains also can add unexpected
pressures for both. Little wonder, then, how confusing it is for the
average person to make sense of the swirl of good and bad feelings
and outcomes of all our culture's recent changes.

Still, changes are happening in our society as a whole that make
efforts in the direction of continued transition urgent. Many women
are changing. And men also are being called by other men, as well
as by women, to be different—like it or not. Our culture is at a
hinge in history, where more and more men are becoming aware
of their needs and deficiencies in the relationship spheres of their
lives.

Therapists are in a unique position to help. This book is about
empowering female therapists to work as effectively and confidently in engaging men in the process of change as they do with
women.

## Men's Language for Feelings

It is easy to assume that only women suffer when their relationships are unsatisfying. My experience says clearly this is a misconception. It appears to be the case in part because of the differences
in men's and women's socialization about relationships and in
part because of men's ways of discussing their responses to encounters with others. Although men may talk about their discom-

fort in a different, more stereotypically masculine voice, they still experience pain when these relationships are problematic, often being unaware of its source. Because they have been socialized away from feeling and toward productivity, the amorphousness of emotions can make feeling all the more frightening for them. Men expect to be in control, and to be unable to name something is to feel out of control, uncertain what to combat. So they typically try even harder to control their feelings. Ergo, another vicious circle is created.

Consequently, to best help, therapists must begin by learning to identify when men are telegraphing feelings, even though they are not using feeling words or concepts that are standard for women. Through this effort, we eventually can help clients begin to identify for themselves when and what they are feeling. Thus, men can begin to acquire the legal tender—feelings—that makes a relationship rich. Otherwise, when couples cannot exchange feelings, the relationship becomes bankrupt at worst, or simply a business partnership at best. For specific tools that therapists can use in teaching people about feelings, see Appendices A, B, and C.

## Two Case Examples

The voices of two clients beginning treatment illustrate men's way of languaging emotional experiences.

### Murray

Murray was referred to me by his physician, who for several years had prescribed both antidepressant and antianxiety medications to him with minimal effect. Finally, both doctor and patient accepted that merely medicating his problems was not solving anything, and Murray called to initiate psychotherapy. In his mid-40s, he was struggling with the natural developmental imperative to find meaningful, and not just vapid, work. Levinson (1978) delineated this conflict in his now classic study of men's development. In the following excerpt, Murray is taking stock of his vocational life and finding significant deficiencies that simply cannot be outweighed any longer by the many facets of his personal life that give him much pleasure. Formerly whenever these thoughts and the attendant feelings would start to surface, Murray would short-circuit them through one or another of his symptoms, which he simply would pop a pill to quell. Now he gingerly approaches identifying the fuel for his symptoms. Spoken approximately 2 months into individual therapy, the following words illustrate his dawning realization of the reality of many of his choices.

*Murray:* I'd like to be happy earning a living, doing what I'm happy at earning a living. But if I did that, a lot of people would be unhappy. . . . I tell the kids to do something they'd like to be doing and not worry about the money, just be happy. But my dad always contradicts that, so I'm trying to counteract [his influence].
*Therapist:* These are some pretty profound thoughts you have! Are they new?
*Murray:* Probably not.
*Therapist:* How long have you thought this then?
*Murray:* Probably since law school.
*Therapist:* Why do you think you've never acted on it?
*Murray:* I don't know. Maybe I never had the guts.
*Therapist:* I'm hearing a lot of wistfulness and regret about lost opportunities.
*Murray:* Maybe.

These words, fairly typical of those spoken by men early in treatment, indicate to me a wealth of emotion hidden beneath the surface of a highly intellectualized defensive structure and style of delivery. Because Murray's socialization as a male has conspired with his experience in his family of origin to proscribe any expression of feeling, Murray defends himself by literal oblivion about anything substantive related to his internal experience. Therefore, it is easy to see in his comments a nearly total lack of comprehension of his experience or of the impact of it. However, his words belie a depth of emotion about regret over some of his choices, sadness over missed opportunities, and fear about making any changes in his life. Bringing these embedded emotions to the surface will form our follow-up work in the sessions to come.

## John

John's words provide another example. He was a previously successful salesman whose business had gone sour, just at a time he was contemplating moving in with his very successful fianceé.

It would be a second marriage for both and would include her three children from a previous marriage, so it was good sense to seek premarital therapy. The following is an excerpt from one particularly difficult session for John.

> *John:* I'm The Provider, and I'm not doing it right now. I've always been able to provide for me and everybody else. It was part of what I had to do. That burden carries a lot of weight, and it doesn't feel good. But sharing it, too, doesn't feel good. I've always felt I had to provide.

John's words demonstrate a common double bind that men get themselves into who are trying to make the changes that relationships of our era are requiring. He alludes to pain of inadequacy and fear of failure at not being able to fulfill the standard male role, even though he does not yet have the words to express it directly. And yet, at this point, he is doing all he can to improve the situation of his stymied business. I suspect his being unable to do even more contributes to an even greater sense of failure.

## Summary

The focus in the early stages of therapy is on active listening, so men can learn to hear and eventually identify for themselves the feelings embedded in their typical cognitive expressions. The process for teaching men and their partners to work with this new mode of expression will be discussed in depth in later sections of the book.

## Fears About Intimacy

Every year, people in the Western world spend billions of dollars on making themselves attractive. Why? In hopes of being pleasing enough that people will want to be with them. I firmly believe one of the most terrifying human conditions is feeling totally alone. Linda, the formerly married single mother described at the opening of this chapter, surely knew that! To feel alone when one is "supposed" to feel togetherness generates both cognitive dissonance and emotional angst. So people often will go to great lengths to avoid being alone, sometimes believing just being in a relationship will salve pain. Then they are sorely disappointed when it does not.

For those who are fortunate enough to have modeling from their parents or others for what a good relationship is, finding one seems like a virtually effortless task. Yet, others seem hapless and hopeless at ever getting it right. This accounts for such common human traps as the revolving door of relationships, addictions that block pain, or spouse abuse to remain in control so the other will not leave. Many of these people can't stand to be alone; but they can't stand to be together, either.

From infancy on, feelings of abandonment stir stark terror. And yet, people have an equally primitive need tugging them in the opposite direction: to be separate and apart. Humans have an intuitive sense that in order to develop psychologically, they need a strong sense of themselves as autonomous beings who can function without the need for anyone else. This innate tendency, which Mahler, Pine, and Bergman (1975) refer to as the psychological birth of the human infant, has its seeds at approximately 4 to 6 months of age. Here, children begin to know the difference between self and other, usually learning this first with the mother. Children whose separation and individuation processes are somehow truncated carry that developmental arrest with them on into their adult lives, and of course, into all their relationships. These people as adults are extremely fearful of any relationship compromising their ability to carry on as separate and autonomous adults. When that fundamental developmental arrest gets carried on into adulthood, even though those individuals may grow chronologically, they remain stuck at some very primitive developmental levels. Our job is to isolate and treat those developmental arrests, as discussed in more detail in Chapters 4 and 5.

Ackerman (1958), considered by some to be the grandfather of family therapy, reminds us the only true autonomy is in togetherness. By that, I think he means the best way to learn about ourselves is in bumping up against and interacting with others, for only then can we learn in a real and experiential way who we are. A significant source of tension and conflict in relationships for most people is the effort to find that happy medium between autonomy and togetherness.

## A Thumbnail Sketch of Catastrophic Expectations

Feldman (1979) offers the concept of catastrophic expectations as a way to understand what propels us away from intimacy even as we seek it. This will be discussed in greater depth in Chapter 9, but a cursory explanation now will illustrate the push-pull that occurs in most significant relationships.

Feldman posits one reason significant relationships, such as marriages, can get so frenzied is people's unconscious fears that disaster will happen when they get close. This is counterbalanced by the fear of what will happen if they get too far away. Feldman lists the following five common catastrophic fears and believes each of us experiences at least one of these fears on the most primitive, preverbal levels. It is our job as therapists to help clients verbalize which of these plagues them so we can help them learn to work with them.

Fear of abandonment (being left bereft)
Fear of merger (being swallowed up)
Fear of exposure (sharing too much and then being rejected)
Fear of one's own destructive impulses (rage)
Fear of attack (persecutory attack and annihilation)

Thus, couples experience two parallel struggles simultaneously: to be in a close, intimate relationship so they do not have to feel alone, but not to be so close that their catastrophic fears are piqued. Hence the jockeying back and forth, as both partners try to do what comforts themselves most. After a time, people either settle in with the comfortable closeness they have found or begin to conclude they cannot meet their own or each other's needs in the relationship. In this case, the relationship begins to deteriorate, and either constant, unresolved cycles of conflict, stony silence, or divorce ensue.

## Working With Catastrophic Fears

What makes the situation so hard for therapist and client alike is that the very thing that comforts one member of the couple often makes the other the most anxious. Most couples are like salt and pepper: a matched pair. For example, people who fear abandonment usually choose to couple with someone who fears merger. This makes absolutely no sense, you say? On a conscious level, that is true. But those unconscious choices protect us from another fear emerging into consciousness. And making that choice may help people continue to play out an unconscious script that comes to them from their family of origin. Complementarity may have many psychic benefits for both parties in a relationship, even though it is the crux of most couples' conflict. This notion of complementarity will be developed further in Chapter 9; what is most significant to know now is that couples mutually develop an unconscious contract that dictates to a large degree the nature of their relationship choices. Hence, it does no good to lodge the blame for their discord in one or the other member of the couple.

How does this relate to men? Both the degree and the compelling nature of the fear are hard concepts for both women and men alike to comprehend, or harder yet, to admit. But if the fear is hard for women to own, when they are socialized to operate on a feeling level, it is prohibitive for men to acknowledge, for they are socialized to believe admitting fear is being weak. And who of us of either sex likes to feel weak?

## Men and Fear

It is difficult for many people to own, to articulate, and to appropriately manage their fears. But for men, this can be an even more difficult proposition. It is no secret men have long used physical or emotional distance as a way of getting away from inner pressures. The following example illustrates how difficult it is for men even to recognize that fear is what they are experiencing, to say nothing of share it. In it, we meet Katherine and Sam, from whom we will hear again in the couples chapter.

Katherine and Sam have been married for 8 years and are in their late 30s. They presented for treatment when once again Katherine became depressed and anxious, fearful that during Sam's frequent business trips out of town she would become more and more unable to manage. Her frequent angry outbursts usually seemed to be catalyzed by Sam's emotional unavailability, whether he is in town or on the road. The following excerpt begins with Katherine's beginning to contemplate the option of divorce.

*Katherine:* I feel like I'm really willing to ask the question [about divorce]. . . . And I'm willing to start taking action. But it's scary.

*Therapist:* (To Sam) What would it feel like if her journey led her out of this marriage?

*Sam:* I'd feel like a failure. It would be a failure. I would have lost about the only things I've ever had that are important to me.

*Therapist:* What does it feel like to say that?

*Sam:* It's heavy. It weighs a lot.

*Therapist:* Can you tell her about your emotions, rather than your physiology?

*Sam:* There's sadness. We have shared so much, invested so much. And I think we really care about each other.

*Therapist:* Do you have a response, Katherine?

*Katherine:* I hear just the surface. I'd wish to hear how lonely you'd be without me, or how you'd miss our friendship. You make it sound like a business deal.

*Sam:* [That's ] not what I'm trying to say at all.

*Therapist:* Try again, then, Sam.

*Sam:* I'd miss what we'd shared, because we are partners and friends.

*Therapist:* Tell her what you'd feel.

*Sam:* Sadness. I tried to say how important it is that we keep working on this. I love you and do not want to get a divorce.

*Katherine:* (Moving closer to him) I need the inside stuff. That's nice to hear. We're people, here, not just some business deal.

*Therapist:* What's your response now, Sam?

*Sam:* I'm thinking about how close we are now, and it feels real.

*Therapist:* Do you like it?

*Sam:* I don't know if I like it, but I know I need it.

*Therapist:* Because it scares you?

*Sam:* I don't know.

It has been said that women and men of the industrialized West appear to be intimate strangers. This excerpt clearly illustrates this, as it provides a graphic example of several typical struggles between couples. It illustrates the interdependence of a couple on each other for their mutual satisfaction. And although one could reasonably predict the subject of their dialogue would generate a great deal of fear in Sam, none of that is obvious, even with questioning by the therapist. By inference, we see how his fear of inadequacy prompts him to hide his feelings and keep his distance, even after he was coaxed into timidly expressing them. Then we see how his halting attempts at experiencing and expressing his feelings leave Katherine feeling alone again, until he finally reluctantly begins to get to his emotions. Finally, the couple is able to taste a moment of emotional connection that allows them to reaffirm the commitment between them. But even then, Sam is loath to admit to feeling fear.

If fear is the impetus for much relationship dysfunction, and men are socialized not to know and certainly not to admit fear, then they are at a distinct disadvantage in relationships, because they are enjoined from taking the very action that would help alleviate the problem. Hence, our task as therapists is to weave a tapestry whose background is a climate of security and trust, such that both men and women can begin to explore behind the doors they have long ago closed. Only then can they become emotionally available for relating. Only then can they attain a truly equitable relationship in which both are free to actualize their full potential.

I do not see Sam being initially unresponsive because he is an insensitive cad; quite the contrary. Rather, it is because of the effects of a combination of his socialization as a male in our culture plus precedents in his family of origin that preclude his emotional expression at this stage of therapy. Therein lies the work of therapy with men: to attempt to remove the multiple stumbling blocks that have preempted their ability to be intimate.

## A Conversation With the Reader

Before we proceed any further, you as the reader would do well to ask yourself: What is the nature of change? As a therapist, what do I believe makes for the greatest change in people? Who is responsible for the changes that take place in clients? What is my role in catalyzing change? Do I believe I myself create change in clients? How you answer those questions will have a great deal to do with your theory of therapy and how you derive or derived it. The seasoned therapist perhaps will have ready answers to these questions. Those who do not are encouraged to pause and grapple with those questions before reading on.

Now that I've said all that, the discerning reader is probably asking herself what will form the backbone of the approach about which she will be reading here. I predict the answer to that question will be even more controversial than a book on men written by a woman.

A basic assumption I make is that the reader who has picked up this book did so out of an interest in helping to create change, regardless of exactly what she believes regarding the nature of change. My core belief is that to change something responsibly, we must first know it in context. Little can be changed substantively if we fail to understand how dysfunctional responses developed. That is, along with social factors that influence people's ways of being, we also need to place an individual and his or her relationships both in historical and contemporary context. This will make for the greatest, most broad-sweeping sense of empowerment and therapeutic leverage for ourselves and with our clients. Decontextualizing relationships reduces therapy to a set of flashy techniques that may or not prove to be of lasting value or of enough significance to change relationship patterns potentially for generations to come. Another obstacle to effective treatment is the tendency to take men's behavior (such as their anger or violence) out of context, while at the same time placing women's behavior (such as why a battered wife stays) in context. This leaves men without the requisite compassion and support for facilitating change that women usually readily receive.

Some readers may discover themselves chagrined that I will not emphasize removal of symptoms. Of course, I care that this happens; being uninterested in the resolution of symptoms would soon put me out of business. But symptom resolution is never my ultimate goal. It comes as a by-product of my work. Instead, I am interested in helping people to build bridges between the lost parts of themselves and to one another by reconstructing unresolved or lost pieces of their past, as well as by experiencing authentic relationships with each other and with me as the therapist. In addition to helping clients genuinely to understand, this emphasis has helped me as the therapist to build a theoretical foundation for my work, rather than merely "locating [myself] in the shifting sands of technique" (Luepnitz, 1988, p. 4).

Therefore, the clinical method I propose here is firmly grounded in psychodynamic theory, with its key feature being to help clients to become sensitized both to their own and their family's uncon-scious life and collective pasts. I am fully aware that for some readers, the book's psychodynamic underpinnings may be even more controversial and difficult to accept than its cross-gender orientation. Nonetheless, I believe this approach offers people the power to change much more than just themselves. They can change their family patterns by being better able to understand and challenge their self-deceptions. This permits clients to make better, more mature, more functional choices and aids the thera-pist in empathically understanding how clients developed their problematic behavior, rather than further blaming them for it. Thus, the past is seen as a treasure, not as a relic to be cast aside or traded.

## What Constitutes a Psychodynamic Approach?

Luepnitz (1988), whose approach to understanding gender is-sues is also psychodynamic, offers us a definition of psychodynamic therapies in a nutshell. She defines psychoanalytic therapists as those who "believe that the more unaware people are of what the past held, the more likely they are to repeat it—that is, only if unconscious conflicts are made conscious can they be transformed" (p. 192). In another section of her book, Luepnitz states, "Psychoanalytic the-ory, then, makes everyone's concerns the things that have culturally been the concern of women: the emotions, sexuality, childhood, relationships, bodily functions, and the irrational" (p. 22). Empha-sizing and teaching men how to value these concerns is the core of what generates the qualitative shift in worldview that the ap-proach I am outlining can catalyze.

In contrast to the richness afforded therapist and client alike by a psychodynamic approach, technique-oriented methods, which can seem facile anyway, can be particularly problematic when used with men. This is because men are socialized to fix problems and to do so by themselves and with the greatest efficiency. So the more flashy technique-oriented approaches to treatment inadver-tently can end up reinforcing the very worldview that itself is problematic with men because it bolsters their socialization, rather than seeking to help them examine and to change it. Fur-ther, this narrow focus on symptoms often prompts the recurrence of problems in other places in other guises. Instead we need to help both men and women get behind their ways of behaving and discern the fuel for these choices from both social and historical perspectives. Only then can we help people to free themselves and to truly, deeply change their lives. What is significant about this approach, then, is that it combines attention to both social and historical factors that conspire to keep both men and women stuck.

## Another Conversation With the Reader

According to Heesacker and Prichard (1992), "After centuries of attributing evil to women's nature, this relatively new . . . movement's perspective seems to have shifted the attribution of evil to men. This perspective is as unviable as the woman-is-evil perspective" (p. 278). This concept is in consonance with Doherty's (1991) calling attention to the "deficit model of manhood." To all three thinkers and to me the cause of building bridges between the genders is ill served by such divisiveness.

In truth, the problem does not reside only in men or their lack of emotionality. The problem regarding women, men, and emotions from this perspective involves a lack of awareness by women and especially by men regarding who and what a man really is. So, before we proceed into the meat of the book, I would invite you to ask yourself another set of questions that can be useful in clarifying what you believe about women, men, and relationships. These can help you adopt a frame of mind that says neither sex is solely at fault for the pain between them, and go on to develop a perspective conducive to the introspection required to maximize the book's effects for yourself and for your clients. These answers may begin also to help you reach for some very important insights that will inform your psychotherapy practice, and perhaps even your relationships with men, for years to come.

I will echo the question posed by Kelly and Hall (1992) and ask you to begin by asking yourself: Who are these men that I treat? Do I really know them? Or do I see them only through the lens of my own experiences with men? What are my feelings about men? about women? Do I secretly believe that masculinity is a sickness to be cured? Do I secretly believe that men are inherently less "therapizable"? How do I feel about men in general? Do I favor them? protect them? blame them? fear them? feel intimidated by them? act seductively with them? Bottom line, do I believe men really are emotionally deficient and inferior to women?

These are key questions about which to search your soul if you are to provide nonsexist counseling or therapy with either women or men. If you are unsure of how you would answer any of these questions, I invite you to keep a journal of your reactions as you read this book, paying particular attention to the sections that stir up particularly strong (countertransference) responses in you. This ability to introspect, as much as any technique or approach you might garner, will improve vastly your effectiveness with both female and male clients.

## A Final Word

More and more, psychotherapeutic services are being delivered by women. This is happening at a time when men increasingly are coming to recognize the limitations of the messages they got from their families and from our culture about what it is to be a man. Therefore, unless we deliberately limit our psychotherapy practice to women, we will be working with more and more men. And even when we work exclusively with women by design or by default, we will be operating indirectly with men, by virtue of men's impact on or place in these women's lives. Women all have fathers—or figures of fathers in their heads—as well as co-workers, bosses, and friends, if not husbands or lovers. And further, any time we work with couples, we need to be sensitive to how to work with men without blaming them for their own—or for our culture's—sins.

Changes are happening in our society that make efforts in this direction urgent. I invite the reader to join me and many of my colleagues in this quiet revolution.

## References

Ackerman, N. W. (1958). *The psychodynamics of family life: Diagnosis and treatment of family relationships*. New York: Basic Books.

Bepko, C., & Krestan, J. (1990). *Too good for her own good: Breaking free from the burden of female responsibility*. New York: Harper & Row.

Doherty, W. (1991). Beyond reactivity and the deficit model of manhood: A commentary on articles by Napier, Pittman, and Gottman. *Journal of Marital and Family Therapy, 17*(1), 29-32.

Feldman, L. (1979). Marital conflict and marital intimacy: An integrative psychodynamic-behavioral-systemic model. *Family Process, 15*(4), 389-395.

Heesacker, M., & Prichard, S. (1992). In a different voice, revisited: Men, women, and emotion. In K. Kelly & A. Hall (Eds.), *Journal of Mental Health Counseling, 14*(3), 274-290.

Kelly, K., & Hall, A. (1991). Toward a developmental model for counseling men. *Journal of Mental Health Counseling, 14*(3), 257-273.

Levinson, D. (1978). *The seasons of a man's life.* New York: Knopf.

Levinson, D. (1990, July). *Adult development of women and men.* Symposium presented for the Cape Cod Summer Symposia, Eastham, MA.

Luepnitz, D. (1988). *The family interpreted: Feminist theory in clinical practice.* New York: Basic Books.

Mahler, M. S., Pine, F., & Bergman, A. (1975). *The psychological birth of the human infant.* New York: Basic Books.

Part I

THE PERSON OF
THE THERAPIST

# What Women Must Be and Do to Work Effectively With Men

This chapter boils down to the barest minimum what the remainder of the book elaborates in rich detail. My purpose is to proffer a series of guidelines in abbreviated form that will be fleshed out throughout the rest of the book. Hence, there are few of the case examples and other amplifications that typify the remainder of the book. The reader may find herself frustrated with this sparseness, eager and wanting more. I hope that those whose appetites have been whetted will feel rewarded with the more thorough discussion of both the theory behind the approach proposed here—one that can readily be translated into practice—as well as a plethora of case examples to give the theory vitality. The aim for this chapter, however, is to provide a succinct discussion, with further elaboration as the book unfolds.

## Our Changing Cultural Context

Many of today's men want to change. This is clear both to women in their lives and to the growing legions of men who want more personal fulfillment from their lives. It is less clear that female therapists can play a special role in facilitating that change.

Based on my assumption that women most surely can work effectively with men, this chapter, then, is about what a woman must be and do to work effectively with men. I am convinced that there are unique contributions a woman can make to a man's psychotherapy growth, if she knows and is confident of what she is doing.

In fact, women most certainly can work with men. More and more, they will be called upon to do so. This is due to a combination of at least two factors: More and more men are recognizing the need for change and are seeking psychotherapy as a vehicle to help them do it; and women are entering the helping professions in increasing numbers. According to Fowler (1991), the chief executive officer of the American Psychological Association:

> For most if its first century, psychology, like most professional disciplines, was heavily male dominated. As educational opportunities became available on a more equal basis, the proportion of women in all professions increased, but few have changed as dramatically as in psychology. In 1960, women earned only 17.5 percent of doctorates awarded in all fields, but by 1984 more than one-third of all Ph.D.s were earned by women. . . . In 1984, the number of women earning doctorates in psychology equalled men and increased to 56 percent by 1989. (p. 3)

With the numbers of women steadily increasing and already outstripping men in the field, it is imperative that women learn to be as knowledgeable about and comfortable with male clients as we are with females.

## Two Major Requisites as Backdrops for This Work

Because women and men are socialized to operate with such different styles, there are two major considerations for women who want to work effectively with men to bring the best of our femaleness to our work. First, for clients' sakes as well as for ours, *we must not abandon the elements that make us women,* such as warmth and nurturing, in an attempt to gain acceptance by becoming honorary men. Both sexes need our nurturing and support. And yet, we must be able to demonstrate that we also can join and relate to men as men. *We must learn to do what traditionally has been considered the man's prerogative and responsibility.* We must exercise leadership and operate with a task focus. When we can do both, we have two forces on our side. One, we can capitalize on our being women and provide what so many of our clients—both female and male—are lacking: nurturance. And two, we can lead, showing men people-affirming, equitable ways to be. This experience offers a model for demonstrating the basic ingredients of new relationships with spouses at home and peers at work.

## Chapter Overview

The first topic will be a brief discussion of why change can be so hard for men. Then I will move on to introduce the central theme of the chapter, namely the therapist as an instrument for change, followed by a discussion of both the personal competencies and the therapeutic skills that are helpful when women work with men. Distilling the essence of this chapter into two central constructs, women must *be* clear about their own personal issues and how those influence the treatment process, and what they must *do* is strive to operate free of gender bias—about women, or men, or themselves.

Of course, many of these same skills and attributes are helpful when we work with women, too. However, if we are to reach and engage men in family change, we must be mindful of certain of these that are essentials, so we don't step onto mine fields and jeopardize both treatment and the man's growth and change.

## Why Change Is So Hard for Men

Some detractors may say that men have such trouble changing because they are rigid. Others say that men do not want to give up the power and privilege they have enjoyed for centuries. Still others may say that men do not care about anything but accumulating more wealth and the attendant power it brings. Perhaps. Or maybe there is another, more hopeful but still formidable explanation. In many ways, what we as therapists and men's partners are asking them goes beyond merely learning new skills by acquiring affective competencies. Rather, we are calling them to change their worldview.

To help men accomplish this aim, the female therapist needs to pay special attention to developing certain rudiments as a daily part of her response repertoire. She also needs to have a healthy respect for how formidable a task this is for men. Thus she can maximize the chances that they will be able to create the adjustments that allow the development of a new set of skills and allow them to undergo basic changes in themselves, in their relationships, and in their values and priorities regarding the meaning of such basic issues as work, partnering, intimacy, sex, friendship, parenting, and leisure, to name a few. Looked at this way, the changes this new epoch require are far-reaching, awesome, and potentially frightening indeed.

## The Therapist as an Instrument for Change

Before we consider the clinical benefits that accrue for client and therapist alike from seeing ourselves as therapeutic instruments for change, some introductory comments are in order.

### The Benefits of a Perspective Broader Than Just Techniques

In our profession, there are ample daily opportunities for foundering, discouragement, and self-doubt. None of us is immune to these afflictions, despite our fondest wish that we could be. It makes no sense, either for our clients or for ourselves, to take on such potentially difficult work without having done everything that would make us adequately prepared. It only erodes our self-confidence and makes us feel bad about ourselves when we feel unprepared or when our feelings rise uncontrollably in sessions.

Yet, many therapists' idea of preparing themselves is to learn all the theories and techniques they can accumulate, because it makes them feel adequate and confident. What about preparation for our own personal feelings rising uncontrollably in session? If we are to be the best possible instruments of change, we need to study ourselves, too. Not being already conversant with our own personal issues is not reason enough to avoid work with men, but we need to be willing to devote some energy to understanding this facet of ourselves in the context of our work. This will make it more rewarding and less precarious for both therapist and clients.

## Research on the Therapist as Instrument

In her presentation at a recent national meeting of family therapists, the feminist author and researcher Judith Myers Avis (1990) synthesized the results of a 2-year study on what is required of therapists in order to engage men in family change. Her most striking finding was that the most salient ingredient of effective psychotherapy with men was the therapist's own personal perceptual and conceptual skills. This bolstered my conviction that all the fancy treatment techniques learned in training programs or at conferences go for naught if the therapist is not clear herself about her own issues and beliefs, particularly about men themselves.

Yet, all too often, she is not. In fact, I sometimes wonder whether students are even trained *away* from developing themselves as therapeutic instruments by supervisors who are threatened because of the work they themselves may not have done. When this happens, all of us significantly miss the mark, and our clients either suffer, or at least fail to derive maximum benefit from our services.

## Extra Steps Required for Preparation of Therapists

It is optimal for the therapist in any situation to be personally clear, but it is particularly significant for female therapists who work with men. Having blind spots about ourselves and our feelings toward men leaves us in a particularly precarious position with them as clients regarding potential boundary problems—a topic that will be discussed in much greater depth in the next chapter.

These potential quandaries warrant discussion for two sets of reasons. One concern is for the protection of our clients and their significant others. The other relates to our own personal vulnerability. Both must be considered before answering the question of what a female therapist must do and be in working effectively with male clients, in order to maximize our effectiveness and to enhance clients' growth. Working with this population has many potential depth charges and emotional overlays inherent in it, warranting an additional measure of introspection. It would be advisable to exercise the same degree of caution and preparation that is needed with other highly charged issues such as AIDS, abuse, rape, loss, or any number of situations fraught with angst that can stir up the therapist's own countertransference reactions.

## In Our Clients' Behalf

Volumes have been written on the impact of the therapist's own family on the treatment process, particularly by the late Murray Bowen (1978) and his followers. One such book by Kramer (1985) examines in depth the multiple layers of a clinician's life that are affected by the patterns we both knowingly and unknowingly adopt from our family of origin. She sees the impact of one's personal experiences and the issues they generate fanning out to affect one's supervisees, colleagues, partners, and children, not merely one's therapy clients. The template for what is "supposed" to be that rides around in our heads can become a time bomb for the unaware clinician and in turn for the client. Some of these effects are manifest in the male-female dynamics found whenever men and women are together, regardless of the context. And some are manifest in the therapist's unknowing replication of her own experiences in the treatment room.

These automatic and natural dynamics are fundamental whenever women work with men in any context, and unaware therapists risk getting caught up in them. When that happens, at most therapists do nothing for their clients, and in far too many instances, the outcome is worse than benign. As was emphasized in the first chapter, women who have not carefully examined their beliefs and feelings about men actually may be psychologically dangerous for men, as well as toxic for those men's significant relationships. There is an understandably even higher risk when the therapist's experiences with men have been hurtful, involving for example abuse, alcoholism, or abandonment. If a woman is fortunate enough to have been reared in that one third (Lewis, 1979) of intuitively healthy families, she may for that very reason hold high expectations about what men are "supposed" to be, which can overshadow the treatment process for the unaware.

A personal example may illustrate. I am the youngest of eight children. My father and I had a very close relationship until his sudden and unexpected death when I was 9 years old. I have no doubt that our bond is a major contributor to my sense about men that informs this work.

But there is a flip side to this coin. I have only two brothers. Both were graduated from high school and left for college shortly after I was born. So after my father died, I literally had no direct, daily interaction with men. This has left me, on some levels, with a void in my understanding about what men do. My point is that my family experiences with men both aided and detracted from my work with men, and I need to be mindful of both.

## In Our Own Behalf

In developing an intimate therapeutic relationship with us, many clients, both female and male, experience for the first time the kind of attachment that can be curative for both themselves and their relationships. And yet, when a woman works with a man, the chances are great for a transference reaction either to stump or defeat the therapist. Therapists who are not aware of and conversant about their own issues and how these interact with clients' issues can end up reacting like Ping-Pong balls, unable to sort out these reactions either for themselves or for their clients. Thoughtful planning of interventions and meaningful expressions of empathy lose a great deal of their potency when overshadowed by the therapist's personal dynamics interacting with the client's.

Because of the intimacy and the strong connection to the therapist that usually develop, particularly in individual therapy, there can be a special kind of vulnerability for both client and therapist of which the therapist must be aware. In this work, where the aim is to teach men intimacy skills, her best tool is *showing* them. And yet, if she cannot keep her own issues and feelings straight, she inadvertently puts herself in a precarious position, especially regarding the highly charged issues of vulnerability, sexuality, and overresponsibility. And this, of course, has the capability of jeopardizing the entire therapy process and of hurting him.

It is no secret that inability to keep clear boundaries is a primary contributor to therapists sexually abusing their clients. The key therapeutic task, then, is to develop enough intimacy to be therapeutic while maintaining enough distance that neither the therapist nor clients are at risk of crossing the appropriate sexual boundary, but not so much distance that the therapy becomes simply a business proposition. Difficult to modulate, you ask? No doubt. However, it is essential for safe and yet effective cross-gender treatment.

For an in-depth discussion of these very precarious issues, readers are encouraged to study the next chapter carefully. For our purposes at this point, it is sufficient to say that these issues are difficult and require special thought for the therapist to avoid overcompensating on one extreme or the other.

### Case Example

Although any number of issues can be problematic, especially treacherous for the therapist and confusing for men is when the transference reaction includes sexual attraction. An excerpt from a men's group session facilitated by my female cotherapist and me illustrates this quandary for most men and how we handled this particular instance. In this session, the discussion turned to how men see women in general and the two female facilitators in particular. First, I offer an example of how I discussed such a situation, rather than avoiding it. An example follows of a man's response to the issue having been brought up.

*Therapist:* One of the things that I think is a common complaint of women about men is that men tend to sexualize all relationships with women. They can't see a woman as a woman. They see a woman as a sex object or see a woman's sexuality first and foremost. And what we are saying here is that part of that is real normal. I think women do that, too, but we don't seem to fixate on it or talk about it quite so much [because] we don't have the socialization to immediately think that way or to talk about it if we do. But it is normal to have that response. Usually when it can be acknowledged, at least to ourselves, it can be gotten out of the way. Then it isn't a barrier. Otherwise, it sits there like a neon sign flashing.

Mark then took the permission given by the above intervention and made the following comment a few minutes later in that same group session.

*Mark:* (To the therapist who spoke above) To say . . . you're an important person in my life right now and I need you are all things that I feel.

> But to have to put them on the table right now is a really hard thing to do, because it makes me vulnerable. It makes me need somebody, and I've spent a good deal of my life avoiding needing people so I won't get hurt. And it makes me feel those feelings of sexual attraction for someone, by putting feelings in the forefront instead of pushing them away and ignoring them.

Here Mark tentatively describes his experience of beginning to bring to the surface and work with sexual feelings that he confesses having since the beginning of treatment. This kind of client disclosure can be parlayed in many directions to explore how the man sees the therapist, women in general, his spouse, his children, or his colleagues; that is, of course, provided the therapist is comfortable enough with her own issues and her own sexuality to permit and to facilitate those discussions.

Other ways in which the therapist's own issues can affect the treatment process are perhaps not always as highly charged and precarious for the therapist as sex and sexuality, but they are significant nonetheless. If we are unaware of ourselves, we cue clients about what is both significant and permissible to discuss, just by what we choose to focus on or redirect away from in sessions. So if the therapist is not mindful, she can inadvertently end up working out her own issues through her clients, or because of her own discomfort, prevent their working on theirs.

Perhaps another example from my family of origin will illustrate this common dilemma from which therapists can tend to hide. I grew up in a family whose rule about anger is that it simply does not exist. Happy emotions such as love, belonging, accomplishment, and the like were permitted and encouraged. But not "bad" emotions like anger or sadness. We covertly were trained to act as though these emotions did not exist, because everyone had to "get along so well," which was another family rule.

Thus, as a beginning therapist, I became extremely uncomfortable whenever I thought clients might openly conflict. In my head, I knew that conflict can be healthy if managed in constructive ways, and that it was my job to teach them to do this. But my guts would scream, and I would nearly jump out of my chair to stop disharmony, even if it were slight, at the least chance that it would become overt. As long as conflict remained covert, as it had in my family of origin, I could tolerate it. However, the covert, itself often the reason for the dysfunction, usually has to be made overt for its secrets not to become toxic. To my great chagrin, this meant I had to learn to tolerate and even encourage open, expressed conflict.

My strategy for learning to endure this to me highly unnatural act initially took a great deal of effort and concentration. I literally had to sit on my hands or put one hand over my mouth to remind myself not to leap inappropriately or prematurely into the conversation to redirect it. Although I must have looked ridiculous, people didn't seem to notice, because they were so engrossed in their own usually necessary struggle. Gradually, I helped myself learn not to steer my clients to a contrived truce. I am happy to report that now I not only encourage conflict, but I also sometimes join the fracas myself, if it seems like that is the only pathway to create change.

### Summary

By now, it is apparent that there are many potential hazards when female therapists work with men. These will be elaborated in greater depth in the next chapter. In the next sections, we will consider some specific, critical attributes and experiences that are optimal for women who want to work effectively with men. The reader will see that although being naturally gifted with these requisite tools and attitudes is fortunate, for those of us who are not so blessed, it is possible to work to develop them. And it is important that we do, for they are a sine qua non for effectively doing this cross-gender work. Furthermore, in some ways, those of us who have had to strain to gain our insights may be even more effective. In this way, our struggle to understand echoes men's parallel challenge to fathom and internalize the fundamental changes that they are being called to make, the changes that are ushering in a new millennium for our culture.

## What a Woman Must Be to Work Effectively With Men

Building on the theme that has pervaded the chapter so far, the best therapeutic tool we have as women therapists is ourselves. So this next section directly answers the question: What must a woman be to work effectively with men? The list that is proffered here is by no means definitive, but a list-in-progress of guidelines to which the reader is invited to add her own.

However, before we can discuss the specifics of what a woman needs to be to work effectively with men, we must first discuss a significant caveat which, if unheeded, also can obstruct therapy.

### Beware of Being Too Good for Your Own (or Anybody Else's) Good

As taking care of relationships typically has been primary for women due to eons of socialization, the unaware can fall into the trap of being, as Bepko and Krestan (1990) suggest, too good for her own good: "Out of necessity, women become relational experts. We've developed the capacities to be sensitive, intuitive, generous, nurturing, and focused on the emotional and physical comfort of others. 'Never hurt anybody' seems ingrained in our psyches" (p. 32). Women learn what these authors call a Goodness Code, and are inducted into following it by a lifetime of silent edicts from our culture.

### What Is Being Too Good for Your Own Good?

According to Bepko and Krestan, "To be too responsible is another name for being too good. . . . The underlying message . . . of the Goodness Code or the Women's Code of Responsibility . . . is that women are responsible for the pleasure, happiness, comfort, and success of the others in their lives" (pp. 98-99).

These authors further state some specific provisos with regard to men that leave our clients, our therapy, and ourselves in jeopardy. They articulate the implicit belief of many women that, "We women can save men from themselves if only we are good enough" (p. 13). Being unaware of this ingrained tendency can spell eventual harm for the therapist who will burn herself out, as well as do her clients no good, because she will keep them stuck.

### Ways to Keep This Debilitating Tendency in Check

If a woman is not to be too good for her own good and still capitalize on the very reason she was sought for therapy in the first place—her femaleness—what can she do? How can she keep this potentially debilitating tendency in balance so that she is truly helpful and not crippling?

Mason (1991) summarizes what is necessary to be a mature woman, which can be extrapolated to the attitude required of a responsible, but not overresponsible, female therapist: "To become mature, we need to separate our sense of connection from our sense of self-sacrifice; they are not the same. . . . Women can be connected and available to others, and at the same time, hold on to their separateness" (p. 38).

Bepko and Krestan (1990) offer another remedy to this potentially debilitating condition that can help the female therapist keep a balance. They advocate her empowering herself and others, and state that she can do this by nurturing:

> To be nurturing is another antidote to being too good and too responsible. . . . Nurturing can have many expressions. It can mean talking, it can mean listening. It can mean encouraging, supporting, validating feelings. It can mean teaching, helping, guiding. It can mean letting someone know that you think they're special and important to you. Sometimes it can mean simply being with a person, being a supportive presence as they cope with a problem that is uniquely theirs. Basically it means communicating caring and concern. It means the act of cherishing and valuing and encouraging the separateness experience and growth of the other person. (p. 86)

Because of our socialization as women, we have finely tuned, highly developed sensors that are adjusted to relationships and to picking up the emotional wants and needs of others. This allows us to bond and to nurture quite readily. But as Bepko and Krestan (1990) warn:

> These qualities are strengths and resources for our entire culture— ones that need to be celebrated and enjoyed. [But] they are qualities that need to be cultivated more in all of us. But being uniquely equipped to do something is not the same as being required to do it for someone else's benefit. And because women can move comfortably within the emotional domain of life, they are not automatically responsible to inhabit and populate that domain for everyone else. For women, being emotionally skilled becomes confused with being responsible. The two are not the same. (p. 111)

In this appeal to more than women to cultivate these relational skills, I heartily agree. And truly, only when women are not the sole—or even the primary—ones responsible for the maintenance of relationships will we have made the substantial progress that our era demands. Thus, our work with men to assist them in learning relationship competencies takes on ever increasing urgency.

### Drawbacks of Not Keeping This Tendency in Check

Several drawbacks are common if the therapist cannot keep in check her tendency as a socialized female to be too good for her own good.

*Getting Trapped by the "Make Relationships Work Injunction."* Because our socialization as females trains us toward relationships, we also have been fed, according to Bepko and Krestan (1990), a "Make Relationships Work Injunction" (p. 34). The most insidious effect of this dictate is that it gets women believing that there is something wrong with them if relationships do not work. Although extremely painful in personal life, it can be even harder to shake in professional life, where we are *hired* because of our relationship skills. Who of us can honestly deny wondering what we did wrong when people leave treatment disgruntled, convinced they have been inadequately treated? Because of our socialization, it takes maturity to not see ourselves as bad when that happens. It is easy to forget also to parcel out the clients' part in the downfall of the treatment.

We would be wise, when we begin hearing those internal messages that are destructive to our self-esteem and certainly do nothing to enhance our clinical effectiveness, to remember the "Make Relationships Work Injunction." This is a way to unhook from these fruitless expectations of ourselves and from the over-responsibility they generate that otherwise can erode our clinical confidence and competence.

A distinction is in order here. Asking ourselves about our part as well as taking stock of the client's part in the downfall of the treatment is responsible. Taking total responsibility for its demise is overresponsible and therefore counterproductive.

*Overresponsibility Is Being Overly Concerned With Clients' Feelings.*
Another drawback of a therapist being too good for her own good
is that she becomes too involved with others' feelings. It is easy,
then, also to become preoccupied with clients' reactions to us. This
often results in our seeking their approval, instead of doing our
job. And this is particularly problematic when doing our job
involves telling clients what they do not want to hear but need to
for the sake of their own health and relationships. In those instances, being too good for our own good traps the therapist into
silence or making nice, and further entangles the client into repeat-
ing his problematic patterns.

*Therapist Burnout.* Still another liability of being too good for our
own good is the increased chance for burnout among therapists
who take too much responsibility for people's lives and for the
outcome of therapy. People who are too good for their own good
expect perfection of themselves and therefore assume they can
and should give perfectly. There is no better formula for therapist
burnout than this impossibility.

*Higher Risks for Therapists From Dysfunctional Families.* Although
overresponsibility can be problematic for any female therapist, it
can be especially harmful for professional and patient alike when
the therapist comes from a dysfunctional family. In these situations, the tendency toward overresponsibility and caretaking endemic to these types of families interacts with the Woman's Code
of Goodness and can make therapy less effective at best or crippling to both client and therapist at worst. When she fails to recognize that helping too much is not really helping, that often it is not
in others' best interests to take care of them, a therapist's attempts to
help will harm. This is because systemic overresponsibility in one
person virtually guarantees underresponsibility in the other person. Again quoting Bepko and Krestan (1990), "Being too good for
your own good means being so overresponsible that the other people
in your life take less and less responsibility for themselves" (p. 107).

Now we are ready to delineate what a woman must be to work
effectively with men.

## What Women Must Be

*1. Able to Create a Holding Environment.* A female therapist is in a unique position to incubate the optimal conditions for growth in men, because of her socialized knack for nurturing and for helping people feel safe. Borrowing a concept from Winnicott, Leupnitz (1988) describes the holding environment as a facilitating environment, an ultimately safe and secure place in which people can regress and reexperience events if need be, as they progress to making the changes they wish to make in their lives. "It refers to the atmosphere of safety and trust that the parent provides for the child, and analogously, the therapist provides for the patient" (p. 187). This provision of security and trust for the client is analogous to the security a child requires from a mother in order to develop adequately.

The role of the therapist literally is to contain or hold the family's pain, just as the mother contains the distress of the infant. This sends the message that the child's feelings have meaning, are bearable, can be contained, and can be resolved. Leupnitz (1988, p. 187) goes on to make another statement with which I agree. If patients do not feel sufficiently held by the therapeutic environment either, they will not feel free to make changes.

In short, then, the essence of good psychotherapy, regardless of the sex of the client, is being compassionate and creating healing through the therapist-client relationship. This, again, underscores the centrality of the therapist refining her skills at using herself as an instrument. But the question may legitimately be asked: What relevance does this have for men? Two major issues, discomfort with intimate feelings and with their aggressive urges, cause them to stay stuck and us to shy away from treating them. But these are the very therapeutic issues on which they need our help. So it is critical that we learn appropriately to manage and create a holding environment especially for those very strong feelings in both them and us. Otherwise, therapy is rendered ineffective at best, or even harmful.

This sense of a holding environment is the outcome of the therapist's having successfully accomplished the suggestions listed previously. A primary element that makes women working with men so extraordinarily potent relates to the fact that women have traditionally been the sources of nurturance for men and women alike. A woman who is able to create this environment is able to capitalize on this ever-present dynamic and to create a place of great safety. This makes risk taking in therapy and therefore in relationships ever more conceivable and fulfilling.

2. *Responsive.* A good clinician is able to hear what clients are saying, taking it as a statement about them and not about her. According to Bepko and Krestan (1990), "Responsiveness is a skill that can be practiced only where there is a basic assumption in a relationship that 1 person is not responsible for the other's feelings, needs, expectations, or tasks" (p. 83). The idea is to cultivate the skill of being able to respond to clients' words and affect without reacting to them or making them a statement about you the therapist. That is, you hear what clients have to say as a statement about them, and not about you. A basic ingredient of responsiveness is empathy, and women, because of our socialization, are trained to become very good at this, provided they do not "feel guilty, ashamed, or responsible for the other person's feelings" (p. 83). This makes it essential that the woman has unhooked herself sufficiently from the Make Relationships Work Injunction that she can practice this skill without a sense of undue concern for others' feelings, needs, or expectations of her. If you are responsive, you convey the message that you understand how what they are trying to express feels.

> The process of being responsive requires that you be in touch with your own feelings and not reactive to theirs. You don't feel the heavy weight of having to be good or to "do something" in response to their feelings. Since you really can never solve someone else's problems for them anyway, it feels good to be free of that burden and still let them know that you care. (Bepko & Krestan, 1990, p. 86)

3. *Comfortable Being a Woman.* This attribute is central for the female therapist not to feel one-down or in any way competitive with her male clients. She needs to not feel apologetic for or regretful about being a woman. It matters not whether she sees herself as feminine, but she does need to develop a comfort level with her own identity as a woman. And since identity is

based on one's sex, she needs to have integrated this into her view of herself.

4. *Comfortable Around Men*. It seems obvious to say that for a woman to work effectively with men, she needs to be secure or at least comfortable around men. One dimension of this is that men who try can be intimidating, even for those women who understand their own interface issues about them. So for those who do not understand their own personal reactions to this sort of man, these reactions can be unnerving indeed. Rather than advise those women to give up treating men, I encourage them to learn the etiology of their reaction. And yet, for some, this can be easier said than done. For women who have not devoted the requisite attention to examining their own fear reactions, or even for women who understand their own interface issues about men, these men can seem too intimidating. Men who have learned to win by intimidation or competition can be truly abhorrent for women to take on, for even with them, women must communicate that we can hold our own and be in charge of the therapy, without having to throw our weight around to do so. That is the only way men will feel safe with us, even though they may repeatedly test us to see what they can get away with.

A woman can help herself get comfortable with men by being able to talk in ways to which men can easily relate. For some, this is "locker-room" talk, which may include bold language and swearing or metaphors like "You act as if this is a sudden-death overtime, and the clock is ticking." For others, this means being able to talk financial lingo, with such phrases as "The legal tender in relationships is emotion, and when there is none exchanged, the relationship becomes bankrupt." For still others, analogies from the corporate world are useful, such as "Your wife is telling you that if she can't begin to feel a connection with you, there is about to be a corporate raid, and you won't even have a golden parachute." Metaphors about building can be useful to help more concrete-minded men comprehend and join into the therapy process, such as "Sometimes, in remodeling a house, you can just add a room; but sometimes, you have to level a section to the foundation and start over." There are many facets to consider in indicating comfort around men. But however it is done, it is important to do. And then if you still remain intimidated by men, that is a supervision or consultation issue.

5. *Comfortable Discussing Uncomfortable Topics.* Paradoxical as this
sounds, a woman must be able to tolerate the discomfort that often
accompanies topics that both client and therapist tend to avoid
bringing into the therapy. She needs to learn to be comfortable
responding to and even bringing up sensitive topics such as sex,
sexuality, homosexuality, and clients' sexual responses to her. For
some, an even more difficult topic than sex is money. Open discussion of such topics is laden with societal taboos, overlays from
family of origin, and dysfunction that result from each. With all
such topics, the therapist needs to develop a freedom about handling her own discomfort so that she does not inadvertently cue
clients to keep certain concerns to themselves. I have learned a
rule of thumb: Topics that are the most difficult to handle for both
therapist and client are those with which the most therapeutic
mileage is made. Yet, because many of these topics can be fraught
with emotion and therefore risk for most therapists, it would be
ideal for trainees to have standing invitations to bring those concerns into supervision. Alas, many do not feel free to do so. In the
absence of this, the wise therapist, whether novice or veteran,
seeks supervision from someone sensitive in these areas or consultation from a trusted colleague. This can help ensure that our
own land mines are not detonated by clients' issues to such an
extent that we become nontherapeutic.

6. *Able to Model Both Dependent and Autonomous Functioning.*
Gilligan (1982), in her landmark work on women's development,
states that in order to be a fully functioning adult, either sex must
be capable of being truly separate and yet connected in discrimi-
nate ways. Typically men, because of both their socialization and
the vicissitudes of the psychological separation and individuation
process, assume they are separate and may or may not move
toward connection, whereas women assume connection and may
or may not move toward separation. For maturity, men have to be
helped to tolerate total intimacy and women have to be helped to
tolerate total separation (Rosenberg, 1990). I would venture to say
that most individuals and couples who become part of a clinical
population are there because at bottom they are stuck at one or the
other end of this apparent polarity. Our job as therapists is to help
them resolve this split so that they are capable of both ways of

functioning and can become fully adult. And to reiterate, our best therapeutic tool is modeling these abilities ourselves.

*7. Capable of Both Masculine and Feminine Functioning and Personal Style.* For a woman to create a safe place for men to explore their interior worlds, she must be capable of playing roles that have typically been associated with both male and female functioning. And yet, multiple studies (Correa et al., 1988) of the effect of sex of the leader on group and organizational functioning yield the same results: women have the most difficulty leading men, for these followers resist allowing the leader to exercise her authority. Therefore, the first item of business when any man enters treatment with a female therapist is to establish authority so that he can respect her enough to listen and follow her leads. She must present herself as capable of being agentic (Correa et al., 1988) and strong. Eagly (cited in Correa et al., 1988) defines the agentic dimension as consisting of one's assertive and controlling tendencies characterized by personal efficacy and independence from others. Correa et al. (1988) cite evidence that people tend to view men as more appropriate than women for task leadership and that people describe most leadership behaviors, including competence, as masculine attributes. Therefore, a woman who is capable of demonstrating only those behaviors and attributes that are typically associated with the feminine will have great difficulty establishing credibility with men. And even when she is capable of both, she can anticipate difficulties with finding her rightful place. As a consequence, encouraging men to join in creating family change at best will be difficult, at worst, impossible if she cannot succeeded in establishing her credibility with men.

However, although nurturance is desired from therapists of both sexes, women are never forgiven for lack of it, because of a complex of psychological factors. "Neutrality and objectivity are desirable; coldness and indifference are unacceptable" (Rosenberg, in press). In fact, to not capitalize on the very traits for which we have been socialized for millennia is to miss one of the major therapeutic tools at our disposal in empowering men to begin to face themselves and to plumb their depths. For optimal effectiveness, a woman must be capable of both agentic and nurturing functioning. When she lacks either, she is not forgiven by either gender.

*8. Firmly Benevolent.* To wrap all the foregoing characteristics into a phrase, we might say that the female therapist must be capable of firm benevolence (Rosenberg, in press). That is, she must be capable of carrying out organizational functions without sacrificing her more nurturant dimensions. She must be able to both confront and comfort. She must both set limits and give latitude. She must be able to encourage dependence and foster emancipation. Although these attributes and skills may seem hard to acquire, they are nothing more, nothing less than those that make for optimal development and functioning in all individuals and relationships. So it is critical for ourselves and our families, as well as our clients, to work to develop these requisite arrows for our quivers.

## What a Woman Must Do to Work Effectively With Men

Although who a woman is and her understanding herself can be of utmost importance, especially in working with men, what she does is central as well. She must be able to communicate a sense of competence and confidence. Otherwise, men will not feel secure in her presence. A rule of thumb may be helpful in clarifying the difference between what women need from a female therapist from what men need.

In general, I have found that what women need to feel safe with a therapist is *sensitivity;* what men need to feel safe with a female therapist is *sensibility.* That is, although understanding oneself and being understanding are necessary conditions for effectively doing this work, it is not sufficient to engage men in the process of change. The therapist also needs to be capable of certain specific skills that transcend the bounds of any particular school of therapy. Regardless of one's therapeutic orientation, despite the particular situation or motif on the table in any given moment, the therapist needs to be capable of acting in certain ways to be successful in treating men.

Again, this is not to say that women do not have similar needs of their therapists. However, to reach and join men, it is essential that these elements be experienced by men at the outset for them to feel safe enough to venture into this foreign territory of psychotherapy, let alone with a woman. In fact, I have concluded that with most men, we have one to two sessions to establish our credibility and to engage them in therapy. Otherwise, they likely will go elsewhere or give up trying. These competencies need to be experienced by men in order for them to respect a therapist enough to take risks and feel safe with their emotions. When men, who usually keep their emotions so well in check, start experiencing them boiling, they can feel overwhelmed. And if they do not feel safe in the hands of a strong therapist, they will shut those feelings back down.

These are generic skills and competencies that any competent therapist—male or female—must have or work to acquire. However, for women to work successfully with men, these considerations take on extra significance. For the absence of these can be the therapist's undoing, regardless of the degree of her training or expertise in her preferred treatment modality.

As before, however, there is a caveat in order about women and competency. Again referring to Bepko and Krestan (1990), competence has become the new standard of excellence for women. When applied to women, it directs women to have the unlimited capacity to do well, without help, and without ever feeling or showing vulnerability. This injunction is another factor that leaves women at risk of attempting to be too good for their own good. And it further reinforces our already-present tendency to act as if our own emotional life takes a backseat to everyone else's. Thus "a woman no longer knows what it is to be and feel like a human being" (Bepko & Krestan, 1990, p. 37). Further, when we go overboard on being competent, several very dangerous results can happen. One, it becomes easy to see all feelings as weak and shameful, and thus we devalue those parts of ourselves as females that do feel and make us uniquely human. Also, we cue our male clients that feeling is weak and to be avoided, thereby fueling their already strong socialization against emotions. We leave ourselves at grave risk of burnout. And we undermine the very reasons we were sought for therapy, our gender.

Now we are ready to consider the skills and competencies required for women to work effectively with men.

## What Women Must Do

*1. Communicate Competence and Confidence.* Gilligan (1982) tells us that women tend to reach identity through attachment and identification with others; men do so through separation, independence, and achievement. Because of their different styles of information processing, men often worry, with women's emphasis on relationship and feeling, that our thinking is diffuse and inconclusive (Rosenberg, in press). Further, what men tend to fear most is engulfment. Emphasizing emotions and connection in the therapy exclusively or prematurely can generate intense anxiety in a male and can seem to him as if the therapist is siding with his partner. And yet, to have only endless intellectual discussions is to leave him where he was when he came in: miserable and detached.

To establish our credibility, therefore, it is wise as soon as possible to join the man where he is. The therapist does this by establishing clearly yet noncompetitively that she is in charge of the therapy, that she can hold her own in an intellectual discussion, and that she does not need the man but rather he needs her skills as well as her innate abilities by virtue of her socialization as a woman. I do this, for example, by making sure not to bend over backward to accommodate male clients' schedules except in emergencies, by dressing professionally without always wearing suits, and by clearly stating in the first session my expectations regarding payment for and frequency of sessions. These sorts of signals establish that I intend to win the battle for structure (Napier & Whitaker, 1978) of the therapy.

However, I do not want to be or to appear cold or indifferent either to the man or to his partner. So I am careful to join her as well. For them both, I tell people that I prefer that they use my first name, I respond empathically wherever I am genuinely moved to do so, I pat knees and shoulders, I hug after particularly poignant sessions, and I have decorated my office to be warm yet not frilly. These elements are all my conscious attempt to signal to clients that we are going to work to establish a relationship as a part of this therapy. I prefer to do treatment with people rather on them. Each of these conscious considerations is an attempt to telegraph to clients that they can feel secure knowing that they are in the presence of someone whom they can respect and who is strong enough to take care of them. All these behaviors demonstrate and model that the therapist is capable of the opposite style of relating from what she is socialized to do, yet she still is a warm human being.

2. *Like Men.* For women to work effectively with men, they need to be clear enough on their own issues that they can honestly say that they like men. This is not to say that they prefer men to women. Nor that the therapist must be heterosexual. But a therapist must not dislike men or have an ax to grind with or about them. Otherwise, the male client is at great psychological risk simply by being in that therapist's office. In addition, liking men will enable female therapists to help the women in the man's life find a balance, as discussed in Chapters 6 and 9, where differences are neither bad nor good. Women who have had negative experiences with men that they have not resolved need to be helped to at least neutralize their feelings about men in order to do this work, if not resolve those troublesome feelings. Then individual male clients can have a chance to be liked or disliked on their own merits. Otherwise, men will continue to feel and be seen as peripheral to the therapy, or still more counterproductive, they will be found at fault for all the family's problems. In those unfortunate instances, we and they will be missing a great opportunity for creating personal and family change.

3. *Have a History of Some Satisfactory Relationships With Men.* The female therapist need not be married or even be heterosexual, for that matter, to do this work. However, it is extremely helpful if she has had some positive experiences with males on which to draw. It is optimal if the men in her family of origin offered her good practice at learning how to relate to men, because it is a fundamentally different kind of knowing when one has grown up exposed to and experiencing good relationships. It is also helpful for her to cultivate relationships with men as friends. Still, it is possible for a woman to do this kind of work even without the benefit of this kind of knowing. One way would be through therapy, supervision, or consultation from a male who is clear and competent to help her work with this sparseness of positive experiences with men. Another way to acquire compensatory experiences with men is participating in a mixed-gender therapy group. This way men in the group can offer her a different model and practice at seeing males and relating to them differently.

4. *Don't Be Afraid of Men's Power or Anger.* It is widely accepted by clinicians and laypeople alike that men are socialized away from

all feelings. Men have been given the message that they are allowed only one emotion, anger, and this leaves them with a tendency to load all their affective responses into anger. It is also widely acknowledged that women are socialized not to feel anger or any other emotion that carries with it power, because that is not "nice." Therefore, when a man experiences and expresses his anger, it can be a frightening experience for a woman indeed. And yet, if men are to be helped to express emotions in general and to learn functional ways of handling anger in particular, we must encourage them to bring their angry feelings into treatment. And we must be confident and able to demonstrate that we can hold our own when they do. If we ourselves are frightened by men and by their anger, we will subtly or not so subtly discourage their expression of this perplexing emotion. If that happens, both partners miss a significant opportunity to learn about how successfully to manage that emotion. Further, to whatever extent a man's anger covers his other emotions, the route to those emotions is through and past anger. For therapists to disallow anger out of our own anxiety or fear is to replicate the logjam in the man's life and relationships and therefore to severely jeopardize the outcome of the treatment.

## A Final Word

There are certain attributes and skills that a female therapist must have in order to effect life-changing work with men. If a woman does not innately possess all of them at this reading, she is encouraged to seek the requisite help so that she is able to develop each of them. This can be done by therapy, supervision, or consultation. Although the therapist's own struggles can inadvertently obstruct the treatment, they also can be used for therapeutic gain *when she understands them.* Whether her own personal issues will facilitate treatment or detract from it depends on the extent of her motivation and of her self-knowledge.

We have seen the characteristics and skills a female therapist must possess in order to be optimally effective in working with men. In the next chapter, we will consider some of the pitfalls for her to anticipate and to avoid in her work with men.

# References

Avis, J. M. (1990, June). *Working effectively with men in therapy: Report of a Delphi study.* Paper presented at the annual meeting of the American Family Therapy Academy, Philadelphia.

Bepko, C., & Krestan, J. (1990). *Too good for her own good: Breaking free from the burden of female responsibility.* New York: Harper & Row.

Bowen, M. (1978). *Family therapy in clinical practice.* New York: Jason Aronson.

Correa, M., Klein, E., Stone, W., Astrachan, J., Kossek, E., & Komarraju, M. (1988). Reactions to women in authority: The impact of gender on learning in group relations conferences. *Journal of Applied Behavioral Science, 24*(3), 219-233.

Fowler, R. (1991, April). Though number of women in field has grown, still room for more! *APA Monitor, 22*(4), 3.

Gilligan, C. (1982). *In a different voice: Psychological theory and women's development.* Cambridge, MA: Harvard University Press.

Kramer, J. (1985). *Family interfaces: Transgenerational patterns.* New York: Brunner/Mazel.

Leupnitz, D. (1988). *The family interpreted: Feminist theory in clinical practice.* New York: Basic Books.

Lewis, J. (1979). *How's your family? A guide to identifying your family's strengths.* New York: Brunner/Mazel.

Mason, M. (1991). *Making our lives our own: A woman's guide to the six challenges of personal change.* San Francisco: HarperSanFrancisco.

Napier, A., & Whitaker, C. (1978). *The family crucible.* New York: Harper & Row.

Rosenberg, P. (1990, June). *Group: gender: power.* Symposium conducted at the Minnesota Psychological Association's Friday Forum, St. Paul, MN.

Rosenberg, P. (in press). Comparative leadership styles of male and female therapists. In B. DeChant (Ed.), *Women, gender, and group psychotherapy.* New York: Guilford.

# 3

# Pitfalls When Women Work With Men

Therapy is a unique setting where people are offered an extraordinary experience. Clients' hopes can be raised and dashed—often many times within the same session—as they struggle with issues and feelings that usually are shared only with their closest intimates, if at all. In fact, with its intensity and focus on sharing otherwise private thoughts and experiences, the therapeutic relationship is one of the deepest, most intimate that most people can have. This situation lends itself to intense emotion of all kinds, with which the therapist must be prepared to deal.

The wise therapist knows that these emotional crosscurrents are a natural part both of life and of the therapeutic process. In fact, a well-respected family therapist who treats many sexually offending therapists, Maloney (1992), remarked in a recent presentation at a national family therapy meeting: "We are very vulnerable to how this [abuse] process starts if we deny that it could ever happen to us, if we insist that it happens to 'those guys.'"

Well aware of the price of a repressive, punitive attitude toward normal human feelings, the therapist knows how to manage this emotional caldron therapeutically. She is well aware of the risk for therapists and clients alike if this situation happens. But she also knows realistically that we all make mistakes. This is not to excuse mistakes, but to empower ourselves to learn to monitor ourselves and our responses to clients in the therapeutic process.

In the current litigious climate, with growing monitoring of our clinical judgments of all kinds from many different sources, I fear that many professionals will adopt a defensive approach to acknowledging and addressing their mistakes or their questionable behavior. If this happens, both their clients and themselves are at risk. Again quoting Maloney (1992), "As laws become more stringent and rigid, we risk these issues going underground." This will not serve our clients who need us to learn from our mistakes just as we expect them to learn from theirs. This situation has the potential to leave therapists preoccupied with their own security rather than willing to take reasonable risks that could in fact be powerfully healing for clients. And perhaps my biggest fear is, as Peterson (1992) predicts, the future will see us "isolated, afraid, and [will] further erode the professional-client connection" (p. 5).

My purpose in this chapter, then, is to help the reader negotiate her way through the maze of responsibilities and directives that are inherent in the therapy relationship in a way that is clearly therapeutic for her clients, without compromising her spontaneity and ability to maneuver as a professional, but protecting her reputation and her livelihood.

## Chapter Overview

The focus of this chapter is on examining the crosscurrents that predictably get stirred up between client and therapist in treatment. I will discuss the therapist's vulnerabilities, occurring anytime she enters the treatment room, but particularly manifest when a female therapist treats a male client. And then, in the final section, I will offer guidelines for female therapists who treat male clients.

## A Conversation With the Reader

You may be asking yourself: Doesn't every therapist take this emotional maelstrom into account? The answer is no. Shouldn't therapists have had training that would make them aware of this and of how to work constructively with these therapeutic dilemmas? Without doubt, but unfortunately in many cases, they have not. And finally: If this emotional vortex exists in any therapy situation, aren't the crosscurrents greater when female therapists treat male clients? That's the point: Women who work with men, especially in the intimacy of individual therapy, need to be especially circumspect.

In this chapter I will attempt to fill this gap. The discussion will help therapists protect both themselves and their clients from getting caught up in these undercurrents that are potentially damaging for everyone. Put more proactively, I will attempt to help the reader clarify for herself how she might approach these potentially very precarious situations and use them to generate greater therapeutic growth for clients. Handled appropriately, many of these emotional eddies can generate much fruitful discussion that can help clients turn the therapeutic tide in their lives.

## On Clarifying One's Own Beliefs and Style

I am well aware that some of the statements I make in this chapter will be controversial and subject to differing opinions on what is right and wrong. I make no attempt to present *the* definitive statement on how a therapist must think or operate. That would suppress thought and creativity, rather than stimulate it. Instead, my first goal is to open new therapeutic avenues for clients, as readers increase their therapeutic artistry in handling what would otherwise be precarious moments in treatment that they usually would avoid. My second goal is to break the conspiracy of silence that shrouds this vital issue, and my third goal is to empower therapists to know and to become comfortable with their own style as therapists. These considerations all will help readers use themselves as therapeutic instruments confidently and creatively.

Many of the on-the-spot clinical decisions I make reflect my own style as a therapist as much as anything else. The reader will need to make her own stylistic decisions. For example, after we have established some therapeutic intimacy, I frequently use the nicknames I hear people call themselves or each other, like Bobbie for Barbara or Jamie for James. Or I use terms of endearment like "Toots" or "Sweetpea." These are some of my ways of forging an intimate working alliance with clients, male and female. They fit my style, so they are comfortable for me. They may not fit the reader. So she is encouraged to develop and stand by her own unique style. And yet, I agree with Peterson (1992) when she says, "Endemic to the concept of professionalism is self-restraint" (p. 30). How can the professional find a happy medium that meets her style and at the same time operate with the needs of the client first and foremost? Establishing some clarity on how to navigate between this Scylla and Charybdis is the focus of this chapter.

## Key Terms Defined

Central to translating the ideas in this chapter into practice is understanding two key terms: *transference* and *countertransference*.

In psychoanalytic theory, the feelings that occur in the patient in the course of treatment are thought of as *transference*. The assumption is that the patient transfers onto the therapist reactions from other experiences in life. In that way, the therapist becomes a surrogate or a stand-in for other significant people in the patient's life as the patient begins to play out old dynamics (Edelwich & Brodsky, 1991, pp. xvi-xvii). Both client and therapist then can examine those behaviors and see whether they offer the best course of action. Usually, however, they are anachronistic and need to be changed. The situation is more potent and easier to work with when clients are not just talking *about* relating, but are communicating *as if* they perceive the therapist as, for example, a parent. Hence, discussing and understanding transference reactions can be very therapeutic.

*Countertransference* is the therapist's own personal experiences that become activated in response to the patient. According to Edelwich and Brodsky (1991), "Any emotion (including anger or resentment as well as sexual desire) can be transferred from past life situations. Thus, the entire range of feelings that a therapist and patient can have about each other can be understood as examples of transference" (pp. xvi-xvii).

These concepts, then, make up the backdrop for all the ideas in this chapter. In the next section, we will see examples of countertransference reactions that can be used either therapeutically, or potentially can undermine treatment.

## A Day in the Life of a Clinician: Clinical, Teaching, and Supervisory Examples of Countertransference Responses

The following examples illustrate typical situations that a seasoned clinician and academician encounters on a daily basis. They are proffered to encourage the reader to contemplate experiences that although commonplace, may not receive their appropriate attention precisely because of their mundaneness.

### Another Conversation With the Reader

Before you proceed any further into the chapter, I would encourage you to stop for a moment and reflect. Ask yourself questions such as these: What are my greatest concerns as a female working with male clients? Where have I got stuck with male clients in the past? What scares me the most when I contemplate working with male clients? What do I enjoy the most? How comfortable am I with expressing affection with male clients? How confidently can I set limits on aggression? How comfortable am I with intimacy of all kinds in my own life? Do I have any axes to grind with men? If so, how do I keep them out of the treatment room? Or don't I?

You may even want to write a few notes to yourself before you proceed. The more clear we are as therapists on our personal (countertransference) issues, the better the treatment we will provide, and the safer we and our clients are when they enter our offices. It is really true that "The unnamed remains the invisible" (Bograd, 1988, p. 33). Remember these questions and your responses to them as you read on.

### A Clinical Example

Don was a 40-year-old always single[1] man whose relationship with his mother was highly sexualized. Although she never literally molested him physically, he came to realize as the therapy progressed that her subtle behavior and verbal messages toward him always left him feeling as though she had. For example, there were no doors on his or his brother's bedrooms. When he began shaving, obvious proof of his budding manliness, he felt he had to hide the fact that he was shaving and conceal grooming supplies like deodorant from his mother. Always puzzling to him before, he realized through treatment that this was so that he could protect himself from her further sexualizing him and that rite of passage into manhood. Just describing this caused him repeatedly to shudder in disgust. Probably what sent the greatest shudders down his spine was his telling me how, after he had left home as an adult, she often would begin letters to him by writing, "I'm up here lounging on your bed." They felt like love letters to him. Once, to his dismay, she did a strip tease in front of Don, then adolescent, who was frozen in horror at the sight. His father was buried on Christmas Eve day 1 year before Don began therapy, and that evening after they had opened each other's gifts, his mother asked whether he wanted to go to church. When he declined out of grief, her immediate reply was, "Oh, you want to be alone with just the two of us."

Because it is a universal tendency to see our family's way as normal, he truly had no idea how inappropriate and intrusive her behavior toward him was. Nor did he grasp how totally repulsed he had been by her encroachment and covert sexual messages all his life. He managed this level of oblivion by developing a reaction formation to defend himself against her early on. A reaction formation evolves as a way for individuals to defend themselves against feelings that would otherwise be overwhelming by replacing an unacceptable drive with its opposite. For example, people who develop a reaction formation against anger feel compelled to be cheery all the time, whether the situation or their responses to it warrant this or not. My client's only awareness was that he felt it mandatory to protect himself by keeping his distance. Not surprisingly, this translated to a rigid need to keep his distance from all women.

After one fairly routine session about three months into the therapy, I was startled to find myself feeling as though I had been sexually fondled in the session. Of course, I knew that I had not been and that neither he nor I had behaved inappropriately in any way. What, then, was generating this rather disturbing countertransference reaction in me?

I hypothesized that my experience reflected how Don must have felt in the presence of his mother. This is known in some circles as projective identification, where clients telegraph how they feel by projecting it onto the therapist. In other circles, this phenomenon is called parallel processing. This is where the therapist's feelings come to parallel the client's. Regardless of the name, in both processes, it is as though the client is telegraphing his or her experience to the therapist, who then picks it up and feels it. The key clinical question that will help the therapist work with this puzzling clinical phenomenon is: Whose reaction am I feeling—my client's or my own?

I decided to very carefully bring my experience into the next session. With great embarrassment and repulsion, Don was able to begin to glimpse that this was exactly how he had always felt toward his mother; that it was against this that he had developed his reaction formation toward his mother; that he had unwittingly but understandably transferred this way of coping with closeness to all women. We then had a major clue to why he felt compelled to stay so distant from women. Although it was a very delicate and awkward matter for me to bring up, I felt that doing so was essential to his treatment and to his future relationships with women. And in fact, it fostered a major turning point in his view of himself, in his relationship to me, and in his view of women.

## A Training Example

I designed and teach a course in a master's program in counseling psychology for the purpose of engaging students in thinking about the treatment process on a metalevel, rather than becoming preoccupied only with techniques, as beginners are wont to do. The focus is twofold to assist these beginning counselors to (a) integrate the patchwork of theoretical material they have acquired throughout the program into a usable treatment approach that is idiosyncratic to them and (b) conceptualize the process of change and their role in facilitating it. In an anonymous pre/post student survey, I recently asked the following question: "What are your concerns about working with the opposite sex as a beginning therapist?" The sex ratio in the class was about two females to every male, which reflects the current trend toward the feminization of the field of psychology.

*Female Students.* The following is a representative sample of the responses the female students gave on the postcourse survey.

Boundaries for physical expressions of affection and caring, hugging [and] touching, that they not be misconstrued.

My own unresolved issues. How to remain "neutral" with a male client (a) who acts like (or worse than) people in my life, and (b) does or doesn't do the same things that are "hot" buttons within my own relationship with my significant other.

I hope I am able to break down my stereotyped image [about] the way men are and not treat all men alike just because they are men.

Physical attraction.

Their resistance to my expertise because I'm a woman.

Men are usually not as in touch with feelings.

Being judgmental; being intimidated.

I am not terribly relaxed around men since I have little exposure to many men other than my husband and social friends.

Blaming men as a result of my own issues, unconsciously siding with women or wanting subtle forms of "revenge" against male clients because of my past experience.

I have abuse issues (personally) which I'm working on in my own therapy. However, my ease and comfort with the opposite sex is impaired, and I'm aware this will affect my work with male clients.

That I won't be able to talk in their language (i.e., using terms [and] phrases that they are comfortable with).

I don't have any.

*Male Students.* What follows is a representative sample of the responses of male graduate students who similarly were polled.

Bias against men, touch issues, and my bias of wanting to "take care of" hurt women.

Either being so sensitive to issues that no work gets done, or not aware enough that a whole bunch of "male" stuff will be thrown on me.

My issue of "saving" women in trouble.

Not being accepted by the client.

Problems with intimacy.

I do not have much concern.

*Conclusions One Might Draw From These Responses.* At the most optimistic, some of these counselors-in-training, both female and male, perhaps will be less apt, simply by virtue of the awareness they articulate, to fall into the gender trap in the treatment they provide. Alas, for some, both males and females, their treatment likely will be overshadowed by the all-too-popular deficit model of men that is based on the assumptions that men are emotionally deficient and inferior to women. These students will need to take steps that go beyond the purview of a graduate school classroom to be prepared adequately to meet the clinical challenges they will face.

Some apparently intuit that reality. Nevertheless, just articulating for themselves what their concerns or issues might be is not sufficient. Most will need to go the next step and clarify in concrete terms just how these issues can encroach on the therapy they provide. And because biases run deep, optimally they will receive help to clarify these potentially highly charged issues. Otherwise, they will be no better off for their awareness. It is hoped that their early supervisors will be attentive to this need as well, or these fledgling therapists may founder in the crosscurrents of these perilous eddies.

If the reader found these novices' concerns echoing her own, I urge her to take immediate action to remedy this situation. Otherwise, she likely will be rendered ineffectual even before she opens her mouth with clients. And even if she vows to work only with female clients, those same troublesome attitudes about men, no matter how covert she vows to keep them, will creep into the messages she gives women about men. Biases cannot be disguised totally, and we all have them. Thus, although a therapist may succeed in helping women to feel and to function better on their own, she will have accomplished little in the direction of teaching them how to acknowledge and work with their natural interdependence with men.

And to the reader who senses she has been successful in navigating around the shoals that are likely to remain potential obstacles for many of these students: Ask yourself how you will know when you have succeeded. Kelly and Hall (1992) offer the following bench marks that have certainly held true in my own clinical practice:

> How will we know when we have succeeded? When our counseling technology has advanced such that we have more men coming in for counseling than appointments available, when we see at least as many male clients as female clients, and when men report to us that

they feel heard, validated, and valued for the first time, we will know
we have reached our goals in counseling men. (p. 271)

I encourage male clinicians reading this text to ask themselves
if they could hold themselves to these same standards.

## A Supervision Example

As a practicum supervisor for a school of professional psychology, I once supervised an extremely talented and mature doctoral
student who came into my practice to do her 9-month practicum.
She had held many responsible jobs where she herself had supervised others and had successfully treated countless clients who
had been considered intractable by the system. So, although she
was technically a student, she was a seasoned therapist.

Because she was such a gifted therapist, she and I both fantasized about her joining the practice after completion of her degree.
Alas, her heart was on the West Coast, and she and her family
planned to move back there when she finished the year. This, then,
would mean that not only would she have to terminate with the
clients she had worked with in the practicum experience, but she
would have to leave my associates and me as well.

One session about 3 months into her practicum, I thought I
noticed her keeping an uncharacteristic distance both in supervision and as she talked about the cases she was working on. This
was puzzling to me, because I had experienced her as an unusually
warm and open person and therapist. The first time I asked her
whether she was feeling a need to keep an emotional distance from
a certain client, she denied it. So the supervisory hour proceeded.
But I was still puzzled by her unusually bland and detached affect.
Although I believe I would be concerned about this presentation
in any event, I was particularly perplexed because the case she was
presenting involved a couple in which the man needed to be
worked with directly on his repressed neediness and intimacy
fears, and to do so would mean to move in emotionally with him,
rather than to hold back. So I believed that she was staying
detached to protect herself, and that this countertransference reaction likely would have serious ramifications with this particular
case, possibly even rendering her totally ineffective. It, therefore,
would represent a kind of seduction of the clients. By that I mean,

they would keep coming back to her because they liked working with her and thought they were being helped, but at base, they would not really be doing the work they needed to heal their very dysfunctional marriage.

What would you do, as this woman's supervisor? I decided to press the issue of her detachment. When I asked about it again, she burst into tears and talked openly about how hard she could already tell it would be for her to leave in another 7 months. Then she could see that, without her realizing it, she already was steeling herself for that eventuality by staying aloof. It then became clear to both of us why, even though her therapy was technically sound, it felt hollow. The direction of supervision then changed. In addition to helping her clarify her treatment focus and what her own countertransference reactions might be in general, we began to routinely guard against this self-protective mechanism creeping into her work by discussing it directly. Then, the therapy would not be contaminated by her needs and processes. As therapists, we have a responsibility to guard against that and to make certain that we are operating on our clients' behalf rather than protecting ourselves from our own vulnerabilities.

### Summary

Whether as professors, supervisors, and clinicians we identify it or not, our own countertransference reactions are factors in our work. We need to be courageous enough to acknowledge that, vigilant enough to keep those responses in check, and wise enough to try to instill a similar clinical sensitivity in those whom we have a responsibility to teach.

## Potential Barriers to Successful Treatment

Through trial and error over years of working with men, I have learned many practical tips on how to structure and orchestrate therapy when men's emotional constriction and couples' inability to intimately connect are central to what brings people to therapy. Clearly, struggles in these areas are powerful enough to cast a pall over the whole of people's lives. This section will clarify some potential quandaries and provide some practical hints on the pitfalls related to gender that can compromise treatment for the unaware therapist. First, I will discuss general snares when women treat men. Then I will consider potential snags endemic to couples therapy.

## General Pitfalls

In addition to the snares of which the therapist must be aware in working with men in couples therapy, there are some pitfalls in working with men in general, regardless of the treatment modality the female therapist uses.

*Failing to Take Into Account the Effects on Men of Their Socialization.* Miller (1986) summarizes the central difference in men's and women's socialization when she says that in our society, a woman's identity has traditionally been based on her capacity to develop and maintain relationships, whereas a man's has centered on autonomy, competitiveness, and success. Mick, whose words we hear throughout the book, speaks to the wearing impact on him of trying to follow these societal injunctions. One can easily speculate on the impact of this mentality on his relationships and on his physical health.

*Mick:* It's tremendously overwhelming to always have to put the mark higher on the wall. There's never a sense of completion or satisfaction. There's always more, better stuff, higher, faster stuff. This is the safest place I've ever been, 'cause I can just come here and be. As males, we skip that class, that part of life that gets us in touch with our feelings.

Because of our socialization, both men and women are bewildered about the new rules for male-female relationships. Aggravating this situation is men's socialization to know and adhere to rules. A critical step in transcending this problem is understanding that men and women are different, with different modes of expressing themselves and different emphases for what is important. It serves no purpose other than to further polarize the sexes to judge either gender's way of being as inherently right or wrong. Meth and Pasick (1990) offer a perspective that I heartily endorse: "If men and women believe that they must learn each other's languages, and that neither has the sole possession of The True

Way of Life, then it becomes possible to begin building bridges to each other" (p. 85). Clients must be helped to use these differences constructively in ways that enhance the relationship, rather than further driving a wedge between them.

*Temporary Increase in Isolation for Men Who Break the Masculine Code.* Although it becomes clear to most men early in treatment that they have paid dearly for adhering to the unwritten, unspoken code of masculinity, those who are in transition to the new identities they are hoping to evolve also can experience discomfort from the transition itself. For although there are many women who are pining for an emotionally available man in their lives, they can seem to be difficult to find. Even more rare for men who have been touched by emotion are male peers with whom to relate. Most men are able to hug their friends after winning a sporting event, because their masculinity has just been validated by participating in, and winning, the game (Swain, 1989). In those instances,there is clearly an emphasis on activities as a way to communicate among men. But until they incorporate an identity as a sensitive man and find kindred spirits, men who now are learning to communicate with words and physical affection can experience increased loneliness for a time. Swain (1989, p. 72) states, "Perhaps the most consistently reported difference in men's and women's friendships is in men's preference for joint activities and women's preference for talking." So when a man learns how to communicate with words and physical (nonsexual) affection, he joins a minority of men. This can itself be frightening and isolating, and the therapist needs to be aware of this situation and prepared to help. The words of Mitch, age 39, who had participated in couples, individual, and men's group psychotherapy with me, speak to this issue. A physician in a large, thriving practice, he describes the response of one of his colleagues, who saw him having lunch with his best male friend. It is worthy of note that the friend also had been a participant in couples, individual, men's group, and an extended family of origin therapy with me, and Mitch was referred to me by this friend. So this in itself would facilitate their being able to go to deeper levels of communication with each other.

*Mitch:* I had an interesting lunch the other day. I met my friend, and we sat and talked about emotions. And my [business] partner was sitting at another table. I could see he was wondering what the heck was going on. When we got back to work, he asked, "Who was that?" I said, "My friend." He said, "What did you talk about?" I said, "Feelings." He said, "I mean, what was the agenda?" "Nothing. We just talked." Even so, somebody will come up to me and ask if we can go to lunch, and I'll wonder, "What is this about? Is it insurance? Is it kids? What is this going to be about?" Going into it, I still feel we've got to have an agenda, and we've got to go through this stuff. And I don't want to do that. I don't want us to get together and have an agenda to talk about.

Here we see that, even when a man has learned how to do friendships differently, and even when he has no doubt that he wants to, his socialization creeps in and sets up a cacophony of messages with which he has to reckon. We also see how a man must steel himself for social sanctions, subtle and otherwise, that big boys don't need anyone, and that men who like men surely must be gay. All these contingencies press on men who decide not to play by the old rules anymore but rather to evolve into more responsive, less constricted, more relational human beings, and we need to be prepared to help them make this transition if they falter.

*Resisting Us Because of Our Sex.* Sometimes the fact that we are female can be an asset in working with men because they often feel less threatened sharing vulnerabilities with women than they do in risking a repeat of the locker-room humiliation many felt from their peers growing up. But for a host of reasons that usually boil down to societal messages and their relationships with their mothers, some men have difficulty giving credibility to women. And just because we are in a position of authority by virtue of being therapists does not guarantee that a man automatically will extend credibility. It is up to us to warrant it.

How does a female therapist warrant credibility without becoming an honorary man in the process? I believe there are some significant ways. One is learning to speak a man's language. This can mean using locker-room language, as in the time I told a male client, "I wonder if pissing people off on purpose is the way you feel loved." It can also mean using metaphors from the man's work world, as when I told a physician and his nurse wife after months of getting nowhere in therapy that if they didn't start to look at what they were doing to each other, their marriage nearly was a DNR (Do Not Resuscitate), and would become a DOA (Dead on Arrival). Another phrase I often use is we will need to Roto-Root the pipes that are clogged to get communication going again. Metaphors such as these can act like indirect hypnosis in that they provide a direct line to the unconscious and bypass conscious resistance. They also indicate that I am willing to enter the client's world.

I also establish credibility by challenging clients. As a rule, I find that this is much easier to do pointedly with men than with women, because men are used to communicating directly and in a rough-and-tumble way. It helps a man realize that the therapist is a force to be taken seriously. And sometimes it is the only way to break through people's patterns of resistance. For example, Jeremy, a 30-year-old therapist from whom we hear in the chapter on loss, spoke the following in a session where I insisted that he stop talking *about* his sadness about his mother's death when he was 7 and start feeling it so he could finish it.

*Jeremy:* I do a very good job of making it sound like it's coming from my gut, but it's all disconnected. And I've gotten away with that with everyone else, because no one challenges me like you do. Shit! What you learn about yourself! All this time, I've thought I was pretty good at feeling and articulating my feelings. Shit! I thought I was good at that! And all this time, I've thought I was doing myself a service, but it's not been full service.

Because men are accustomed to speaking directly to other men, I find little or no difficulty in confronting men, putting them on notice that they have work to do. However, my experience is that women, because they are less accustomed to that kind of directness, can become extremely angry when confronted with the need to do their own work rather than continuing to blame the man for all the relationship's woes. Confronting rigid and controlling women can be much more precarious. However, not to take on a person's defensiveness perpetuates the problem. I continue to believe that if all the therapist does is nuzzle clients' defenses, she accomplishes nothing and deserves not to be paid. It is a judgment call based on clinical experience whom the therapist confronts, how strongly, and when.

*Credibility Difficult to Establish.* By whatever means that are ethically at her disposal, the therapist must establish her credibility with all clients as quickly as possible. That is what Minuchin (1974) called joining. As I have said, men are likely to be skeptical, perceiving therapy as a woman's world, especially when it is provided by a female. To be effective, it is imperative that the female therapist refine her own skills at joining male clients. There can be special considerations involved. For example, men who are a great deal older than the therapist may be more comfortable relating to her as a daughter or comparing her to a Betty Grable pinup than seeing her as a competent professional. In this case, she is likely to feel patronized, or even harassed. And if she does not short-circuit this, the therapy will be rendered ineffective. Also, depending on the era and life experience of a man, being treated by a female professional can seem odd, and his expectation may be that he will receive less effective help than if he were being treated by a male. This is unlikely to happen with our own clients, because men with those views would tend to seek out a male therapist to begin with. Furthermore, many with these views would not acknowledge the need for therapy at all, because until relatively recently, therapy was seen as the province only of crazy people. The female therapist is most likely to run into this attitude when she brings a father into an extended family of origin session. Then it is especially important that she establish credibility quickly and effectively, given the time-limited nature of the sessions and because many fathers brought into these sessions are old enough to be her own father.

An illustration is provided by one father, who spontaneously volunteered the following comment on his way out the door the day of the last session. To me, it was high praise, especially coming from someone who had no previous exposure to or respect for psychotherapy. He was a burly, rather coarse, self-made, tattooed man in his late 60s who I worried prior to the sessions would have great difficulty engaging in the process. His comment, I am thankful to report, proves me wrong.

*Dad:* I just want to say that I just couldn't conceive of how this was going to work. But I can see it really did. And with a lady doctor, too!

However she does it, a female therapist must establish her credibility. She does this by being scrupulously attentive to how she handles herself; how she discusses the agentic topics that are typically men's bailiwick, such as structuring treatment and payment for sessions; even by how she furnishes her office. Specifically, I do this by making it clear that I am in charge of the sessions, by introducing, starting, and stopping them.

For a man to feel safe to explore his inner geography, both he and the family need to feel that they are in a safe place and that the therapist is strong enough to provide a holding environment for him to do that. Joining and providing a safe context is a sine qua non, especially for effectively treating men.

*Our Own Unexamined Biases About Men.* A thorough self-analysis of our assumptions about men is required if we are adequately to treat them. Among too many of us, an implicit pathology model prevails that implies that maleness is a sickness to be cured. In countering this bias, I agree with Kelly and Hall (1992):

> It is assumed that men have chosen not to participate in a [treatment] process that has not promoted their development. Instead, mental health counselors [need to] ask themselves, "What have *we* done to make counseling inaccessible to men, and how can *we* change to accommodate their needs?" and make the necessary changes.

Just as is needed with women, nonsexist treatment approaches for men must be adopted by all of us if men are to be treated effectively and with respect.

It is impossible for therapists to be bias free; that would be inhuman. Rather, it is our *unnamed and unexamined biases (counter-transference issues)* that pose the primary threat to the efficacy of the therapy. Every therapist needs to be aware that she is not merely doing therapy *on* people; she and her client(s) together are creating an emotional system (Kramer, 1985). Whether she knows this or not or wants to acknowledge it or not, it all makes up the subterranean drama of therapy. And when this covert drama goes on totally outside the therapist's awareness, then both the client and the treatment she provides can be jeopardized.

Earlier I reported my students' responses to a question about their concerns in working with the opposite sex in therapy. I believe that the two students who said they had no concerns are downright dangerous. They are at great risk of not only unexamined but unacknowledged biases bleeding into the therapy. Paradoxically, the student who worried about her own unresolved issues, such as how to remain neutral with a male client who pushes her "hot" buttons, is much safer to her clients. She is much more likely to be aware when her own issues are affecting the treatment negatively. The women who were troubled by their acknowledged tendency to blame men because of their own experiences are also a better bet. However, for those women to provide adequate treatment to men, they would be well advised to seek supervision in addition to therapy. The dictum, "First, do no harm," is compulsory here. Unfortunately, too few people—men and women—have a clear grasp of their own issues, and they use the treatment room to make their own point or even subtly to seek revenge, as another student courageously admitted. This is a cardinal example of inability to separate their personal feelings from the professional demands of the situation, and it is particularly risky for clients when therapists have a covert agenda of which maybe even they themselves are unaware. Then "male bashing" takes on very dangerous proportions.

*Being Seduced Into Disliking Clients.* There are many subtle seductions employed by people who seek, and yet are terrorized by, intimate connections. And not all of them have sexual ends in mind—probably more have control of the relationship as the goal. These clients attempt to lure us into relating to them (transferentially) the way many other significant figures in their lives have. This leaves them comfortable by virtue of their knowing exactly what is expected and often gives them the perfect rationale for staying the same. This unconscious wish to remain the same unfortunately often does not stop their chiding us for not helping them change, perhaps because it is easier to work on transforming someone else's life than on closely probing one's own.

    Edelwich and Brodsky (1991) offer a perspective on this clinical conundrum so vexing to the therapist who is sincerely trying to avoid the trap:

> The term "seduction" encompasses a broader range of interactions
> that occur not only in therapeutic relationships, but in all human

relationships. It is of the nature of human interchange that people
are drawn into emotional involvements, positive or negative, which
support or interfere with the avowed purposes of individuals involved.
One may be seduced into antipathy as well as attraction. (p. 11)

Just how susceptible a therapist will be to either positive or
negative seduction will depend on several factors. Perhaps first
and foremost are her own beliefs about and needs for intimacy. If
she *needs* clients, then letting them go, whether prematurely or
not, will be difficult for her. Further, if the pragmatic therapist is
anxious about what the loss of this client could do to her caseload,
perhaps she will find herself working extra hard to pander to the
client who is trying to seduce her into a fight. Likewise, if the
therapist has merger issues that she copes with by staying detached and reserved, rather than seeking intimacy, she is susceptible to clients who will stir up angry responses in her so that both
"legitimately" distance. And these types of clients are experts at
making themselves targets for mother's disapproval and even rage!

Rather than give in to our natural human tendency to throw
these cantankerous clients out of therapy, it is preferable to see
whether they can be helped to learn another way of operating. My
suggestions are threefold: (a) examine your own behavior to make
certain that you are not in fact providing shoddy treatment; (b) help
clients understand their feelings and what you both could do better
to avoid and learn from the discomfort; and (c) if you honestly
believe that you are taking their individual needs into account to the
best of your ability and there are still complaints, leave the struggles
with the clients, where it belongs. Either they will resolve it, or they
will drop out of therapy. On the bottom line, after examining your
contribution to the quagmire, if your conscience is clear, accept their
threat or wish to resign from the treatment. I prefer this to termi-
nating the treatment myself, because it minimizes the client's
feeling abandoned by yet another authority figure. Whatever the
route of termination, it is a relatively safe bet that it is only a matter
of time before these issues resurface. And if you have left the door
open, sometimes people will come back to see you. And if not, they
may begin with someone else. However, the same scenario is
likely to repeat if that therapist decides to be honest and not
coddle them. But maybe after another unsatisfactory experience,
they will face the need to deal with themselves.

Forty-three-year-old John provides a clinical example of a positive outcome of struggling with this clinical quandary. Here, my sticking with him through what I experienced as his obnoxious behavior became therapeutic for him. John was referred to me by both his girlfriend and his best male friend, at different times former clients of mine. He had denied the need and the suggestion repeatedly, until his girlfriend broke off the relationship, tired of being unable to establish an intimate connection with him. For three sessions, he rambled on, alternating between occasional tears, which he would quickly stuff, and theatrics the likes of which Cecil B. deMille would have applauded, carrying on in a way that seemed to be only for my benefit, about how wronged and hurt he was. At first, I listened to him, doing my best to forge a working alliance with him. As he prattled on, appearing to try to please me with his display of how distraught he was, even his expression of emotion came to seem to be a distancing maneuver, as every time I would zoom in and ask him to elaborate on what he was feeling, he would take off with more theatrics.

Having great difficulty developing a working alliance with John, I began to feel as though I simply did not like him. Recognizing that I would not be able to work with him if this continued, I confronted him when I could stand no more. It was either that or throw him out of my office. I told him in no uncertain terms I was having difficulty in liking him, that I thought he was using his slick salesman self to sell me rather than being genuine, and he had the balance of that session to get me to like him, or I was done trying to treat him and would cheerfully refer him elsewhere. With that, the facade came down, and he began to tell me of his sadness, hurt, and fear in some genuine ways. Because he stopped, at least for the moment, presenting his false self (Masterson, 1988), by the end of the session I felt without a doubt that we had now forged a working alliance and contract.

My confrontation so early in the therapy was a gamble. But if I had not made it, I would truly have been unable to treat him, which would have been to his detriment. So it was a risk I believed I had to take. Later, as we got into the meat of our work, I shared with John exactly what I had been responding to initially, and he readily acknowledged what he had been doing, volunteering that he was mighty glad that I had taken that chance.

A follow-up note: As John worked through much emotional underbrush, our bond became very strong. He started to incorporate what is commonly called a "good enough" parent experience with me that was reparative of his traumatic experience with his alcoholic parents. As evidence of that, when he occasionally would telephone between sessions, he would start the conversations with "Hi, Ma, this is John." His acknowledging his positive transference reaction and our bond indicates that we were able to forge a strong, safe working alliance.

*Finding Intimacy the Therapist Needs Through Clients.* If the therapist is frustrated about finding the intimacy she wants and needs in her own life, she is at risk of seeking intimacy vicariously through or even actually with her clients. Here where both the client's and the therapist's vulnerabilities can be exploited is perhaps where the greatest sexual dilemma for the therapist occurs. Because we are not superhuman and therefore not above the emotions that affect all human beings, therapists whose needs for intimacy are unexamined and unfulfilled are at the greatest risk. The fact is that therapists and clients do have feelings for each other, and well they should. These feelings are important for healing in the psychotherapy process, as they provide the learning that makes the therapy successful—if they are handled appropriately by the therapist. For a female therapist to avoid compromising her position and ethics, she must be on the alert for markers that might indicate that she is using the intimacy of the therapy setting to meet her own intimacy needs. If she finds she is doing so, for her clients' and her own good, she needs to seek help in understanding her own life.

*Experiencing Seductive or Sexual Responses From Clients.* When clients become seductive with therapists, I believe they are looking not so much for sex as for the nurturance they have lacked in their lives and do not know how to find. Or they are hoping to feel a sense of specialness that they either had and lost or never had at all. Either way, they have learned to use sexual wiles or prowess as the primary way to stroke their battered sense of self. Not only is it *not wrong* for male clients to act seductively toward us; rather, they can be expected to do so (as can female clients with male therapists). Clients can act seductively without our allowing ourselves to be seduced. In fact, it is the job of the mature, centered therapist to manage such situations in a way that neither crosses the appropriate boundary nor shames the clients, who need to understand why they act this way and learn better options.

Bograd (1988) describes a meeting of seasoned family therapists that she convened to talk about the taboo subject of sexual nuances in therapeutic relationships; she quotes an anonymous female therapist who said,

> On the days I lead [men's] groups, I dress as if I'm a female eunuch. I am sometimes irritated that I feel compelled to make such a choice, but this way I can insure that I can get some therapy done, rather than dealing with the men in the group flirting with me. (p. 33)

This response of avoiding the crosscurrents she could obviously feel in the group is unfortunate, for she leaves herself extremely and unnecessarily uncomfortable, thereby compromising her own effectiveness as a female leader. And her timidity is causing the men to miss a very valuable learning experience. Discussing these issues directly is grist for the therapeutic mill. Through this issue, many men could learn about how they are seductive with women in general, which undoubtedly forms a barrier in their lives. And had she the courage to raise the issue of seductiveness, she would attain more, rather than less, credibility in the group and with the individual men.

We as a culture have socialized males to believe that it is acceptable for them to need and want sex but not comfort. For far too many males, *intimacy equals sex*, and they have no concept that it can be otherwise:

> Seductive behavior is to be expected from clients. It should not be seen as being directed at the therapist personally, or as cause to respond in anything other than a professional way. The therapist's job is not to pass judgment, but to help clients find better ways to satisfy their needs. Since a client's behavior in therapy reflects inadequate coping strategies learned elsewhere in life, sexual overtures toward the therapist can be explored therapeutically to shed light on the client's characteristic responses outside of therapy. (Edelwich & Brodsky, 1991, p. 26)

Because clients are hungry for what we, especially as women, can give them, they will tend to detect mixed messages or read into our words what they want to hear unless we are very clear. It is our responsibility as therapists to draw that line so that there is no doubt of its existence, without shaming or rejecting clients for their responses to us. Otherwise they will learn nothing. And worse yet, they perpetually will hide their needs and neediness in shame, as though needing were something of which they should continue to be ashamed.

A clinical example illustrates how the therapist might handle this awkward issue. An interchange early in the course of a long-term therapy with Aaron, whose words we also hear elsewhere in the book, illustrates how and why men can get so confused. The only son of a father who virtually abandoned the family when Aaron was 11 years old, he was given the overt message that he had to be the man of the family. He took this to mean that he was to need nothing from his mother or his younger sisters and that he was to take care of them. The following interchange took place in the first phase of therapy when he was learning to allow himself to open up and to trust me.

*Aaron:* I didn't know how to define a self, so I defined my self by what I wasn't. Now I'm trying to find out who I am, not who I'm not. Living in the house with just women, I was scared to death I'd become a homosexual. So I learned how to be a womanizer. Without my father there to teach me, I couldn't be a man's man, so I learned how to be a ladies' man. Every time I'm with a woman, I'm womanizing.

*Therapist:* Do you womanize with me?

*Aaron:* I'm afraid I do, because it's become a habit now.

*Therapist:* When you hug me, are you womanizing?

*Aaron:* When I'm afraid, I womanize so that I'm not afraid. Then I can take control of the situation. If I'm not seducing, I feel nervous. (Pause) I didn't know what I was doing. Damn! That's not a nice thought! I'm not a shit!

*Therapist:* No, you're scared.

*Aaron:* I've gotten so good at womanizing, that I'm really scared of myself. I define myself by the women I date, so I can't tell if I have a genuine interest in them. . . . Women have always been a mystery to me. Although they're a mystery to me, I still feel more secure around women than I do around men. It's OK if I want sex, but not solace.

Later that session:

*Aaron:* That's why I'm much less sexually active now. I'm questioning my motives. Friday nights I stay home alone now. I feel much more at peace with myself, because I don't have my dick leading me around the room anymore, doing dumb stuff.

Rather than shaming men like Aaron for the coping style they developed to survive psychologically, the role of the therapist is to help them examine the roots and consequences of this behavior. Only in this way can they be helped to change both their worldview and their behavior.

*Not Working Constructively With Clients' Reactions to Us.* Whenever men and women are together, there is a sexual charge. Often, therapists do not recognize the subtlety and nuance that indicate that this is happening. And we are even less prepared to respond therapeutically when the response is made overtly. And yet, this is a very normal, natural part of male-female interaction that exists in every situation, whether it is acknowledged or not.

Perhaps the major reason that therapists are so skittish about this topic is the fear that they will be unable to draw the line between these normal feelings and unethical acts. This is needless worrying once the therapist is clear with herself and is able to indicate plainly to her clients where the boundaries are on their interactions. Therapists who are definite and unambivalent need not overcompensate by denying nonsexual, nonexploitative intimacy in their offices.

Even if a woman is not particularly physically attractive and is old enough to be a man's grandmother, men still can have a physical response to her. This is part of the transference reaction that is inherent in any therapy. For example, in one men's group session where we were discussing men's sexual responses to women in general, one man openly confessed to my portly cotherapist, who is 25 years his senior, that he would love to see her in a hot pink bikini.

Given their socialization, most men first automatically check a woman out physically (not necessarily sexually). And if women are honest, they will acknowledge that they do the same. Then they usually have one of two reactions to what they have just done. One is to repress and deny their feelings, fearing acknowledging that they have responded this way. Or they operate with their sexual awareness staring them in the face, trying to push it aside because it feels wrong to have those feelings.

Neither of those responses is necessary when this checking out happens in the presence of a courageous and skilled therapist. These normal, human responses can be surfaced, talked about, and got out of the way. Female therapists need to learn to do just that, if they are going to work effectively with men.

A men's group session in which my female cofacilitator 20 years my senior insisted that the men talk about their responses to me illustrates this. She is identified below as Therapist II.

*Therapist II:* Let's bring this issue of attraction to women back in here. How do you handle your feelings toward Beth? At least half of you are in love with her.

*Mick:* Half of us? (Laughter around the group)

*Therapist II:* (Smiling) I should have said most.

*Oren:* Beth is probably the third or fourth woman in my life that I haven't thought of as a sexual person as opposed to being a woman I can respect for nonsexual reasons. And I think that's because . . . we talked about that right from the beginning. She made it very clear in the first 20 minutes of the first session that we were not going to have an affair.

*Gary:* I put up a wall when I came in here. She was the therapist I was going to work with, and that was all. It wasn't till I acknowledged that this is a human being across from me that I found physically attractive that she became real, became a person. And she is also a competent therapist. I don't know how many sessions we were into therapy when I was able to acknowledge this.

*Norman:* (To Therapist I) I didn't actually feel real comfortable with you until my wife and I had some sessions where we had some hard, gripping things and we hugged. I hugged you. That's when I really felt you as a real close friend and there wasn't any question mark anymore about sexuality there. And it was a good feeling, because it showed me that I can hug another woman and be a friend without it being sexual.

*Mitch:* I don't think there's a woman that I've met in my life—I just thought about this in the last 2 minutes—that I haven't checked out physically. I can't honestly sit here now and say (pause), there isn't a woman, I don't care what age, that instantaneously I haven't checked out physically, which is the same as sexually.

*Therapist II:* Women do the same with men. I do it all the time. And I know Beth does. That's part of the fun of being with them. That's part of relating. It's a human response to a human being, and it's a good feeling to have it. And you don't have to do anything about it. You can just enjoy it.

*Gary:* If you had gone around the room 5 minutes ago and asked me if I had done that, . . . I would have said, "Oh shit! No!" But when you stop and think about it, you are doing it all the time, but you're probably not aware that you're doing it.

*Mick:* There's a line between availability, and as you say, checking it out.

When these normal feelings can be talked about, they can be got out of the way of the therapy. And if talking about them does not accomplish that, then the therapist needs to seek consultation— for her own as well as her clients' protection, for she has not yet won the battle for structure (Napier & Whitaker, 1978). In such a case, it probably would be appropriate to refer the client elsewhere. However, in all my experience, this has never happened.

*Mistaking Transference Reactions for Personalized Invitations.* Whatever the nature of men's reactions to us as women and not just as their therapists, I see them as transference reactions. It matters not the actual physical attractiveness of the therapist. Rather, the intimacy that is generated in therapy, particularly individual therapy, is a hothouse for these sorts of very natural feelings. Failure to recognize this leaves us at risk of being seduced. And clients are at risk of being ashamed about these normal feelings and humiliated when their overtures are spurned. In any case, when these matters are bungled, an important opportunity for growth is lost.

There are subtle seductions that I often do not even choose to comment on to clients. But it behooves me to make a mental note of them lest I become caught up and to use them as diagnostic information. Then I can decide what, if anything, needs to be done with them therapeutically. For example, one particularly good-looking man in the initial stages of his individual therapy would sit on the couch opposite me, leaning back in a particularly alluring pose. This went on for two or three sessions and stopped without comment from me, once he figured out he could get nurturance from me that would not be sexual. Another young, attractive, jet-set executive fantasized aloud about my going to London with him on his next business trip, and another time, about how much he had wanted me with him one night when he cried. In these instances, I did not choose to comment either. I see situations such as these as markers of clients' loneliness and need for nurturance that they are as yet able to voice only indirectly. And I see the statements of the second client as indicators that illustrated several key elements about the therapy. First, I was becoming a transitional object for him, in the psychoanalytic sense, so that he could begin to learn what he was looking for in a relationship with a woman and identify when he had it. And second, he was finally allowing himself to trust someone, particularly a woman, enough to let himself in on the needs he had denied his entire life thus far.

Such instances give the therapist an important toehold for gaining greater ground toward men's full admission of their repressed feelings and needs. I recognize them as markers that the treatment is progressing as it should.

Another incident illustrates the kind of covert comment a client makes. My response was simply to gently and clearly reiterate what he was already acknowledging: that our connection, though real, would go no further. Nor was he asking it to.

Harry was an attractive, separated man exactly my age. Growing up in an emotionally barren family where his father was literally absent for the first 5 years of his life and his mother was emotionally unavailable to him left him feeling abandoned and starved for nurturance. And so it is no surprise that he married an emotionally barren woman, thus perpetuating his family of origin pattern of deprivation. One day, as we began to explore the depth and duration of his deprivation, he made the following statement. It illustrates how close the client wants to be and how imperative it is that the therapist maintain the boundary between them. Harry's words were simple and succinct:

**Harry:** It feels good to be intimate and still respect the bounds of our relationship.

If I had not previously and repeatedly made it clear that we would not cross the boundary required for him (and by inference, me) to be safe, this situation could have been confusing and risky. Instead, it was a lovely shared moment.

*Exploiting Clients' Need for Us by Undermining Their Autonomy.* Although most therapists would be loath to admit it, they can find themselves in situations in which for one reason or another they need their clients to keep coming to therapy. Perhaps they work in private practice and their ability to pay their mortgage depends on their hours worked. Or perhaps they practice in an agency where tenure and raises are dependent on their ability to complete a specified number of client hours. Perhaps they simply enjoy seeing a particular client. Worse, maybe they have come to be dependent themselves on seeing certain clients. I always check myself out on this score when I find myself looking forward to seeing a client. These situations, potentially toxic for any client, can become particularly problematic for male clients because it catches men in an area where most feel particularly vulnerable: becoming overly dependent and losing their ability to function autonomously. Often, this makes them reject closeness in relationships. Lacking assurance that closeness will not be suffocating and that psychological merger will not take place, who would dare try it?

Men's dependence is an extremely charged issue. Facing just how dependent they can be runs counter to the socialization and the psychological development of males in our culture. It can be quite threatening for most men, and they simply steadfastly refuse to risk it—with us or their partners—if they cannot feel confident that learning how to be functionally dependent will not compromise the autonomy that makes them men.

Being able to help a man protect and preserve what has made him a man is the only way to reassure him that exploring the side of him that craves connection and intimacy will not eclipse his previous autonomous self. Then we can help men change by facilitating their seeing how they have constrained their behavior and affective range in the service of gender definitions. Miller (1986) correctly summarizes this split for men:

> [Men's] greatest source of fear is the totally false belief that [the pull toward other people] will reduce them to some undifferentiated mass or state ruled by weakness, emotional attachment, and/or passion, and that they will thereby lose the long-sought and fought-for status of manhood. This threat . . . is the deeper one that equality poses, for it is perceived erroneously not as equality only but as a total stripping of the person. (p. 23)

The following excerpt illustrates how a positive transference reaction to the therapist can be emotionally corrective for a client. Further, his feeling for the therapist is instructive in that it helps him identify what he is looking for in a relationship with a woman. And it is useful for the therapist diagnostically in gauging how the treatment is progressing.

Terry, a 42-year-old divorced man, had been unsuccessful in establishing a long-term relationship with any woman except his female best friend. Divorced after an affair approximately 10 years ago, he still dated that woman but remained unable to commit to a relationship with her. But he could not seem to live without her, either. Their living in this twilight zone, neither truly in their relationship nor able to leave it, was brought about in part by his complete denial of his needs and neediness. And yet, he would become like a petulant child when his needs were not noticed or met. So the treatment was aimed at enabling him to understand his conflict about his needs and give him an emotionally corrective experience that could then allow him to do his relationships with others differently. About 3 months into the therapy, he reported:

*Terry:* I left here last time feeling, for the first time, that I'd been really, deeply understood.
*Therapist:* What was that like?
*Terry:* It was liberating, hopeful.
*Therapist:* What was liberating?
*Terry:* It was liberating that now I can shed that skin, and that you can help me make the necessary adjustments for my life. Now I realize how nice it would be to call and say, "I need some reassurance. I'm scared." Somebody like you, for instance. Somebody whom I knew would have my best interests at heart, who wouldn't take advantage of me.
*Therapist:* So how does it feel to let yourself in on needing me?
*Terry:* Fine! I have this conviction now that if I can let myself need you, that you'll help me.
*Therapist:* And you're not scared that you'll get too dependent?
*Terry:* You won't let me. You're not going to want me to call you on Saturday morning and tell you how my date was.
*Therapist:* You're right. And you took a quantum leap this week!
*Terry:* I don't know. All I know is I feel different.

The way to engage men in family change is to reassure them that it will not mean a total revamping of self, that the person they have known will not be lost. If not given those reassurances, they will be loath to explore and experience their long-repressed needs and longings for connectedness.

*Becoming the Receptacle for Men's Immaturity and Unexamined Prejudices About Women.* "The devastating fact is that most men are fixated at an immature level of development" (Moore & Gillette,

1990, p. 13). Sometimes female therapists are beset with male clients whose idea of masculinity equals domination. To set such a client straight, the therapist needs to help him understand the concept that Moore and Gillette (1990) describe as Boy Psychology: "Boy Psychology . . . is charged with a struggle for dominance of others in some form or another. *And it is often caught up in the wounding of self, as well as others. . . .* [italics added]. Man Psychology is always the opposite. It is nurturing and generative, not wounding and destructive" (p. 5).

It is important that the therapist unequivocally believe that a man remains a boy not because he wants to but rather because that is the only path he knows. Treatment is aimed at helping him reckon with the multiple prices he has paid for this way of being and at helping him gain the requisite skills and attitudes to change those more destructive, self-defeating modes of operating. Our task is to lead him into healing experiences so that he can explore and actualize the inner world of masculine potentials (Moore & Gillette, 1990).

The intake session of a physically abusive, perfectionistic, domineering, 48-year-old man who had a physically abusive, perfectionistic, domineering father illustrate his beginning realization that he was fixated in an immature state of domination. He was forced to recognize his abusiveness, his immaturity, and their effects when his wife of 20 years finally announced that she was leaving him for another man.

*Perry:* I don't understand how I let my abusive behavior go on so long, without dealing with my feelings. And I have no idea where to start, but it's time I grew up! After this first surfaced a couple of months ago, I've been on my best behavior. But it was already too late.

*Therapist:* What are the feelings that go with saying that?

*Perry:* I feel like a failure. My wife worked so hard on this, but I didn't try at all.

*Therapist:* If you have, I think correctly so, linked your abusiveness to your inability to express emotions, then we've got to help you express your emotions as emotions and not act them out.

Moore and Gillette (1990) clearly articulate what is needed of us as therapists:

In the present crisis in masculinity, we do not need, as some feminists are saying, less masculine power. We need *more* of the *mature* mas-

culine. We need more Man Psychology. We need to develop a sense
of calmness about masculine power so we don't have to act out
dominating, disempowering behavior toward others. (p. xviii)

It is our job as therapists, both male and female, to midwife the
rebirth of this Man. What that takes is firm limits on his abuses of
power while we work to get up underneath his defenses to find
the more gentle, tender human emotions that are there but have
been cauterized long ago by early life experiences. Accepting this
perspective, I hasten to add, *does not excuse* a man's misbehavior.
But it does allow both him and us to have a nonpunitive, non-
shaming way to begin to work with it. No one can hear that he
needs to change if he must at the same time defend himself for
what he has done. If it is important to learn as therapists how *not*
to engage clients' defenses if we are to be therapeutic, it is essential
in situations in which their defenses are already high. In order to
perpetrate violence, they are defending against feelings of fear
and powerlessness. Yet, when they have done violence, unless
they are sociopathic, they feel ashamed and out of control. It is
essential that the therapist grasp the swirl of feelings that underlie
dominating behavior and that she not shrink from it.

## Obstacles in Couples Therapy

When people present for couples therapy, one of the first diagnostic considerations is to clarify the source of the dysfunction
between them. For those of us who think systemically, it is easy to
place the locus of the dysfunction in the system. But what exactly
does that mean? Where the therapist goes from there depends on
her theory of therapy. All too often, she misses the role of gender
in the genesis of the dysfunction and instead pathologizes a client
or the system. This does not serve a constructive function either
for the clients' lives or for the therapy. In this section I will detail
the pitfalls related to gender as it affects treatment.

*Categorically Blaming Males for Relationship Dysfunction.* Often even
when therapists identify gender as a contributor to couples' difficulties, they frequently place the cause of the problems in the lap
of the male simply because he is male. And yet, because of the way
marital relationships are structured in our culture, men often are

automatically in a one-down position. According to Goldberg (1987), "In the way it is constructed, marriage is essentially a feminine institution. Its requirements for success are heavily weighted toward qualities more highly developed in the feminine spheres of consciousness" (p. 59). This makes it very difficult for men to participate as equal partners in the emotional arena of marriage.

Therefore, it almost inevitably appears to be the male who is the cause of relationship problems. But this can be too simple an assessment, and I challenge therapists to look more closely at the etiology of people's dysfunction. The woman inevitably has contributed to the relationship dysfunction too, because it truly does take two to tango. But even when it appears that a man's behavior is at the root of the problem, he usually is doing what he has been socialized to do. So he experiences his own crosscurrents arising from his difficulty in reconciling his socialization as a male with the new cultural imperatives for what a man is to be.

For example, consider the following excerpt from an extended family of origin session. Oren, whose words we hear throughout the book, invited his father to come and end the estrangement that had existed between them for 30 years. Their interchange illustrates the tragic impact of a father's buying into societal expectations for how a father teaches his son to be a man.

*Oren:* I always had this image of you being tough and powerful. I was afraid you'd be disappointed if I didn't get things done, so I used to hide.

*Dad:* I couldn't have been a very good dad.

*Oren:* I think I now have words for what I wanted then. I just wanted you to be involved with me. I always remember I was afraid . . . of just not doing a good enough job.

*Dad:* I must've been an insensitive person in those days, to not recognize what you needed. I just can't get over right now how that's upset you. I didn't know any better. I just thought I was making you a fine young man. If I'd ever had any idea what I'd done, I sure would've done something. I miss you. I've missed you. The way I was brought up, work was happiness.

*Oren:* And I thought, "I'm not worth it. He'll be too busy."

*Dad:* If there is anything that would help us get together, it would be worth it. I'd like to be a dad as much as you'd like one. I probably worry more about rejection than you do. I just thought of this! I wonder if that's why I work so much. I wonder what I'm running away from. But whatever it is, we're here together now. . . . I was the responsible one. There's just no excuse for what I did.

Meth and Pasick (1990) similarly state:

"To be a man" requires him to constantly prove himself in a highly structured, competitive arena. Manhood is not merely a static, developmental milestone. Rather, it is a status that must be earned repeatedly. He can "be a man" one moment, and if he fails to meet a challenge the next can just as easily lose the tenuous designation (in his own mind, if not in the opinion of others). (p. 203)

These examples illustrate how men are behind the eight ball when they enter marriage having internalized societal expectations for being men. The wise therapist knows this, factors it into her assessment and ongoing treatment, and avoids pathologizing the man for doing what he has been shown to do to be a man.

*Appearing to Favor One Client Over the Other.* No matter what they announce their purpose to be, most couples who come to therapy do so in frustration over failed attempts to find intimacy with each other, either sexual or emotional. It is the therapist's job to assess the factors that contribute to the situation and to decide where she will start to intervene in this painful condition. It is usually women who express the most pain from this failure to connect, and because of men's socialization away from feelings and intimacy, who would be surprised by that? According to Meth and Pasick (1990), the message that men hear is,

Being a "private person" euphemistically expresses one of the cardinal rules men subscribe to: Pay little heed to your feelings or, better, deny them altogether. At least, keep them to yourself. . . . Most wives are not privy to all their husbands' private thoughts. Men learn not to discuss feelings since this will reveal vulnerability, weakness, and suggest a more "feminine" orientation. (p. 203)

Little wonder, with messages like that, that it is usually the man's defenses that pose the initial challenge and focus for the therapy work! The pitfall here, however, is that working initially with him can leave the woman feeling left out, threatened, or ignored. And it can leave him feeling shamed and blamed for their problems. The situation is particularly precarious if the woman grew up in a family where her needs for nurturance were ignored, leaving her voraciously hungry. For her to have to watch him get the therapist's appropriate attention can leave her feeling like a starving person who is forced to watch others eating a banquet. At the same time, if the therapist begins to focus on the woman and her concerns, she must be aware that the man may feel that his initial fears are coming true. He then may feel that the two women are siding with each other, ganging up on him, and leaving him stranded.

So where is it safe for the therapist to work? How does she stave off the feeling that each may have that my needs do not count and that I will not get my due? It is of central importance that she go back and forth in highlighting the issues of each of them that warrant attention. She may alternate several times within one session. Or she may alternate sessions. Or she may do a series of sessions focused on person before she shifts to the other. However she does this, the therapist must be prepared clearly to demonstrate that she has no favorite and has not forgotten about the partner on whom she is not currently focusing. Often, even when people are being reassured of this, they deny the need for reassurance. I continue in my reassurances all the same, so that even if their conscious mind resists the acknowledgment, their unconscious mind can hear it.

The key therapeutic challenge, then, is to focus on the partner whose issues appear to be the most conspicuously responsible for the blockage between the couple *at that particular time,* while reassuring both as to two very important factors: (a) just because one partner is the focus of attention in any given session or moment does not mean that she or he is to blame for all the couple's problems; and (b) even if one partner is not receiving attention at the moment, this does not mean that that partner's concerns are unimportant. Although these reassurances ought to go without saying, people whose passions are piqued may be functioning in those moments at some very primitive emotional levels. So I no longer take the chance of my behavior being misinterpreted, but explicitly explain what I am doing.

The words of Kari and Mark, both highly competent physicians in their mid-40s, illustrate this dilemma for both the couple and the therapist and how carefully the therapist must work to keep the balance.

*Kari:* (To the therapist) I'm fearful that you can awaken in Mark some parts that I can't.

*Therapist:* Can you say some more about that?

*Kari:* A sense of excitement, joy, pleasure in himself. How do I say it (pause), things that were there once upon a time between us that went away. A sense of excitement that comes with sharing with someone else. This has been gone a long, long time from our relationship.

*Therapist:* What's your understanding of why I'm doing that? (Deciding to take no chances) I'm doing it for you both, not for me. Are you worried that Mark and I are going to get carried away sexually? Because we're not. That simply is not going to happen. I'll see to that.

*Kari:* No. The adult person in me knows that. Maybe it's a broader concern. If I can't push those buttons and you can, someone else can come along who will. (To Mark) If that soft part of you stays hidden, then you are mine. And if you show this, the world will see you and want you. And then you'll look at me and say I'm not the person you want to be with. (Pause) But there's also the possibility that you could end up saying I'm the one you want to be with. And then it gets better for us. So I just wanted to put this on the table and say I'm scared.

*Therapist:* Thanks! I'm glad you let us know where you are.

*Kari:* It's also scary for me when you two get close, because the little kid in me is scared. I wonder if you're going to love him better than me. And that scares me. So I wanted to warn you that I really want you to do this. But it really scares me.

*Therapist:* Can you talk to her, Mark, and help her with this?

*Mark:* I have a lot invested in you, and I love you. And if I find that other people love me, I'm not interested. I have a true desire to share my life with you, to be close. It's a spiritual need I have, too, to be close to you.

*Therapist:* Mark, tell Kari what you're feeling right now.

*Mark:* Happy. I'm happy that you're being honest with me about your feelings. I feel sometimes like we're going through this big sea of garbage. We're in this little boat in a big storm, and we're rowing through it saying, "We have this big moment, and we're together, and that's all that counts." That's the only important thing. We have each other.

*Kari:* I take that a step beyond that and say, "But when we get through this storm, we'll have to ask if we still want to be together."

*Mark:* That's a scary thought!

*Kari:* But then it means more.

*Mark:* Yes. Because we're doing it because we choose to, not because we have to or because we possess each other.

Here we can see the crosscurrents of primitive fears and jealousies that get stirred up in the woman about both her husband and the therapist. Even when what she wants is a more emotionally available husband, she may still have her own negative feelings

about the process of his becoming that. Such feelings, if unacknowledged or unattended to by the therapist, have the capacity
to undermine the treatment. And yet, not to provide the help the
man needs to become more emotionally available to the woman is
to perpetuate the dysfunction that pains her the most. So it is
imperative that the therapist have the ability to walk a fine line,
balancing both people's needs and feelings.

*Confusing Emotionality With the Ability to Be Intimate.* Meth and
Pasick (1990), in an effort to debunk the myths that constrain both
men and women in relationships, list as their first myth to dis-
credit, that women automatically are good at expressing feelings.
This lore is particularly illusory in that women, who are socialized
to feel and express emotions, usually can express a wider range of
passions than men who usually are permitted to express only anger.
But the savvy therapist knows that merely being able to express
emotion does not automatically build pathways toward intimacy.
Sometimes effusive expression of emotions such as anger can
serve as a distancer when it prevents and protects one from having
to express more vulnerable, intimacy-generating feelings such as
hurt and sadness.

The words of 25-year-old Heidi illustrate this fallacy. The highly
talented and gregarious child of three generations of alcoholic
men, she thrives on crisis and is stuck on effusive emotion as a
way to connect with people. When her fiancé began to discover
his own emotional life and express himself, she had a very strong
negative reaction—even though it had been at her insistence that
he began therapy with me in the first place. Worn down by constant, unresolved crises marked by torrents of emotion, he finally
left the relationship. The following dialogue occurred in a session
in which I was attempting to help her pick up the pieces of her life
after he ended their engagement:

*Heidi:* If a man is sensitive, he is weak. And if he were there for me, he
  wouldn't meet my need for crisis. And as we've figured out, I need
  crisis. And besides, Bob would've seen sides of me, because of his
  sensitivity, that I hardly ever show. So I'd be afraid of his finding the
  private me, instead of the public me.
*Therapist:* And if he found that, what are you afraid would happen?
*Heidi:* Oh, fear. Fear that he would abandon me, of course. I guess I just
  didn't trust him. And I just didn't trust myself. (Sadly) I wish I

could've spent this couple of years feeling what I could from him, rather than spending all my energy demolishing it!

This excerpt illustrates that women, who generally appear to be more open, trusting, and expressive initially, may well be just as fearful of genuinely expressing emotion as men. It is up to the therapist to screen carefully for this subtle incongruity. It is not always because of men's failure to express themselves that relationships sidetrack or rupture. It is an interactive effect.

## Danger Zones for Therapists

When a therapist approaches a danger zone for herself, she automatically places both herself and her clients at risk unless she is clear as to how to negotiate through this potential mine field. It is essential that the therapist be well versed in how to deal with this subterranean drama that goes on in therapy whether it is recognized or not. Anyone who works in any capacity in a clinical context must have a working mastery of these highly charged issues, for at the core, they involve the person of the therapist. It also goes without saying that these same perils exist when men treat women.

Although many of the delicate issues discussed here involve sex, not all of them do. Some involve the therapist's need to monitor her own countertransference reactions in general to the intimacy of the therapeutic setting. Even a therapist who would not consider having sexual relations with a client faces challenges and dilemmas that affect her in the work. And of course, these in turn can affect her clients unless she is aware of them and knows how to work effectively with these potential quandaries.

This discussion is vital because, although our gender may be the reason we are sought for therapy by either sex, it can pose traps for the unaware. I raise several questions to challenge the reader to find answers to as she reads this section. If after she has finished, she still has some confusion, it would be in her own and her clients' best interests that she seek supervision or consultation to answer them before she steps onto what could potentially be a mine field. For in the caldron of a therapy hour, that confusion could translate to some potentially disastrous actions from which she needs to protect both herself and her clients. It should be noted

that these same sorts of issues can be expected to surface when
client and therapist are the same sex, if the sexual preference of
one or both is for same-sex relationships.

How do therapists handle a client's sexual attraction to them?
How do therapists handle a client's flirtation with them?
What do therapists do when they find themselves sexually attracted to
    clients?
What is an acceptable boundary on therapeutic intimacy?
What level of physical contact is appropriate, particularly with clients
    who are attractive to you or who might be attracted to you?
How do therapists assess whether the personal feelings that arise be-
    tween therapist and client enhance the therapy or undermine it?
When and how is it appropriate for therapists to share the sense that
    there is a sexual undercurrent between them and the client? Is it
    ever?

"Every act represents a choice, and part of a helping professional's
mandate is to transcend personal feelings when making choices that
affect a client's well-being" (Edelwich & Brodsky, 1991, p. xxiv).
In this section I will attempt to help the therapist establish her own
framework for making her intervention choices.

As is reflected in the chapter on individual therapy, I believe that
the relationship a man has with a female therapist can become the
prototype for successfully relating to other women. Yet, in order
for that degree of intimacy to develop and still be safe for both
client and therapist, there are some safeguards that a therapist
must install. To do this, she must be clear herself about her own
style and her own limits.

## The Special Vulnerability of the Impaired Provider

Again quoting Maloney (1992), "The connection must be made
between personal problems and professional vulnerability." That
is, the therapist is especially at risk when she is struggling with
nodal life events herself, such as death or divorce. Of course, nodal
life events like these cannot be prevented automatically. Therefore, when a therapist is experiencing these, in order not to be an
impaired provider, she needs to seek consultation or therapy for
herself so that she and her clients are protected from her needs and
biases spilling over into the treatment.

### Risks Greatest in Individual Therapy

There are several danger zones for a female therapist when she treats male clients, particularly in individual therapy, where no one else is present to dilute the intensity of or monitor the emotional responses that flow back and forth between therapist and client. And yet, no safer laboratory to practice intimacy skills exists than a therapist's office—if the therapist can take steps to ensure everyone's safety. For men are uncomfortable with, and often inept at, intimate relating because they avoid it; and they avoid it because they are uncomfortable and inept at it (Meth & Pasick, 1990).

## Boundaries: A Key Concept

Before we consider danger zones, a discussion of the concept of boundaries is necessary. A complete analysis of this very complex issue of boundaries and boundary violations is well beyond the scope of this one chapter. However, clinicians should be well versed and confident in this very precarious area. I encourage readers to study, for example, Peterson (1992), Edelwich and Brodsky (1991), and Simon, Stierlin, and Wynne (1985) as grist for more thorough contemplation of how sensitive problems develop and effectively might be handled.

Still, limited discussion of the issues is warranted here. Specifically, four questions will be answered briefly: (a) What are boundaries? (b) What are boundary violations? (c) Why are boundaries important? and (d) What are characteristics of boundary violations?

### What Are Boundaries?

Peterson (1992) defines boundaries simply as "limits that protect the space between the professional's power and the client's vulnerability" (p. 4). Elaborating on this basic definition, she says boundaries

> protect the space that must exist between professional and client controlling the power differential in the relationship. . . . [Then quoting clients] "They define where I end and you start," said a therapist. "It's a way of saying what is mine, what I will allow and what I won't. They mark the territory between us." (p. 46)

Simon et al. (1985) offer another definition: "Dysfunctional families show disturbances of boundary differentiation. Boundaries allow for the differentiation and development of structures. A disturbance in boundary formation is thus synonymous with pathological structure" (p. 26). That is, boundary disturbances interfere with the healthy functioning of a system. It is especially incumbent on us as mental health providers to be vigilant about not promoting pathology by our own behavior, however wittingly or unwittingly we do so.

## What Are Boundary Violations?

Again relying on Peterson (1992), "Boundary violations are acts that breach the core intent of the professional-client association. They happen when professionals exploit the relationship to meet personal needs rather than client needs" (p. 75). She elaborates:

> Boundaries are the limits that allow for a safe connection based on the client's needs. When these limits are altered, what is allowed in the relationship becomes ambiguous. Such ambiguity is often experienced as an intrusion into the sphere of safety. The pain from a violation is frequently delayed, and the violation itself may not be recognized or felt until harmful consequences emerge. (pp. 74-75)

Perhaps the main problem with boundary violations is that they replicate for the most susceptible their experiences with role reversal in their families of origin. Thus, instead of a corrective emotional experience, our conduct with those clients offers a replication of these early, familiar, very damaging encounters

It should be noted that many boundary violations are initiated by clients who consciously or unconsciously try to reduce the window of their own vulnerability by equalizing the power differential in the relationship. These situations, too, are our responsibility to manage appropriately to prevent the client's having yet another experience with being hurt by those who are supposed to help.

## Why Are Boundaries Important?

Again to quote Peterson (1992), "While these unspoken and less visible boundaries monitor the inequality between [therapist and client], they also create the safety net of understanding that joins us in an agreed-upon and common purpose" (p. 48). This under-standing protects client and therapist alike from being suspicious of the therapist's intent and motives in making the interventions that must be made, for there remains little doubt in whose best interest they are being made.

Peterson's (1992) work goes beyond a focus solely on clinicians to consider these same perplexing issues for teachers, clergy, law-yers, and physicians. In her comprehensive coverage of the issue, she defines boundaries this way:

> Boundaries regulate our interactions. . . . These demarcations pro-vide us with a sense of personal privacy and safety. Operating within the boundaries that define a healthy professional-client relationship produces the consistency and predictability in behavior that lowers the risk to clients. . . . They allow for a safe connection based on [clients'] needs, not on those of the professional. Boundaries regulate our interactions. These demarcations provide us with a sense of per-sonal privacy and safety. Operating within the boundaries that define a healthy professional-client relationship produces the consistency and predictability in behavior that lowers the risk to clients. (p. 46)

As we have seen, perhaps nothing has a more significant impact on creating a safe place in the therapist's office than clear, firm, fairly enforced boundaries.

## What Are Characteristics of Boundary Violations?

Peterson (1992) uses an interesting analogy in discussing the problem of detecting a boundary violation. "[It] is difficult, be-cause it is a process, rather than a single event. It grows like a cancer beneath the surface of the relationship's legitimate purpose and is hard to recognize until it emerges as a serious, blatant problem" (p. 72). She lists four characteristics of a boundary violation that can serve as early warning signs for the vigilant professional. According to her, as integral parts of the whole, all are interconnected and become a dynamic system that has a wayward life of its own. She elaborates on these characteristics in great detail in her book, but space limitations allow only mentioning them here:

1. The Reversal of Roles
2. The Secret

3. The Double Bind
4. The Indulgence of Personal Privilege

Whatever the exact nature of the boundary violation—many of them begin as good, well-intentioned acts—there will be consequences to the therapeutic relationship and to the client(s). When both practitioner and client are unaware of the consequences of this behavior, many violations proceed to dangerous proportions before they are checked. Wise therapists have considered the potential ramifications of many such acts, and take adequate precautions to protect their clients and themselves.

**Summary**

Boundary violations and the potential abuses that can result are serious problems which practitioners of all kinds must carefully explore and understand. As I have reiterated, understanding the self of the therapist must be a very important part of the novice professional's training, But alas, with rare exceptions, it usually is not. This leaves both practitioner and patient at grave and unnecessary risk, especially in cross-gender treatment, whether the therapist is female or male.

With this abbreviated discussion of boundaries as a backdrop, we can turn to a discussion of avoiding general pitfalls that can have deleterious effects on the treatment we provide.

## A Baker's Dozen Guidelines for Women Working With Men

I will close the chapter by listing 13 guidelines that can become signposts in attempting to learn more effective ways of working with men. They are proffered as pointers, rather than definitive rules for how this very delicate and sometimes electric treatment is conducted. The reader is invited to massage the ideas before she makes them her own, rather than accepting them wholesale.

1. Begin with a thorough self-analysis of your own assumptions about women, men, and the process of change. We need to ask ourselves first whether we subscribe to a pathological model

that sees maleness as a sickness to be cured, or whether we approach both men and women from a developmental model that asks what is in their way that blocks more healthy functioning. All too often, counselors adopt the latter perspective about women but still pathologize men. How they manage to justify and reconcile this inconsistency is beyond my ken, but one can only wonder about the treatment they provide.

2. Establish your credibility from the beginning. With women, therapists establish credibility by sensitivity; with men, it is by sensibility. The chief executive officer of a multinational corporation will watch for different elements that make you a credible resource than the physician who is chief of staff at a large teaching hospital. Likewise, the kindergarten teacher and carpenter will have different measures from each other and from either of these. However, they will all need to see that you have established your credibility.

How does a female therapist accomplish this, without being defensive or aggressive?

A. Be prepared from the intake call on, to establish that you are a professional in your own right. For example, *you define the playing field*. That is, you decide whom you want to see and in what order, rather than allowing a client to dictate, for instance, that individual therapy will be done when it should be couples work. I have lost cases in the intake call because of my steadfast refusal to do individual therapy on couples issues, but that is more palatable to me than the ineffectual therapy that would be done if I lost the battle for structure from the beginning. Men especially will appreciate this take-charge attitude. And if they do not, be grateful that you did not have to fight a losing battle with them to do the work.

B. Establish your credibility silently, in the way you decorate your office. If you choose a soft, frilly decor, men will probably feel as if they have stepped into a bedroom rather than a professional's office. Even if you work in a setting where the furnishings are provided, you can choose accessories that communicate competency and strength, such as bold or dark colors. Shelves lined with books you have read or intend to read in the field indicate that you are a professional.

C. How you dress can also make a statement. Obviously, it is important that you not dress seductively. Neither do you have to dress like a eunuch to be taken as a competent professional. Your clothing can make a statement. I do not necessarily wear suits to do this, although they can give an immediate message. I have some of what I call my "doctor clothes" that I wear on the days I make presentations, or appear in court, or have intake sessions, particularly when I know in advance that I am seeing highly professional and competent people, male or female. For example, once I did an intake session with a couple in which the man was an upper-level manager in a multinational corporation. Although it is usually my custom to check my schedule for intake sessions when planning what to wear, I had forgotten about the session. So I wore a uncharacteristically casual skirt and blouse to the office. Even in that session, it was clear to me that they would not be back. Perhaps it was that our chemistry was off; perhaps they simply did not like my philosophical approach. However, I also think that, whether they fully were conscious of it or not, I had simply failed to present myself as a competent professional in the way I had dressed that day.

To summarize, in whatever ways you do it, you must establish yourself as capable and strong in your own right, without being aggressive or competitive in doing so. Then and only then will men feel safe enough to be vulnerable.

3. Know your limits and set them firmly with both yourself and clients. This is also a way to establish your credibility. As has been repeatedly stated, it is especially important to clarify the parameters of acceptable expressions of affection. You must also know the boundaries of what you will accept in other physical expressions of emotion, such as physical aggression. I often explicitly state something like the following: "I'm not going to let you hurt yourself, or me, or anyone, or anything in this office."

For example, I once worked with a hulking and brawny Vietnam veteran who had learned karate as a Green Beret. About 20 minutes into the intake session, I detected a hint that he could become violent with himself, but that he also had won in the past by intimidation. He reported that he had literally lost count of his successful "kills" in the war, and so I surmised that this was part of his agony. However, it was also what made him a force to be contended with wherever he went. I also knew that he had been in two other therapies with women, which he had found ineffectual. The combination of those two factors prompted me to take a big risk.

Halfway through the first session, I identified his violent urges, demanded that he not become violent, said that I would not tolerate violence to anyone, and commanded that he give me a no-suicide, no-harm contract. Although I was a bit frightened when I figuratively stood toe to toe with this hulk so early in the therapy, I felt I needed to in order for him to feel safe. And in fact, my gamble paid off. He burst into tears, promised me he would not hurt himself or anyone, and told me this was the first time he had felt safe in years.

Only when you can set clear, unequivocal limits on the expression of any emotion can your office be a safe place for all involved.

4. Do not deny or repress personal reactions that flow between client and therapist; these are normal. Men are typically maligned for relating to women as sexual beings or for having or stirring up sexual responses in women when in reality those feelings are part of every male-female interaction. Of course, sexual feelings with clients are not to be acted upon. In fact, whether or not one chooses even to bring any of these responses into session is a minute-to-minute decision based on the therapist's best clinical judgment at that time. However, when the therapist has carefully considered the issues in advance, she is less likely to make misjudgments that could have disastrous consequences for herself or her clients.

5. If sexual undercurrents continue to intrude into the therapy, seek supervision, consultation, a cotherapist, and maybe even therapy. In general, there is no need to be alarmed at being attracted by or attractive to a male client. However, as members of the helping profession, we have a higher standard of conduct to uphold, regardless of how provocative or attractive a client is. As professionals, it is our responsibility to refrain from acting on these feelings. And according to Peterson (1992), "The burden imposed by this responsibility restricts our freedom, because we have to put the client first in the relationship" (p. 53). Therefore, be responsible both to yourself and to your clients by seeking assistance with those feelings, should they become intrusive and bothersome or should you experience increasing difficulty not acting on them.

6. Be careful not to shame men for their feelings or allow them to shame themselves. Feelings don't have thoughts; they just are. That is, they are neither right nor wrong. And they can be highly illogical and irrational. But when people try to control them by talking themselves out of them, they almost certainly increase the potency of those feelings.

Our job regarding strong and messy emotions is threefold: (a) to create a safe enough place that people feel free to expose their highly vulnerable and often shameful feelings; (b) to help people articulate their feelings in that safe place; and (c) after holding those responses up to the light of day, to help people make appropriate choices for what to do with those troublesome emotions. It is what people *do* with their feelings that is critical, not that they have them. Clients count on us to help them learn to understand and titrate those vexing emotions. If we shame them, those feelings will go back down into the caldron and boil over somewhere else, unfortunately often in violent reactions.

7. Accept the fact that sexual feelings are a natural part of any male-female interaction. Men are not to blame for the fact that sexual feelings sometimes enter into the therapy equation. Feelings, even these precarious ones, always need to be acknowledged, at least to oneself, in order not to become their own roadblock. And sometimes, they need to be expressed carefully and directly with clients so that they can be gotten out of the way. In doing this, however, be certain that you reaffirm the appropriate boundary between you so that confusion is minimized.

    If the therapist reminds herself that these, too, are part of an overall transference reaction, she is likely to feel less awkward or self-aggrandizing in bringing them out. Further, seen from this perspective, discussing them is clearly part of the therapy and not merely a mutual flirtation. Otherwise, both therapist and client can get stuck in yet another spiral of repression that can have disastrous consequences in crossed boundaries, client abuse, and therapists' damaged careers.

8. Don't run away from problems with clients. Running away from problems only provides clients with yet another bad model for dealing with the problems of life. Bring the difficulty into the treatment and work with it. It may be difficult to do, particularly with a recalcitrant client or one who has made up his or her mind to orchestrate to fire you, but try to see these points of contention as opportunities for growth from the following vantage points. First, if clients are able to articulate to someone as powerful to them as their therapist what they want and need in a relationship, they will be better equipped to do this with others. Second, if clients are having

this difficulty with you, it is also likely a replication of their way of relating outside therapy. Avoiding personalizing the problem and encouraging them also to work from the same perspective can give you the mileage you need to help them examine their ways of relating. If they can be helped to see their patterns of relating are dysfunctional, they will be better able to change them with others. And after all, is that not what they hire us for?

Although the conventional wisdom is to refer such clients elsewhere, my approach is, wherever possible, to work out the problems with clients so that treatment can continue. Otherwise, they will have learned little of substance when it comes to making a better life. And, when termination of treatment is not our initiative, they are prevented from feeling abandoned. Only when you are certain through supervision or consultation that you cannot resolve the impasse should you refer a client elsewhere.

9. Don't let men hide behind their typical ways of relating to women as they interact with you. Men have been taught to associate with women in many ways, such as putting them down, womanizing, protecting, patronizing, or becoming ineffectual themselves. When they relate that way to us, they are showing us how they do their everyday lives, and that can help us know where to intervene, for therein likely lies the genesis of their problems. When we allow them to persist in those ways of relating with us, we are missing a golden opportunity to help them learn to operate in more emotionally available, equitable ways with women.

10. Be vigilant about not fostering ways of being that are antithetical to the new male-female relationship. Because you are working so hard to help clients develop new, more equitable, more emotionally satisfying ways for women and men to relate, be on the alert for ways you inadvertently may be working at cross-purposes with yourself.

11. Learn how men communicate. Rather than putting men down for thinking and expressing themselves like men, learn to respect their ways of speaking and use your knowledge to engage them in treatment. The analogy I frequently use in couples therapy is that she speaks Russian and he speaks Polish, and they both need interpreters. Neither language is right or

wrong. It is merely different. To work effectively with men, you must learn how they express their emotions and thoughts so that you can teach them a new, relationship-building lexicon. Initially, this may mean that you will need an interpreter yourself! For example, when you have tuned your ear to hear it, there are plenty of feelings embedded in a statement such as "I always thought I had to be perfect." But men have not learned the language of feelings, so it comes out sounding like an intellectualized thought. Seize the opportunity, when you hear statements that you as a clinician know inevitably have feelings behind them, to help them label the emotions they are telegraphing. Then they can come to know them for themselves. This allows them to go the next step and learn to share feelings with the significant people in their lives, such as spouses, children, parents, siblings, friends, and sometimes even co-workers.

12. Try not to "know" in advance who is to blame for relationship dysfunction. In truth, no one is to blame; both are responsible for contributing to the problem. It is our job to ascertain each person's part in the problem, to help each understand the other's contributions to it, and to help both learn to do something different. This includes not allowing couples to blame each other. This is the advantage when the therapist works systemically with people. As this approach is so central to the adequate treatment of men, a separate chapter called "A Primer on Systems Thinking" will be devoted to helping the uninitiated reader understand these concepts.

13. Relax. There is no reason to be intimidated or feel awkward or inept around men simply because they are men. They are just people. And if you do feel any of these feelings, seek consultation or supervision or even therapy for yourself. Remember the dictum, "First let us do no harm."

## A Final Word

When we understand ourselves and how to capitalize on our relationships with men in therapy and avoid the pitfalls that can occur, we are much more effective change agents for both women and men. When women seek therapy for painful relationships

with men, we do them no favors by understanding only their perspective and not comprehending and interpreting men's as well.
Behaving and believing in a one-sided way is gravely dangerous
for each partner in a couple, as well as highly toxic for their
relationship and for the health of their family as a whole.

## Note

1. I am indebted to my friend and colleague Karen Gail Lewis, A. C. S. W., Ed.D.,
for making me aware of the deficit language often applied to single people, for
example, phrases like "never married" or "not married." Hence, although the term
"always single" is not a perfect solution to the linguistic dilemma, I prefer it over
the alternatives.

## References

Bograd, M. (1988). Behind the family mask. *Family Therapy Networker, 12*(2), 30-34.
Bowen, M. (1978). *Family therapy in clerical practice.* New York: Jason Aronson.
Edelwich, J., & Brodsky, A. (1991). *Sexual dilemmas for the helping professional.* New
     York: Brunner/Mazel.
Goldberg, H. (1987). *The inner male: Overcoming roadblocks to intimacy.* New York:
     New American Library.
Kelly, K., & Hall, A. (1992). Toward a developmental model for counseling men. In
     K. Kelly & A. Hall (Eds.), *Journal of Mental Health Counseling, 14*(3), 257-273.
Kramer, J. (1985). *Family interfaces: Transgenerational patterns.* New York: Brunner/
     Mazel.
Maloney, B. (1992, June). *Issues in treating the sexually offending psychotherapist.*
     Presentation given at the annual meeting of the American Family Therapy
     Academy, Amelia Island, FL.
Masterson, J. (1988). *The search for the real self: Unmasking the personality disorders of
     our age.* New York: Free Press.
Meth, R., & Pasick, R. (1990). *Men in therapy: The challenge of change.* New York:
     Guilford.
Miller, J. (1986). *Toward a new psychology of women.* Boston: Beacon.
Minuchin, S. (1974). *Families and family therapy.* Cambridge, MA: Harvard Univer-
     sity Press.
Moore, R., & Gillette, D. (1990). *King, warrior, magician, lover: Rediscovering the archetypes
     of the mature masculine.* San Francisco: HarperSanFrancisco.
Napier, A., & Whitaker, C. (1978). *The family crucible.* New York: Harper & Row.
Peterson, M. (1992). *At personal risk: Boundary violations in professional-client relation-
     ships.* New York: Norton.
Simon, F., Stierlin, H., & Wynne, L. (1985). *The language of family therapy: A systemic
     vocabulary and sourcebook.* New York: Family Process Press.
Swain, S. (1989). Covert intimacy: Closeness in men's friendships. In H. Risman &
     P. Schwartz (Eds.), *Gender in intimate relationships: A microstructural approach*
     (pp. 71-86). Belmont, CA: Wadsworth.

# Part II

# THE ART OF TREATMENT PLANNING

# Overview of the Tapestry:
# The Grid for the Model

Until recently, individual and family psychotherapy orientations have been seen as mutually exclusive approaches whose differences are fundamentally irreconcilable. I personally confess to holding that rather naive belief when I first learned family therapy. And indeed, it requires a wholly different worldview to think truly systemically. Nevertheless, both my thinking and the field of family therapy have evolved, and the tide is rising to reconcile the once-rejected ideas of individual therapy with a family systems perspective, typified by the work of Feldman and Pinsof (1982), Feldman (1992), and Moultrup (1990). Likewise, a more nascent current seeks to blend group and systemic couples therapy, represented by the work of Coché and Coché (1990).

## Chapter Overview

In this chapter, I will detail the multiple and variegated threads that make up the theory and philosophy behind my model for the diagnosis and treatment of men. This model provides an integrated, comprehensive framework that is idiosyncratic to each case and relies heavily on ever-evolving diagnostic assessment as treatment unfolds. It is comprehensive in the scope of the clinical concerns addressed, ranging from here-and-now problems, such as management of sex, children, or finances, to there-and-then problems, such as childhood relationships with parents, siblings, or peers.

No single description of an approach can be comprehensive enough to deal effectively with every single situation with which therapists and clients are faced daily, and although there is a grid that underpins my clinical decisions, still no two courses of treatment are alike. Thus, I think this model is "systematically eclectic . . . and rests upon the twin assumptions that each modality and orientation has its particular 'domain of expertise,' and that these domains can be interrelated to maximize their assets and minimize their deficits" (Pinsof, 1983, p. 20).

In this chapter I advance a set of premises and decision rules for applying the different treatment modalities and theories synergistically. This composite maximizes the potency of each individual piece in a way that would be unlikely were any one of them the only arrow in the therapist's quiver.

A word of caution is in order for the reader. Because the medium of writing is linear, the components of the model must be presented separately. This may seem to imply that there is a sequence. But in practice, they cannot be thought of linearly, because they interact in a circular fashion. Because I hope to empower the reader to implement these ideas, I will attempt to articulate *how* I actually think and *what* I actually do in common clinical situations when I am treating men, whether individually or with others. In this chapter, as I attempt to delineate the underpinnings of the approach that I have come to conceptualize and practice when I treat men, the reader will at least have an outline to consider in clarifying her own methodology. I will discuss the components of the approach, and when use of each component is indicated.

It should be noted that a family systems perspective is the lens through which I view any case, whether clients are seen with anyone else or individually. Whatever individual or group work is done must make sense for the client *in the context of his relationships*. Thus, a family systems perspective both gives birth to and develops from the individual or group work. This ensures that treatment will not end up a hodgepodge that baffles therapist and client alike. My way of thinking relies on the belief that the therapist's primary role is that of consultant to and about the man's relationship networks past, present, or future.

## A Note to Clarify

Whereas this chapter covers an integrated approach to the creation of treatment interventions, the next chapter, its companion piece, will answer the question: What is the process of therapy? By that I mean the emphasis will be less on integrating multiple theories and instead on describing the stages through which most clients pass as they experience this approach. This ideally makes for the qualitative shift in worldview that can result from an emphasis on generating psychological development.

## The Therapist's Role

The process of integration that forms the metatheory for this treatment relies on coordination of treatment by a single therapist on three levels simultaneously. That is, to use this paradigm, the therapist must consider a case from three angles. The first involves an understanding of the presenting problem as defined both by the client(s) and by the therapist. That is, the therapist must consider how to assess what the client identifies as his or her issues, clarify the concerns that might both underlie and fuel the presenting problem, and help the client(s) shape or reshape their formulations of the problem if their perspective is incomplete or facile. The second perspective juxtaposes multiple theoretical orientations from both family and individual psychologies in such a way that the individual is very much put back into the system. The third aspect employs multiple therapeutic modalities where appropriate (individual, couples, family, family of origin, and group). In some cases, all these modalities are applied; in others, only some are. The therapist needs to have an overarching conceptual framework for deciding which are to be used, in what order, and why.

Thus, the role of the therapist as treatment coordinator is vital to the success of this very complex model. Her primary roles are to clearly and comprehensively conceptualize the case, taking into account historical, social, and current factors that might have a bearing on the presenting problem. This ensures that a coherent therapy will be provided, regardless of which modality or theoretical orientation is being used at any given time. Working truly integratively requires a greater measure of clinical competence than approaching every case with one therapeutic orientation and preferred modality. Here, we must be competent in multiple approaches, each of which requires considerable time, energy, perhaps even additional training to learn. But possibly the single most important requirement of us is personal maturity, which includes knowing when we are in over our head and need to refer to another professional who is more competent in a given area.

The therapist must act as the loom that holds the multiple strands and threads together while the client(s) do the work of weaving and assembling the tapestry. I see the job of a good therapist as being in many ways analogous to that of a good parent: to teach the skills required for living and to move gradually into the background as treatment progresses. When clients have internalized those skills and the therapist herself, treatment has been completed.

## General Considerations in Designing Treatment

Where and how does a therapist begin? Just as no two clients are alike, no therapist or therapy can be "one size fits all," either. Therefore, no attempt will be made to delineate *the* blueprint for women treating men. We each have to decide on our own paradigms on the basis of our own beliefs concerning the nature of change, the role of the therapist in sparking it, and the theoretical approach that best facilitates it.

The purpose of this chapter is to help the therapist think about how to design treatment strategies, so that treatment will be a truly comprehensive, idiosyncratic, and creative improvisational process, rather than a paint-by-numbers or cookbook exercise. To that end, the reader is invited to consider the following questions:

> How does the therapist take hold of a case when she wants to practice improvisationally and truly integratively?

What are appropriate theoretical bases for making such decisions?

What issues specific to men does the therapist need to be aware of?

How does she weave together issues that are idiosyncratic to a particular case that must be resolved for clients to feel that treatment has been a success with those that are generic to and therefore essential in the treatment of men across the board?

## A Caveat

Having said so much, a warning is in order. No therapy, particularly one whose cornerstone is modeling how to build relationships, will be effective if it is centered around what Pinsof (1990) calls technolatry, or the worship of technique. He goes on to state that some of the assertions accompanying technolatry are that "treatment is a set of techniques. [That] it has nothing to do with the relationship. [That] change is easy to accomplish with the right technique, the right reframe, the right paradoxical intervention, focus on the appropriate solutions. [That] people stay changed once the cycle is broken" (p. 10). This way of thinking is very limiting for therapist and clients alike and is antithetical to what I believe is good therapy with any population. That is, when we do therapy on rather than with clients, we border on abuse.

## A Word About Improvisation

What is the place of improvisation in effective psychotherapy? As the family therapist and jazz musician Moultrup remarked, "The basis of effective psychotherapeutic technique is disciplined improvisation. Effective psychotherapy cannot be conducted without the ability to improvise. . . . The art of improvisation is endlessly complex, even when it appears to be basic or simple" (1990, p. 90).

If improvisation is central to any good therapy, it is particularly significant in the treatment of men. I can only echo Pinsof and Moultrup in saying that attempting to do therapy emphasizing technology rather than relationship is to invite treatment to become isomorphic, allowing and encouraging men to perpetuate in the therapy the ways of operating for which they have been socialized their whole lives.

What constitutes disciplined improvisation? How does the therapist prevent treatment as complex as that proposed here from becoming a disjointed jumble? Effective improvisation that unfolds in a coherent and integrative way has at its center a consistent theoretical core provided by "a therapist who has a defined self, and has brought it to therapy. This is in contrast to the therapist who has latched onto one static model and clings to it past any usefulness" (Moultrup, 1990, p. 108).

Developing the skill of improvisation will enable us to elicit more emotional reactions than cognitive ones. And as I have stated, this ability is particularly important in working with men. "A psychotherapist may conduct psychotherapy with a variety of different clients having a variety of different complaints, but there will be a thread of familiarity that runs through the work" (Moultrup 1990, p. 91). This thread will be a blend of how the therapist conceptualizes her own work, combined with her view of the specific salient issues that are central to the treatment of a client's particular problem.

I emphasize that this book comes about as a result of my experience and improvisation as I have worked with men. I do not propose to write the definitive statement about how treatment with men should be conducted; rather, I am attempting to share what I have learned as a result of my experience and to encourage readers to experiment in their work. "The need for improvisation in the therapist is similar to the task of therapy for the client. If the client is going to effectively eliminate the unhealthy and destructive life choices that brought [him] to therapy, [he] obviously is going to have to change. If the therapist is clinging to old patterns of behavior, old ways of thinking and old ways of doing therapy, [she] is going to be modeling the opposite of what [she] expects from the patient, and [she] probably will have less empathy for [her] patient's dilemma" (Moultrup 1990, pp. 108-109).

## Emotions Must Be Wed to Intellect

Throughout the process of choosing interventions, the therapist must keep in mind that the entire background of the tapestry is the marriage of emotion with intellect. All too often, clients request our help in making yet another try at changing, still hurting and dysfunctional after clocking countless hours in therapy. They lament continuing miserable feelings but hasten to protest that they have already talked about many of the issues we want them to address. That's just it; they have talked *about* their experiences ad nauseam. But they remain unable to break free of their grip. I believe that this is because they have been unable to reconcile their emotional responses with their cognitive understanding. Empty insights devoid of emotion only serve to bolster clients' typical defenses of rationalization and intellectualization. And because for many men, most expression of emotion except anger tends to be socialized out of them at an early age, this defensive style can be particularly problematic, especially for those in a clinical population.

The core assumption on which this approach turns, then, is that human emotions function as facilitators in problem solving and that repressing or otherwise mishandling emotions is a chief contributor to individual and family developmental arrest and resulting dysfunction. Conversely, the greater clients' ability to experience and channel their emotions appropriately, the clearer their attachments, the stronger their feeling of connectedness with life, the higher their degree of satisfaction in all facets of their lives, and the greater their ability effectively to meet and solve life's problems.

## Integrating Orientations

A clear conceptualization is required if efforts at improvisation or integration are not to become a jumble. Some facets of the approach presented here, such as family of origin sessions, may be optional depending on the therapist's skill, training, interest, and assessment of the client's needs. After years of experimenting, however, I have concluded that other dimensions, such as teaching affective skills, attending to gender-related issues, and doing family of origin exploration if not actual extended family sessions themselves, are essential to thoroughly and effectively treat men. In this section, I will consider the following questions:

What are the major threads of therapeutic orientation that must be woven into the therapy with this population?

Which components are optional?

How can these seemingly disparate orientations be braided together into a unified whole?

## Essential Elements in the Treatment of Men

There are three essential elements to the empathic and effective treatment of men: (a) attending to gender-related issues and understandings, (b) taking a developmental perspective, and (c) operating from a psychodynamic systemic frame. Each will be described below.

### Gender-Related Issues

The most fundamental element in the treatment of men is attention to socialization of both women and men. Clients need us to interpret this for them, for a host of reasons. One is that it helps to put words to and therefore reify their experiences. Two, it helps remove the tendency to blame self or others for behaving in gendered ways. And three, it makes the idea of having choices over what has seemed prescribed or foregone more real and possible. "Given the profound ways in which the female-male situation is inscribed into all of life, all the necessary change is not likely to occur readily or rapidly" (Miller, 1986, p. xi). When we study gendered behavior and intimate relationships, it becomes readily apparent that many forces mold and influence both females and males in both arenas.

More often, the primary reason men need or seek psychotherapy from a relationship-oriented psychotherapist is that there has been some disruption in their lives that has caused them either to acknowledge a problem with their way of living or to accede to someone else's perception that there is a problem. Just as women have much to gain from a nongendered world, so also do men. Though often not recognizing it on a conscious level, this "new man" who is lying dormant within many males, especially those who seek treatment, is attracted to being free to parent, to express intimacy, and to escape the strictures of rigid role prescriptions for which he has been socialized. And yet, he is extremely frightened of those changes. Our job is to help him free himself from those strictures so that this repressed man may emerge.

Therefore, although I might like to see all elements of the way I do treatment with men as essential, only one is truly critical: a focus on gender issues. Two dimensions make this motif indispensable: how gender issues affect the therapist and the treatment she provides; and how gender issues need to become the subject of the therapy because of what men and their partners need to understand and work through.

*Gender and the Therapist.* The opening paragraph of Meth & Pasick's (1990) trailblazing book states:

> The attainment of manhood is both a unique and complex experience often misunderstood by the therapeutic community. As there are many facets of masculinity, we need to understand male development within social, psychological, legal, cultural and ethnic frames of reference. What does it mean to be male? What are the myriad factors that determine man's development? What are the messages about masculinity that significantly influence the development of male identity? Finally, what are the specific affective and behavioral characteristics of being male that influence men individually and in their relationships? These are questions that we believe underlie much of the challenge in working with men in any psychotherapeutic context. (p. 3)

To work effectively with men, all clinicians must grasp and have empathy for the impact of men's socialization on males. And if this is the case for all therapists, it is of central importance for women therapists, as we have been socialized very differently from men and therefore will not know, at a visceral level, what it truly is like being a man. Although being male has its privileges, it is vital that we realize that along with those advantages come constraints that often eclipse a man's full and equal functioning in relationships of all kinds, that jeopardize his physical and psychological health, and that even compromise his work functioning—the one area in which he supposedly has the edge over women automatically. A central therapeutic task, then, is to help men to realize these multiple impacts so that they can begin to make other, presumably better choices for themselves.

In fact, although clearly men stand to gain much from working with male therapists, I continue to believe that they have a qualitatively different experience when they seek therapy with women, for several reasons. First, if men can find healing with a woman therapist, they can have an emotionally corrective experience (Yalom, 1985) that positions them to have qualitatively different relationships with women. Second, women generally are better able to consciously admit feelings of weakness or vulnerability.

Even when weakness is real, we are accustomed to drawing on our experience with it, turning it into a strength, and moving in to work with and encourage it. Thus, the man can see that what at first seems a weakness can be turned into a strength. And because of their socialization, at the start of treatment, most men are preoccupied with not appearing weak. Miller (1986) talks about this male-female difference:

> In Western society, men are encouraged to dread, abhor, or deny feeling weak or helpless, whereas women are encouraged to cultivate this state of being. The first and most important point, however, is that these feelings are common and inevitable to all, even though our cultural tradition unrealistically expects men to discard rather than to acknowledge them. (p. 29)

That women are usually much more able to tolerate and encourage these frightening, needy feelings in themselves and in others can make a man feel safer sharing his. Greater ego strength comes from his sharing and from the accumulated experience that says it is acceptable to do this rather than flee from these needy feelings before he experiences them. Aaron's words describing in the termination session his relationship with the therapist illustrate Miller's point. At the start of therapy, he was by his own admission a womanizer who literally could not stay with only one woman at a time, even though he would profess with as much conviction as he could muster that he would remain faithful to his girlfriend of 4 years. In the course of therapy, first individual and then with Laura, he was able to commit to and marry this woman to whom he had learned to remain faithful. In his termination session, then 30-year-old Aaron spoke of how he experienced his relationship with the therapist. Often the degree of trust and security that people can find, usually for the first time, with either a male or female therapist can allow them to go on to seek those healing experiences with others. If the therapist is female, the male client has the added advantage of having a kind of safe dry run for relating to a significant woman. These were among the ingredients that became Aaron's springboard to commitment to his new wife.

*Aaron:* I don't think I would have changed if I hadn't seen you. I don't think I'd have learned to become . . . deep-down happy, no, deep-down satisfied with myself and my life.

In a later session:

*Aaron:* You were such a steady force in my life. I knew that nothing catastrophic would happen in my life, because I could come back in to see you, and we'd figure it out. This was home for me.

Third, "Women, both superficially and deeply, are more closely in touch with basic life experiences—in touch with reality. By being in this closer connection with this central human condition, by having to defend less and deny less, women are in a position to understand weakness more readily and to work more productively with it" (Miller, 1986, p. 31). The words of 34-year-old Mick to his therapist illustrate his growing comfort with and acceptance of vulnerability. They also speak to the role of the therapist in creating the essential sense of a holding environment that made it possible and acceptable for him to experiment with losing control so that, paradoxically, he could gain genuine control of himself and of his life.

*Mick:* I now experience a big difference between feeling threatened and feeling safe. And there's a long distance there! You taught me you *can* lose control and get all the feelings out, and then straighten your tie and walk out. *That's* what being safe is to me now. It's so damned unfair, that we [men] have had to be so tight and so in control. (With tears in his eyes) It's so sad!

*Gender and Clients.* "Ours is an age of personal and gender identity chaos" (Moore & Gillette, 1990, p. 102). Knowing and understanding the bewildering impact of this fact on many of our clients is important. Along with the new strength that comes of loosing the shackles of our socialization come new areas of vulnerability. As these men are slowly learning, there is no absolute invulnerability, no matter how hard they might try to control. However, intellectually knowing that and learning to accept and work with it often are very different matters.

Surely this sense of chaos also affects women. But its impact on men who are socialized to be in charge, to fix everything by themselves and for their loved ones, never to be unsure, to be in control, and to cover their fears is massive. They may feel a heightened sense of vulnerability when feelings surface, because they are taboo. In a termination session after approximately a year of treatment, 38-year-old Marty, a recently divorced plumber, spoke about this experience. Although his experience of our relationship would have been essential for his healing given his idiosyncratic issues, his words also speak to what men need from their therapists in order to be willing to endure the new kind of vulnerability and unfamiliar reactions to it that introspection and relationship intimacy require.

*Marty:* You've been the parent I've never had. You've taught me a lot about how to do it for myself now. It's a dimension I've stepped into. It's being my own parent. It's like crossing a threshold.

It is no secret to say that although while women are pushing for men to become emotionally available and join them in equitable relationships, men's socialization runs counter to that experience. And even when they want to join us in those types of relationships, doing so is often very difficult. So the first task for the therapist is continually to remind herself of this, and minimize her tendency to blame a man for doing what he is socialized to do.

*Clinical Examples.* Two men speak to this pervasive sense of bewilderment in the following excerpts.

Sam is a 40-year-old married man with four children. High school educated, he owns and operates a successful business. His wife was at her wits' end because of the accumulated effects of Sam's earlier alcoholism, extramarital affair, and general emotional aloofness and unavailability. Empowered by participating in a women's group that I facilitate, she finally was able to make good on her repeated threat to end the marriage if he did not change: She made plans to live separately. This finally prompted him to call to reinitiate treatment.

The initial phase of the treatment was standard work: decrease intellectualization and all other types of resistance, and position the client to begin the requisite depth work, particularly on family of origin issues. This excerpt, as Sam begins the ninth individual session, indicates that I now have a highly workable client.

*Sam:* It's completely different, coming in here and having to switch. Big sigh! It's hard to get into it.
*Therapist:* Can you say more?

*Sam:* Sure. I had lunch with my bankers right before I came here. And they're nice. But there's a distance. (Pause) And then to come in here and switch, when I've been trying to keep myself away (pause), it's hard.

*Therapist:* Keep yourself away from what?

*Sam:* From just not wanting (pause) from opening up fully. It's difficult, after I've been in that mind-set, to make a turnabout and be human. Just like when I leave here, it's hard to go right back and think. Now, I always make sure I have a few errands to do on the way back to work, so I don't have to go think right away.

*Therapist:* And isn't that interesting. What comes so unnatural on the way in here is being human, which is what ought to be natural for all of us!

*Sam:* Um hum.

*Therapist:* And that's sad!

*Sam:* Um hum. But I'm more human now than I was!

That this dialogue occurred at all is significant. Sam is beginning to glimpse what he has lost in his years of responding to life as a socialized male. And that it occurred in the ninth session indicates that the treatment has begun to take hold. After much verbal arm wrestling, we have moved from the first phase to middle-phase treatment.

Paul, a 40-year-old architect who was recently divorced and also declared bankruptcy also illustrates a dawning realization of the degree to which his socialization as a male has wreaked havoc on his life. Here, he begins the fourth session by taking stock of the shaky foundation on which he has built his life. What catalyzed his seeking treatment was his growing realization that his modus operandi was jeopardizing yet another significant relationship, shaking him to the foundation.

*Paul:* I was taking the net worth path.

*Therapist:* Tell me about that.

*Paul:* When I was being an architect, I didn't like the job so much. I liked it in the classic, ideal sense of being a master builder. But the real world bogged me down. And so I took the path of the businessman, the provider. But I didn't know where I was going or why.

*Therapist:* No wonder you became emotionally bankrupt!

*Paul:* Really! But I don't know how to do anything different. That's why I'm here.

Just as it is important that we fully appreciate the impact of gender on men, so also is it important that we help them learn it also.

*Gender as It Interacts With Dysfunction.* As we have seen, messages about gender socialization have enough power to compromise functioning by themselves. But sometimes they interact in very powerfully destructive ways with a man's psychological dysfunction that would exist regardless of his gender, as a result of family of origin rules and precedents. That combination can be degenerative for both the man and his relationships. Treatment that ignores either a man's gender-related issues that compromise his functioning or his own psychological profile will be ineffective at best, dangerous at worst.

Daryl, age 47, is an example. A highly responsible mathematician for a government agency, he has been plagued with migraine headaches for as long as he can remember. He has no memory whatsoever of events that happened before seventh grade, and he protests that nothing bothers him. His wife, sensing that she was nearing the end of her emotional rope with the marriage, requested individual therapy for herself to help her lose weight and decide whether she should leave the marriage. As I discuss in detail at the end of this chapter, I always request couples sessions in such instances, even when the problems appear to belong to only one member of the couple. This allows both people to join forces in attacking the problem and neither of them is stuck being identified as the culprit. For reasons I will explain later, I see problems often being relationship issues that masquerade as one person's problems, so I play it safe and request the presence of both partners.

This time was no exception. I requested that Margaret ask her husband to join us for therapy, which he reluctantly agreed to do. From the time they began treatment and for many months, Daryl was bemused about his needing to be there, taking the position that this was Margaret's therapy. However, after spending several sessions trying to help him see that perhaps he had some concerns that could be addressed and he might even be contributing to Margaret's unhappiness, I decided to overlook his protests and the three of us settled down to work. In an effort to cement my conviction that each was making a contribution to the dysfunction, I did family of origin exploration for both and in the process of doing so, discovered that both of Daryl's paternal grandparents had committed suicide in his childhood. Daryl had no recollection that these events had ever been discussed or that much attention had been paid to them. In a couples session approximately 7 months after treatment began, the following dialogue occurred between Daryl and me.

*Daryl:* I think I've conditioned myself to shut everything down. I tune everything out.
*Therapist:* What's your sense about why that is?
*Daryl:* I'm hiding. I want to get away. It's like locking myself in my room.
*Therapist:* Any ideas about why you might do that?
*Daryl:* Um (pause) I think it has something to do with feeling safe, with being in control. . . . Maybe. I don't know. Like I've said before, *life* scares me to death!

To see this case as only an issue of gender is to miss that there is greater cause for concern. The whole of this man's functioning, physical and emotional, has been compromised by his inability to deal effectively with his feelings. But to miss the gender-related concerns that have exacerbated his rigidity is to miss an opportunity to reframe the dysfunction in a way that both is more palatable for clients and is in fact true. Although one can easily see family of origin precedents in his emotional withdrawal, one can also see how they are confounded by his gender socialization. Both sets of issues must be addressed in order for treatment to progress.

In addition to gender, two other major orientations form the principal strands that comprise several threads in each case: a developmental perspective and a psychodynamic approach. These and the separate fibers that form them will be discussed separately below.

## A Developmental Perspective

In this section, I will review some of the general theoretical assumptions common to developmentalists who theorize about both the family and individual life cycles. Then I consider the major individual developmental theorist of adult development (Levinson, 1978, 1990) whose work has influenced my thinking. Then I will discuss the seminal contribution to the field of family therapy by Carter and McGoldrick (1980), who conceptualized stages of family development. Though a more thorough discussion of development will be included in the next chapter, an overview of basic concepts is necessary here to understand the theory.

*The Concept of Development.* Implicit and explicit in the work of the individual theorists who have influenced my thinking is the belief, now generally accepted, that "All lives are governed by common developmental principles in childhood and adolescence and go through a common sequence of developmental periods. At the same time, each individual life has its own special character and follows its own special course" (Levinson, 1978, p. 3). To these theorists, there is an underlying organization in an individual's movement through life, a sequence, direction, and hierarchical order that are central to the growth that takes place. They further see the aim of all learning as stimulation to the next step of development. Levinson (1990) posits, "We have to have an understanding of what the basic order is, in order to understand the disorders."

My work borrows this premise and transposes it to psychotherapy. I assume that most of those who become part of a clinical population have experienced, for one reason or another, a developmental arrest that places an artificial ceiling on the entire rest of their development. The aim of therapy, then, is to locate and remove these logjams so that the whole of development may continue in the way that comes naturally for humans if there are no impediments placed in the way by life's circumstances.

*A Conversation With the Reader.* As we discuss developmental theory, it is important for you the reader to ask yourself some questions: How do I identify developmental arrests in clients? What are developmental arrests? Do I get so caught up in trying to solve their presenting problem that I forget to wonder what factors are in the way of their doing what developmentalists know comes naturally? Do I take seriously the premise that when clients' development is stuck, no matter what flashy moves or techniques I try, they will remain stuck and literally incapable of substantive movement until their development is freed up? Or do I just keep expecting them to change, and then get frustrated, or angry, or call them resistant when they do not or cannot? These are critical questions that are difficult to ask yourself and more challenging still to answer. But I encourage you to ponder them, preferably in writing, before you read on.

*Clinical Example.* In order to make graphic the effects of a severe developmental arrest, I offer the following case example. As you read it, ask yourself what your own personal responses to Dustin would be and what clinical interventions you would try from the frame of your preferred therapeutic orientation.

In my initial screening, I search for any developmental arrests that may be compromising the whole of a client's functioning. Dustin's case is an example of this. Twenty-five years old when he began therapy this time, Dustin had been in psychotherapy of one kind or another since he was 3½ years old, carrying one diagnosis or another. Because of what I knew from the referring therapist, I deduced that again labeling him mentally ill would have little or no positive effect, and so I began immediately to search for the locus of his individual and family of origin developmental arrests. I was assuming that with a history and a presentation such as his, this was a situation that was rife with developmental arrests. And they were fairly easy to ascertain.

The older son of highly visible and successful professional parents, he had experienced a severely truncated separation and individuation process. In fact, at intake I saw him as functioning emotionally at about an 18- to 24-month-old level. The major contributors to Dustin's severe developmental arrest were related to both of his parents being highly narcissistically removed from him, due either to their literal absence or their extreme self-absorption when they were home. When they did interact with him, they were extremely intrusive with him, invading his personal boundaries either actually or verbally. All this was in addition to their drawing him into their marital relationship as a regulator of both their intimacy and of their conflict. So whatever attention he was able to get was negative, either by his being symptomatic or because of their narcissistic need for him. Hence, his severe developmental arrest.

Because of this complex of factors, Dustin had learned to sabotage his own separation and individuation and remain his parents' object, both in case the parents again required him, and because his own source of security now was totally intertwined with his parents, whom he both deeply loved and hated. Thus, any efforts at separation and individuation that were not undermined by Dustin were actively, albeit unconsciously, hampered by one or the other parent to such an extent that Dustin had introjected an identity based on seeing himself as incompetent.

This situation served both himself and his parents but left him extremely dependent and ineffectual in all relationships. For example, he had been fired from approximately 36 jobs at the time of intake, and after 5 years of college, had not amassed enough credits for a 2-year degree. The following excerpt illustrates his individual developmental arrest, made in the service of the family.

*Dustin:* It's very difficult for me to separate myself from someone, to let go. One of the reasons I depend so much on other people is because I don't have much on my own. It's frustrating me that I'm always leaving myself behind.

*Therapist:* What do you suppose accounts for that?

*Dustin:* Fear—I'm afraid of people's expectations.

*Therapist:* Whose?

*Dustin:* Friends. Parents.

*Therapist:* Tell me about fearing.

*Dustin:* I don't know what they want anymore. Before, the expectation was on having a normal son. But the emphasis was on how abnormal I was.

*Therapist:* How does it make you feel to say the emphasis was on how abnormal you were?

*Dustin:* Angry. I don't want to see myself as so different that people will not work with me. People who have established a definition of themselves walk away from me. How does that relate to my parents? I get so close to talking with them, and then they go away. I just don't want to be alone.

*Therapist:* Tell me.

*Dustin:* Whenever I'm alone, I start thinking about what a failure I am. . . . I feel like a cripple who fell out of his chair. I just can't pull myself up. I don't know how to help me. I don't know how to face myself in any way. That's scary. I'm tired of falling out of my chair!

A follow-up note: after 2½ years of treatment, Dustin had passed the 1½ year mark for holding the same highly responsible semiprofessional job and received a raise and a bonus for his performance, had earned his 2-year degree and matriculated into a baccalaureate program that specialized in adult learners, and had maintained a relationship with a woman for 1½ years—the longest ever for him. And perhaps the most remarkable and satisfying result to Dustin was his cordial, more mutually accepting relationship with his parents that involved pleasant, friendly, even loving exchanges between them, rather than verbal duels or shouting matches. Clearly, removing the roadblocks to his development allowed his growth to progress as it should, as well as helping him solve the daily problems of his chaotic life.

*Summary*

Addressing and correcting developmental arrests ensures not only that clients will have solved the life problem that brought them to therapy in the first place but also that they will be in a position for their developmental process to continue as it normally would have, before he was fixated. This then allows for a higher level of functioning and dealing more effectively with the rest of their lives. And the best news is that developmentalists agree that true development is irreversible; changes that involve increased complexity and competence cannot be undone, as simple behavior change can. So in that sense, happily, growth is a one-way door.

*Men and Development*

Because men are socialized against interdependence and expression of affect of any kind (except anger), their normal developmental process is jeopardized virtually from the start. Therefore, it behooves the therapist to seek to identify the male client's developmental arrests and to unfreeze the whole of his development, or whatever solutions are arrived at to the problems with which men enter therapy will be cosmetic and serve only to lull them into believing their problem is solved when likely it will resurface later in another guise. And this time, another layer of dysfunction will have been painted on by the client as he tries to cope. This chain of events is my main objection to brief therapies.

Perhaps the most significant contributor to conceptualizing men's developmental stages is Levinson (1978, 1990), a researcher for years at Yale University, who concluded that men go through a particular set of stages, and that satisfactory movement through these stages depends on the life structures or choices an individual makes.

What are life structures? These are choices that form the underlying pattern or design of people's lives at a given time (Levinson, 1990). According to Levinson's theory, there are four basic life structures: career, family, recreation, and friends. Of the four, the first two must be in place for people to have the requisite free attention to emphasize the other two. But the important point to underscore is that if people's life structures are unstable or unsound, their lives are on shaky ground, and therefore a developmental arrest will occur.

If adults' development is to proceed in optimal ways, their life structures optimally are freely and deliberately chosen. When this is the case, the lives they build on those foundational life structures can be expected to involve a great deal of satisfaction. Unfortunately, all too many people fall into or back into decisions that often become counterproductive. And even when people are deliberate and wise about their choices, life is not always tidy or predictable. Untoward events like the stillbirth of a child, a chronic illness, a parent's untimely death, the sudden folding of a company where an employee experienced career satisfaction and job security, wishing to marry but failing to meet an appropriate partner all have implications for people's lives and can negatively affect the solidity of their life structures. Clinicians who narrowly focus only on resolving the current crisis leave clients in only marginally better shape to tackle life in the long run, because in such instances, families and individuals must make an additional developmental shift in order to accomplish the life cycle task required to accommodate this change. When neither clients nor clinicians are aware of this, the whole of people's psychological development can become jeopardized.

### Diagnosing for Developmental Arrests

Changes in people's life structures affect their relationships in multiple ways. To help the clinician isolate any developmental arrests that may be plaguing an individual or a family, diagnostically there are several questions to ask ourselves or our clients. The following is a partial list of questions that can help you identify the solidity of clients' life structures. Because the strength and validity of people's life structures will have a major impact on individual and family development, and on their quality of and satisfaction with life as well as on the presence of dysfunction that derives from poor life choices, these are important diagnostic considerations.

1. Did clients make their choices of their own volition, or did they feel as if those decisions were thrust on them by circumstances; by other, more powerful people; or by cultural or family expectations, etc.?
2. How deliberately were life choices examined, or did clients merely impulsively do what seemed like a good idea at the time?

3. What would be required of both therapists and clients to strengthen tottering life structures, and would this just postpone the inevitable and thereby perpetuate the developmental arrest?
4. What is the prognosis for healthy resolution of the problem for which treatment was sought, if relationships are based on faulty life structures?
5. Have there been major events that have occurred untimely or out of clients' control, such as a parent's or spouse's early death, a chronic illness, or an unwanted divorce?
6. How has the individual or family handled and been impacted by these untoward events?
7. After clients resolve the current crisis for which they sought treatment, have they attained the skills that will also bring some genuine satisfaction with life?

Locating clients' developmental arrests and discerning the source of these problems so that they can be remedied is our primary clinical job. Another job, however, is to help clients determine whether life changes they are contemplating are truly in their best interests or are merely efforts to change the subject in a bogus manner to avoid making a difficult developmental transition while seeming to do so. For example, people often get divorced, thinking that change in and of itself will fit the bill for a developmental shift. Although a divorce certainly will create a crisis, it does not guarantee that developmental growth will result without the spouses being challenged to deal with this and the surrounding issues qualitatively differently. By contrast, marriage in a new developmental phase with an appropriate partner cannot be the same, if the spouses truly have changed.

If the relationship does remain superficially the same when change of some kind is needed, each partner and the marriage will become stagnant. Then the marriage compromises everyone's growth. The words of 46-year-old Stewart describe his startling realization that he had stunted his own growth for 20 years by avoiding the inevitable divorce that his former wife finally initiated.

*Stewart:* For 20 years, I sought my wife's approval. So I built houses. I built a successful business. But I never got her approval. I'd have stayed there until I was dead, physically dead. But she finally said she didn't want to do this anymore. But I'd have stayed, still trying to get her approval. My marriage dying was also about my failing. And I didn't want people to know I'd failed. So I'd have stayed until

> I died. So yesterday, when I finally asked myself, "Why am I doing this?" it was a real wake-up call.

If, for whatever reason, people are unable to accomplish the necessary developmental changes successfully, dysfunction will result. When those who present for therapy do not have their developmental arrests identified and treated, the whole of their development remains fixated, sending ripples of dysfunction throughout their relationship networks. That is, although their symptoms may seem modified, the underlying structure of their lives remains fixated. This developmental logjam becomes an artificial ceiling on all the relationships in the family and further symptoms eventually result.

Levinson (1990) suggests in making diagnoses that we borrow the concept of "good enough" from the psychoanalytic literature. That is, although no parent (or life choice) can possibly be perfect, is it good enough, satisfying enough, for the rest of people's growth not to be stunted? I use this notion both to make my own clinical decision and to help people assess for themselves whether this is true in their lives. That is, I do not necessarily assume that an entire life structure has to be dismantled in order for people to attain satisfaction from and significantly change their lives. Often, as I have said, this can be merely changing the subject. However, in some instances, in order for any part of development to proceed as it should, major revamping, and not merely shoring up an existing life structure, is needed. This point has major implications for the length of treatment and speaks in general for the need for long-term work where there has been a significant developmental arrest for either individuals or for the family as a whole.

The experience of 32-year-old T.J., from whom we will hear throughout the book, illustrates this. Five months before he initiated treatment, he separated from his wife of 11 years and moved to another city, his excuse being that he had bought a business locally. Already a millionaire many times over, he had done robotically what his father had taught him to do: make money. The catalyst for his separating was his realization that his wife, too, had that same expectation of him, with what he experienced as little or no personal concern for or connection to him. Although the separation and move generated their own crises, the therapy was sparking an even bigger one, because he was beginning to grasp the depth of his developmental arrest and his personal bankruptcy. The following excerpt occurred seven sessions into the therapy and illustrates the shifting that is beginning to take place in the entire fabric of his life.

*T.J.:* I don't want to lose how good I am at work. I'm losing my edge. But I'm starting to notice other things, though.

*Therapist:* What are you telling yourself about that?

*T.J.:* Frankly, at first I was telling myself you were a shithead.

*Therapist:* I can see why. And now?

*T.J.:* Now I can't. I have an awareness. And I have to find a way to make it work, built on compassion, rather than on a focused greed. You know, "I want, therefore, I am."

*Therapist:* Are you settled with that yet?

*T.J.:* Yes. Because it's beyond the point of my being able to make the other choice—or I would.

*Therapist:* Are you sure?

*T.J.:* No. What I've done is great, but it's binding. The whole garbage can inside is shaking. That's kind of how I view it: I have a garbage can inside that's shaking, and the lid is going to blow off. I had a management consultant who was driving me to be the Ultimate Manager Machine, which is 180 degrees opposite of where you are trying to take me. So I stopped calling him.

*Therapist:* How did you make that determination?

*T.J.:* I realized that 2 weeks ago after I left here, as I was sitting in the parking lot hitting the steering wheel—I realized that somewhere along the way, I had been taken over by the machine. I don't like that. I met this woman who has beautiful blue eyes. I didn't even know what eyes were for! I've been going to the mountains for years, only this time I felt it. I felt! I just inhaled it! Always before I only felt guilt and greed. G squared. That's what I've been driven by. But, Beth, it's driving me nuts! Now what do I do with this?

*Therapist:* You're doing it.

*T.J.:* But what do I do with it? I've got to find a way to pocket it. My whole attitude has changed.

This excerpt illustrates several important elements in the change process. First, it shows that developmental growth and change really are a one-way door. Second, it illustrates the disequilibrium and temporary anxiety that accompany fundamental rather than cosmetic change. And third, it depicts a client who is in the middle of a massive transition, whose life and life-style will never be the same again, for now parts of life aside from just work and money are being explored.

## Theories of the Family Life Cycle

Whereas Levinson believes that there is an underlying and age-linked order to all individuals' development, Carter and McGoldrick's work (1980) is centered on the developmental tasks with which families must successfully grapple in order for their development as a unit to proceed, regardless of the age of family members. They believe that the family, like individuals, passes through a set of developmental stages. The concept of the family life cycle captures a sequence of stages or eras, each of which has its own biopsychosocial elements.

Carter and McGoldrick's central assumption is the premise of Nathan Epstein and his colleagues (1978) that the primary function of the family is to support the development of its members. They believe further that the successful achievement of one individual's developmental tasks is dependent on and contributes to the effective accomplishment of other family members' developmental tasks. Thus, family and individual development are interlocking and highly interdependent.

How is this relevant to a clinical situation? People present for treatment mired in situations for which a shift to the next stage is not natural, most likely because their typical emotional pattern does not promote this modification. That is why symptoms have appeared. These reflect a family life cycle derailment, and therapy aims for change that reestablishes the inherent developmental momentum of the system. Therapy that focuses strictly on symptom relief or on the family's interactions only at the time of crisis will miss the opportunity to help the family position itself for supporting each member's continued growth and thus will likely serve only as a Band-Aid, a temporary fix.

*Clinical Example.* A clinical example of a family case illustrates the far-reaching and multigenerational effects that can accrue because of developmental arrests. Brian, age 44, and Monica, age 48, had been married for 2 years. Each brought two children into the marriage from previous marriages, but Monica's children were old enough to live on their own. Brian's children, both adopted in infancy, had manifested a fairly high degree of distress since their childhoods, but each time Brian requested that professional help be sought, his children's mother refused, denying that there was any problem. Brian finally sought therapy for himself when, after his divorce from his first wife, he seriously contemplated remarriage. However, try as I might, I could not stem the tide of problems with the children. As the degree of dysfunction deepened, I tried all kinds of therapeutic interventions with different configurations of family members. Still, every time Brian made a mistake in parenting, he would become merciless with himself, going on tirades and then pouting in scenes that would sometimes last for hours, sometimes for days.

Because I saw the roots for Brian's logjam about perfectionism in his relationship with his father, I tried several times to help him to examine that relationship so that he could give himself the opportunity to make alternative choices. The first time I suggested that perhaps his father, too, was imperfect, Brian threw a box of tissues and stomped out of the office, threatening never to come back. I tried countless times to get him to reconsider the rather naive view of his father that resulted in his inability to see himself as competent. Finally, the following conversation took place, which he reported later was highly significant and very healing for him.

*Brian*: Dads don't do that.
*Therapist*: Do what?
*Brian*: Make mistakes. They teach their kids. They have profound insight into the world. They are perfect.
*Monica*: (To the Therapist) And to see himself not doing something perfect with his kids makes him crazy!
*Therapist*: (To Brian) What are your tears?
*Brian*: Relief. I guess it's because I'm really ready to see this, to work on this. The good guys always win, and the bad guys always lose. And my dad was a good guy. My value system said that fathers do it right. They do everything. They're a perfect being. They have a great depth of wisdom. They solve all problems. They do it all.
*Monica*: How could anyone live up to that!
*Therapist*: And how does it make you feel about yourself when you can't?
*Brian*: That I've never been adequate. I've never measured up. Intellectually, I know that's not true, but at an emotional level, that's how it feels. I didn't want him to be (pause), I didn't want him to be (pause), I didn't want Dad not to be perfect. And when he'd tell us his troubles, I could see that he wasn't. And I didn't want that.
*Therapist*: What would be so bad about seeing him as not perfect?
*Brian*: It wasn't fair. He wasn't perfect. He was good.
*Therapist*: Can't he be good without being perfect?

*Brian:* I don't know. I have a tough time seeing him as not perfect. It goes
   back to being a little kid. You know, "My dad can beat your dad."
   And it wasn't true.
*Therapist:* What scares you about seeing that? What happened to your
   world when your daddy wasn't bigger and stronger than anybody
   else's daddy?
*Brian:* (Crying quietly) It hurt. I don't think I ever dealt with that. I avoided
   that. I'm sure I avoided that. It wouldn't have been acceptable.
*Therapist:* Yeah. And I'm asking you to deal with that now.

   In this excerpt, we see Brian begin to inch up to the central issue
that had affected his functioning as a father, his performance at
work, and his entire self-concept. In his eyes, compared to his
"perfect" father, he could do no right if he weren't perfect, too.
And yet, although his father's success in life was modest by most
people's standards, to Brian his mark was unattainably high.
Therefore, until he could see his father realistically, he was doomed
to a bone-grinding sense of failure from which he could not
extricate himself.
   A follow-up note is relevant here. After working directly with
that split in two sessions and beginning to resolve it, Brian reported noticing much less tension at work both as a manager and
with his superiors. He also reported a much calmer, stronger, more
rational approach to dealing with his two very difficult children.
And Monica reported a much more mature, calm, and centered
feeling between them. Thus, an individual developmental arrest that
had its roots in his family of origin had been transplanted into two
subsequent family situations and spread its dysfunction. When it
was identified and dealt with, it could be corrected. This change was
a significant contributor to putting this family back on course
developmentally.
   Thus, we see the interactive effects of individual and family
development and how they work either to prompt continuing
development or to arrest it.

## Psychodynamic Systems Theory

   Here I discuss the synergistic connection between the intrapsychic and
the interactional variables in therapy, and indeed, throughout the
life of a family. Moultrup (1990) offers us this perspective on the controversy involved in reconciling individual and systemic concerns:

The interface between the individual and the broader elements of the system remains one of the more problematic points of conceptualization in mental health. This difficulty has often been circumvented by disregarding one level of the system in favor of a useful but incomplete emphasis on the other. Indeed, one of the catalyzing factors for the development of family systems-based therapy was the inadequate attention afforded to the broader system in the field of individual psychology and psychiatry. It is curious to note the frequency with which this tack led to the development of schools of therapy that neglected the individual dynamics in favor of attention to broader systems dynamics. This clearly can be seen as the same mistake from the other side of the fence. (p. 19)

This approach taps the synergy between the individual's intrapsychic functioning and his interpersonal connections: It attempts to help him reconcile the dimensions of his inner life with the multiple relationship systems in which he operates. Specifically, here I will discuss the integration of family of origin therapy with redecision therapy and hypnosis to access and remove early developmental logjams in an individual's life. It is clear that the synergistic effect of being able to work with each of these inner elements and braid them into the approach to the client's outer life is where this integrative model gets its extraordinary power.

*Family of Origin Therapy.* Whereas many of their compatriots appear perennially to have had difficulty in keeping the individual's place clearly in perspective when working systemically, many prominent voices in the field of family therapy have not. Notably, the early work of Bowen (1978), Framo (1982), Paul and Paul (1986), and Napier and Whitaker (1978) spoke to the need for a prominent place in our systemic conceptualizations for individuals. Each of these theorists in addition espoused the belief that the key to unlocking solutions to clients' problems lay in their families of origin. Although a case can be made that this is critical for all clients, it is particularly important for men. Family of origin work is cited as a powerful ingredient for change by Meth and Pasick (1990) as well, because the family is where a boy receives his strongest messages about what it is to be a man.

The key to unlocking change in a man often lies in helping him to gain an appreciation of the influence of his family of origin on ways he thinks and behaves. One of the most powerful and enduring

influences in a man's life is the family in which he grew up. That is
where he received his first training in what it means to be a man.
(Allen & Gordon, 1990, p. 143)

Unless a man is able to understand the messages he received
about masculinity and where they came from, he will be hampered
in relationships. In his early articulation of men's struggles, Fasteau
(1974) discussed the centrality of a man's understanding his roots
to understanding and changing himself now. "Incompetence in
personal relationships is the inevitable result of belief in the masculine ideal, the degree of incompetence varying directly with the
degree of belief" (p. 3). Many of those messages, of course, come
also from the culture at large. The initial training a boy receives in
how to be a man that comes from his family is then reinforced by
the culture. In accordance with this point of view, helping a man
to understand his place in his family of origin is a centerpiece to
successful treatment.

*Clinical Example.* Forty-year-old Sam, whose words we heard earlier in the chapter, offers an example of the central importance of
this idea to the treatment of men. Four years earlier, he and his
wife had attempted family therapy, which he summarily ended
when I lobbied for family of origin exploration. Back in treatment
with 4 years of dysfunction added to his earlier problems and a
wife who was threatening divorce, he finally began to acknowledge that this type of exploration was vital for his journey inward
as well as for healing his interactions with others. He captured the
notion clearly and simply when he spoke of a long overdue conversation with his mother:

*Sam:* I should've known this stuff years ago! I felt like a big piece of the
puzzle was being put into place and tamped down.

Then, spurred on by his emerging interest in his family history, he
initiated another conversation with his mother in which he learned
the rather shocking story of his illegitimate birth in the back seat of
a car, with his naive teenaged mother, unaware that she even was
pregnant, being driven to the doctor for what she thought was back
pain. Although he described his shock and sadness at learning the
truth, in the next session we also hear him express a great deal of

relief at finally having answers to the question of why he always felt a chronic and exaggerated sense of shame about himself.

*Sam:* I'm feeling pretty damn good! I feel like doing this is helping me feel better about myself. I feel more in control of myself and my life. I feel more whole. In fact, it's been two weeks tomorrow that I quit smoking, and it hasn't even been that hard!

Later in that session:

*Sam:* It's pretty awesome to see the patterns from my family that I've repeated. It kinda makes me wonder what other patterns will repeat. But I find myself thinking, what other patterns *could* repeat? (Pause) Oh! My parents divorced right about my age, when we were my kids' ages. And I don't want that to happen!
*Therapist:* What's your sense about what you might do, in order to help that not happen?
*Sam:* What I've been doing here these last weeks.
*Therapist:* Which is?
*Sam:* Trying to figure out myself, so we can both be happier. 'Cause if I'm happier, we both are happier.
*Therapist:* How does it make you feel about yourself, having this information?
*Sam:* More solid. Less—uh—transient. More firmly rooted, perhaps. Maybe it's because it's a fact. It's immutable. There it is. And I also feel like it's a helluva story to tell my kids. 'Cause they've gotta feel whole, too. I now understand that the farther back you know, the more solid you feel. I mean, just knowing [referring to his parents' marriage] "married in 1952, divorced in 1968" helps me to feel anchored. And it's not even that I'll remember the dates. Just knowing them helps me feel anchored. When I look at my genogram, I see so much failure above me. And I don't want it to go on. I am determined to stop the pattern with me.

I see a kind of sequence in the layering of the family of origin exploration that needs to take place. First, I am careful to establish, repeatedly if I have to, the link between historical patterns and the current symptomatology. Clients' being able to grasp this gives me the permission and the access I need to work in a way that appears at first glance to be remote from and even totally unrelated to the problem that clients bring into therapy. Over and over, I loop the current problem to whatever thread of the pattern I can pick up from even a cursory exploration of the family of origin. Although I do

enough historical exploration to tantalize and hook clients, I do
not begin full-blown family of origin exploration until I have a
solid contract with clients that gives me permission to do this
work. This is for two reasons. One, generally family of origin work
contains highly emotionally charged material that often is painful
for clients to discover, to say nothing of resolve. And two, unless
they buy into my view that these patterns are at the root of the
current problem, whatever material is generated very likely will
seem to be empty insights that then can become another layer of
rationalization and intellectualization painted on top of already
considerable defenses. So on both counts, I want their expressed
permission.

For most people, especially men, whose expectations for themselves can be incredibly high, it often takes a long time genuinely
to see the connection at an emotional level between historical
precedents and current events. That is, even though intellectual
assent to an idea may be possible early on, it can take months,
sometimes even years, for clients to come to acknowledge at an
emotional level the connection between an event that happened
so far in their past and their rigidified present.

*Clinical Example.* Mick, whose words we hear throughout the book,
offers an example. At 31 years of age, he presented for marital
treatment with his wife, whose anger from her chronic depression
and her borderline personality disorder was unrelenting. Although
Lenore actually had not been abused herself, she grew up in an
ambience of physical and verbal abuse aimed at her brother. Mick's
experience with physical and verbal abuse in childhood was actual,
though more episodic. His father's emotional storms were usually
intense, appearing out of the blue. However, the abuse and its unpre-
dictability left Mick extremely hypervigilant and fearful of any
discord or intimate contact that might generate controversy. Further, no matter what he or I tried, Lenore would explode in a rage
and threaten to leave both the therapy and the marriage.

Unable to gain much therapeutic ground by working interaction-
ally on their marital issues because of the block that Lenore's profuse
and unrelenting anger and Mick's timidity about it created, I then
attempted to begin family of origin exploration. To minimize their
fears of doing this painstaking work in the other's presence, I also
offered some individual sessions. Predictably, Lenore resisted this

suggestion, too, but Mick used his sessions to begin to touch on the abuse and resulting fear he had experienced with his father. Although intellectual assent to the influence of the abuse on him was easy, his coming to examine it at an emotional level took well over a year. Meanwhile, the dysfunction in his marriage deepened, becoming more and more threatening to him physically and emotionally.

Finally, Mick agreed to deal directly with his parents, as all else with Lenore seemed to be going for naught, and he asked them to fly into town to join us for a family of origin session. (See Chapter 11 for a detailed discussion of this technique.) During the preparatory session just before that meeting, Mick articulated the connection between his role in his marriage and his family of origin for the first time. Sadly, it took Lenore's biting his arm sufficiently hard to leave teeth marks the next day to drive this connection home.

*Mick:* I know I'm very close to divorcing Lenore. And I want [my parents] to know that I've done with her what I learned with them. If my father says I'm worthwhile and I don't need the abuse I'm getting, I can stop being "The Victim."
**Therapist:** Then I guess you'd better ask him to talk to you about that!

Once clients have acknowledged, at a visceral level, the present-day impact of historical factors, then they can begin in earnest to explore for themselves the genesis and the multiple impacts of these patterns. Multiple tactics, such as genograms, open chair dialogues, and letter writing can be used in this effort. The following are two examples of this exploration. One illustrates an experiential technique; the other involves more standard insight-oriented exploration.

*Clinical Example.* Oren, age 50, was abandoned by his birth father at 6 years of age when his mother had an affair with the father's business partner, whom she subsequently married. His stepfather, the classic workaholic, had no time for Oren and taught by example and by expectation that he assumed that Oren would be a worker, too. These patterns left Oren, much to his chagrin, a chronic and extreme overachiever whose excesses were not limited to work. Having five advanced degrees or certifications in different fields, he overdid food, sex, alcohol, schooling, and anything else he did. The crux of his presenting problem at the onset

of treatment was his recent realization that his philandering precluded his having any relationship with a woman, and he desperately wished to change that. The following imaginary conversation
with his stepfather took place 1½ years after he began therapy.

*Oren:* I got to thinking this week, that the only times you touched me were
to spank me. And then the only other time you touched me was to teach
me to fight. (Pausing to cry) Did you even touch the things I was working
with? I don't think you even did that! My intelligence was always book
stuff. Yours was always how things work. I don't remember anything
where you helped me with your hands. I don't remember having
anybody's hand to hold—except women's. I don't even remember
having my mother's hand to hold. Never! The only thing I ever
remember was your criticizing that I wasn't a better football player.
And you said if I didn't shape up my deportment, you'd come to
school and take down my pants and spank me in front of the class! I
know that's all you knew how [to do], but I sure wish I could've had
more than I got! (Sobbing) You knew so much about so many things,
I wish we'd have had time to explore them together. Even working
together would've been nice! There's so much you could've taught
me! I missed not having you there, Dad.

*Therapist:* Oren, I'd like you to tell that little boy inside you that even
though he can't have his dad there, he can have you there always.

*Oren:* Big Oren?

*Therapist:* Um hum.

*Oren:* You mean try to connect me up with them?

*Therapist:* Um hum.

*Oren:* (Chuckling) OK, all you Orens. Even though you don't have your
dad, I'm going to be there for you. (Pause) But now I'm scared
shitless! I'm afraid I won't measure up—because I don't know what
it means to be caring and committed.

Exactly where this excerpt ends—what it means to be caring and
committed—was the major theme pervading much of our work.
Eventually Oren was able to commit both to a woman and to her
child and to attain the requisite confidence that he would be able
to follow through on his commitment of both fidelity and stead-
fastness.

The following excerpt with 30-year-old Aaron, from whom we
also hear throughout the book, and his fiancée, Laura, represents
the culmination of 3 years of therapy. Because he lived in a major
city 8 hours away and chose to commute to see me for therapy
despite my efforts to find him a therapeutic resource closer at

hand, we met for 2 hours every 2 to 3 weeks, depending on our schedules. As stated earlier, at intake, Aaron was 26 years old and was still jumping from woman to woman, much as he had seen his father do before and after his parents' divorce when Aaron was 11. Aaron's mother, an ineffectual parent particularly after the father left, died in a coma from incorrectly prescribed medications when Aaron was 23.

One of Aaron's presenting concerns was his inability to find satisfaction in any of the many relationships in which he had been involved, both with family members and with women. Despite the gargantuan effort involved in his coming to therapy, for many months I felt as if I did not have a working contract with him to do anything other than attend sessions. So I worked from the angle of insisting that he develop a relationship with me as a prerequisite to my being able to help him with any of his other relationship concerns.

Slowly and gradually, Aaron allowed himself to bond with me. As he allowed himself to trust our alliance, he reported a commensurate strengthening of a relationship with one particular woman, Laura. Although their relationship had gone on for 4 years, it had been battered by all his liaisons with other women and by her impotence to take a stand regarding this behavior, for fear of losing him. For several months, we explored his relationship with his mother before and after his father left. We studied the impact of the model of his father's philandering on him. We scrutinized his distanced relationship with his sisters. Finally, he began to seriously consider that a significant element of his life was missing because of his inability to commit to a relationship. At this time, he requested that Laura be included in the sessions, an idea I heartily endorsed, because I could see that their relationship might possibly jell with help to overcome the residue of his rather checkered past.

The following excerpt occurred just weeks before he asked her to marry him and she accepted. It illustrates two very important concepts. First, we see how once a man understands his own patterns and emotions, he then is in a position to own their effects on his relationships and to ask for help in changing them. And second, once the pattern is clarified and his partner is in a position to see how her responses may have inadvertently fed into his problematic behaviors, both are better able to work to change their mutual dysfunctional pattern.

*Aaron:*  I'm worried that if you stand up for yourself, you'll leave. I don't
    want you to leave.
*Laura:*  It's so strange to hear you say that! I'm always the one who doesn't
    want you to leave! It's so weird!
*Aaron:*  I put up this barrier so I'm not vulnerable if you leave.
*Therapist:*  How do you feel about saying that?
*Aaron:*  (Sobbing) Awful! It's a bad habit of mine that I can't get over. I
    have never had anybody *not* leave me before.
*Therapist:*  Tell her about your tears, Aaron.
*Laura:*  That's the first time you ever showed me you could cry! I've never
    seen this before. I'm sorry.
*Therapist:*  What are you sorry for?
*Laura:*  For my part in what kept you from showing me more of what you
    had to tell me, to show me.
*Therapist:*  How do you see yourself doing that, Laura?
*Laura:*  I did what my mom does: go to my room. And I guess that's what
    I was doing with him!

Later in the session:

*Aaron:*  I'm afraid if you do something better than me, you'll go out and
    find somebody better than me. I feel like I have to compete against
    your idea of what's ideal.
*Laura:*  If I'm better at some things than you, that's all it means. I think it's only
    natural for me to be good at some things and you to be good at others.
*Aaron:*  But I want to be good at everything.
*Therapist:*  But you can't be good at everything. We have to help you
    disabuse yourself of that notion.
*Aaron:*  (Sobbing to Laura) I love you. Please don't leave me!
*Laura:*  I'm not going to! I'm never going to! I love you. And I'm telling
    you that years from now, I want us to be together.
*Aaron:*  I'm not used to unconditional love! I love you, and I want to grow
    old with you.
*Therapist:*  Tell her what it's like to tell her how much you need her.
*Aaron:*  It's about time! (Pause) I never told my mother how much I needed
    her. And I only rarely told my sisters. I'm really new at trusting women.
    I'm really hoping that our doing this can help us have a better family.
*Therapist:*  Talk to Laura some more about how your pushing her away is
    tied up in how you pushed your mother away.
*Aaron:*  I pushed my mother away because I was torn between needing
    her as a mother and having to provide some sort of leadership of the
    house. I was the man of the family, and I was told that since I was 11.
    So on the one hand, I had to be an adult, but on the other hand, I had
    to avoid being my father and hurting my mother. So the only way
    I could do that was push them away. So I just reflexively distanced

myself from my mother and my sisters, because I saw my mother needing a man, and I saw myself as having to protect myself from her.

*Therapist:* Now connect the dots and tell Laura how you do that with her.

*Aaron:* Sometimes the way you care for me is the same kind of care my mother did for me. So the only way I could protect myself and you was push you away. That's why my sisters and I are polite strangers. I've pushed them away, too. After the divorce, my sisters and I were given free rein. We were tenants there. It wasn't like a household. That's why I decided, "I don't need anybody." My mother and I started to have major conflicts about her authority and my autonomy. And that's where I learned to fear dependence.

When the couple could each identify their contribution to the impasse *between* them, they were able to move forward both together and in their individual lives. Shortly after this session, Aaron very ceremoniously asked Laura to marry him, and she happily accepted. In the session following their engagement, Aaron offered the following observations.

*Aaron:* The word *give* has become much more important to me lately. I used to think that I am who I am, and she is who she is, and if we get along, that's great. Otherwise, it's no big deal. Now that I'm giving to her, I can see how easy it is and how good it actually feels to make her happy. Now I understand what you meant when you said $1 + 1 = 3$. That's what we get when we give to each other. [Regarding their decision to marry] Now that I feel I've got her, I see no reason to wait for anything. I don't know why, but I believe that having her in my life makes me much more peaceful. I've got so much more mental energy to think about things. I wouldn't be doing any of the things I'm doing. I never realized how much energy always looking took!

Each of these excerpts is offered to illustrate the power of family of origin exploration in breaking patterns that constrict clients' current and everyday lives. These patterns act like transparency overlays that people isomorphically and unknowingly superimpose on their current situations. As such, they are largely responsible for dysfunction now. The therapy, then, is to identify and eliminate these overlays so that people are relating to current, real people, not shadowboxing with ghosts from their past. Each of the men who spoke above told of powerful longings that can be explored, tapped, and channeled now that they no longer need to be denied or repressed.

*Redecision Therapy.* A specific set of techniques for working psychodynamically with the genesis of archaic patterns that have shaped—and misshaped—clients' lives is redecision therapy. It is based on the premise that here-and-now behavior is often an outward manifestation of a repetitive pattern that people learned early in life to survive emotionally, if not actually. The unconscious decisions they made in their past form the basis for their perceptions of events and shape their responses to them. The primary goal of these early decisions was to get needs met in their family of origin. However, what was functional then has a high probability of being dysfunctional now, because it has a child's magical-thinking, irrational quality that impedes and is impervious to rational thought.

The difficult part about early decisions is that most were made unconsciously and therefore remain outside awareness, often impenetrable to the rationality of current circumstances. That is, clients may know all the "right" reasons that they "should" do or not do something and still be unable to do what they know they want to do. This is particularly true of men who seek therapy to learn to become more sensitive to themselves and others. They know that this is what they want to do. They acknowledge that they and others need them to do this. But until they are helped to surface their obsolete unconscious decisions and make different decisions, many will be unable to do it.

Redecision therapy is an approach developed by Mary and Robert Goulding (1979) to help clients address the impasses that have resulted in their lives because of the early decisions they made in order to get along in the home of their childhood. These decisions, often made at an unconscious level, were designed to satisfy the overt and covert instructions that were communicated to them. These early decisions may have been helpful in that they guaranteed the clients' survival in childhood, but they are archaic now. In fact, they likely compromise clients' functioning in adulthood because they were made when the child had only concrete reasoning ability and few adequate emotional defenses.

Simply making an intellectual decision to change for most people will go for naught. Giving intellectual assent to the need to change and attaining the requisite flexibility to accomplish actual change often are two different matters. Ultimately, freedom from the patterns that bind people involves regressing to a typical moment that generated or reinforced that early decision, retrieving the emotions involved, and reworking the decision at that nexus. Hypnosis does not necessarily have to be used in order to accomplish regression, but in the event of an extraordinarily unyielding impasse, it may necessary. More often than not, however, simple depth exploration is sufficient.

Redecision therapy allows the therapist to facilitate clients' experiencing temporary regression to the moment in time when they unconsciously made the decision around which they have unwittingly lived their lives. When they understand the choice they made and its full impact on them, then that judgement can be changed to one that can serve them better in their adult lives. Redecisions can be made that carry the same psychic impact of the earlier decisions. Once the redecision has been accomplished, an individual usually looks, acts, sounds, and feels different, and figuring out new more flexible behavior is made easier. Then the therapist's job is to help people practice behaving in ways that are consistent with their new perspectives and decisions.

Redecision therapy can be especially significant for men. Owing to a combination of socialization learned from the culture and in their family of origin, their emotional range can become extremely limited. They are left constricted and restricted in the ways in which they are able to relate to others, even when they sincerely want to change.

*Clinical Example.* The following example illustrates the developmental bottleneck generated because of an early decision, as well as the redecision work with a client around that impasse. Rob is a 41-year-old, highly successful high-tech salesman who has been divorced for 8 years. During that time, he has had relationships with several women, some lasting for several years. But at intake, he reported still being lonely and frustrated. The precipitant for therapy was his meeting a woman 6 months before who seemed different from the rest. A former client of mine herself, she suggested that therapy might be a tool for both of them to gain the requisite confidence in their ability to form a lasting and satisfying relationship and for him to learn to become emotionally available to her. There are two other complicating variables. One, he is from an ethnic group whose watchwords are stoicism and independence. And two, as a child, he spent many years on his grandparents' farm, because his mother took him and his three brothers there every time his father, a career Navy man, was deployed out to sea. The following dialogue, which took place about 4 months into the therapy, illustrates redecision work.

*Rob:* (With tears welling in his eyes) When my father left for the first time, I guess I must've felt, "Don't share. Don't trust. Hide your feelings." Because my dad retired after 25 years of service, that meant he would've been gone for most of my formative years, when I was learning to build trust. This must've developed in me a wanting not to be left, a fear of being alone.
*Therapist:* Sounds like we need to help you make another decision.
*Rob:* That's what I'm trying to do with Melissa.
*Therapist:* So what would that decision be?
*Rob:* To have feelings with her. To trust her. To allow her in. To allow her to experience those feelings with me. And to take those feelings and make a solid bond, so that she becomes a place for me to go. That hopefully will reverse all the other things I've done, trying to drive her away. And I think I could still do that, by not sharing.
*Therapist:* I'm sure you could. And I'm sure you don't want to. So all this sounds great. But I guess I'm a little concerned that you could think of Melissa as the only place you can go, and that would leave you too restricted. There are other people in the world who are trustworthy, too. In fact, I'd like you to come to see the parts of the world itself as a trustworthy place, instead of a hostile place.
*Rob:* Um hum. And I think I'm starting to do that with my friends now, too, to allow myself to be open with them, too. So I think that's another piece. If you allow yourself to feel and share your emotions with others, it allows you to feel stronger. The more I think about it, the more I think it's because I'm afraid people will go away that I don't trust—I know I need to make sure I can open myself up to many different people, not just Melissa.
*Therapist:* Yes. That sounds like it's another decision.
*Rob:* Yup!

The preparatory work during the previous 3 weeks for getting Rob to this point involved helping him to see the paradoxical effect of gaining greater control of his life by loosening his strict, rigid controls on his emotions. Having had an extremely rewarding experience once he let go of the controls on his feelings, he attained the requisite faith in me, in himself, and in the process to proceed to really extricate himself from his emotional and behavioral strictures. I time the introduction of the redecision work when I hear evidence that a client is beginning to attribute his here-and-now impasses to his handling of early life events. The following excerpt from the session 1 week prior to the one in which we reworked his early decision illustrates how the tone was set to do this.

*Rob:* I felt last week like I went from control to feeling. And I felt like I didn't have any control.

*Therapist:* That must have really scared you, to feel you had no control!

*Rob:* Yes! It did! It scared the crap out of me! But that's OK, because I felt that that's where we've been trying to get me to. I got a lot of stuff out, and it helped me to have a much better week. I'm finding it a lot easier to go with feelings. Just coming in here today, looking at all the things I have to do, it feels better. So I'm learning that bein' in touch with myself and sharing it makes me feel a lot better! A week ago, I was worried about everything. Last week, for the first time, I felt like I was letting go and getting in touch with my inner self. It was hard, but it was good. Last week, I was pretty desperate. This week I'm not. And I think I won't be again.

*Therapist:* I think you've just learned one of the elegant paradoxes of human relationships: When you let go of being controlling, you gain control of your own life. And, rather than being weakened, you actually gain strength by sharing with appropriate people.

Later in the session:

*Rob:* For the last year, I felt like I was kinda hollow. I felt hollow, because literally there were no feelings of any kind. That's why I felt hollow. And that's sad. I started to build up my immune system early in life to protect me from all my feelings. But I don't know why.

*Therapist:* Let's figure that out.

*Rob:* It's probably all the moves and my father not being there. I'm sure out of all that came confusion of feelings, of how to react. Probably early on, I started to get confused and started to build a protective shield.

These excerpts delineate the sorts of cues that clients give us to indicate their readiness to make a new, more appropriate decision than the relics by which they have lived their lives since childhood. Some of these cues are listed below.

1. The client was able to articulate the early decision he had made.
2. He could see that his early decision, which kept him separate and apart from others, was probably rooted in his fear of abandonment.

3. He had empathy rather than judgment for himself, for making such a decision.
4. He indicated in several ways that he no longer needed or wanted the protection that early decision had afforded him.
5. He could see how continuing to live by that early decision was interfering with his life and his happiness now.
6. He had a clear motivation and incentive to do otherwise.
7. He had experienced enough pain from having lived by that early decision that whatever pain he felt in learning to live without that protection would seem a small price to pay.
8. He was starting spontaneously to open up with others besides his lover and could see the benefit from this increased support network.
9. He recognized at both an intellectual and a visceral level that he no longer needed or desired the control he previously felt he had to exercise to maintain his early decision.
10. He had tasted the relief and the connection that comes from sharing emotions, and clearly he liked it.
11. He was tired of feeling perpetually hollow or sad.
12. He recognized that he could make choices for his life that were different from his family's, especially from his father's.

Because good therapy is aimed at helping clients break through their impasses, we need many strategies available to us to help clients do that. Men, often already affectively constricted, can be particularly plagued by the stalemates that their early decisions created.

*Clinical Example.* The therapist may need to use all the techniques at her disposal to maintain the requisite agility to maneuver these roadblocks so that they can be removed. Sometimes that involves being direct, blunt, and to the point. Work with Stan illustrates this. A divorced, 35-year-old factory worker and youngest of five sons of a father whose frequent temper tantrums and emotional outbursts dominated his childhood, he learned that the only safe person for him was his mother. And he reports becoming very emotionally dependent on her, for which he was shamed mercilessly by his father. Thus she became unsafe for him as well. As a result, he made an early decision not only to write his father off but also to become wary of any closeness, especially with women. These historical factors, plus his former wife's habitual infidelities, prompted him to cultivate to a fine art the skill of stiff-arming everyone to keep his distance. In addition, a huge, athletic man, he introjected the societal message that "Big boys don't cry"—or feel, for that matter. In the second session, describing his bitter disappointment with life to date and his abject aloneness, he came dangerously close to tears. Letting himself slip so far that any emotion was apparent to both of us triggered his retreating so that no further real work could proceed. He was adamant. He believed he simply could not allow himself to cry. In the next session after he almost cried, he said the following:

**Stan:** When your voice gets soft when you talk to me, I don't like that shit. I *have* to be in control! If I let you nurture me, that means I'm weak. Monday night at work, I almost broke down and cried. And I can't do that shit! I mean, geez, I work in a factory! That's just not something you do. I can't do that! I am a feeling person. But I know most guys wouldn't understand that. You've got to pay attention to the norms. You've got to remain in control.

As certain as he was that he could not allow himself to cry, it was also clear that to continue his adherence to those norms was to leave himself stuck. Thus, I had the makings of a therapeutic double bind, and whether I came at issues directly or subtly, Stan continued to protest that he simply could not allow himself to cry. And yet, each session, he heartily assured me that he liked working with me and that he was getting a lot out of our time together. I was frustrated, however, that, after nine sessions of exploring, reframing, and even stroking his resistance, he still made no moves to experiment with change. When he returned for the tenth session, he started with the following statement. With that entree, I decided to blitz his resistance.

**Stan:** Are you going to tell me why you were so pissed last time?
**Therapist:** Sure. And thanks for asking. People come into therapy to change, not to get help to justify their intention to stay the same. You are going to have to decide which it's going to be for you. And until you do, I won't feed your defenses. So let me know what you decide.

It was clear within minutes that he had already made his decision in the intervening week. He began to work and was highly workable ever after.

*Hypnosis for Age Regression.* Another specific strategy for working psychodynamically to remove early developmental arrests is hypnosis. It can be used for age regression back to early traumatic experiences that forged the nexus of clients' developmental arrests. Hypnosis has two distinct benefits. First, it allows clients to "see" what actually went on that made that source experience so powerfully damaging. And second, it provides a kind of anesthetic while they experience the pain of recovering those early memories, because it is as though clients get to observe themselves reliving the trauma from afar.

Sometimes disabling events are so deeply embedded in clients' unconscious that they are unable to know at a conscious level what happened. Obviously, if clients cannot surface their experience somehow, everyone is at a loss to work with it; if an experience cannot even be recalled, none of the decisions and emotions that accompanied it are available for examination, either. Then the therapist must try other even more sophisticated tools to gain access to this pivotal information. Perhaps the most elegant tool is hypnosis. When either early decisions or traumatic events can be uncovered in a fully conscious state, hypnosis is not needed and would be excessive. However, when they cannot, hypnosis can give both therapist and client an opening that they would not otherwise have.

Because hypnosis is an extremely powerful tool, caution needs to be exercised in using it. It is not for the untrained, as it is a tool that has the power of major surgery. I urge therapists who wish to incorporate hypnosis into their practice to get both training and supervision in the use of this very powerful tool, in order to do no harm. Simply reading about hypnotic techniques is not sufficient, and therefore I do not suggest any. The only reason for this cursory discussion is to illustrate how a potent a tool it is for resolution of early impasses and developmental logjams.

*How Hypnosis Works.* Hypnosis acts like a laser beam zeroing in on critical incidents, to enable reliving and reworking them, this time with the accompanying feelings that originally had to be repressed or denied. Using this medium, clients are unable to continue to deny the reality of those events, and they can then free themselves of their grip. I employed hypnosis in a case of a woman who was convinced that there had been sexual abuse in her history. Yet, try as we might, we could dredge up no conscious memories of it. We worked week after week trying to prompt, surface, and recall even tidbits that might help her corroborate or shuck her intuitive sense, to no avail, with both of us getting more and more frustrated. Finally one day, she said, "There are no words for my experience." Eureka! In that moment, it became clear that if there had been abuse, it must have occurred at a preverbal age. So I put her in a trance, and what she saw, with the clarity of a horror movie, was her father sexually abusing her from the time she was 4 months old lying in her crib. Although having her suspicions confirmed was a calamitous experience, once that memory was retrieved, she also experienced a great deal of relief. She now could begin to fit the disjointed pieces of her life into place and begin working through the damage that had been done to her.

The words of 33-year-old Lyle illustrate the power of this intervention for him. The purpose of our using hypnosis was to help him to identify both a developmental impediment and the strengths he had acquired in the therapy process that would help him work through this particular stalemate.

*Lyle:* I felt like I could experience *me* more. It was the only time I could see myself. I could experience the different dimensions of me more, even if we didn't talk about it. Hypnosis is really tapping into my gifts.

*Therapist:* What if we hadn't done hypnosis?

*Lyle:* It would be stifling. In this [conscious] dimension, I couldn't have gotten the information I needed. Things I didn't know, I could get through hypnosis. And what I saw was so true, it was unshakable. The unknown is scary. Hypnosis is scary! But it was so easy to do and it felt so right. It felt so good, it was unnerving! I don't want to stay the underachiever any more. That's been my role, but that doesn't mean that that's who I am.

Under hypnosis, people can gain access to heretofore unavailable information with which they then can work to resolve their developmental logjams. When they have no conscious avenue to that information, they remain caught in the paralyzing grip of that early experience. Therapists who believe in the need to help clients locate and resolve their early traumas and who are well trained in the uses of hypnosis will find it a very useful tool indeed for age regression.

## What Factors Can Jeopardize Our Effectively Working With Men?

Probably worse than any other factors jeopardizing our effectively working with men are our own life experiences with men, as even without our knowing it, they constantly shape our work with both females and males. Consequently, it is important that we have a clear understanding at both an emotional and a cognitive level. For example, if a woman grew up protecting her mother against an abusive husband, her natural tendency will be to do isomorphically the same for female clients regarding their spouses. Likewise, if a woman grew up being "daddy's little girl" in a family where the mother was there in name only or where females competed for men's attention, the female therapist's natural tendency will be to ignore the needs of the woman and shield or concentrate on the man. Of course, just because a therapist may have had a less than optimal experience in her family of origin does not automatically disqualify her from treating men—or women. However, she must work diligently to study how her own countertransference experiences might intrude into the therapy.

Not all life experiences are to be kept strictly out of the consultation room. Indeed, many of our experiences can be used to augment our treatment, just by increasing our own knowledge base, even if we choose never to share it with clients. It should be stressed, however, that for the therapist to be as certain as she needs to be that her own history will augment and not diminish the therapy, she needs to have examined herself and her experiences closely. And for the times that she feels stuck with a client, she needs to seek consultation from a trusted colleague. And sometimes, to avoid becoming impaired herself, she will need to seek therapy for herself. Being the object of clients' transference reactions can itself be difficult, and such reactions are particularly loaded when women work with men. So the therapist's own personal clarity is essential to protect herself from burnout and to guard her natural countertransference reactions from bleeding into the therapy.

## Protocol for Integrating Modalities

In this section, I will offer a thumbnail sketch to help the reader clarify how to think about utilizing and integrating each of the main modalities at her disposal: individual, couples, group, family, and family of origin therapy. There will be further elaboration on issues related to implementation of each specific modality in separate chapters later in the book. But for our purposes here, questions such as these will be answered:

How does the therapist know where to begin with a case?
At what points are additional modalities utilized?
Is a particular order followed in adding other modalities?

The chapter is not intended to be a cookbook. Rather, the attempt is to provide some guidelines for therapeutic improvisation.

## Choosing Modalities to Use

As stated above, all three types of treatment modalities are utilized where appropriate: family (which may include nuclear family, family of origin, and couples therapy), individual, and group psychotherapy. It is not a one-size-fits-all proposition, however. Which modalities are used and in which order for each case is up to the therapist to decide, proceeding from a combination of her own personal philosophy and her assessment of each case.

Doherty (1981) offers the following with which I wholeheartedly agree: *"The therapist's control over who participates in family therapy sessions is the* sine qua non *of successful outcome.* This is as close to being a therapeutic axiom as we have in our field" (p. 26). That is, it is incumbent on the therapist to win the battle for structure (Napier & Whitaker, 1978) and stipulate initially how and with whom therapy will be conducted. Otherwise, she has lost before she begins, for people's tendency to strive for homeostasis and equilibrium will work at cross-purposes with any changes the therapist suggests they need to make. Likewise, in excusing key family members, she will lose a valuable resource in affected family members that otherwise could amplify the changes made, rather than homeostatically stalling them.

As therapy progresses and there is ample evidence of change taking place, and a strong therapeutic alliance and a clear working contract have been forged, the therapist can afford to leave it up to clients to decide who should be involved or what modality(ies) will be used next. However, prematurely giving the client discretion has a high probability of compromising the therapy and of rendering the therapist ineffective.

*When Individual Therapy Is Requested but Couples Therapy Is Indicated.* Seeing the appropriate person or people at the appropriate time is key to the success of any therapy. Kramer (1980) offers some clarity on how to conceptualize this vital issue:

> The primary goal of family therapy is to effect changes in the interpersonal relationships among members of the family system. . . . In contrast, the primary goal of individual therapy is change in that person, with changes in the system and in other members seen as secondary, incidental, or beyond the responsibility of the therapist. Stated in this way, the basic difference between the two seems simple and not earth-shaking. Yet, the difference becomes sharply clear when the conceptualization is applied to the practicalities of clinical management. The difference lies in the conceptualization by the therapist, not in the number of people in the treatment room. If the therapist has as his primary goal beneficial changes in the relationships, and if he feels a firm therapeutic commitment and loyalty to every member in the system, then he is conducting family therapy no matter how many people happen to be in the room or what techniques are used. (pp. 101-102)

My personal bias is when the presenting problem involves a relationship issue to begin by seeing all the people who are directly involved. In most cases, I refuse to begin with individual therapy when people request help with a marital issue. I do individual therapy only when couples or family treatment has progressed far enough that tipping the fragile relationship equilibrium in nontherapeutic, uncontrolled ways is unlikely. However, individual therapy is indicated with single, emancipated adults.

Some clinicians opt to be more flexible than I personally prefer to be on this point, or have had to be more inventive because of their difficulty in getting men into their offices. They have found ways to treat the absent spouse, who at least in their experience, is usually the male. For a thorough discussion of an alternative approach, see Lewis's (1991) cogent and useful paper.

If the presenting problem is a relationship issue but the couple is unmarried, I screen in the intake call for the significance of the relationship to the caller. If it is a stable, ongoing relationship, I request that both begin treatment. If the caller is involved in a relatively new, uncommitted relationship and has anxieties or problems with relationships in general, I comply with the request for individual sessions. If the caller simply seems too fearful of meeting with a partner or other family members, I will meet separately a few times to provide strength and perspective before others are asked to become involved. If key family members are resistant to entering therapy, I agree to do a session or two where the focus is on strategizing on how to get the reluctant family member to join us. However, I explicitly state in the intake call, "So that you don't feel later as if I've done a bait and switch, I will want to meet in a session or two with you and your partner." If the potential client still wants to work with me, then I have the seeds of a therapeutic contract and the work can begin. If not, I cheerfully refer him or her elsewhere.

Some special caveats are in order, because doing individual sessions where your goal is couples or family therapy can be delicate to handle. The main stipulation is to be certain that these individual sessions do not compromise the overall direction of the case. The primary goals at that time are twofold: (a) to position oneself in the most advantageous way possible for the subsequent family or couples work and (b) to join with the spokesperson for the system in a way that allows an entree into the system without its becoming an unholy alliance (Haley, 1966). Specifically, that means the following. First, the therapist must be careful not to allow herself to be triangulated onto the side of the person requesting separate sessions. Second, even if the therapist does not become triangulated, the danger of ongoing separate sessions is that both present and absent members may come to think of the therapist as that person's therapist and may not believe or feel she can broaden her allegiance. Third, these sessions are rife with opportunities for the client to dump a secret on the therapist that she or he expects to be kept. To avoid this, the therapist needs to make it clear early on that she does not keep secrets that she believes could have a deleterious effect on the relationship or on the therapy. When I am told a secret nonetheless, I make it an explicit goal to help the keeper of the secret prepare to disclose it to the other(s). This requires laying groundwork for the other(s) to be able to hear it and constructively work with it so that it becomes more safe to disclose the secret.

Writing on engaging resistant fathers in family treatment, Doherty (1981) suggests what can be generalized to recruiting any reluctant potential participant:

> When the therapist believes that of course the father will attend (although it may take a little persuading or pressuring), then that therapist is apt, in my view, to have little problem with absent fathers. Conversely, therapists are likely to have difficulties in this area if they are timid or inconsistent in demanding fathers' presence. (p. 26)

Sometimes individuals requesting treatment are themselves resistant to couples therapy. Usually for reasons of their own, often because of an affair or because of having silently made a decision to end the relationship, they protest that they wish to work this out on their own and leave the partner out of it. In effect, if we agree to this, we are helping them ambush the partner, and beginning treatment without the partner virtually guarantees an end to their relationship. Although I have less concern when there are no children involved, when there are, I believe I have a moral responsibility to attempt to help both people honestly examine both the relationship and the covert decision. This includes attempting to save the relationship first, as Weiner-Davis (1992) suggests.

Questions such as the following help me to induce the participation of key parties, regardless of who is resisting:

> Even if your spouse does not believe he/she has a problem or that there is a problem, would you please ask him/her to join us so that he/she can help me help you?
>
> What do you foresee happening between you if you grow and he/she stays the same?
>
> Can you help me understand what makes you believe that deciding the ultimate fate of your relationship has to be or even can be all your responsibility?

Answers to questions such as these help me decide who should be involved, suggest the turf on which I likely will need to fight the battle for structure, and usually result in my being able to convene sessions with the requisite people. If people opt not to work with me on these terms, we have saved headaches and heartaches on both sides. Usually, these types of questions, plus my persistence and belief that those who are needed will come in, result in my being able to convene sessions with the requisite people. If not, I suggest that the people continue their search for a therapist.

*When Couples Therapy Is Requested.* When a caller requests couples therapy, my decision is usually straightforward, because beginning there is most often my preference. So couples therapy is where I begin. I make certain that the caller and I are on the same wavelength by asking the following types of questions:

Can you give me a thumbnail sketch of your concerns?
Are you currently in a committed relationship?
Is your partner prepared to join us?

When the answers to these straightforward questions are clear, I schedule an appointment with the couple and continue treating them as a couple until further notice. Sometimes individual or group therapy sessions are indicated; often they are not.

*When Individual Sessions Are Integrated Into Couples Therapy.* Whether meeting as a couple was their idea or mine, sometimes as the treatment progresses, it becomes apparent that continuing to meet with the couple perpetuates a dysfunctional united front or is beginning to bog down because of extreme rigidity. In these instances, I will alternate couples sessions with individual sessions for each. There are several purposes for this strategy. Sometimes, I do this to gain access to a closed system. Other times, I do this to help extremely enmeshed couples individuate so that they can experience a different quality of togetherness that makes new levels of intimacy possible. In still other cases, I may offer to meet with people separately if I sense that there is a particularly sensitive or difficult issue that they want and need to discuss with their partner but would be unable to broach without preparation. It should be noted that to maintain the requisite balance and avoid disturbing the therapeutic alliance with either member of the couple, if the therapist meets with one person separately, she needs also to meet with the other before resuming couples work.

Depending on their financial or insurance constraints and my ability to schedule multiple sessions for the same case, I will do a 2-week or a 3-week cycle. On a 2-week cycle, every other week, I meet with the couple. Then during the alternate week, each has an individual session. Or on a 3-week cycle, one week I meet with the couple; the next week I meet with one of them; and the third week with the other. Occasionally, when a couple is in crisis, I will make the time to hold all three sessions in the same week to settle the system and the individuals so that constructive work can proceed. But this is only rarely needed.

If I feel extremely stuck and unable to get a toehold any other way, I may divide a single session into thirds. That allows me to do an individual piece with each client and immediately assess its impact on the couple system. This also can interject some calm into a chaotic situation where tension is escalating in precarious ways or shake up a rigidly homeostatic system.

However I choose to integrate individual sessions into couples work, I make these ground rules explicit: (a) individual sessions are not for talking about the absent partner or for working on couples issues; (b) I will not keep secrets that may be deleterious to the relationship or the therapy: (c) we will focus on each individual and his or her family of origin contribution to the current problem; and (d) we will explore what each of them, and not their partner, can and needs to change.

In general, I strongly encourage the sharing of insights gained and feelings discovered in separate work with the other member of the couple. Nonetheless, it is up to each person to decide what, if anything, from the individual sessions is brought up in the couples sessions or at home, provided that in my judgment not bringing up an issue or sharing a discovery will not adversely affect the couple or the therapy. If necessary, I will prompt and help the individuals to bring up a topic, should they neglect for one reason or another to do so. Out of respect for individuals' right to privacy and confidentiality, I do not bring up issues myself, except in extreme instances. For example, sometimes an individual needs preparation and help to bring up the issue of an extramarital affair or the decision to leave the marriage. I would use individual sessions to help that spouse be clear and prepared to bring up his or her intentions.

*When Group Therapy Is Requested.* Perhaps the key question that vexes any group therapist is determining appropriateness for participation. Questions such as these help me begin my assessment in the intake call:

Are you currently in therapy with anyone?
Have you ever been in therapy, particularly group therapy, before?
Was your participating in a group your idea or someone else's?

I conduct women's, men's, and mixed-gender psychotherapy groups. If callers request group therapy, I do not place them immediately in a group; I meet with them individually first. This is useful for four reasons. First, it helps me screen for appropriateness for group psychotherapy in general. Second, it lets me assess their readiness to participate in a group at that particular time. Third, it allows me to check for compatibility both with me as the leader and with the others who will constitute the group. And fourth, it enables me to discern whether a mixed- or a same-sex group would be more helpful. Even if people have been in therapy before, unless it is with someone whose work I know to be highly consonant with my approach, I do not put them into a group without some preparation beyond the initial screening.

*When Family of Origin Work Is Requested.* In my experience, it is relatively rare for people to request family of origin sessions. When it does happen, it is usually either because the caller is a therapist or has participated extensively in prior family therapy. Those people often know exactly what they want and maybe even what they need. So the therapeutic task is relatively straightforward: facilitate an open discussion so that the family can accomplish a task on which they had previously been stuck.

In the intake call, questions such as the following help the therapist assess the advisability of agreeing to the request for a family of origin session without a surrounding course of treatment for preparation:

What gives you the sense that a family of origin session would be helpful right now?
Have you had any prior therapy? If so, with whom, and what was the approach used?
Has your family tried anything like this before?

Much more common are the family of origin sessions that I initiate in the middle phase of treatment after a good deal of prodding. This urging is usually required because of the degree of pain clients anticipate having to face and which typically is present.

Even if clients do not require a full-fledged family of origin session, my bias is that family of origin issues must be explored. In fact, it is an integral part of this treatment model to assess for and treat unresolved family of origin issues in whatever way possible. Although family of origin sessions are not indicated for everyone, family of origin exploration generally is.

## A Final Word

In this chapter, we have discussed the highly complex process that planning and executing integrative psychotherapy with men is. We have discussed the strands of theory that are woven together into a complete whole, as well as considered the multiple treatment modalities that can be used to accomplish this. However it is done, whatever the theoretical orientation of the therapist, one topic must pervade the work with men: helping them to develop a sensitivity for and understanding of the impact of gender socialization on them. From there, it is up to the therapist to decide for herself how she will weave her therapeutic tapestry.

## References

Allen, J., & Gordon, S. (1990). Creating a framework for change. In R. Meth & R. Pasick (Eds.), *Men in therapy: The challenge of change* (pp. 131-151). New York: Guilford.

Bowen, M. (1978). *Family therapy in clinical practice.* New York: Jason Aronson.

Carter, E., & McGoldrick, M. (Eds.). (1980). *The family life cycle: A framework for family therapy.* New York: Gardner.

Coché, J., & Coché, E. (1990). *Couples group psychotherapy: A clinical practice model.* New York: Brunner/Mazel.

Doherty, W. (1981). Involving the reluctant father in family therapy. In A. Gurman (Ed.), *Questions and answers in the practice of family therapy* (pp. 23-26). New York: Brunner/Mazel.

Epstein, N., Bishop, D., & Levin, S. (1978). The McMaster model of family functioning. *Journal of Marriage and Family Counseling,* 4(4), 31-49.

Fasteau, M. (1974). *The male machine.* New York: McGraw-Hill.

Feldman, L. (1992). *Integrating individual and family therapy.* New York: Brunner/Mazel.

Feldman, L., & Pinsof, W. (1982). Problem maintenance in family systems: An integrative model. *Journal of Marital and Family Therapy, 8*(3), 295-308.

Framo, J. (1982). *Explorations in marital and family therapy: Selected papers of James L. Framo, Ph.D.* New York: Springer.

Goulding, M., & Goulding, R. (1979). *Changing lives through redecision therapy.* New York: Brunner/Mazel.

Haley, J. (1966). Toward a theory of pathological systems. In G. Zuk & I. Boszormenji-Nagy (Eds.), *Family therapy and disturbed families* (pp. 11-27). Palo Alto, CA: Science and Behavior Books.

Kramer, C. (1980). *Becoming a family therapist: Developing an integrated approach to working with families.* New York: Human Sciences Press.

Levinson, D. (1978). *The seasons of a man's life.* New York: Knopf.

Levinson, D. (1986). A conception of adult development. *American Psychologist, 41*(1), 3-13.

Levinson, D. (1990, July). *Adult development of women and men.* Symposium conducted at the Cape Cod Summer Symposium, Eastham, MA.

Lewis, K. (1991). Treating the absent male: Is it possible? Is it ethical? *Journal of Feminist Family Therapy, 2*(3-4), 213-225.

Meth, R., & Pasick, R. (1990). *Men in therapy: The challenge of change.* New York: Guilford.

Miller, J. (1986). *Toward a new psychology of women.* Boston: Beacon.

Moore, R., & Gillette, D. (1990). *King, warrior, magician, lover: Rediscovering the archetypes of the mature masculine.* San Francisco: HarperSanFrancisco.

Moultrup, D. (1990). *Husbands, wives, lovers: The emotional system of the extramarital affair.* New York: Guilford.

Napier, A., & Whitaker, C. (1978). *The family crucible.* New York: Harper & Row.

Paul, N., & Paul, B. (1986). *A marital puzzle: Transgenerational analysis of marriage counseling.* New York: Gardner.

Pinsof, W. (1990). *What's wrong with family therapy?* Panel discussion conducted at the annual meeting of the American Association for Marriage and Family Therapy, Washington, DC.

Weiner-Davis, M. (1992). *Divorce-busting: A revolutionary and rapid program for staying together.* New York: Summit.

Yalom, I. (1985). *The theory and practice of group psychotherapy.* New York: Basic Books.

# The Process of Therapy: To Generate Development or Merely to Teach Skills?

Spoken 4 months into couples therapy, the following words of a 55-year-old man present the essence of this chapter. David, married and father of three adult children, is an upper-level manager in a corporation whose name is a household word.

*David:* I feel like you're taking me on a journey, and I'm not sure I'm going to like it when I get there—and that's scary for me. I ask what's going to be in there when we get in there. It's a journey inward, as you're peeling back the layers. I'm like a kid at an amusement park who's scared and hanging onto his parent's arm, because he's not sure he's going to like it when he gets there. I just wanted to tell you all this.

*Therapist:* What does it feel like to be saying this?

*David:* I guess I feel trusting. I wouldn't have told you if I didn't trust you. I feel like I've told a friend, and I know you won't hurt me with this. A person has to believe in the journey. I've read that for years, but I never really believed it until now.

*Therapist:* What made the concept of the journey click for you?

*David:* Hmm. Gosh, I don't know if I can answer that. Every time I think of where I want to be, I realize that that's not the end. It's a continuum.

It doesn't stop. I've known that for years, but I just verbalized it today
when I realized you were taking me on a journey.
*Therapist:* That's a lot of trust!
*David:* Yes. But I have nothing to lose at this point. When I first came, I
knew I had a lot to lose: my marriage. This is anxious for me, but I'm
doing it. I keep figuring all along that it is going to get easier. Nobody
told me about all the uncertainty along the way. But I'll make it.

It is probably apparent by inference that the approach offered
in this book is not *One-Minute Treatment of Men,* a manual for how
to fix men, or a four-session cure for what ails them. This model
is about engaging them in a *process* of personal and family change.
One can receive a picture postcard of the Statue of Liberty or of
the Grand Canyon and still not have been there. Although the
content is the same, the process, the journey of going to that place,
is qualitatively different from merely having a picture of it.

## What Is the Aim of Psychotherapy?

Gauging successful outcomes of psychotherapy requires first
answering the question: Therapy for what? A central assumption
of this chapter is that one of the major aims of psychotherapy is to
push toward the discovery and establishment of conditions that
foster the development of both individuals and families, not merely
to turn out persons who are capable of performing certain discrete
behaviors. Those changes can be expected to wash out over time,
often in a matter of weeks. By contrast, true developmental growth
changes people's cognitive structures and information-processing
systems such that, as the title of Thomas Wolfe's novel suggests,
You can't go home again.

As is the case with all the psychotherapy I provide, in the
context of this book I am proposing that the aim of therapy is to
help men change their worldview. This will allow them to discover a qualitatively different mode of being in the world that will
make them better, more intrinsically motivated and satisfied partners, fathers, sons, friends, managers, participants, workers, leaders, and followers. And it is our job as therapists of whatever sex
to help them attain the vision necessary to forge this new kind of
man, tempered in the crucible of the chaos and challenge of our

time. As therapists, we need to learn to become effective guides for men who, as Keen says (1991),

> are willing to undertake the spiritual journey beginning with the disillusioning awareness that what we have agreed to call "normal" is a facade covering a great deal of alienation. But it goes beyond the valley of the shadow to create a new vision of manhood—a vision of man with fire in his belly and passion in his heart. (pp. 6-7)

With my focus on interactions between people and on internal processes within individuals, rather than on solutions and specific content, I am proposing a distinctly different orientation from many of the other therapies that are being touted today. Particularly in this era of cost containment, of easy and quick solutions, this approach stands out. This is because of its emphasis on facilitating developmental growth with its resulting change in worldview, rather than more facile approaches that promise solutions in a few simple sessions.

You may be asking whether people will stay put for this kind of treatment, which usually becomes long term. Isn't it commonly accepted that clients will remain in treatment for only 6 to 10 sessions, regardless of the therapist's orientation? Maybe. Or perhaps clients lose hope or interest in a more in-depth course of treatment when therapists themselves do not have the tools or the vision to help them to take the journey toward more deep and substantive change.

Surely, therapists who have not embarked on their own inward journey will be handicapped in being both knowledgeable and believable guides for clients' inner voyages. When I accurately have diagnosed the existence of and contributors to clients' generalized sense of ennui, however, and am successful in illustrating that the ultimate resolution of this malaise is not in a how-to manual, I rarely have difficulty inducing them to take the plunge inward.

## Chapter Overview

In this chapter I attempt to articulate the process of generating developmental growth. This experience can both catalyze and ultimately become a spiritual journey. Clients must undertake this process if they are fundamentally to change the ways in which they meet the world. The central purpose for this work is to help people, and in this context men in particular evolve a new paradigm for more fulfilling, emotionally available, equitable ways of relating and of being in the world. When they do this, men can surrender their restricting, driven, outmoded identities as strictly warriors and workers and learn to discern who they really are.

First I will provide some disclaimers regarding those clients who fit this approach and those who likely will not. Then I will discuss my data sources for the chapter. After that, I will offer some considerations for varying the model that this chapter will detail. Then I will delineate some differences in the course of treatment where process rather than content is emphasized. Following that, I will consider the developmental underpinnings that make this approach distinct. Specifically, I will discuss the elements of a developmental perspective, considering conditions that are conducive to developmental growth, answering the question of how to structure treatment with development in mind, and summarizing the central assumptions that all developmental theorists make. Then I will consider the implications for therapy when this model is used. I will discuss the role of the developmentally oriented therapist in each of the three phases of therapy, the common characteristics of each phase, and some sample questions for each. I will end the chapter with guidelines for the developmentally oriented therapist.

## Disclaimer

Justice cannot be done to such abstract and theoretical ideas as I have listed above in one chapter. Yet, some attempt further to articulate the underpinnings of the approach seems warranted. Thus, although these ideas perhaps deserve an entire book of their own, I will proffer them here as the backdrop for the treatment proposed.

The exception to the wide applicability of these ideas relates to those whose daily survival is in question. For them, the opportunity to contemplate their inner geography is a luxury they simply do not have. Treatment of those clients is of necessity confined to more basic, concrete, and survival-oriented issues. To expect them to contemplate the meaning of life and of their relationships when they cannot ensure their next meal would seem ludicrous and even irresponsible. By the same token, if they can become more secure, it would seem that helping them do just that might enable them to begin to break the destructive, dead-end cycle in which many are caught.

Likewise, the applicability of these ideas is limited for those who manifest such severe cognitive malfunctioning that they fall in the mentally retarded or severely mentally incompetent range. It is a widely accepted premise among developmentalists that cognitive development is a necessary, though not sufficient, condition for all the rest of development. Therefore, those who are severely limited cognitively likely will manifest limitations across the board that render them not amenable to this model.

## Data Sources

Most of the views, judgments, and insights of this chapter are derived from three data sources. Two are highly unscientific: (a) my knowledge of the process of my own spiritual journey, which was made imperative by my experiencing four deaths of immediate family members in 4½ years; and (b) the clients in whose struggles I have been privileged to share, who have taught me enormous amounts about the pilgrimage to become. Thus from both sides of the desk, I am acquainted with the process involved in the dark night of the soul. And because I have taken that expedition myself, I know also that it is by no means reserved for or exclusively the responsibility of men to take. All who aspire to the highest level of development must take their own version of that trip and find their way home to a new place.

The third data source is the developmental literature in which I steeped myself for my dissertation study at the University of Minnesota in the early 1970s. My dissertation was an intervention study designed to promote deliberate psychological growth in the adult educators who participated, and I was able to generate measurable developmental shifts in them. Over the intervening 20 years, I have had countless opportunities to operationalize and refine the theory, transposing it into daily psychotherapeutic practice. This chapter, then, is the result of taking the ideas I used in structuring the teaching intervention that was the core of my dissertation and translating them to psychotherapeutic practice.

## Some Factors That May Require Variations in Approach

There are two primary considerations here: (a) client attributes that may require changes in the timing and pacing of our interventions, and (b) determining when to decline further treatment.

Although at first blush the ideas I've discussed may seem more readily applicable to brighter, more achievement-oriented clientele, my experience tells me that this approach can be applied to a wide variety of people, regardless of sex or socioeconomic or educational level. For example, in addition to a host of white-collar workers, I have used these same basic methods with people from such diverse occupations as homemaker, farmer, laborer, waitperson, and office worker. In these latter instances, how I tackle the case may vary at least initially, but the process and the goals remain the same. That is, the pace is often slower, sometimes because of less cognitive horsepower, sometimes because of low self-esteem, sometimes because of the rigid character structure of clients. Each of these conditions needs to be addressed and the obstacles it presents removed before the more existential issues posed in this chapter can be considered effectively. Nevertheless, I have seen over and over that it is the human condition to want surcease from the existential angst that plagues people who are struggling to answer the question of what the meaning of life is and what they want out of life. In fact, usually these questions are even more compelling to those who have been occupationally or interpersonally frustrated. Further, it is my bias that those who do not ask these questions need to do so, because answering them will lead to richer, more fulfilling lives.

Part of the difficulty in diagnosing that these unanswered spiritual questions are at the bottom of what troubles people is that few enter treatment stating that they do not believe their lives have meaning. Instead, most seek help for issues such as chronic fatigue or backache, depression, trouble with their bosses or company policies, impotence or marital conflict, or acting-out or depressed children. And when we accept their formulation that this is the problem and focus only on solving it and not on resolving the larger, deeper issues that vex them, we do clients no service in the long run. Therefore, in addition to resolving the presenting problem, I define our job as helping clients "get a life," as the current popular expression suggests. It is highly likely that people who come to us with this basic sense of ennui are signaling a developmental arrest that needs to be identified and addressed before any amount of therapy will translate to a truly better, more satisfying quality of life.

On the issue of pacing, the common conclusion among developmentalists of Piaget's ilk is that it takes 3 years to accomplish a change in developmental level. This does not mean that all clients have to stay in therapy for 3 years, but it does suggest two considerations: (a) it is an unrealistic expectation to demand immediate fruits of their and our labors, and (b) trends that are of a truly developmental nature can be expected to remain stable across time but take a long time to be incorporated fully. This means that the therapist has two responsibilities in making her initial assessment. One is carefully to determine who might be willing and able to go the distance in terms of time, energy, and money investments. And the other is to modify her approach for those who cannot, so that no one is left cut open and bleeding on the psychotherapeutic operating table when therapy stops. Even though I heartily subscribe to the premise of the great American educator John Dewey (1916) when he said that any experience that does not contribute to later development is miseducative, it is the therapist's job not to start something she cannot finish. She must keep in mind the covenant we make: "First, do no harm."

## When to Decline Further Treatment

No surgeon would perform an operation in a parking lot except in the gravest of emergencies. Likewise, when conditions for doing our work are not optimal and the consequences of proceeding could be grave, it behooves the therapist to make a sound clinical judgment about when to go ahead and when to leave well enough alone. This section provides the reader with some decision rules for considering the question of when to decline further treatment.

These cautionary notes are particularly relevant for us thera-pists who are systems thinkers. There are two arrows in our quivers that perhaps are among the most potent we have: access to the entire system and knowledge about how to shift the system underneath clients so that they have to change accordingly. This produces what is known as second-order change (Watzlawick, Weakland, & Fisch, 1974). Because this knowledge and the resulting changes it can produce are so potent, we must proceed cautiously.

The primary consideration is whether any factors could keep the client from going the distance. If so, I ask myself: How movable are those factors? If they are changeable, then it is more safe to proceed, as indicated above, but the work first focuses on remov-ing the obstacles. The classic example is when one member of a couple wishes to proceed in self-exploration and healing the mar-riage while the other spouse pouts, sabotages the therapy, and eventually refuses to continue. All of us, no matter how experi-enced and competent, have known the peril of being unable to forestall this rigid homeostasis, and eventually we are rendered impotent to make the system shift. This often results in one spouse exiting the therapy, threatened by the remaining spouse's changes that thereby threaten to change the relationship. Then the primary assessment to make is whether to proceed with the remaining spouse, and how far to go. I discuss thoroughly with the remain-ing client the implications of proceeding and of not proceeding, leaving it up to him or her whether to move ahead or not. How-ever, it should be noted that these discussions need to have begun early enough that the client is not in the midst of the disequilibrat-ing process. Otherwise, leaving the client is at best irresponsible and possibly dangerous.

## Clinical Example

After a course of moderately successful marital therapy for a 30-something couple, the wife refused to go any further or engage in her own journey, but the husband was very interested in explor-ing his psychological development. After two sessions in which he and I met separately and considered carefully the indications and contraindications for his proceeding, he opted to go forward. In those sessions, both he and I were mindful that he had four children under the age of 7 to whom he was extremely devoted and that his explorations could well lead him to question the wisdom of his staying married. And in fact, as he began the work of exploring his inner geography, his first tentative conclusion was that he may well have made a mistake in his choice of marital partner. Predictably, his wife began to experience his changes and felt their relationship begin to shift as a result. When she complained and began to sabotage his efforts, I suggested that he invite her to resume therapy. Once again, she refused.

In the meantime, partly opting for the geographical cure and partly because he was offered a golden career opportunity, the couple decided to move to another part of the country as soon as financing could be arranged for him to start a new and promising business venture. This was despite the obvious uncertainty and unclarity between them, and at least initially, was in many ways because of it.

In the midst of this, however, the husband persisted in his wish for continued individual therapy. Nevertheless, I knew that for him to go any further in his course of treatment would mean his eventually passing a point of no return that could severely jeopardize the marriage. Because of the disequilibrium generated in developmental change, the process would become too compelling to leave in the middle. For that same reason, I chose not to generate a marital crisis. Instead, reluctantly, I opted to suggest that he not start anything he could not finish in the time that they had left, employing the surgical metaphor used above. Further, I cautioned that if conditions worsened when they settled into their new city, as would likely happen, the couple should seek therapy there; I recommended trained family therapists whose names I obtained from my organizational directories. Then, rather than doing a termination session with him at that time, I offered him the option of leaving the door open for the duration of the time before they moved, in case any crisis demanded immediate attention—as was a strong possibility—or in case his wife changed her mind about resuming therapy.

About 3 months before they moved—approximately 3 months after his and my last session—the man, of his own volition, said to his wife that either she had to go back into therapy or he was moving without her. That did it. They came back into treatment, she began the work she had been trying to avoid, and the marriage was solidified enough that all three of us felt confident that they could make the move with a degree of trust in the marriage that neither they nor I had felt before. And by now freely acknowledging the need for further treatment, both agreed willingly to seek the services of one of my colleagues in their new city as soon as the dust had settled for them there.

Not all scenarios turn out as positively as this one did. But I am convinced that had he and I proceeded by ourselves, a divorce that as events unfolded would not have been necessary, virtually would have been guaranteed. And it would have been by default, not by design or necessity.


## Content Compared With Process

Two concepts are central to understanding interactions between people and in therapy: *content* and *process*. Although particularly systems thinkers concern themselves with these notions, all therapists need to, for the concepts have relevance both for any given interactional sequence and for one's entire orientation to therapy. First, we will apply them to a discrete interaction; then to the philosophy of therapy.


### Content and Process in a Given Interaction

I often use this example to illustrate these concepts with my clients. If I say, "Today is Tuesday," in a matter-of-fact way with no particular affect of any kind, I am likely to be perceived as transmitting factual information. However, if I shriek "Today is Tuesday!" at the top of my lungs, I am communicating quite a different message. The listener may not know the meaning of the message, but unequivocally it will be perceived as very dissimilar from the first. This, in a nutshell, illustrates the differences. An emphasis on content is focused on the meaning of the words themselves as expressions of facts. An emphasis on process implies attention to the multitude of other relevant data, most of them unrelated to the content, contained in any communication. Essential to grasp and to work with in any couples therapy, the distinction between these two concepts is elemental to gender-sensitive marital work.

A research finding 25 years ago by communications theorists is now so commonly accepted that it has passed into general understanding. That is the conclusion that only 7% of the meaning of a given communication is contained in the words; the real meaning is contained in the remaining 93%, which is composed of tone of voice, volume, nonverbal cues, and so on. This is particularly important in light of the fact that it is the processes between people that mar beautiful content. Whether people are tuned in on that dimension or not, process is always occurring. One of the skills we need to teach clients is how to learn to monitor interactions on the process dimension.

The point in making the distinction between content and process is simple and yet at the same time subtle and complex. At the foundation is the belief that relationship difficulties and misunderstandings come out of the polarized and unconscious defensiveness of men and women, not merely out of lack of communication skills and functional behaviors. Of course, those become factors, too. But emphasizing them to the exclusion of the underlying processes that are operative for women and for men is to allow ourselves to be seduced. Let us not be persuaded to believe that a marriage can be fixed in 10 easy steps just by focusing on behavior change between couples.

Although a focus on behavior change can be stultifyingly simplistic for the effective treatment of any problem, it is particularly problematic when part of the explicit contract is to help men make qualitative changes. This is because approaches that promise results in a month, for example, only bolster men's already considerable defenses while further feeding into their common tendency to avoid intimacy by focusing on fixing and on how-to solutions. What people are really saying when they seek this approach is: I want a solution that I only have to do, that won't touch or change who I am. If we pander to this way of operating, then we are contributing to the socialization of men that trapped them in the first place while we leave women stuck in their socialization, alone on the emotional process dimension.

## Content: Chasing the Illusion of "How-To"

An emphasis on content in relationships is based on the belief that change is a matter of motivation, awareness, and behavior modification. It focuses on how-to and answers questions that even from a logical standpoint are much too big to solve quickly and easily. When we facilitate a simple solution to a complex and dynamic problem, we are fostering a pseudosecurity from that mechanical solution that at first placates but then ultimately can defeat. It unconsciously reinforces the problem between the couple as each new how-to seems to be the answer for a while, until it stops "working." Meanwhile, the problems often subtly and insidiously become progressively more intractable and hopeless, often resurfacing in some other area of life.

So when we attempt to help people solve problems by making changes in the content of their life, we have been corrupted by the same hopeless pursuit that an obese person chases with one more diet or a sexually frustrated couple seeks in learning only the mechanics of sexual arousal. This approach denies the function of the symptom as a marker of a deeper dynamic that must be understood and worked with, not simply glossed over or got rid of. True and lasting happiness means basic change in the way people operate, not learning one more panacea.

When individuals' internal processes are not altered, then the process between them becomes stymied. And the attempted solutions themselves spawn more problems, because people have been lulled into thinking their problems are solved, whereas in fact the problems are deepening outside their awareness. "Content is the seducer or the web that pulls others in. The process is the 'poison' that distorts and then destroys relationships" (Goldberg, 1987, p. 85). How-to solutions are thus paths away from confrontation of the inner self, from which true and basic change emanates. "When [people] enter this sacred space within, . . . they can emerge from the inner space seeing what they need to do about a problem and knowing how to do it" (Moore & Gillette, 1990, p. 110).

## Process: Learning to Look Within and Between

Process is the invisible element that in reality either creates the problem within and between people or generates true and lasting satisfaction. Therapists who emphasize process understand this. They attempt to help men and women understand *how* they relate, not just *how to* relate. They acknowledge that it is not simply *what* people do that is the problem. Rather, it is their own internal process and the relationship dynamics this generates that are the focus of the therapy.

The pain of communication breakdowns illustrates how the relationship process transforms and ultimately jeopardizes beautiful content. Inattention by both therapists and clients to this process dimension jeopardizes relationships, for most couples start out optimistic and in love. But progressively, the content basis of the initial attraction and open feelings is eroded by unconscious processes within individuals that eventually contaminate what passes between them. *It is important to underscore that it is an interactional dynamic that occurs between the couple that generates this; it is no one person's fault or even responsibility.* Content changes that are not integrated at a process level will be misleading at best, disillusioning at worst.

Intelligence and wit can easily solve a content problem. But much more is required to focus on process. It takes willingness on the part of the sage therapist to examine and understand her own processes and then the foresight to lead her clients through an examination of theirs. This also requires the judgment on the therapist's part to ride out the disequilibrium of clients that Piaget (1932/1948) warned us comes from and is required for making developmental shifts. This sense of upheaval results from the uncertainty generated by learning qualitatively different responses and processes.

In contrast to a process approach, which at least initially usually is disquieting, the allure of a content approach can be compelling. Because there is little or none of the cognitive dissonance and disequilibrium that so characterize process-oriented, developmental change, therapists and clients alike can experience feeling good immediately. For example, a 30-something highly successful man (by outward standards) once left treatment with me after five sessions because he demanded that I be, in his words, a "Doctor Feel-Good," and I would not. That is, he wanted me to tell him how to fix his conundrum of a meaningless life while only making him feel good in the process. After several discussions in which he attempted to explain to me the error of my ways, he correctly discerned that I resist a simplistic content-oriented approach, and he appropriately chose, with my blessings, to leave treatment. Not only do clients want to feel good immediately, often without having to work toward it, but therapists like to appear to be wizards and fixers themselves. So both clients and therapists can be attracted to the ease and neatness of a content-based, solution-oriented, fast approach.

Snippets of sessions with two different men illustrate what it is like for men to cross the process threshold and begin to value and allow themselves to experience life on this wholly different dimension, rather than remaining riveted on the content plane as they are socialized to do. The first words of T.J., from whom we heard in the previous chapter, illustrate what it is like as he begins to cross over to a new worldview; a second excerpt speaks of his beginning to root himself there; and a third quotation, from the next session after he began to realize he had traversed into another dimension, speaks of his beginning to become firmly planted there. We can see his realization of the metamorphosis occuring in most aspects of his life as a result of his exploring and embracing developmental growth. I also have included an excerpt from a second man, speaking in his termination session of his different worldview, so that the reader can see that developmental growth is not the sole province of well-educated, achievement-oriented people.

T.J. is a 32-year-old Ivy League educated, highly successful entrepreneur. Spoken 2 months into therapy, the first words given here illustrate the panic that people can experience when they begin to realize what is required of them if they truly are to change their lives. Although glimpsing the change often is exhilarating, it is not uncommon for people also to be intimidated when they first grasp the shift in worldview that they are experiencing.

The first quotation illustrates what T.J. felt as he began to sight what lies beyond the content dimension. We see his very understandable and appropriate disorientation and disequilibrium, which Piaget (1932/1948) postulated always accompany true developmental change. He spoke in a somewhat agitated state:

*T.J.:* I realized 2 weeks ago after I left here—that somewhere along the way I had been taken over by the machine. That's what I've always been driven by.
*Therapist:* Wow! That's an awesome realization!
*T.J.:* But, Beth! It's driving me nuts! Now what do I do with it?
*Therapist:* You're doing it. And that's lovely to see.
*T.J.:* But what do I *do* with it? I've got to find a way to pocket it. My whole attitude has changed, and it's great. But it's a departure.

A second remark 3 months later depicts his beginning to incorporate these new ideas. This is indicative of developmental change taking place and the concomitant shift in worldview that can come from examining internal processes rather than focusing on content. This time when T.J. spoke, his affect was calm, more centered, more objective, less reactive.

*T.J.:* It's $40 million this year, and $100 million next year, and so what! The few things that made me happy, like skiing, I quit because it didn't help my balance sheet. But none of this makes me happy.

The third excerpt is from a session approximately 5 months after the second, 9 months after the inauguration of therapy. In its richness, it offers the reader countless markers that indicate that T.J.'s view of his world, his place in it, and the standing of others who matter to him have changed dramatically. Set against developmental theory, it shows a shift to greater abstractness as indicated by his ability to reflect on his experience, his integration of different values and priorities, and a greater centeredness and inner peace. His words may seem like a soliloquy because I began the session by inviting him to reflect on what he was currently experiencing.

*T.J.:* I'm calming down. I'm settling down. I realize that I can't control it all. And I'm suddenly aware that I feel some happiness now. What I came to [regarding my business] is that I'm not going to be able to manipulate, guide, or steer it. It's too big. And that's just the way it is. And I realize that this applies to my personal life, too. All of a sudden, I realize my relationship with my children is different; I can't manipulate and control them. They're not like making beds. And so what that's done is open me up to a whole range of things I never knew were possible. I lived in such a narrow band of experience before! And it makes me sad to realize that. I feel an (pause) a rebirthing. I can't deal with that smirk on your face anymore. Tell me what's on your mind.

*Therapist:* I'm delighted! That was what I was telling you last session: You're coming out the other end of the tunnel. Remember when you used to worry that you never would, that it would always be so dark and confusing for you? This is what I knew would happen if you stayed in the struggle.

*T.J.:* That's good.

*Therapist:* Yes, it is. Tell me more about what feels so different.

*T.J.:* We talked last time about the difference between alone and loneliness. And I guess I now realize it's OK to be lonely. There are times when it's OK—to be at one with craving my kids, or with wanting to curl up next to [his estranged wife]. There are parts of loneliness I'm living with, no, I'm dancing with. I realize now that I'm always gonna have some loneliness, whether I'm with somebody or not, and I need to live with it, not force it away or cover it up. I need to dance with it. And you're not allowed to laugh when I say this, OK?

*Therapist:* (Chuckling) OK. I'll laugh now.

*T.J.:* I can tell the difference now between sex and passion, a hug and a grope. And I always felt like I was more of a man if I could fire answers and decisions off. Now I realize that I need to marinate. (Pause) Just as I know now I don't have to prove that I love you by having sex with you, I don't have to *prove* to my board [of directors] that I'm a good leader. And I've never even noticed an election before. (Pause) I have enough sense of feeling now to be disgusted with the games going on. It is [also seeing] that part of me that I don't want to be that just increases my disgust. (Long pause)

*Therapist:* What do you think about what you're saying? What are your reflections on your reflections?

*T.J.:* There's relief. (Pause) And deformity. You know, when a new baby comes out, they're all squished. [How I feel] is like that. But there's a lot of oxygen now. Before, there was almost none.

*Therapist:* God, T.J.! This is wonderful!

*T.J.:* And I feel like I need to be here.

*Therapist:* (Clarifying) What do you mean by "here"?

*T.J.:* I needed to get where I am. And I feel like it's not a moment too soon. (Pause) I'm not afraid anymore. And that means a lot! That means I can close my eyes. (Chuckling) And it means I can open then. And I feel real lucky. I feel lucky to have you. And I feel lucky that things peaked as they did, 'cause it forced me to squish out.

Later the same session:

*T.J.:* (Regarding his and his wife's decision to divorce) I long to pour cereal for my children in the morning. (Smiling) It's ironic. I used to hate getting up in the morning with the kids! And I keep hearing the ring of my dad's voice when he said to me, "She can't be as bad as your mother!" That is so sad—for them and for me. (Pause) Where were we going? I lost my place.

*Therapist:* It's OK. You're just reflecting. Keep going.

*T.J.:* I feel! I feel! I really feel! And sometimes it hurts. It really hurts. (Smiling) We need to help me get some balance. We need to work on that. I use the teeter-totter analogy. I've always lived my life at the center, with not much sadness, but not much happiness. What a pathetic state! It's like always having bologna sandwiches for lunch, and then every once in a while, getting a peek at a Chateaubriand.

And you know, sometimes everything isn't OK. And that's a whole new kettle of fish for me. I can now say, "It's not my responsibility" and stop trying to fix it. There's self-love now that I give to others. I can now say, "I don't tread on me, so you shouldn't, either."

*Therapist:* Yeah!

*T.J.:* For example, my mother will say stuff to me now, and I now will say "That hurt me." It's just three words, but they are very important. And I have to sort through and figure out how to make a home for my children and me. That's my absolute top priority. I need you to help me with that. I have to nest. I have to make a place that is *my* place where I go and am comfortable there. There are little things that are important to me, like I need to be able to sit in that place and see touches with the past and touches of the future. And it has to be a past, present, and future that includes my children.

Later the same session:

*T.J.:* And I've learned that there's aloneness, positive loneliness, and negative loneliness. And I've also learned what to do about it and what not to do: don't pick up the phone, and don't turn on CNN.

Although these words would be significant coming from anyone, when they are the impassioned utterances of a man who used to personify the male machine, they are startlingly refreshing. Before treatment, this man had no relationship with his children other than being a paycheck; described himself as everyone's American Express card; kept a fax machine in his bedroom; worked predictably from 6:00 a.m. to 10:00 p.m.; was a master manipulator by his own admission; would twist himself like a pretzel to placate and pacify; had few real friends, merely acquaintances who would salve him in his frenzy to avoid himself and his aloneness; and constantly created business crises to avoid emotions, intimacy, and, paradoxically, separations.

The second voice signaled readiness to terminate treatment in a 35-year-old carpenter who was a high school graduate. This excerpt illustrates that he clearly grasps the power he now possesses to change his life, now that he understands and operates on the process dimension.

*Matt:* As I was writing in my journal this week, I kept thinking, "Hey, I finally got it!" I think I got the answers for dealing with the rest of my life: When a problem comes up, face it, deal with it, and go on. So

> I don't have to carry around all that extra baggage anymore. Now I can experience every moment I possibly can. I believe I have most of the tools I need to take care of myself for the rest of my life. And for that I am truly grateful and will remember and carry it with me for the rest of my life. So in the future, I will come back here in my mind to help me to relive those experiences, to see them for how I want them to be seen and felt, so that I have the proper perspective to carry on the rest of my life in the way I want to. My brain got a shower when I finished writing that!

Only change on the process dimension will shift people's inner geography enough to make relating truly meaningful. This is the difference between first-order change, with its emphasis on content and not on structure of the relationship system, and second-order change, with its emphasis on basic structural shifts that virtually preclude going back to the same, more simplistic behavior (Watzlawick et al., 1974). With second-order change, the defenses that tend to polarize men and women will have broken down sufficiently to make connection meaningful and not just a matter of transacting information or of modifying behavior. Until then, women and men will continue to use different languages and live in different worlds, having been lulled into believing that theirs is a shared experience when in fact it is probably a mutual bolstering of defenses. Unless this deeper, inner experience of men and women comes together so that they can begin to experience life similarly, they will be unable to really hear each other, no matter how lovingly or intently they listen. It is the therapist's job to clarify that this is her orientation and then to help clients consider whether it is one to which they can subscribe. And if it is, then she has a mandate to help couples aspire to life on this new plane.

## What Is Development?

Perhaps the easiest way to define development is to say first what it is not.

### Development Compared With Learning

The difference between *development* and *learning* is a critical distinction here. Development implies genuine changes in thinking, feeling, and behavior toward more complex functioning; learning suggests mindlessly adopting behavior, a fad, or even a new "snake oil remedy," without fundamental growth (Erickson, 1976). Development involves structural transformation in one's thinking and a fundamental reorganization of thought; what is genuinely developmental can be contrasted with learning, where one simply acquires new behaviors or attitudes.

John Dewey, undoubtedly one of the foremost educational theorists and philosophers of the United States, foreshadowed the now classic work of Piaget. Writing in 1916, Dewey distinguished between learning and development stating that one can learn something not necessarily worthwhile, for example, how to be a burglar or a storm trooper. By contrast, an experience that is genuinely educative induces growth and development through experiences that promote greater competence in living.

Jean Piaget (1932/1948) is probably the single most influential theorist in the area of cognitive development. Through countless hours of observation of children, he was able to produce a map of the stages of cognitive growth. He concluded that these stages are distinctly different from one another; that development is the transformation of basic cognitive and affective structures; that adult cognitive structures are radically different from and develop out of childhood structures; and that the developmental process is sequential and invariant. Thus, each new, evolving system is a major qualitative transformation of those that have gone before (Erickson, 1976).

Development, then, is assumed to be a progression toward greater abstractness. Development toward higher levels assumes an increased availability of alternative concepts, or schema, for coping with the same stimuli by rendering the individual less stimulus-bound, more relativistic, and less unilateral. It allows perception of more varied goals and more means for their attainment. Thus, greater development provides more adequate means of establishing an internal locus of control, greater independence from an external locus of control, and greater mastery over what otherwise would be an omnipotent environment.

## Three Key Concepts

Understanding three key terms is crucial to conceptualizing the developmental process: *progression*, *arrestation*, and *temporizing*.

Each will be briefly defined below (Erickson, 1976), and an example will be given to illustrate each.

## Progression

In its most general form, progressive development involves emergence of a more abstract conceptual schema for relating two basic orientations that may be seen as opposing poles of a given concept. Integration of these conflicting differentiations generates the emergence of the new concepts required for development. Growth toward greater abstractness is characterized as becoming progressively less stimulus-bound, more relativistic, and less unilateral (Harvey, Hunt, & Schroeder, 1961).

### Clinical Example

Dustin, the 27-year-old whose words appeared in the last chapter, had been in therapy with one type of mental health professional or another since he was 3½ years of age. Along with severe learning disabilities and attention deficit hyperactive disorder, he had developed extremely low self-esteem because of those conditions, because of his desperate dependence on others, and because of his being never quite able to do anything adequately. This was extremely painful for him and his parents, both highly acclaimed, competent professionals. Dustin's repeated failures, of course, exacerbated both their and his sense of hopelessness that he ever would have a productive and satisfying life. For example, when he called to arrange therapy for himself, he was seeking merger by bed hopping with woman after woman whenever he could, had been fired from 36 jobs since moving to the city 3 years previously, had flunked out of college, and was so desperate about his life that he would spend most nights sleepless and literally screaming at the top of his lungs at his image in the mirror for what seemed hours before he exhausted himself enough to sleep. I must confess, I got a sinking feeling in the pit of my stomach as he intoned his various fiascoes and failures. Would I be any better able to help him than the hordes of therapists and educators who already had tried?

My first task was to draw a boundary around the therapy. That is, I returned a long-distance telephone call to the hovering, intrusive, overprotective parents, attempting to calm the understandable anxiety they also had that this effort at therapy would be no more fruitful than the other attempts. I needed both to reassure them and to state clearly that I would do the therapy in accordance with my assessment of Dustin's needs and problems. This related to my second boundary, which was to respond to their request that I do career counseling with Dustin. I stated clearly that it was my assessment that he did not need this approach at this time, and in fact, it would be counterproductive because he would not be able to capitalize on it given his current state. I assured them that if when we finished our work he remained unemployable, I would help him find such a resource. But in the meantime, we would be working together in the way that I saw fit, which did not include emphasizing his inability to hold a job or any of his repeated failures, for that matter.

With them reassured, or at least backed off, I proceeded to identify Dustin's developmental arrest, which I located at between 18 and 24 months of age. And then I worked to correct his truncated separation and individuation process with a combination of family of origin work Bowen-style, helping him to understand the function of his dysfunction both for himself and for his entire family, and to see how he perpetuated his own dysfunction and lack of differentiation in his current life. The following is an excerpt from a session 2 years after Dustin began weekly psychotherapy sessions:

*Dustin:* I love my girlfriend, and by the way, it's been almost a year that we've been together, but it's not worth giving up my sense of myself for it. It's a question of setting limits. And I try to make it clear to her that it doesn't mean that I don't love her. But I *have* to hang onto myself. If being in a relationship with her—or anyone else—is dependent on my giving up my sense of myself, forget it. I'm not going to mutilate myself anymore. I'm not going to be a mutant anymore. A lot of things are happening at once. I'm defining myself. I'm becoming more acquainted with my family, and this helps me define myself. In his own way, my dad is trying to impart to me who he is. And I'm able to talk with my sister and brother now like we're related. As I define myself more fully, I am able to establish myself more fully. And I think what's different with my mother is I am able to set limits. And that allows me to have the space to deal with her without mutilating myself. I am

> able to breathe more. And now I'm setting limits for my girlfriend, and we're getting along beautifully. And I have more friends now.

Although the astute reader may see this with a somewhat jaundiced eye, saying it is too good to be true, the clinical evidence is that these changes have held up over time. At this writing, nearly 3 years after the initiation of therapy, this client remains in his relationship with the woman whom he has been dating now for approximately 20 months and plans to marry her. He now holds a full-time, semiskilled job in the health care field at which he has been promoted several times. He has completed his associate of arts degree and has enrolled in a baccalaureate program that specializes in adult learners with special needs. With the credits he already accumulated from his associate of arts degree and from his previous failed attempt at completing undergraduate school, he has only 7 more months of schooling to complete his baccalaureate degree. And he sees his parents both in town and going home without anyone's getting crazy or regressing.

Now with only check-in sessions at 4- to 6-week intervals, in his most recent appointment, Dustin spoke the following, which illustrates his successful individuation:

**Dustin:** I'm experiencing my parents as my mother and father now who live in Indiana whom I see occasionally, not as my mommy and daddy on whom I'm so dependent.

To summarize, there is both anecdotal and factual evidence to demonstrate a developmental progression that has resulted in a much healthier degree of separation and individuation for Dustin. And paradoxically, it is because he has separated that he can now afford to connect with others.

## Arrestation

If environmental pressures are out of synchrony with the conceptual structures required for emergence of a more abstract synthesis, arrestation, or fixation of development, occurs. This prevents further progression by producing one positive and one negative pole. The result is that the negative pole is ignored (Harvey et al., 1961), and thus no new integration can take place.

### Clinical Example

The words of Aaron, a man in his late 20s from whom we have heard elsewhere in the book, illustrate plainly and simply the developmental arrest that took place for him around his mother's death 3 years prior to his initiating treatment. When he presented for treatment, he was extremely well defended, using anger, material excesses, and seduction of women as his primary coping mechanisms.

*Aaron:* I lost my purpose for being when my mother died. When I found out she died, my first thought was, "I have no future anymore." Something was taken away, snatched away. I felt like I lost a large part of my identity.

We see here evidence of two layers of developmental arrests. Not only do we see the fixation that his response to his mother's sudden death generated, but also we see vestiges of incompletion of his much earlier separation and individuation process. Had this been completed, her death, though painful, would not have had to be so devastating.

It should be noted that clients do not always perceive as clearly as Aaron that they are stuck. However, even in his obvious crystal clarity, he remained oblivious to the full impact of what he was saying. Over the next several months of biweekly 2-hour sessions, we identified the multiple effects of his trauma on him and began to resolve his loss so that his individuation process could continue. This would allow his development to proceed.

## Temporizing

Sometimes people experience being overwhelmed and overcome either by the changes they are making or by those they contemplate needing to make. When this happens, it is quite normal that they will shut down so they can regroup and recoup their energy. Known as temporizing, this is a suspension or even reversal of growth. It is a pause, sometimes for a year or more, where the individual is quite often well aware of the step that lies ahead but is choosing to wait, as if gathering forces to make it.

This often looks like retreat or escape, and it requires clinical acumen to diagnose whether it is just temporizing or whether it is fixating. However, if true developmental change has occurred, the arrest will be only temporary while the individual gains the requisite strength to proceed. The therapist's clinical astuteness is also required to titrate the amount of disequilibrium clients need to deal with. Sometimes it is best for the therapist to pour on the steam so that clients do not hide or lose their momentum; at other times, it is better to encourage and support their need to rest. Keen and sensitive clinical judgment is required to discern which is which.

### Clinical Example

T.J., from whom we have heard earlier in the chapter, entered treatment asking me to help him clarify his best course of action regarding his marriage. However, on some level, he must have known that he was seeking greater depth than just a solution to his marital dilemma, because he interviewed six other therapists and was dissatisfied by the superficiality of the approaches each offered. He already had separated from his wife and moved to another city to nurture a new business venture and to experience separation before he could decide anything. After 3 months of meeting only with him, I finally persuaded him that the best way to know was to quit "arm chairing" their relationship and get her to come to town for some sessions or go to her therapist with her. As the couple had already been to her therapist with what T.J. experienced as a highly unsatisfactory outcome, he instead asked her to join us. She readily agreed, signing a release of information form allowing the two therapists to consult.

In our first 2-hour couples session, they agreed to meet six more times to see what could be done to solve their problems and whether positive feelings about her and for the marriage could return for T.J. Feeling certain that she wanted to stay in the marriage was not an issue for her. She earnestly and desperately wanted this. In the meantime, both continued their individual therapy, she in her city, he with me. This required frequent contact between the two therapists, who were able to forge a reasonably workable relationship that allowed us to head off most attempts at triangulation.

Although the couple clearly were able to learn much more cooperative, respectful ways of interacting with each other and of solving a host of mutual problems, instead of warming to his wife, the experience left T.J. even more convinced of his decision to proceed out of the marriage. Now he could see that he had married her for all the wrong reasons: somebody else's. Finally, after a full year of agonizing, he tearfully divulged his conclusion to his wife. Although we had not met for the number of sessions to which they had agreed, the wife refused to come back to therapy and demanded that they go see another widely acclaimed counselor who touts cures for marriages in four sessions. This behavior only convinced him further that their worldviews were vastly different and that divorce was the direction in which he needed to go. However, as soon as he stated this to her in a joint session and then repeatedly to me in our follow-up session, he began to manifest the psychological equivalent of a physical shock reaction. He became withdrawn, vacant, tearful at inappropriate times over nothing in particular, and most of all numb. In the second follow-up session, he made a direct request that I discerned I could not refuse: "Give me 90 days." Although in this context, time was not mine to give, I interpreted his request as a plea that neither of us expect him to take action yet on what he knew full well he would have to do. In my clinical judgment, it would have been a grave error to push him, for that likely would prompt a fight-or-flight reaction, and either fight or flight would invite a developmental arrest. So I readily agreed that temporizing was what he needed to do.

Sometimes clients' temporizing is not as conscious a choice as this man's was. However, even if clients do not make their intentions and needs explicit, we have two jobs at that point: (a) to help them articulate the need so that neither therapist nor client feels as if he or she were regressing or running away; and (b) to continue to monitor the process carefully to ensure that temporization is not truly, nor does it become, fixation.

## Experiences Conducive to Developmental Progression

This section will answer the question: What sorts of experiences can be expected to generate progression? The answer turns on the assumption that development toward higher and more complex modes of cognitive and affective functioning is a central objective of psychotherapy. The wise therapist reading this will anticipate the next section and begin immediately to translate this developmental theory into practice. Then we will move on to describe the role of the developmentally oriented psychotherapist in generating development.

How can a therapist decide what types of interventions are more likely to promote progression to the next level than others? What indicates that a given strategy is more likely to generate cognitive restructuring than everyday activities or those that emphasize mere learning (Erickson, 1976)? The developmental literature suggests that six generic types of activities are critical for developmental progression to take place. These activities can become organizers of both the content and process of developmentally oriented therapy.

## Experience Plus Reflection Cycle

Long ago, John Dewey (1916) posited that people learn best through continuing cycles of genuine experience along with structured examination and systematic reflection on those experiences. This cycle becomes a constant in structuring developmentally oriented interventions. Sprinthall (1973, p. 361) concluded after long research, "Raw and unexamined experience merely affords the opportunity for self-knowledge. . . . A [reflection] format helps the learner to discern meaning and internalize the experience." Experience followed by reflection becomes central to the organization of therapy on two levels. First, the therapist facilitates experiences in each session with clients. This is followed by careful reflection immediately and in follow-up sessions on the impact of those interventions over time.

For instance, I routinely begin my second session by asking clients, "What were your reflections on our first session together?" This allows me to assess several dimensions. First, I am able to hear directly, rather than leaving it to assumption or guess, how effective I was in joining (Minuchin, 1974) them. Thus I can see how likely they are to take to me and to the approach I am offering. Second, it gives me my first opportunity to gauge how slow or fast they will be in embracing my ideas and approach. And third, it offers them the opportunity to reflect in session if they did not do so between visits. Prompting their reflection allows both them and me the opportunity to gain insight on how the course of therapy will go. This heuristic framework allows and eventually prompts spontaneous, careful analysis and evaluation of experiences as they occur, because it requires people to confront continually their assumptions and competencies. Once people genuinely engage in this operation, usually they automatically begin to see the need to do so on a regular basis.

### Clinical Example

Sherman is a 53-year-old physician who had been in treatment approximately 2 months at the time the following dialogue occurred. One of the reasons he sought treatment was his chronic, vague, generalized sense of low-level depression. Another was that he experienced himself as totally incapable at either finding or sustaining a meaningful relationship with a woman. This understandably lowered his self-esteem and increased his depression in an ever-worsening vicious cycle. He had tried three other therapies with male psychiatrists with nominal carryover. Although he had been married to the same woman for 23 years and had several children, he reported feeling alone and lonely all his life. Now divorced, he realized that he used sex with women and work as his two drugs of choice. However, realizing that did not mean he was able to stop. He entered treatment to get help to do that, so that eventually he could settle in with a relationship with which he could experience the genuine happiness that he believed was possible but had never experienced. By then accustomed to reflecting on his experience, he spontaneously began a session by sharing what he had been reflecting on during the previous week.

*Sherman:* I ask myself, "What is so difficult about being comfortable talking with people that's not if I take off my clothes? What gets exposed when I talk that doesn't get exposed when I take off my clothes? Why is it easier to think about that, when the real problem is just being comfortable talking?"

*Therapist:* These are great questions! How did you answer them?

*Sherman:* The only thing I can think of is that maybe there isn't anything there. Maybe I'm empty inside. When people ask me what I do when I'm not a doctor, the wall is white—and if I can't be cute and funny, I feel like a nonperson. So I suppose this is a lack of contact.

*Therapist:* Can you say more about that lack of contact? It sounds to me like you're feeling your loneliness again. Or maybe for the first time.

*Sherman:* I'd probably even have sex with a man for comfort! And I don't do that.

*Therapist:* God, you're that hungry!

*Sherman:* Yes, I guess I am. I lead with my genitals. That's how I remain in control.

Sadly, what this man's reflections are showing when they take him inside is his desperate loneliness and emptiness. As frightening as this is for him, the good news, however, is that now that he has begun his journey inside in earnest, he can begin to find more constructive ways of filling and fulfilling himself. And his ability to reflect on his internal experience will be key in that process.

## Empathy Building by Role Taking

A central assumption of Piaget (1932/1948) is that a crucial element in promoting developmental growth is empathy or role taking. Kohlberg (1969) asserted that experience in a variety of social roles will produce significant and positive change. He believed that a program that deliberately increases experiences with social roles and requires the ability to understand and experience problems from another's point of view may be the necessary means to nurture growth. Hence the value of debate. The higher one's developmental level and the more abstract one's functioning, the greater the capacity to "act as if," that is, the greater one's ability to empathize. This ability to take another's perspective, in turn, sparks increased development.

### Clinical Example

In the termination session after approximately 7 months of marital therapy, 50-year-old Larry revealed the following learnings:

*Larry:* All this stuff (pause), my confrontations and stuff, just don't work anymore. Remember in the first session, I said sex was my right? Well, I don't believe that anymore. And I used to say to people, "You pissed me off, so I'm not even going to talk with you." But now I realize that was what my father used to do to me, and I hated it. And now that I realize that, I'm not going to do that anymore. And remember I used to say that I wanted [my wife] to take the initiative with sex? Well, she does that more now. And I think it's because she's more relaxed and because she knows now that she has the option to say no and I'll respect that. Before, that was a personal affront to me, but now I'm not taking it personally. I'm trying *real* hard to be different.

*Therapist:* That's very good, Larry.
*Larry:* (Chuckling) Hey, I'm trainable! I'm seeing this stuff and understanding [that] there's a connection here between this and how I was raised.

Here we have evidence of Larry's ability both to reflect on his past behavior, and in light of his realizations, to change it. His ability to empathize allowed him to recognize and to acknowledge how his odious behavior was just like his father's. How that had felt for him provided him with a new vehicle for understanding and changing his own impact on others.

## Promoting Openness of the Individual's Conceptual System and of the Marital or Family System

Building trust within the couple or family and in the therapist is another critical operation. This is what promotes openness of systems. Gaining access to an individual's conceptual system is identical to the process of establishing a therapeutic relationship. A way of operationalizing trust is clients' willingness to give credibility to the therapist. That is, the therapist must provide the optimal environment by promoting intrinsic trust first in her and then work to establish this in the couple, family, or group members. It is common knowledge that therapy is severely compromised when it is not possible to accomplish this. But if therapy in general is jeopardized, that which is done with an eye toward generating development through embarking on a spiritual journey is rendered impossible without it.

### Clinical Example

Perry is a 45-year-old real estate developer whose life was a house of cards that collapsed around him shortly before he began treatment. He was recently divorced with three children. His rather sizable financial empire had dwindled to nothing, taking with it his self-esteem and sense of competence and confidence.

The initial stage of therapy was couples work to help the pair clarify the best course of action regarding their marriage. Then, after a pause of a couple of years, Perry requested individual therapy, which later evolved into his participation in a mixed-gender therapy group. Perry's comments in the termination session of the group therapy illustrate the evolution of trust in the therapist that must take place in order for treatment to be effective, however quickly or slowly it happens. He also discusses his ability to parlay his trust in the therapist into trust in the group.

*Perry:* (To the therapist) When I first met you, I thought you were the enemy. Now I leave here seeing you as a friend, mentor, and even savior. (To the group) And what the group has done for me is give me people I can trust. I'm in a totally different spot than I was 20 weeks ago, and it's really alien territory. And I've found that if I take care of myself and my stuff, I wake up confident every day. I'm a little scared because I'm so used to feeling bad. But I can do it.

The examination of more complex and threatening issues is predicated on first having established an ambience of trust and intrinsic acceptance. For clients to be willing to experience cognitive conflict, they must first trust and feel supported. And the issue of building trust has a second dimension. In order to generate that kind of climate, trust-building activities themselves must be sequenced. Initial interventions should involve a low level of threat so that clients do not feel denuded. Then gradually the therapist can ask clients to engage in experiences that generate greater and greater levels of disequilibrium.

## Examining the Relativity of Perceptions

The ability to deal adaptively and flexibly with multiple dimensions hinges on several beliefs. First, one must be committed to the idea that there is no one right way to see an event or to answer a question. Then one must be able to change set, to take another's perspective. One also must be able to tolerate the dissonance generated by allowing alien inputs into the system. All this requires the greater abstractness associated with few stereotypes and great flexibility in the face of complex and changing situations. Harvey (1966) concluded that this valuing of diversity is the most central prerequisite to differentiation and integration and hence to greater abstractness.

*Clinical Example*

The following segment occurred almost exactly one year after Margaret and Daryl, a couple from whom we have heard elsewhere in the book, began joint therapy. Both were in their early 40s. Their 15-year marriage had long since grown stale when they presented for therapy. This, in turn, contributed to the already substantial developmental arrest that each of them brought into the marriage. They presented jointly for treatment at my insistence when Margaret's depression deepened to such an extent that she began to scare herself with her rapid and out-of-control weight gain and increasing sense of despondency despite the Prozac she had gotten from her regular physician. Only after they had been in treatment a while did Daryl confess that virtually constant migraine headaches plagued him. At first, their rigid distance was readily apparent from their clipped, intellectualized style of conversation and refusal to talk with each other, each riveting attention on the therapist. But eventually as I employed systemic concepts to teach them each one's part in the malaise and how each could take responsibility for change, they began to experience a gradual building of trust, first in the therapist and then in each other. In the following excerpt, they are discussing some of the factors that made it possible for Margaret to acknowledge to herself and then to share with Daryl for the first time an experience she had with date rape when she was a teenager.

*Margaret:* Now I feel comfortable telling you I had a dumb reason for doing stuff. I didn't really know that I presented a certain face to people, so I suppose I presented a face to you. And I didn't realize that.

*Therapist:* So, Daryl, what's your part in why it is working for her to share now?

*Daryl:* What's my part?

*Therapist:* Yes. Because if you have a part in why she wasn't sharing, then you have a part in why she is now.

*Daryl:* I'm not really sure. I'm probably a little bit, or maybe it's a whole lot, more accepting than I was. Other than that, I don't know.

*Therapist:* What's your thought about that, Margaret?

*Margaret:* (To Daryl) Now I think you realize (pause), even if things seem trivial to you, you'll listen.

*Daryl:* The first 3 nights after you told me about your rape, I started shaking.

*Therapist:* What was that, Daryl?

*Daryl:* Anxiety! I didn't know how to feel. Then I told her a couple of days later that I felt sad that she had to go through that. Usually when I feel, it's depression. But this wasn't that. It was just plain sad!

*Margaret:* That was such a different response than you've ever had before. Just to know that you felt something about me! To know that you felt *anything* about me! That's encouraging. And my part is, I've never given you a chance to respond to me, for fear of how you'd react. I expected you to react in a certain way. And I'm realizing more and more now that I never have given you a chance, because I was so sure about how you'd react. But I'm finding out that now I'm usually not right about how you'll react.

*Therapist:* Daryl, what's all this like for you?

*Daryl:* I feel closer to Margaret than I have ever! And that's very positive (pause) and it's not a pity thing. It's a sharing thing.

*Therapist:* Have you ever shared like this with anybody, Daryl?

*Daryl:* No!

*Therapist:* I didn't think so.

Here, we see the results of a focus on becoming more aware of a complex series of contributors to human behavior, including their own. Learning open-minded, nonjudgmental perceptions of behavior gives one the capacity to transcend one's own narrow perceptions and truly enter the world of another. This has the capacity to generate a great deal of intimacy between partners while increasing the developmental level of those individuals involved.

## Differentiating and Integrating Concepts

At every developmental level, the potential for regression is determined by a person's capacity for making new differentiations and integrating these parts. What do these terms mean? According to Harvey et al. (1961), differentiation is the breaking of a novel, undifferentiated situation into more clearly defined and articulated parts. Integration is the relating or hooking of such parts to each other and to previous concepts. The two processes may occur simultaneously, but differentiation may occur separately. However, the outcome of this combined process is increased abstractness. What does this mean in operational terms? Therapists with an eye toward development help clients make distinctions between terms commonly used but little understood, for example, success and failure, failure and mistakes, assertion and aggression, love and dependence, needs and wants, having needs and being needy, dependence and interdependence, commitment and habit, and so on. The more differentiated and integrated systems are assumed to be more abstract; those that are less so are considered more concrete.

### Clinical Example

A woman in her mid-30s requested individual therapy to help her cope with her highly disengaged marriage. As usual, I explained that I do not work in that way and that she would have to get her husband to join us. I agreed to meet with her one time to strategize about how to get him to my office, but that would be it. When she succeeded in getting him there, they disclosed that this was their second attempt at couples therapy. Stewart had refused to continue with the first therapist, saying that Katie was the one who needed it, but later confessed a lack of confidence in the previous therapist. Their marital issues at intake were fairly typical: female dependent and desperate; male cold and aloof. The following exchange took place approximately 3 months after the couple began treatment.

*Katie:* I told Stewart that I felt like I had seen a long-lost friend last session. And he said, "You like to see me human." And I said, "No, vulnerable." I haven't seen that since we were first dating. And that night, I even felt sexually attracted to him. And it was the first time in a long, long time.

*Therapist:* Stewart, what was it like for you last session?

*Stewart:* Tough sessions. These are tough sessions. But they force introspection. Tough issues. But I felt good afterward. Vulnerable, I guess. But I resist the word "vulnerable" if it means shared weakness. But it did feel more balanced.

In sum, a major strategy for moving conceptual systems toward greater abstractness is challenging clients to engage in continuing cycles of differentiation and integration. The reader will notice the ample opportunity afforded the therapist to capitalize on the disequilibrium created by the making of these distinctions. It is at the therapist's discretion to decide when to increase the disequilibrium, so that differentiation is required, and when to decrease clients' experience of being off balance, so that integration is possible, or at least, so that arrestation is not invited. This assimilation of new, dissonant information in turn brings about changes in cognitive structures.

## Examining Options and Making Choices

Once clients' conceptual systems have developed to a point that the people can recognize and foster diversity, they can begin to seek personalized solutions to their problems. Now there are several possible alternatives rather than just one "right" answer. The therapeutic task is to provide environmental conditions that will maximize openness and developmental progression, not to teach "answers." To do this, we need to orchestrate the environment so that clients can discover for themselves the solutions that fit best for them without overwhelming them with the resulting disequilibrium in the process.

The primary tasks of the therapist at this stage are: (a) to clarify situations where choices are necessary, (b) to refuse to choose so that clients must, (c) to provide feedback on both the confusion and the clarity she is hearing from clients, and (d) to titrate the amount of disequilibrium the client must tolerate at any one time. Thus the therapist enables clients to straighten out their own thoughts and make decisions for themselves.

### Clinical Example

Molly is a 47-year-old woman who has been married to John for 27 years. Because John's style has been to withdraw into depression that has been chronic for him since early childhood, or to retreat into work, Molly experiences having been, in effect, a "married single" her whole married life. When their last child left for college, the silence around the house was deafening, and this very involved mother of three could no longer tolerate the void of her marriage that their empty nest pointed to so poignantly. So she vowed to move out, both as a way to get John's attention and to experiment with whether divorce was what she wanted.

Although she had been acknowledging her loneliness to herself and to John for years, asking for his involvement and forewarning him of her possible action if nothing changed, he seemed shocked by her decision to get her own place. Panicked and infuriated by her plan to move, John requested treatment for himself. As is standard for me, I agreed to one session with him alone, stating that he would have to get her to come in with him for me to take the case.

He cried for most of our first session, expressing his shock and disbelief that Molly would be taking this action, even though he acknowledged that he had basically ignored her his whole marriage because work and making money were more important. After that first session, he readily agreed to ask Molly to begin couples therapy. However, he remained adamant that if she moved out, that was it; the marriage was over.

My goals during the first couples session were twofold. One was to join Molly so that she could feel that I could be her therapist, too, as she had not met with us the first time. And the other was to intervene on John's rigid stance about her moving out. This was for three reasons. One, he was inviting an emotional cutoff that would only intensify his pain, not stop it as he believed it would. Two, Molly seemed firm in her resolve to separate, so my assessment was that my trying to dissuade her would have compromised her own development. And three, sometimes in highly dysfunctional marriages, living apart can give a fresh perspective as well as allowing feelings to return, or to develop if they genuinely never were there in the first place. So separating is often something I encourage.

In that first session, I carefully explained all of this to John. Though it was a struggle, I got him to agree that following through on his threat to end the marriage immediately if Molly moved out, before they both had a chance to understand themselves better and until we had a chance to work on the marriage, would be foolish and unnecessary. Reluctantly, he agreed to back off from his ultimatum and give therapy a chance to work.

We then designed a plan for intensive therapy, at Molly's request. This was due primarily to two factors. One was her sense of urgency to figure out what she wanted and what the actual possibilities were for her marriage. And the other was, now that her children were no longer there as buffers or companions, she was terrified of continuing to live in the emotional desert in which she had existed for years. Thus we agreed to alternate couples sessions with individual sessions for each, and decided that both would participate in a group. Molly would be in a women's group, and John would join a mixed-gender group. For a further explanation of the rationale for this clinical decision, refer to the chapter on groups. The following dialogue took place in an individual session with Molly approximately 2 months after the initiation of treatment. It should be noted that this dialogue actually happened without interruption, but because Molly's thoughts both in this excerpt and in general at this stage are so jumbled, and yet she is struggling mightily with huge issues that are not limited to her marriage, I will present the dialogue in pieces. This will allow me to provide the reader with a conceptual framework for my interventions as I try to help Molly sort out her profound and pervasive sense of confusion. Further, as the reader will see, Molly's thoughts are so scattered that she readily admits that she is in no position to decide anything yet. And at this early stage of treatment, the reader undoubtedly will recognize her jumble as being fairly typical, particularly with such huge life changes at stake. However, I hope that this dialogue with my explication will illustrate the probing and clarifying the therapist needs to do with clients who are in the process of examining their options and making choices.

*Molly:* I don't think men are so strong. I think men need to be taken care of.

*Therapist:* You think men need to be taken care of.

*Molly:* Not *think.* I *know* that.

*Therapist:* What makes you assume men are so weak that they need to be taken care of?

*Molly:* Somehow I got it in my head that men don't listen and women know the answers. My mother's friends used to say that they'd never seen a more competent woman. But as soon as my dad was in the room, she'd turn helpless.

*Therapist:* What message did that give you?

*Molly:* That I shouldn't be able to take care of myself, it's not OK. And I also got the message that the only reason a woman works is because her husband can't take care of her.

*Therapist:* And what would that mean [if he couldn't]?

*Molly:* That I've chosen poorly.

*Therapist:* So you've got yourself coming and going!

*Molly:* Yes! I didn't realize how emotionally attached I was [to John] until [I started] the group. But I'm always there. When everybody said they're like Siamese twins with their husbands, I feel that. And yet, I look at a woman like you, and I see your strength. And I certainly feel your strength! So I don't understand that. It gets me all mixed up with me.

Given the beliefs about men that we hear Molly talking about here, little wonder that she has difficulty trusting her husband— or any man. If she believes men are inherently weak, what would allow her to believe that she could be emotionally taken care of? Yet, being a "good girl," she has abided by the messages that she got from her mother's example that a man's job is to take care of women instrumentally, and that her job is to not threaten him by being competent or strong. And as a result of all of the conflicting messages she got and in turn gives herself, it is no surprise that she has difficulty trusting herself and her ability to make choices for herself.

*Molly:* My parents had a boy right before me who died. And so they wanted to have another boy when they had me. And they wanted to have another boy, and then they had my younger sister.

*Therapist:* How does that link to your messages about competence?

*Molly:* They thought my dead older brother was brilliant. So maybe I thought I'd better not surpass him. In fact, I missed 57 days of school in kindergarten because my mother said I just didn't have to go. And that continued throughout school.

*Therapist:* Both [of these factors] would also be why you'd figure you'd better not be competent. (Seeing her tears) What are you feeling?

*Molly:* Sad. I guess I feel sad. I know I was a disappointment to my mother. My dad once told John that he always thought of me as two children in one.

*Therapist:* The girl and the boy?

*Molly:* Yes.

*Therapist:* So which are you more: the boy or the girl? I think, because you don't see yourself as feminine and pretty, you think of yourself as a boy. But then, I think you think, "Oh no! I can't be competent!" so you go back to being incompetent and the girl.

*Molly:* You can't be both. But you try. But then you don't have to be competent [if you're a woman]. I hold myself back, because if I don't, I'm the man. And then I think, too, if I really get competent, I might make more money than John.

*Therapist:* And what would be so bad about that?

*Molly:* That would mean I married wrong. If he said he wouldn't go to therapy and then would bow out, that would be OK. But if I said I was leaving because I could take care of myself and do better than what I am used to (pause). . . .

*Therapist:* Then what?

*Molly:* It would be like deballing a man. And another thing is, my sexual needs and desires have always been more than John's.

*Therapist:* What happens then?
*Molly:* I'm more the man. But I get rejected a lot.
*Therapist:* And then what happens?
*Molly:* Then I flip into this pouty female.
*Therapist:* No wonder you're confused!
*Molly:* I *am* confused! I flip-flop all the time. I get strong, and then I think, "Oh my God! This is too much!" (Pause) But I do find that, now that I've moved out, I feel my creativity coming back. My mind is clicking. (Pause) But it's not OK to be smarter than the man. Somehow I think it's not OK to be smart or smarter than the man. (Pause) But I am afraid though!
*Therapist:* What are you afraid of?
*Molly:* If I *were* successful, what would I do? Because then I'd be strong. And I'd be a man. And I can't be feminine.

Here Molly's confusion about the mixed messages and double binds she got from her family of origin are approaching astronomical proportions. Sensing that she could become overwhelmed with the resulting disequilibrium, I begin to search for some avenues for her to start having some tentative answers. (The astute reader will notice that I did not say "The Answer.") Then she can use these pathways to reach two very important goals. One is they can be building blocks for helping her ultimately make her huge and compelling decisions about her marriage and about what she wants out of life. And the other is they can serve as tools for defining a clear, coherent sense of self, rather than one that is so diffuse, riddled with confusion and contradiction.

*Therapist:* Do you think your mother gave you that message?
*Molly:* Um hum. And I think my mother was much happier after my dad died.
*Therapist:* What does that tell you about your paradigm for relationships?
*Molly:* That my life will be better if I get rid of John. Because he just doesn't feed me, sexually or any other way.
*Therapist:* You've got some big decisions to make, don't you?
*Molly:* Yeah, I do. And I'm just kind of hanging around because I'm afraid.

In an effort to begin to give her a framework for understanding her confusion—even though she is in no way ready to take any action yet—I am attempting to help her understand her family of origin precedents. This will not only help her comprehend her choices in life, but also her scripting about how relationships "should" be. Once she grasps that and how she has lived by unspoken dictates and maintained strict loyalty to them, she eventually will be in a position to make different choices. It should be noted that those choices will not automatically take her out of her marriage, although they may. Equally possible is that they will allow her, with her husband's cooperation, to create a new way of being within the marriage that works better for both.

*Therapist:* Let me just try something out on you, OK? What if I were to say that you may have already made your decision?

*Molly:* To leave?

*Therapist:* Yes.

*Molly:* I think I have.

*Therapist:* What does it feel like to say that?

*Molly:* Safe, here. But I'm not ready to tell John yet.

*Therapist:* I know. And I don't think he's ready to hear it yet, either. And if you try to tell him before you both are ready, it'll only drag you back in.

*Molly:* And the fact that he's coming here and really working, really makes me respect him.

*Therapist:* And then I'll bet that really confuses you, too.

*Molly:* Um hum.

*Therapist:* Which is another reason you're not ready. But we'll all get you ready.

*Molly:* Oh God!

*Therapist:* What's "Oh God?"

*Molly:* It sounds like so much work. I want to climb back in bed.

*Therapist:* And be incompetent?

*Molly:* Um hum. I just always knew I'd be taken care of. (Pause) But we pay the price, don't we? (Pause) I've been working so hard. I've been fighting for survival. But we're helping the real Molly to come out.

Now that the dynamics that generated some of her major developmental impasses have been articulated, she can begin to see that she does have options. And yet predictably, as soon as the option to leave the marriage, which she had thought she wanted, was put on the table, she swung to the other side of her ambivalence and began to state reasons to stay.

At this early stage of treatment, the therapeutic task is to guide clients to see that they can learn to make choices without deciding for them, while helping them tolerate the disequilibrium that questioning brings. This can be especially difficult at those times, unlike this instance, when it seems patently obvious to us what clients need to do. Particularly then, if we are working on both levels of helping them solve their problem while they gain developmental growth, it is essential that we resist the seduction of telling clients what to do. Clients and therapists alike must learn that their and our not immediately answering questions can facilitate developmental growth.

## Journaling to Promote Developmental Progression

Before we leave the section on experiences that are conducive to developmental change, journaling as a tool to promote growth needs to be mentioned briefly. I encourage the reader to peruse the book *Life's Companion: Journal Writing as a Spiritual Quest* (Baldwin, 1990) for some suggestions about the uses and the power of journal writing as a tool for introspection and growth. Having my own journals going back to 1970, my personal experience as well as my clinical practice tell me that this medium is second only to the therapy session in its power to generate change.

In addition to offering clients an intensely introspective experience, often for the first time and from a developmental frame, journal writing supplies a composite of all six of the elements necessary to generate developmental progression as discussed in the previous section. First, journaling gives people the experience of writing on which they can reflect while they are also reflecting on their experiences and encounters with life. Second, it facilitates empathy building both for themselves—especially crucial for men, who tend to disown and judge their feelings—and for others as they learn to empathize while working to understand. Third, it promotes openness of the individual and of the system as people begin to grasp, through their reflections on sessions and on their adventures in living, the significance of what they are doing. Fourth, it offers them a secluded place to examine the relativity of their perceptions, allowing them to contemplate their beliefs, values, and attitudes and confront themselves in privacy on paper. Fifth, it provides a solitary place either to extend the differentiating and integrating that they have begun in sessions or to begin to grapple with this process that is so central to true developmental growth and change. And sixth, as people begin to examine options and make choices, they have a sequestered place in which to try out their thinking. Thus, it is easy to see how all this enhances the experience obtained in the therapist's office.

How do we teach clients to journal and to value it? This is an important question, because I have learned that clients rarely will begin this part of the journey the first time it is suggested. We can speculate on all manner of reasons for this resistance, but each client's excuses are idiosyncratic. The question is, even in the face of their resistance, how do we induce clients to avail themselves of this device?

The first, easiest way is to believe in it and do it ourselves. Modeling that this is of value and is a priority for us can be extremely helpful. The next is in the way we present this homework. I usually ask people to go buy a special book that fits their style, so that it is inviting to them to come to it. For example, for very obsessive-compulsive personality types, I suggest they might be comfortable with a notebook that has tiny lines, maybe even graph paper, so that they can write neatly as they use this as a device to clarify and order their thoughts. To people who are expansive and highly expressive, I suggest that they seek out a blank book with unlined pages and just the right design on its cover. For executive types, I suggest that they seek out leather-bound blank books that they would not feel awkward carrying in their briefcases. For the more frugal or those whose life-style is unadorned, I suggest a 99-cent spiral-bound notebook from the drugstore. It does not matter what people choose; it only matters that it be inviting and feel personal to them. In all cases, I discourage loose-leaf pages, as making it harder to see and to keep track of the sequencing of the development of their thought and feeling. And I encourage people to carry their journals with them, so that when their reflections generate a dramatic discovery or when a piece of a thought suddenly comes clear, they can capture its essence before it slips away.

Once people realize the power they can find in journaling, it is no longer necessary to remind them of or even mention the need to do it. For example, many people come to sessions a few minutes early to sit in the waiting room and read the week's entries as a way to help them focus on where they need to work for that session. Another example is two men I once had in men's groups. Although they were both high-powered attorneys whose hourly rates were astronomical, both reported that their first order of business on arriving at their office daily was to get a cup of coffee and write in their journals. They came to find this necessary to center themselves and clear their minds for the day's work.

When clients resist getting started, there are certain tacks that we as therapists can take to enhance their cooperation with this suggestion. First, I repeatedly recommend that they do it, and I even good-naturedly call it nagging. Second, I suggest that they write even when they believe they have nothing to say, continuing to write until something of substance appears on the paper. In fact, I even suggest that they write how dumb an idea they think journaling is and how they have nothing to say, until they think of something to say. Third, if people continue to resist the suggestion, I even take a few minutes in session teaching people how to reflect on or amplify what they have written. In ways such as these, they can begin to see the intrinsic value of doing something that starts out as homework with only extrinsic value.

## Summary of Central Assumptions of Developmental Theorists

In reviewing the work of major developmental theorists, a set of common assumptions emerges. Theorists who take a developmental view agree that:

1. There is an inner logic to the way humans progress that forms discernible and predictable patterns. Individuals do indeed pass through a natural sequence of stages.
2. Developmentalists see cognitive structures as integrating principles, the framework through which affective experiences are interpreted. These cognitive structures render the individual selective in which stimuli are relevant and therefore affect perceptual, affective, and behavioral outcomes.
3. All developmentalists identify the structure of thought by focusing not on the referents, or *what* individuals think, but rather on *how* they think about an issue. In other words, the focus is not on what individuals believe but rather on how abstractly and relativistically they hold their beliefs.
4. Development involves structural transformation in one's thinking; what is genuinely developmental can be contrasted with learning, where one simply acquires new behaviors or attitudes.

5. Although the extent of development depends to some degree on organismic capabilities, the environment is even more influential. Development is seen as the product of interaction between the person and the environment. A combination of readiness within the individual and certain elements in the environment is assumed necessary for growth to occur. Further development is stimulated by interactions of the individual with the environment facilitating experiences that promote openness of the system to new differentiations and integrations.

6. Development is arrested or fixated when an individual resorts to minimizing the conflict between present beliefs and incoming information so as to reduce the imbalance or disequilibrium.

7. Once a concept or predisposition to believe in a certain way develops, it becomes an experiential filter or psychological prism. This renders the individual selective in what is more relevant and consequently in how he or she senses, interprets, feels toward, and responds to a given person or situation.

8. Higher stages of development are qualitatively different and "better," in that they provide individuals with more complex and therefore more adequate skills that increase their capacity to interact effectively with the environment.

9. Therefore, stimulation to the next step of development is the aim of both education and of psychotherapy.

These central premises form the backbone for the approach described in this book.

## Structuring Treatment With Development in Mind

Looked at in a developmental context, there are three phases of treatment. This section will answer the following questions: How are phases of treatment demarcated? What is the role of the developmentally oriented therapist? What are the major tasks for therapist and client at each phase? How are those tasks different as treatment progresses? How do clients predictably respond to the experience at each phase? What sorts of questions typically mark each phase? For each phase, I will discuss the major tasks of the therapist, the common characteristics of the phase, and sample questions at each phase. The word "phase" is simply intended to denote the beginning, middle, and termination of treatment.

## Phase I

*Major Tasks of the Therapist.* The first major task is the same as it is in any therapy: establish trust in the therapist and between the people participating in the therapy. This will set the norm of supportiveness necessary for people to engage in the sometimes painful, sometimes exhilarating process of change. To do this effectively, the therapist must gain credibility. Important in any therapy, it is critical when men seek therapy with women. As a woman, not only must she appear knowledgeable, but paradoxically, as a developmentally oriented therapist, she must be careful not to provide the pat answers that people who function at more concrete levels have come to expect and demand. At first, there is confusion and restrained—and sometimes not so restrained—hostility toward the therapist as clients learn that not immediately answering their questions can facilitate their progress. Clients must experience a change in their definition of the role of the therapist in order to move toward changes in their own roles. A third major task here is to encourage people to verbalize their internal struggle, without fear of being "wrong" or "bad." Once people forfeit their fear of being judged, the real work of therapy can begin. And a fourth major task is helping people identify their own contributions to the relationship dysfunction for which they are seeking help. When people stay riveted on the other person's transgressions, they give away all influence they have to change the situation. Instead, they render themselves powerless, having to wait for the benevolence of the other person to create the necessary change. Though it logically would seem as though it would put people down to admit their contributions to a problem, instead it gives them maximum leverage for changing it. Then, although they need the other's cooperation, they are not totally dependent on anyone to influence their situation.

*Common Characteristics.* One characteristic of the first phase is the expectation that the therapist will talk while the clients wait to be enlightened. This is particularly predictable in certain situations. One is if clients have been in paint-by-numbers therapy where results are promised within a month. Another is if clients are therapy virgins who have never been in treatment before. And sadly, it is often even true if they have had years of therapy. For example, I once treated a therapist who continually reminded me during the first phase of treatment that she had been in her own therapy for 16 years. The effectiveness of those therapies to promote genuine growth is suspect, in that she was needing therapy again and still, and in that she had few clues about how to put this approach to use for herself. My assessment early on was that her behavior in her other therapies—and indeed, in her marriage and in her life—had been carefully orchestrated to keep her away from any thoughts, feelings, or relationships she could not control. So I had to monitor carefully the amount of disequilibrium that she experienced. My purpose was to help her avoid further fixation by providing enough support and encouragement that she could stay in the process, without offering so much salve that she could resist further the disequilibrating experience that is the cornerstone of developmental growth. But either way, people usually do not know how to put this sort of process to use for themselves.

At this stage, typically, there is no challenging of the authority of the therapist, although I encourage that early on and see it as a positive sign if people do, provided the challenge is not an excuse to fixate. In any event, the therapist can expect expressions of unfamiliarity and discomfort with the process.

In sum, the therapist's main job at this stage is to titrate the amount of disequilibrium that is being generated in the system. She must not introduce so much that people once again choose to fixate rather than to progress, but she must introduce enough that people's systems become open to change. More than anything, she must establish that this therapy will be supportive without coddling, that it will be a struggle and clients should expect that, but that she will take the journey with them. I explain clearly to clients that I do not do therapy *on* them; I do therapy *with* them. Therapy at its best is a partnership. Finally, clients will struggle ever more vocally to learn the value of and skills for genuine reflection and introspection. For clients to engage in the disequilibrium that they gradually are experiencing, setting the norm of supportiveness is critical.

*Sample Questions.* The few questions included here are only to provide the therapist a flavor for the kinds of queries she might use to open the system to developmental change. Because of my conviction that good therapy is a combination of insight (cognition) and catharsis (affect), the questions that elicit a cognitive response are listed alternating with those that generate affect. This prevents the appearance of a bias in favor of one or the other. Obviously, there is no way to provide an exhaustive list for the reader, because good treatment relies on therapeutic artistry and improvisation, not on a technician's rote application of basic skills. If the reader already asks these sorts of questions suggested for each phase, she may want to consider the responses they elicit in a developmental frame. This will get her even more therapeutic mileage from them.

> What is your understanding of your part in your current situation/
>     dilemma?
> What is the feeling that goes with those tears?
> How is your having this problem helping you?
> How are you feeling/did you feel about the piece of work you did last
>     week?
> What do you notice happens after you do X?
> What are you feeling confused about?

## Phase II

*Major Tasks.* By now, the sessions begin to take on a tone of relaxed inquiry. Several factors account for this. One is that the therapist will be working to generate the maximum disequilibrium possible, particularly affectively, so that clients are compelled to resolve their dilemmas in a qualitatively different way. Yet, a supportive atmosphere will be prevalent. This, however, does not mean that clients are only coddled and never confronted. But even when they are confronted, an ambience of trust has been established so that it is clear that this challenge, too, is done out of concern for the client. This trusting ambience is attributable to several factors. One is clients' changing view of the role of the therapist and of therapy in helping them resolve their dilemmas in a qualitatively different way. Another is clients' increasing ambiguity about their old roles and increasing comfort in relinquishing them. Still another is their uncertainty as they try on new roles. The analogy I often use is that clients in this stage feel like turtles without their shells. They know they want to give them up, but learning to live without them can feel extremely vulnerable and frightening until they adjust to the new experience.

Just as potent are clients' new role-taking experiences as they learn empathy skills. Progress is promoted as clients are encouraged to reflect on their successes and on how they experience them.

*Common Characteristics.* As people venture their deep feelings and strong opinions, a paradoxical experience happens: They begin to feel sure enough that they can risk sharing what they are uncertain of. I think of this phase as the working phase of psychotherapy. By *working phase* I mean the following. One is that a solid, clear therapeutic alliance and contract are established that involves shared goals, sense of directionality, and mutual ownership in the therapy. Another is that the therapist trusts clients just as they do her, thus giving her the maximum movement with her interventions. In sum, there is maximum comfort and trust as clients experience their difficult though exhilarating journey. By now, the preliminaries are out of the way, and people unequivocally and irrevocably have begun their journey inward.

*Sample Questions.* Because this is the working phase of therapy, the following kinds of questions are typical here. Again, I alternate those that tap cognitive understandings with those that foster affective experiences.

   What is your current understanding of what factors account for your insight/conclusion/behavior change?
   Even though there may be many external markers that tell you that you are successful/happy/worthy/loved, how do you really feel deep down about that?
   What do you think would happen if you tried to go back and be the way you were before you started therapy?
   What are you feeling now about X choice/behavior/event?
   How would you have responded to X situation if it had happened before you started therapy?
   When is the first time you remember feeling like this?

**Phase III**

*Major Tasks.* By now, the major task of the therapist is to facilitate the internalization of experiences and concepts. Here clients are struggling to begin to use what they have discovered. And the final task, a clear need for any therapy relationship but even more critical where depth has been shared, is to facilitate termination. My rule of thumb is that the longer and more intense the therapy relationship, the more critical it is that attention be paid to a careful, planned termination of treatment. In those instances, clients usually request a spacing out of appointments before they actually terminate, to allow for time to practice before the safety net is removed. If they don't request that, I suggest it, because it has the added benefit of allowing the opportunity for guided integration of concepts. But even when clients do terminate, I reassure them that if they ever need to come back for a psychological tune-up, I am available. Even in the termination session, I am helping clients reflect on the experience and integrate it into usable knowledge that they can take with them. This increases their confidence level and amplifies their successes.

*Common Characteristics.* The most obvious characteristic is personalization and sharing of the concepts discussed. By now, clients usually are aware of what they need to do, even if they choose to temporize, resting a while before they begin to do it. And there is usually a mix of exhilaration and sadness as the therapy ends. I make it clear to clients that even though the therapy is ending, our relationship does not end, even if we never see each other again. Relationships, once they are meaningfully and deeply established, do not simply end, even without contact. Having an adequate termination experience is particularly essential for those clients who have unresolved losses in their history, so that this, too, does not replicate their earlier experience. In such cases, we can help them to have a qualitatively different, emotionally corrective experience with a loss.

*Sample Questions.* In this phase, the focus is on helping clients reflect on their therapeutic experience so that they can consolidate their gains, claim their successes, and be aware of potential pitfalls. Questions typical of this phase are:

What have you learned that will stick with you the longest?
What has been the best part of this experience for you?
What changes do you see in yourself and in your life since you began this journey?

What would you say will be the best/hardest part about ending therapy?
What would be some early warning signs that you might be getting
  yourself in trouble, and what could you do to help yourself with
  that?
On the whole, how do you feel about your experience over the time you
  have been in therapy?

## In Summary

Although certain specific competencies are required of the therapist at each phase of treatment, there are some generalizable skills
and attributes as well that are worth mentioning. First, the therapist
must realize that she teaches by modeling. If we demonstrate a
healthy respect for questions as well as for answers, then clients will
be much better able to tolerate the disequilibrating experience in
which they are engaged of giving up the illusion of finding "right"
answers. It also is extremely helpful if the therapist has embarked
on her own journey so that she is capable of higher levels of
functioning herself. Otherwise, she will be neither a believable nor
a knowledgeable guide.

## Guidelines for the Developmentally Oriented Therapist

I will end this chapter by suggesting some principles that can
guide the therapist who is learning to work from a developmental
perspective. Of course, these are in no way presented as the
"right" way to do therapy. Rather, they are proffered as proposals
that learners can use to shape their behavior to be more consonant
with a developmental approach.

  1. It is advantageous to have some knowledge of developmental
     theory so that you can clarify for yourself your style in inte-
     grating this theory into therapeutic practice. This will help
     you avoid the tendency to get seduced into emphasizing only
     skill development without keeping your eye on the larger
     picture. If you are a novice in developmental theory, begin
     with any of the authors noted in this chapter. They all are well

known and highly respected for their work in the area, though Piaget's work is seminal to all other developmental theorists.

2. It is helpful if you yourself are capable of operating at a higher developmental level than your clients. If you have made your own pilgrimage to your inner self, the chances are good—though not guaranteed—that you can function at a higher developmental level. If you are not sure, it would be advisable to begin fearlessly to ask yourself those existential questions that you may have avoided. Remember that we teach by modeling, whether we intend to or not.

3. Learn to manage your own continuing cycles of differentiation and integration, and teach your clients to handle theirs. Because this is the basic process that is necessary for clients to progress developmentally, learn to invite clients' reflections along lines that will encourage it. People's developmental progression is determined by their capacity for making new differentiations and then integrating these parts, the result being increased abstractness of cognitive functioning. What might otherwise seem hairsplitting to the unaware can in fact be a useful therapeutic strategy for the developmentally oriented therapist.

4. Develop the clinical skills necessary to promote disequilibrium as well as to provide support. Most in our field were drawn to it because of great concern about and sensitivity for people. Classic research that was done by Truax and Carkoff (1967) clearly bore out that warmth, genuineness, and empathy are essential attributes of an effective therapist. However, in addition to those attributes, it is equally important that therapists know how to promote disequilibrium. Sometimes this is done by confrontation, other times by persistence in tracking clients who might otherwise avoid uncomfortable, disequilibrating issues, and still others by encouraging clients' differentiation and integration of concepts. In any case, learn to develop skills in these areas. Above all, toughen your skin for the times that clients' reactions to their disequilibration process are unpredictable.

5. Learn to tolerate clients'—and your own—disequilibrium. We do no service to our clients or to the therapy process when we feel compelled to jump in to rescue people from this naturally

occurring experience. I have learned over the years that when I find myself tempted to do this, before I intervene, I must first ask myself whether it is in their best interests or mine. If they need to experience being off balance to resolve the issue under scrutiny in a wholly different way, then therapists do no service by attempting to take that away, even if doing so might make all of us temporarily more comfortable. Most people love to be seen as fixers, and therapists are clearly no exception. Yet, the need truly to unravel issues only will surface again, likely in even more compelling ways, because more and more dysfunction accrues when people wallpaper over unexamined and unresolved issues. By contrast, for the times that intervening would be simply a countertransference reaction to ease my own discomfort, I have learned to take one of two courses of action: (a) bring my reaction into the therapy, if I believe that we can use it to further clients' understanding of themselves and of their impact on others; or (b) keep my mouth shut, which sometimes literally includes sitting on my hands or putting them over my mouth until the urge to protect both my clients and myself from their discomfort passes.

6. For the second-order change that is created by a shift in the family system to have its greatest effects, attempt to combine that with developmental growth for the individuals involved. In this way, the changes that are created likely will last the longest. Both the family's developmental processes and those of the individuals within it can then continue to progress. Second-order change itself can be a very disequilibrating experience. Learn to capitalize on it.

7. Learn to discern the differences among avoidance, arrestation or fixation, and temporizing. It is understandable that from time to time, people will want to slow down the process of change if they feel overwhelmed by it or out of control of it. At those times, temporarily pausing is not only necessary; it is therapeutic. However, we need to distinguish between that and avoidance. When people are avoiding, they are attempting to escape an unpleasant truth that they need to face. Over time, this virtually guarantees fixation. In addition, it may be a marker that the whole of the individual's development has become arrested.

8. Remember that not all clients will opt for this in-depth course of treatment. Try as I might, I sometimes cannot adequately demonstrate the advantages of this type of approach such that people are willing to take the plunge. In those instances I have two choices: either do the piece with them that I can delineate and see if I successfully can lay tracks along the way that may induce them to take a deeper look, or send them on their way to someone who will work more simplistically and superficially.

9. Be aware that sometimes clients in reality do not have a choice about whether to resolve their crisis or merely to fix their problem. This is particularly true when clients present for treatment in the midst of a relationship crisis that may be indicative of an unresolved developmental crisis. In those instances, how you assess the situation could make or break a valuable opportunity for your client. If you choose to go the route of solving the problem in as brief a time as possible, the precipitants for the crisis likely will pop up again somewhere else. And then the client will have to wait for that next opportunity to make fundamental change, meanwhile tolerating the sense that their life is just not quite right.

10. *Be patient.* Remember Piaget's conclusion that it takes approximately 3 years to make a stage change. This means that sometimes we will see the fruits of our and our clients' labors, but sometimes the client will be long gone. If it is change that is truly developmental in nature, our work will take effect, even when we are not around to see it.

## A Final Word

The model being proposed here is a long-term treatment process, in that fundamental developmental change cannot happen overnight or in a fortnight. Just how long the process takes varies with many factors: the motivation of the client(s), the depth and duration of the dysfunction, the numbers and reactions of others involved in and affected by the changes that are required, and the vision and the motivation of the therapist to push for and lead clients to fundamental developmental change, to name a few. Not all clients are candidates for long-term treatment, for one reason or another. But those who are sincere about wishing to make the longest lasting changes need to be offered this approach. For a more thorough consideration of appropriate candidates for long-term treatment such as that discussed in this chapter, see Appendix D for a discussion of clinical presentations that may indicate long-term treatment.

## References

Baldwin, C. (1990). *Life's companion: Journal writing as a spiritual quest*. New York: Bantam.

Dewey, J. (1916). *Democracy and education*. New York: Macmillan.

Erickson, B. (1976). *An evaluation of a curriculum intervention: Conceptual development in in-service education*. Doctoral dissertation, University of Minnesota.

Goldberg, H. (1987). *The inner male: Overcoming roadblocks to intimacy*. New York: Signet.

Harvey, O. (1966). *Experience, structure and adaptability*. New York: Singer.

Harvey, O., Hunt, D., & Schroeder, H. (1961). *Conceptual systems and personality organization*. New York: John Wiley.

Keen, S. (1991). *Fire in the belly: On being a man*. New York: Bantam.

Kohlberg, L. (1969). Stage and sequence: The cognitive-developmental approach to socialization. *Harvard Educational Review, 4*, 449-496.

Levinson, D. (1978). *The seasons of a man's life*. New York: Knopf.

Levinson, D. (1990, July). *Adult development of women and men*. Symposium presented for the Cape Cod Summer Symposia, Eastham, MA.

Minuchin, S. (1974). *Families and family therapy*. Cambridge, MA: Harvard University Press.

Moore, R., & Gillette, D. (1990). *King, warrior, magician, lover: Rediscovering the archetypes of the mature masculine*. San Francisco: HarperSanFrancisco.

Piaget, J. (1948). *The moral judgment of the child*. Glencoe, IL: Free Press. (Original work published in 1932)

Sprinthall, N. (1973, May). A curriculum for secondary schools: Counselors as teachers for psychological growth. *School Counselor*, pp. 361-369.

Truax, C., & Carkoff, R. (1967). *Effective counseling and psychotherapy*. Chicago: Aldine.

Watzlawick, P., Weakland, J., & Fisch, R. (1974). *Change: Principles of problem formation and problem resolution*. New York: Norton.

# Part III

# BACKDROP FOR STRUCTURING TREATMENT

# A Primer on Systems Thinking

Recently I completed treatment of Oren, whose words the reader will find laced throughout the book. At intake, he was a 47-year-old man who was twice divorced. His presenting problem was not atypical for men who present for treatment: inability to be in or maintain an intimate relationship. The primary manifestation was his philandering, often literally getting out of bed with one woman and immediately moving on to the next mark. With a combination of pride in his prowess and shame for his actions, he confessed his sexual exploits and the hollowness and loneliness he felt as a result of them. He was referred to me by his individual-oriented male therapist, who believed Oren needed family of origin work and wisely recognized his own limitation in this area. Twenty minutes into our initial session, after Oren had detailed his exploits sufficiently for me to get the picture and for him to sense that I was not going to be horrified or titillated or run away, I announced, "You and I are not going to have an affair. Now are you prepared to get to work to help yourself?"

Months later, he reported two realizations from that conversation. One is that I was the first woman whom he had not viewed as a sex object, because I had made it crystal clear that he would have to relate to me as a person and that anything sexual between us was totally out of bounds. The second realization, stunning to both of us, was that I was his 16th therapist. A few were group therapies; most were individual therapies. He readily acknowledged that in most of them he had learned some useful information, and he also admitted that he probably had not been really ready to help himself before. But he also attributed some of his success this time to me and to my approach.

What, then, was so different? Because the previous therapies had all been based on an individual perspective, he had learned to further pathologize himself without seeing himself or his behavior in context. This compromised his ability to change his behavior, because he only felt more ashamed and became even more compulsively out of control, resulting in yet another cycle of compulsive acting out and the resulting shame. So his individual-oriented therapies, despite the therapists' best intentions and laudable efforts, unwittingly contributed to his dysfunction. By contrast, when he learned a family systems perspective and was able to see the multiple factors contributing to his difficulties, he was able to stop his promiscuous behavior, eventually marry, and commit to fidelity with his wife. At termination of treatment nearly 3 years later, he had maintained his pledge to his wife—and to himself.

## Chapter Overview

We can never effectively examine men and their gendered behavior without seeing them in context. For the matrix of healing is our facilitating a combination of changes in the individual and in his relationships. Therefore, first I will briefly compare an individual and a family systems orientation. Then I will go on to consider the stumbling blocks to effective treatment of men that the family systems perspective can remove. Next, to help orient the fledgling systems thinker, I will begin with an in-context glossary. I will go on to discuss the advantages to therapist, clients, and others in the clients' relationship networks when the therapist works from this philosophical stance. Finally, I will summarize how these concepts particularly are elemental in the treatment of men, regardless of the gender of the therapist.

The central focus of this chapter is to assist the reader in thinking systemically. This will help her guard against her natural tendency as a woman to blame men and side with women, and will give her tools that will invite men and their partners to engage in long-lasting, basic change. The material will be organized around these two threads: leverage the therapist can garner from a family systems orientation, and advantages to the client from learning to think systemically.

What follows is an attempt to distill basic family systems concepts down to their most basic level. Those readers well steeped in family systems thinking will doubtless want to speed through or even skip this chapter. But those who do not think and practice systemically are encouraged to read it carefully and critically. This chapter discusses "the pattern which connects" (Bateson, 1972), and its purpose is to help the reader "think systems." To work effectively with men, I believe a female therapist needs to conceptualize her treatment in terms of relationship networks—past, present, and future—rather than focusing only on individuals and ignoring the contexts in which they developed and live.

## Systemic Perspective Essential in Treating Men

The crux of the outlook I offered to Oren that made the difference was looking at his relationship problems *in context* and teaching him to do the same. This is the nucleus of a family systems perspective and what makes the approach so unique and robust. Why? Because if everyone has a part of the problem, then everyone can join forces to solve it, rather than waiting haplessly for the individual elected to have the problem to be beneficent enough to change. And if it is ever important that therapists are capable of taking a systemic view, it is a prerequisite in working effectively with men because it is simply too seductive and facile to label any one person the cause for problems in relationships.

What makes this recognition so important in doing therapy with men? Because men are socialized away from relationships and women are socialized toward them, women have an orientation that gives them more practice in relating. Taking a linear and therefore more superficial look, it is easy to conclude that men are responsible for relationship dysfunction. After all, when they do not want to share and they seem impatient about understanding, it seems easy to diagnose them as causing the dysfunction. For example, it is easy to place the blame for family dysfunction at the feet of a cold, distant father without looking up the generations to the model he had in his parents' marriage and at how his wife's behavior inadvertently also may contribute to the perpetuation of that style of relating. But systems thinkers know that to attribute problems to any one person in the system is a facile conclusion, for we conceptualize relationships qualitatively differently. That is what this chapter is about.

In order for therapists, especially female therapists who may have their own biases and beliefs about men to begin with, to be able to work effectively with men, we need to see beyond a man's blatant contribution to the problem, to search also for everyone else's part, rather than to lay blame for all relationship break-downs only at his feet.

Kelly and Hall (1992) make the following statement, which I heartily endorse: "Remember the rules of the playground: it takes 2 to have a fight. Mental health counseling interventions for men that do not consider men in systems are not likely to help men or their families" (p. 264). In fact, I would extend this premise and predict harm for all involved if men are not treated systemically. Being unable to take this perspective in working with men is to risk doing harm to our clients, both male and female. Of course, it is hurtful to the man to be blamed for all the relationship's woes; but it does the woman no good, either. Even if the ingenuous therapist anoints her "right" in a given situation, what a hollow victory it is if it defeats him and the relationship is compromised and eventually jeopardized! How motivated will he be to partner with her in those circumstances? Further, even if she is to coax him to try to change in those circumstances, inducing change through guilt, blame, and intimidation, how long lasting will those changes be if they involve modification only at a superficial level?

Thus readers who will have the easiest time translating the ideas in this book into practice are those who already think systemically. It is for those who do not that this chapter is written. These readers are urged to get training or supervision in this area if they are committed to being able to work effectively with men—or with couples and families, for that matter.

## Summary of What Constitutes a Systems Orientation

What does it mean to think systemically? In contrast to individual therapy paradigms where the thinking is linear and the rationale for explaining outcomes is that A does a given action that *causes* B to react, systemic thinking takes into account the contributions of each individual in the relationship network to a given outcome. That is, any given situation is looked at holistically, with an effort to identify each of the multiple contributors to any given outcome. These concepts are so pivotal that they will be discussed in depth later in the chapter.

## Individual Perspective Versus Systems Orientation

Until the mid-1950s, the universally established point of view was that psychological problems reside solely within the individual. Dilemmas in relationships between people were seen as deriving from pathology within the individuals involved. This naturally gave rise to the belief that change can be brought about by diagnosing and treating the individual who manifests the problem. Although systems thinkers have clinical and empirical evidence that this is too simple a stance, among many mental health professionals this point of view still prevails.

Unfortunately, the perspective that labels and focuses only on individuals' pathology does not reckon with several key factors. One is that the orientation leaves the onus on that one individual to change, even though others may be contributing to and affected by the problem. Two, the individual's will to change is expected singlehandedly to outweigh a system's covert and sometimes overt agenda and inertia. Three, others in the system are rendered powerless to influence the problematic situation in any direct and involved way; they are dependent on the identified patient's beneficence and motivation to change. And four, the remainder of the system may be adversely affected by decisions and changes an individual makes in a vacuum, as often happens when a spouse in individual therapy unilaterally decides to end a marriage on the basis of conclusions drawn about who is to blame for the marital dysfunction.

When a therapist believes she can decide in a relationship who is healthy and who is not, she is ignoring the interlocking nature of the partners' problems. Although the axiom "It takes two to tango" may be accepted without question, all too many therapists do not internalize it, which means seeing the interrelatedness of the contributors to dysfunction in relationships. Though I believe that grasping this premise is central to any good psychotherapy, subscribing to it is a prerequisite to effective treatment of men by women. This, perhaps more than any other single concept, will help mitigate the human tendency we all have to level blame.

### Systemic Perspective Neutralizes the Tendency for Different to Be Seen as Wrong

What makes this point of view pivotal when female therapists treat male clients? Although there are threads that connect men's and women's experience, we are fundamentally different by virtue of both our biology and our socialization. And this differentness itself can become a major stumbling block to effective cross-gender treatment. It is a universal human tendency to label that which is different as pathological. In the introduction to *Ethnicity and Family Therapy*, McGoldrick, Pearce, and Giordano (1982) comment on the unconscious programming that people internalize because of their ethnicity. These same concepts are applicable to gender differences. "The Russian word for a German is *nemetz*, which means 'one who is mute,' reflecting the belief that those who could not be understood could not speak at all. We tend to label that which is different as 'bad' or 'crazy'" (1982, p. 5).

And indeed, women and men are so different that sometimes it seems as though they speak entirely different languages and come from entirely different worlds. Attention is now being paid to these gender differences in language and communication style by people such as Tannen (1990) and Meth (1992). Their approaches suggest that good relationship therapists must learn to act as interpreters, as bridges between men's and women's experiences. And yet, if we are to be adequate interpreters of those dissimilarities to our clients, we need to understand and respect those differences ourselves without falling into the trap of labeling the one who is different from us, the man, as pathological because of his way of being.

This universal tendency to pathologize those who are different is yet another reason that in order for the female therapist to treat men effectively, she must be secure in her own identity. Only then will she not have an ax to grind or an agenda of her own to act out. Again borrowing from the literature on ethnicity:

> If people are secure in their identity, then they can act with greater freedom, flexibility, and openness to others of different cultural backgrounds. However, if people receive negative or distorted images . . . or learn values from the larger society that conflict with those of their family, [they] often develop a sense of inferiority and self-hate that can lead to aggressive behavior and discrimination toward other . . . groups. (McGoldrick et al., 1982, p. 5)

Although most people are averse to admitting bias or prejudice of any kind, the wise female therapist who is treating male clients is savvy enough to identify and keep track of her own. Only in this way can she facilitate change and growth and not unwittingly perpetuate abuse. The dictum, "First, do no harm" is an important one to remember when women are treating men—or anyone else, for that matter.

## Glossary

The following is a list of key concepts for this way of working with men. As words define our reality, they define our world. "We organize our lives and our worlds by concepts, by our thoughts about them, and we can only think in terms of words. In this sense . . . words make our reality and make our universe" (Moore & Gillette, 1990, p. 53). Thus, understanding the following terms is key to working effectively with anyone, but especially with men.

### System

Two questions that may be going through the reader's mind are: What is a system? and What makes for systems thinking? *System* is a word bandied about now in most therapeutic circles, but few seem genuinely to fathom its meanings and subtleties. Yet, truly grasping the vital assumptions behind this word will vastly improve your clinical practice, particularly with male clients. So each of these very important questions will be answered below.

*What Is a System?* According to Simon, Stierlin, and Wynne (1985), a system is defined by a central concept. "The premises of systems theory are based on the insight that a system as a whole is qualitatively different, and 'behaves' differently from the sum of the system's individual elements" (p. 353). Weiner-Davis (1992) says it another way: "Family members act systemically in highly predictable patterns in order to preserve an equilibrium or maintain balance" (p. 70). Later, she offers a further clarification: "The behavior of the individual family members could best be understood when associated with the actions of other family members" (p. 71).

I know from my teaching experience that genuinely comprehending the concept of a system is among the most perplexing notions for inexperienced therapists to grasp. So if I were to say in one word the key concept that characterizes a system, it would be the word *interlocking*. Once the therapist can see that a family's behavior and interactions are interlocking, rather than attributable only to one person, then she can begin to think systemically.

*What Is Systemic Thinking?* Again, Simon et al. (1985) are helpful:

> Traditionally, psychology has viewed the individual as a unity, and the individual's developmental features and processes have been considered to be part of this unity. [By contrast], within the framework of family therapy and theory, the individual is viewed as being a part of the larger system of the family. This view changes the models used to explain an individual's behavior. *This wider framework does not view behavior as being independent of environmental conditions and as the by-product of intrapsychic processes, but as the result of the interplay of reciprocal processes between interactional partners* [italics added]. The behavior of the family as a whole is determined by the rules . . . applicable in the family system, as well as by the structure of the family itself, in other words, by the type of reciprocal relations that exist between the members of the family. (p. 354)

Being able to fathom this concept and to internalize the attitude that there is an inevitable interplay or reciprocity between family members when it comes to creating and addressing problems will enable the therapist to think and intervene systemically.

Specific to the requisite mind-set for effectively treating males, Kelly and Hall (1992, p. 272) agree that a systemic approach is required: "Instead of examining male behaviors in isolation, mental health counselors [must] consider the function a given behavior plays within a family or cultural system." Believing this, we will not run the risk of taking men's—or anyone's—behavior out of context and blaming and immobilizing the individual as well as fixating the system's growth.

## Family

Whatever your specific definition, I suspect that most would agree with this general one: A family is a set of interlocking interpersonal relationships that form a powerful emotional system in which every person is linked in an interdependent way.

But individuals' definitions of *family* may vary greatly. Some would match the vision of the traditional family: two parents in their first marriage living in the same home with X number of children. With all the variant family forms making up the U.S. landscape, that definition has become too limiting and simply no longer matches reality in all too many cases. We need an alternative, more inclusive definition of family that will match to a much greater extent the families who frequent our offices today. Kramer (1980) offers us such a definition:

> A group of people with a past history, a present reality, and a future expectation of interconnected transactional relationships. Members often (but not necessarily) are bound together by heredity, by legal marital ties, by adoption, or by a common living arrangement at some point in their lifetimes. *Whenever intense psychological bonds and continuing emotional investments exist among intimates, the concept of "family" can be used* [italics added]. (pp. 43-44)

Systems concepts about family turn on two pivotal premises. One, there is no "right" way to be a family. And two, particularly because adequate treatment of men requires exploration of men's roles in their family of origin, this perspective considers generations—not just the individual—in its conceptualization. That is, in this context, men as sons, partners, and fathers are taken into account. This does not always mean that each generation is brought into the therapist's office, but it does mean that they are factored into the treatment at least in the therapist's mind. A well-trained family therapist can do family therapy with only one person in the room: "Family therapy is defined by the conceptual goal of changing the system, not by the number of people in the interview room" (Kramer, 1980, p. 45).

### Health Orientation

To systems thinkers, families or individuals are healthy until proved sick. According to Pinsof (1983), rather than asking what is making the patient or patient system sick, the family systems therapist asks: What prevents this patient system from being healthy or adaptive? This *orientation to health* rather than pathology is a key differentiating factor of systems thinking. The reader easily can see how consonant this orientation to health is with a developmental perspective. For example, rather than labeling a woman who is enraged at her husband's emotional unavailability a hysterical female, systems thinkers would seek to account for the factors in the marital system, in his personality, as well as in her own makeup that would explain her seemingly erratic behavior. This orientation minimizes the likelihood of blame being leveled by therapists and felt by clients. Further, it lessens the probability of the therapist taking sides with some clients against others. It also lessens the chances of clients being perceived as fragile and helpless because of their "pathology." Further, it mobilizes hope and installs incentive in clients, which is one of the therapist's primary motivational tools and clinical obligations. Having this perspective, we do not demotivate people; we empower them.

### Circular Causality

A family system can be defined as a group of individuals interrelated so that a change in any one member affects other individuals as well as the group as a whole. These effects, in turn, affect the first individual in a *circular chain of influence*. Every action in this sequence is also a reaction. Causality is thus seen as circular rather than linear (Walsh, 1982). This means that it is impossible to determine a finite start or endpoint for a given action. People's behavior and responses come from and give rise to multiple factors. By contrast, linear causality assumes only one possible cause for any given behavior. Therefore, one individual can easily be blamed for dysfunction, because in this way of thinking, one cause can lead to a given outcome. This belief tends to pervade individual-oriented therapies and usually is highly obstructive to effective therapy.

## Nonsummativity

*Nonsummativity* is another key systems concept. This is the idea that the whole is greater than the sum of its parts and is a synonym for the common term *synergy*. By this, I mean that the family system cannot be understood merely by summing up the characteristics or attributes of its individual members; the parts as well as the composite picture must be examined separately. "When the parts or components are examined separately, the results or findings cannot simply be added together in order to determine what the whole will look like. The whole must be examined as a whole, as a system, rather than as the sum of a number of parts" (Nichols & Everett, 1986, pp. 67-68).

This concept speaks to the interdependence involved in relationships. Looked at this way, 1 + 1 = 3. The central point here is that the therapist's focus needs to be on patterns, not on individual or finite parts. The therapist must search for what Bateson called "the pattern which connects" (1972).

## Communication

All behavior is *communication*. Even silence transmits messages, and therefore, it is impossible not to communicate. Communication defines relationships because it establishes roles and rules. In ongoing relationships, communication cannot be left chronically unclear without disastrous consequences. This is important not only with regard to what the therapist observes in clients but also in what she wittingly or unwittingly communicates about herself.

For instance, it may seem old hat for the therapist to observe how close couples sit to each another. But does she also pay attention to where she herself sits with relation to each of them? By doing so, she can telegraph several messages. For example, she can indicate that she will take a balanced point of view, or that someone will be favored. She can show that she is willing to become involved in building a relationship, or that she wants to keep her distance, hiding behind her professional title and tasks. If she has a bias against men and favors women, or if she encourages men and ignores women, or if she blames parents for clients' current problems rather than holding the clients themselves responsible for their continued choices, all of this will be communicated to clients, ultimately harming clients and compromising the therapy.

### Family Rules

All relationships over time develop *rules* that determine explicitly or implicitly who can do what to whom when. This is why the first few years in any marriage can be so stormy, because people are in the process of developing a consensus for what their new rules will be. Often, however, the negotiating for these guidelines occurs covertly, embedded in such heated issues as relating to in-laws and children or how to handle conflict. These rules have a dual function. They serve as stabilizers and protectors of the equilibrium of the system because, however covertly, they stipulate the expectations that guide daily family life. The advantage of rules once they are hammered out, is that life becomes predictable and therefore safe. However, when rules become rigid, their effect can be stultifying, in that they deny the family the requisite flexibility for making normal developmental shifts. This has dual implications for the therapist. In addition to assessing for, and if necessary, helping the family rewrite its outmoded and counterproductive rules, she needs to be aware that the rules from her own family of origin form an unconscious template for how relationships "should" be. Unless she is aware of and vigilant about this, she accidentally can infringe on clients' needs out of loyalty to her own preprogrammed notion of what is right and good. For example, if in her family of origin the rule was to protect mother at all costs, she will tend toward doing that with clients. This is likely to mean either that she will protect the woman in this family, or that she will shield the clients' mothers by avoiding necessary family of origin work. Likewise, if only men in her family were to be trusted, she may unwittingly align with men and ignore women. To protect the health of her clients and of the treatment, the therapist needs to clarify her own blueprint for relationships and be vigilant about superimposing that on clients.

## Homeostasis

Both systems and the individuals within them have homeostatic mechanisms at work. It is important that the therapist learn to recognize the presence of *homeostasis* and to take it into account in order to work effectively.

*What Is Homeostasis?* All individuals and systems seek to maintain a balance. Welwood (1990), though not a systems therapist, describes that phenomenon very nicely: "Every time we repeat a habitual pattern, we wear 'grooves' in our psyche. By the time we reach old age, these grooves have become deeply etched" (p. 18). Over time, both individual and system come to experience these "grooves" as optimal for comfortable and normal functioning. To maintain this steady state, homeostatic mechanisms, such as family rules, communication patterns, and so on, reinforce the maintenance of this state.

*How Does Homeostasis Act in Families?* Once a family arrives at what it intuitively considers to be optimal functioning, it has found its preferred homeostasis. Then, the family becomes like a well-oiled machine, calibrated to operate within certain grooves, based on the rules the members have worked out. "Pathological systems are characterized by excessive rigidity, a lack of flexibility, and limited potential for change" (Simon et al., 1985, p. 186). Only so much deviation is tolerated in the system before a family's (or an individual's) homeostatic mechanisms kick in to restore its former balance, because homeostasis helps people and systems cope with the anxiety generated by change. This push-pull is the genesis of the contradictory messages that therapists pick up regarding change; it does not mean that we are on the wrong track, but occurs because of the anxiety that good feelings and new behavior can generate. Often, in fact, I predict aloud that a family's homeostatic mechanisms will engage following a good piece of work to restore its former and familiar balance. My verbal prediction is not an expression of any lack of faith; rather, it serves three very important functions. First, it lessens clients' disappointment and hopelessness if they backslide, because that now can be seen as a normal response to change. Second, it offers clients the chance to resist their own resistance to change. And third, it makes explicit that they do have choices about whether to backslide or not. Thus, both therapist and clients gain a small measure of control over the zigzag path that is the journey of change and growth.

*What Is Homeostasis in Individuals?* Obviously, the degree of flexibility in systems is greatly affected by the amount of adaptability of the individuals within that system. When individuals in those systems are strictly governed by their own set of internal rules, the amount of variance allowed before the individual's and therefore the system's homeostatic mechanisms engage will be limited. And yet, we all have our own homeostasis or defenses, to a certain extent. What prevents us from living more fully and having more enriching relationships is a set of narrow, limited notions about who we are and what is permissible. These defensive postures, originally crafted to shield us from pain, have now become dead weight, keeping us from fully engaging in life. "Since these old ways of doing things fight for dear life to maintain their hold on us, it takes intention and effort to break loose from their grip" (Welwood, 1990, p. 16).

*How Does Individual Homeostasis Interact With Systemic Homeostasis?* It takes dedication and work to break out of these patterns that constrict both systems and individuals. Whether we actualize our innate potential or allow it to remain arrested, as was discussed in Chapter 5, depends entirely on whether or not we deliberately remove obstacles to our growth. Yet, by the time we start to become aware that we have such choices, a great deal of baggage has already accumulated in our lives. So systemic homeostasis now begins to reinforce destructive individual defenses, and the seeds of our humanity become encased in harder and harder shells. To quote Welwood (1990) again, "Unless we bring our larger intelligence and awareness to bear on our defensive postures, they will harden further, freezing us into a living rigor mortis" (p. 18).

*Clinical Example.* Burt, a 50-year-old male, provides us an example of this pattern of changing and then retreating to change back. He recently disclosed how comforting exhaustion is to him, because it saves him from the confused jumble of emotions that emerges when he allows himself to be rested enough that he can have emotional responses. This means that despite his coming into therapy asking for help to feel better physically and emotionally, he is terrified of feeling better. His rigidity about maintaining homeostasis makes him highly resistant to treatment, as is apparent in his consistent pattern of arriving at least 15 minutes late to every session, even though he then vociferously acknowledges his need and desire to be there.

*Summary.* Just as individuals have their own homeostatic mechanism, relationships do as well. These are apparent when, for example, women drag men into our office because they want their partner to change, and yet when he begins to do so, those same women balk because of the commensurate need to transform themselves. This means that even when people come to our office begging that we help them change, there is a competing, usually unconscious, message that demands that we not change a thing. It is our job as therapists to help people learn to manage this tension between the forces that would have them stay the same and those that contain the seeds for change, so that people do not spend their lives half asleep, leading what Thoreau (1854/1962) called "lives of quiet desperation" (p. 1156). Management of homeostasis is one of the key skills that a therapist needs to develop to gain clinical savvy. Obviously, to manage it effectively, she needs to understand the phenomenon and be prepared to accommodate it.

## Isomorphism

*Isomorphism* concerns the tendency people have to replicate in every system of which they are a part the roles they learned in their family of origin. When those roles are benign, people are in luck.

But often the roles are less facilitative and are probably what brings people to therapy. For example, although people frequently promise themselves they will not parent in the ways that their parents did or fight the way their parents did, they often are horrified to recognize themselves doing just that. Another facet of isomorphism is that just as clients can behave isomorphically, so can therapists. The responsible therapist has studied her own family of origin sufficiently to be cognizant of the patterns she learned there so that she will not replicate with her clients the role she learned growing up or superimpose her own material onto clients' situations.

## Triangulation

In their glossary of family systems terminology, Simon et al. define *triangulation* as "The expansion of a conflict-ridden, dyadic relationship in order to include a third person (child, therapist, etc.), which results either in a 'covering up' or a 'defusing' of the conflict" (1985, p. 364).

The tendency for the therapist to triangulate or to be triangulated is strong when she works with two persons, because a three-person system easily degenerates into a triangle at points of stress in the system. And because effective therapy will generate a certain amount of distress because of the pain and anxiety involved in change, there is an ever-present risk to which the therapist must attend or she and the therapy will be undermined. The risk becomes particularly strong when there is a chance that the couple relationship will disintegrate; couples will attempt to "solve" their relationship dilemma by ignoring it and by drawing in a third person, often the therapist. The therapist may become the repository of displaced anger, and the therapy will be sabotaged unless she can help the couple direct their anger where it belongs. Or one partner may attempt to seduce or induce the therapist to be on his or her side against the other partner. The wise therapist recognizes these perils and plans interventions to accommodate them. Otherwise, the therapy becomes like an affair and both it and the marriage are obviously in jeopardy unless she can detriangulate herself.

Triangulation is a hazard when therapists of either sex work with a couple, but there is particular peril when a female therapist is sought particularly because of her ability to engage men in family change. Then the possibility that treatment will be experi-- enced as an affair is greater. Couples in a clinical population manifest dysfunctional ways of relating; that is why they seek out treatment. Further, even as they learn more functional ways of relating, because of homeostasis and anxiety about change at many points along the way they can look very dysfunctional as they struggle to learn more appropriate ways to be. Clients must rely on the skill and wisdom of the therapist to guide the treatment so as to minimize such difficulties. To do this, the therapist capitalizes on therapeutically effective forms of triangulation, as when the therapist "uses the strategy of entering into different coalitions and acting as a 'go between' in order to challenge and change the structure of the system" (Simon et al., 1985, p. 365). Thus, she can *choose* to triangulate to affect positively the course of treatment, but she constantly must be cautious about being triangulated and therefore co-opted by one or the other partner.

## Advantages of Systems Thinking

Taking a systems perspective and teaching clients to do the same has many clinical advantages for both therapists and clients.

### How a Systems Perspective Helps Therapists

Adopting a systems point of view allows for many advantages that otherwise likely would elude the clinician.

*Aids in Enlisting People to Change.* To become engaged in family change, people need to be helped to learn two assumptions that systems thinkers make as a matter of course. First, that everybody, however innocently, has a part in the creation and perpetuation of the problem. This is an outgrowth of the concept of circular causality, where there are multiple contributors to an outcome, not simply one cause. And two, the corollary that everybody can have a part in the solution. When clients come to see this, they can have great influence over the troublesome situation they brought to therapy in the first place.

Dave's plight provides an example. His wife, Barb, was referred to me by their family physician, who recognized that the relationship was contributing to her ulcers, as this symptom unequivocally can be seen as based in emotions. An individual-oriented counselor likely would have worked with her separately, focusing on her stress management skills, expecting her to change her situation in a vacuum. As a systems therapist, I chose a very different approach. One, I insisted that her husband participate in the therapy, and two, I identified factors in her relationship systems that contributed to her stress. This included assessing her marriage, her parenting, her family of origin, her business relationships, and her friendships for stress factors. In other words, I did a thorough systems analysis. This is particularly helpful for clients like this woman who have been in individual therapy before and yet have made few inroads into genuinely getting to the heart of their problems. The following dialogue occurred in the fifth session of the joint therapy. My focus at this early stage was on helping Dave remove his own barriers to intimacy so that he could learn to give Barb what she needed. My assumption was that this would greatly diminish her stress level and their conflict, both of which were sources of great distress for each.

*Dave:* She's the emotional half of the family, and I'm the other half.
*Therapist:* I guess I wonder if you're aware of the price you've paid for only doing and being half.
*Dave:* Most of my relationships are at arm's length. I used to think nothing, that there was no price I paid. But now I see that it's hard on Barb because I always funnel everything through her. We're talking about having a close relationship, and that doesn't exist. I either internalize everything, or funnel it all through Barb.
*Therapist:* And what's the price you both pay for that?
*Dave:* Her stomach problems. My headaches. Pain in my back. Increased stress on both of us. Stupid fights. Being unable to give her what she needs.
*Therapist:* How does it make you feel that you can't give to her?
*Dave:* Lousy!
*Therapist:* Can you find some feeling words for lousy?
*Dave:* Uh (long pause), I feel sad that I can't fill that void that she has. And I feel inadequate. Even knowing before that this void existed, I've been unable to change.
*Therapist:* Then how does that make you feel?
*Dave:* Like a failure!
*Therapist:* Do you know what you're feeling right now?
*Dave:* (Sighs) I feel like a bad person that I don't know how to deal with these issues. I just don't know how to do this. But if we knew what

all the answers were, we wouldn't be here. And I don't even know what the questions are!

*Therapist:* And that must be hard for you, too, because as a male, you're supposed to know how to fix everything.

*Dave:* Exactly! And I don't. And that hurts.

In addition to enlisting all relevant family members to do their part to change the dysfunctional pattern that precipitates the symptoms, it takes the onus off the symptom bearer to do all the changing.

*Aids in Diminishing Clients' Natural Tendency to Blame Self.* People tend to do two kinds of blaming, both of which are counterproductive to problem solving and developing intimacy: blaming self and blaming others. People who blame themselves for their problems are caught in an endless feedback loop of self-recrimination and failure that results in constant assaults on their self-esteem. Clearly, this is counterproductive, and we as therapists must intervene when we see clients engaging in this very destructive behavior. Likewise, people who hold themselves harmless and only castigate their partner are just as stuck. They must wait helplessly for the other to be insightful, motivated, and beneficent enough to change what in reality is their mutual plight. Murray provides an example of how crippling self-recrimination can be. A 50-year-old real estate tycoon successful until recession hit, he now is faced with a tottering empire. Although intellectually he knows that changes in the law and the economic picture have had a profound impact on his industry as a whole, he still relentlessly blames himself. This leads to depression, which leads to diminished functioning, which leads to depression. Caught in that endless cycle, his physician finally persuaded him to try psychotherapy again. The following exchange occurred approximately 2 months after he began therapy. The reader will note the evidence that his gender socialization for success that is also part of what cripples him.

*Therapist:* Listening to you, I hear that you have a terrible double standard. You judge other people on who they are as humans. But you judge yourself on bottom lines and balance sheets.

*Murray:* I probably do. You're probably right. I judge myself by these external standards.

*Therapist:* Why do you think you do that? You give your kids permission to be who they are, and all kinds of credibility when they experiment. But you don't give yourself that same benefit.

*Murray:* I suppose. I see myself kind of like Swiss cheese, full of holes. And I don't know what to fill them with.

*Therapist:* What are your holes?

*Murray:* All through school, I got crummy grades. I didn't feel like I measured up to what my dad or my mother or my uncle thought were successful. And I don't have anything to make up those deficiencies. Whatever I do, it's just not enough.

*Therapist:* And it never will be enough until you can move from your head down into your feelings. Because when you start feeling, you will start filling in the holes. That's why it's so important for you to start feeling.

*Murray:* But I don't like to see my holes. When I see them, I want to run away from them.

*Therapist:* And as long as you do that, you'll never fill the holes.

*Murray:* Maybe. But I don't want to think about it. I just put those thoughts out of my head.

*Therapist*: So you stay alienated from yourself. No wonder you feel lonely!

*Murray:* But how can I think about that? I'd rather bite a plugged-in electrical cord than do that!

It is apparent from Murray's resistance that he has a long way to go before he can truly come to accept himself. It is also clear that he must go the distance. The route to helping him for the therapist is to be Johnny One-Note, that is, to persist in the theme that he must make friends with himself and feel his feelings of sadness and self-loathing. Only then can he find the self-acceptance that will give him relief from the agony that his depression rheostats down to a dull roar.

*Helps Teach Clients to Minimize the Habit of Blaming Others.* As I have stated, when people blame the others in their lives for their problems, they give away all opportunity to influence the situation in a more positive direction. Unwittingly, they leave themselves in a situation where they only can sit and wait for the other to solve the problem that is in reality a shared one. In addition to this being an invitation for much frustration for all involved, blame also becomes a homeostatic mechanism that militates against the finding of a successful solution. According to Meth and Pasick (1990), "Sometimes it is easier to complain about what we do not have than [to] adjust our own behavior to help foster the desired results" (p. 188).

The words of 38-year-old Tara illustrate the conundrum that she unwittingly created for herself. For years, she begged her husband to change, blaming him for their problems, waiting helplessly for him to change. This impotence understandably fueled her increasing anger, which had infused the marriage with so much toxicity that the well of feeling between them had become poisoned. Here we see her begin to realize how she, too, has blocked their communication and given away her ability to influence the situation by her own defensive actions and reactions.

*Tara:* (With profuse tears) If I shared my loneliness and it took him back to his, I couldn't handle it.

*Therapist:* Because?

*Tara:* Because I want him to do that, but something in me says that I want him to be strong, too. So there's this push-pull within me. And it's really hard.

*Therapist:* I'm sure it is.

*Tara:* But I guess I can see now what you've been saying (pause), that I get in the way of his working on his stuff. Earlier in the week when he was sharing more, it was great. But then I started having trouble with that.

*Therapist:* So inadvertently you shut him down.

*Tara:* I guess I did. I never realized that. Seems like I'll have to do some new things. (Pause) I guess I have been doing new things. (Pause) But I guess I've been doing more new things with others, and I need to be doing new things with myself.

*Therapist:* You've realized a massive piece today. Good work!

Meth and Pasick (1990) endorse a statement by Rubin that I, too, ratify: "Male avoidance of closeness can save women from facing their own difficulties with closeness" (p. 204). The previous excerpt illustrates Tara's dawning realization of the degree to which she inadvertently and unconsciously has obstructed her getting what she wants and needs from her husband. The extent to which she realizes that she has worked at cross-purposes with herself and why she does so is the measure of influence on her previously intractable situation that she will recover. Each person in a relationship working on his or her own part in the problem will give all a greater sense of control over their own life.

### How a Systems Perspective Helps Clients

Just as a systems perspective can facilitate our job, it also can make life in general and relationships in specific more functional for clients. The first benefit of this perspective helps therapist and clients alike: It mobilizes hope and minimizes isolation. And perhaps the primary benefit accruing to couples from this perspective is minimizing conflict between people and maximizing communication. Researchers have established that communication is a significant variable making for long and happy relationships (Marano, 1992). Additionally, a systems perspective helps people to feel empowered along three dimensions that are relevant to this discussion. First, clients feel more empowered within themselves, so that taking corrective action in their lives is more conceivable. Second, they feel more clear and potent in their intimate relationships. And third, they are helped to seek emotionally corrective experiences within the context of their families of origin. Each of these benefits will be elaborated below.

*Mobilizes Hope and Minimizes Isolation.* The belief and the experience that nobody can or will understand are truly crippling, contributing to a bone-grinding sense of isolation and loneliness, with despair the result. Because this is an experience that is universally terrifying, people will go to great lengths to avoid the ordeal of facing themselves. This is especially true when they believe that they will have to face their internal abyss alone, as they have done their whole lives. The therapist's job then is to mobilize hope so that clients survive this ultimate existential encounter and move on to a more full life that is not overshadowed by terror and avoidance. She does this by offering to be there with them as they confront themselves and the totality of their feelings, usually for the first time.

Forty-year-old Don, from whom we heard early in the book, presented for therapy when he began to realize that the isolation in which he had placed himself for self-protection was becoming intolerable. These words, spoken 5 months after beginning therapy, illustrate his nascent understanding of the adaptation he felt he must make in order to survive his mother's intrusiveness and the emotional aridity of his family of origin. They also depict the slow and gradual dawning of his realization that a major element in his life has been missing.

*Don:* My ideal was to never need anyone. I was going to live in the woods alone. My heroes were always those who never needed anyone. Yet, at the same time, I desperately wanted to count on someone or have someone to take care of me. And yet, I wouldn't ask. My ideal was that people were going to come to me because they wanted to be with me. But no one ever did.

*Therapist:* And so your protection of yourself never worked, did it?

*Don:* No. Because that scenario was incompatible: wanting desperately to be taken care of, and yet wanting to be alone.

Later in the session:

*Don:* So much of my emotional life is vicarious. It's so much more real through movies and stuff. It's been kind of shocking to realize that. And it's depressing, too. It was all there. I had to feel those feelings somehow; I had to have an outlet. So I went to books and movies for that.

*Therapist:* So now Don has to learn how to feel for Don, and not some character in a book or movie.

*Don:* (With tears in his eyes) Yes! I think it's true that I'm feeling more now. I'm kinda peeling things away that have stopped my feelings. But it's hard now, because there is a lot of yucky stuff under there. And I don't want to look at it.

*Therapist:* I understand. But you can do it. And I'm going to be there with you.

This excerpt illustrates the powerful synergistic effect of a male's socialization to be strong and not need anyone with a family of origin that reinforced those messages by its extremes of both disengagement and emotional void, and intrusiveness that bordered on incest. These conspired to shape a man who was exceedingly and rigidly out of touch with his feelings, with himself, and with others when he began therapy. The first several months were aimed at simply helping him to attach to the therapist so that he could learn to connect with others. Slowly and gradually, he began to do so, and an ability to relate to others followed.

*Minimizes Conflict and Maximizes Communication.* It is no surprise to most of us when couples explain what brought them into treatment is inability to communicate. And couples who cannot communicate are handicapped in adequately solving their problems. And yet, what relationship is without its problems? Therefore, helping couples communicate adequately so that they can solve their problems and experience pleasure in the relationship is always an implicit goal, regardless of the treatment orientation of the therapist or of the specific manifestation of the couple's problems.

How does a family systems orientation help clients communicate? Because of the belief in circular causality, where everyone is a part of the problem and therefore can and should become part of the solution, the tendency to blame one's partner for all problems is minimized, as has been previously stated. When people stop blaming and start communicating, this yields understanding and in turn promotes an increased ability to solve mutual problems, thus creating a positive spiral.

A clinical example of a couple, both 35 years old, illustrates this experience. Barry is a dentist; Tamara cares full time for their two children, although she is a registered nurse. They presented for treatment 4 months prior to the session in which this conversation took place, when Tamara was at her wits' end, stating that she was planning to take the children and move out West. The first several sessions predictably were heated, as Tamara spewed forth her pent-up anger and Barry, mystified yet stoic, sat and listened. Immediately, I began the slow, gradual process of helping them to identify each one's part in the communication impasse that was patently obvious, and the feeling between them began to soften. Eventually, I was able to ask them to begin to take emotional risks with each other. The following excerpt illustrates the positive effects of this approach in thawing frozen communications and softening hearts.

*Barry:* You learn what you see. But I learned what I *didn't* see. I was just never taught to emote. But since my great exposure last session, Tamara has been nicer than she's ever been.
*Therapist:* What do you make of that?
*Barry:* I think she saw me as vulnerable.
*Tamara:* And then, there's a lot more to love! He was more real.
*Therapist:* (To Barry) Was there any part of that that was scary for you?
*Barry:* Oh, no.
*Therapist:* (Smiling) Oh.

*Barry:* Yeah, right. You don't believe me! OK. (Pause) It was scary, because then I might have to reciprocate. And who cares if Barry has emotion? Who cares! It goes back to my self-worth, I guess.
*Therapist:* That sounds sad.
*Barry:* Yeah. I guess it is. There have been times in my life where I just haven't bothered to share, because I just wasn't sure I was worth the bother to people. This is all related to whether or not I'm willing to share with people.
*Tamara:* It sure is easier to share with you when you're a real person, not a brick.

As the excerpt above illustrates, a systems perspective neutralizes the tendency to blame and instead helps people take responsibility for themselves and their behavior. This goes a long way toward helping people attain a new quality of communication and greater depth of intimacy than they previously were capable of, or in most cases, thought was possible.

*Helps Clients Feel Empowered Within Themselves.* Whatever the therapist's orientation, it is her job to help clients mobilize their resources and change their lives, in addition to the explicit and specific requests clients make of us. This is a place where we can capitalize on our socialization as women. Whereas men are socialized to tell, women are socialized to support. Men order people to become; women encourage and nurture people's becoming. A female therapist, then, can quite naturally provide the environment for her clients to *become* different—not just learn different behaviors. When we can help clients change, our mission has been accomplished and they are ready to terminate treatment. And a systems perspective is particularly conducive to this because of the multiple factors discussed in this chapter.

An important distinction needs to be made explicit here. Helping clients take responsibility for their own lives and happiness is *not* the same as blaming them for their predicaments. In fact, both in word and in concept, "blame" needs to be expunged from language and thought. It only demotivates action and assaults self-esteem. This means that both therapist and client are to be discouraged from thinking or speaking in terms of blame. Instead, the therapeutic task is to (a) intervene when we hear people blaming self or others, and (b) help people see the areas in which they could change their situations by taking responsibility for themselves. This is a natural outgrowth of systems thinking, because of its emphasis on circular rather than linear causality.

When clients can learn to redirect the natural human tendency to blame others for their plight, they can take hold of their own life. They can see that it is truly their responsibility to get themselves happy. The following excerpt illustrates this process of realization for 29-year-old always single Sandy. It illuminates how she has chosen inappropriate men in the past and then automatically blamed the failure of the relationship on the man, without assuming any responsibility for the outcome. The oldest child in a family with seven children and two highly perfectionist parents, she had learned to keep everyone at a distance. Thus, the flaws she knew she had would never be detected, keeping her safe and acceptable to her parents. What she did not know was that she was following their recipe for loneliness and isolation.

*Sandy:* Last time, you used the metaphor of detonating land mines. I've been thinking about that, and I can see that there are a lot of my land mines that we've detonated. But so much in me really has changed, that when I look at it, it can be really uncomfortable.

*Therapist:* Like what?

*Sandy:* For example, I've begun to realize that probably the only man I've ever met who was capable of intimacy, I pushed away. I said, "Oh no! I can't have that! But we can go to movies together." (With profuse tears) He was the only man I had met who was kind and gentle and capable of intimacy, and I pushed him away.

*Therapist:* What are your tears?

*Sandy:* It hurts!

*Therapist:* I'm sure it does hurt to be realizing how you have hurt yourself over the years. But the good news is that now that you're figuring this out, you can learn to do something different.

*Sandy:* It hurts to realize that I always made the choice to keep disconnected from people. I can see now that the situation I've put myself in was never to choose to be with anybody. How could I have lived so long without living? No wonder it's been so sad!

*Therapist:* Exactly.

*Sandy:* But it's the pattern I've been taught. And so for years, that's exactly what I've done. I've cut people off before they could even get connected. That's what I've done! I've cut them off before they even *want* to get connected. It's not normal to do it any other way for me! This has been a lonely, scary place for me to be. Man, this hurts! This is the existential loneliness of starting to figure out who you are and what you've done.

*Therapist:* Yes, it is. You've unknowingly put yourself in a Catch-22. When you've pushed away the people who could be good for you and who would be with you, you have relegated yourself to only being with people who are not good for you so you'd be alone.

*Sandy:* I see that now. Wow! I feel better already! I've been smoking too much and walking around with a knot in my neck for 2 weeks. But I feel better already! This is great!

Although discovering what she had been doing clearly was painful, it was also empowering. Now she could begin deliberately to monitor what she otherwise would do reflexively and start to make other choices. To have remained unaware, she would have continued to render herself powerless to influence her situation. And she would have continued to project blame for her state onto cold, emotionally unavailable men whom she inevitably would choose.

The ultimate goal of therapy is to empower people to empower themselves. When clients begin to see their own unwitting complicity in their misery, it is usually a painful realization. And yet, no true change can happen—regardless of how much they may want a better life on a conscious level—until they can see the ways they have sabotaged themselves. Then and only then can they get out of their own way and get themselves happy.

Self-validation and assuming responsibility for self are both the process and the outcome of effective therapy for all, regardless of gender.

*Helps Clients Empower Selves in Intimate Relationships.* When people comprehend and accept responsibility for their actions, the counterproductive cycle of blame and stuckness and then blame for the stuckness can end. This frees people from the endless snare of rebukes, retribution, and remorse. Thus, they are able to achieve an outlook that allows them to take a metaperspective on an otherwise hopeless, entangling situation. This enables them to size up the truth of their plight and make some conscious choices that would improve their situation one way or the other. Sometimes from this metalevel, they can see multiple avenues for improving their dilemma that they never knew existed. Sadly, other times, they can finally see that the only salvation for both parties is to end the relationship. However, from this vantage point, they will get clarity about the relationship, once and for all. No longer will they have to languish in the purgatory of a terminally unhealthy relationship.

Peter is a 63-year-old executive who had committed what he called business suicide multiple times by getting himself fired just when he started to succeed. He reluctantly began marital therapy again when I stated that I would not see his wife without him. Already hopeless and worn out after 42 years of unsuccessful trying in the marriage, both in and out of therapy, he had long since given up on his life getting any better. Because his wife had been referred by their physician, whom they both respected, when Peter refused to come in for at least an initial session, I called the doctor to request his support in getting Peter to come in. Fortunately, Peter had a doctor's appointment scheduled within the week, because not only were his ulcers acting up and his back was locked in pain, now he was experiencing heart palpitations that were scaring him. With his doctor's endorsement and encouragement, he finally reluctantly agree to come in for a session. Just one session, he reminded me.

Peter's depressive affect and closedness were starkly apparent that first session as he sat huddled by the wall and began to intone how he had known since a month after his marriage that he had made a horrible mistake in marrying his wife. Primarily because he was steeped in a religious tradition that forbade divorce, he felt that he was consigned to stick it out dutifully. Four children and 42 years later, his depression and physical symptoms had become so compelling that he could no longer ignore them. However, prior to beginning therapy, he could think of no recourse but continuing cycles of blaming himself and her, and giving up. And this attitude of giving up had contaminated his entire life. Because I was able to convince him in that first session that I had no preconceived notions about what he must do with or about his marriage, and because I was able to show him that I could and would help him make those decisions for himself, he was motivated to begin therapy. Finally, he could foresee a way out of the impasse that he was increasingly less able to tolerate, as illustrated by the continual worsening of his physical condition and the deepening of his depression. It was easy to diagnose the degree of the inertia that had immobilized both him and his wife, who also understandably was clinically depressed. To help them get a new perspective on their situation, I facilitated their deciding that living separately, at least for a time, would be clarifying. Then, after 7 months of a combination of couples and individual therapy for each, terrified that if he spoke extemporaneously he would lose his nerve, Peter prepared and read the following statement to his wife in what was to be their last couples session.

Susan,

Years ago, my lifelong habits of direction and control of my emotions and actions were formed by my family, by the church, and by many other outside sources I had no control over. I never knew, understood, or even dreamed that something was wrong or that I would someday experience a need to understand . . . what happened and why. . . .

Then three things happened that changed all of that: 1) my increasing depression; 2) Beth became my counselor; and 3) our separation. These have allowed me to uncover the causes of my depression, to understand what happened and why, and to see how I have been molded and controlled by others.

My whole life has been affected by the total suppression of my real emotions by myself, and these were then controlled by others.

I can now help myself to not be ashamed to express emotions outwardly—positive and negative—to control my victim personality, and look forward to the future happening, rather than despising and fearing each day.

Our separation has allowed me to focus clearly on my problems and our problems. The entire process of investigation and analysis let me focus on our relationship as it is rather than how you or I think it should be or [on how] it is perceived by others. . . .

[Now I see that] you and I have never been friends and that our major and maybe only sharing is the kids, and they are wonderful. We both share this failure of [having] no friendship equally.

Companionship was there on rare instances, but [it] usually ended in anger, alienation and negative feelings on both our parts. [It] almost never [ended] in exhilaration or joy. Again, we both share the responsibility.

Intimacy was non-existent [sic]. Neither of us knew how to share deep feelings. Even today, we only know how to be intimate about selected things with Beth present.

Sex was good. [But] all other factors were missing. And we both share the responsibility for this. It is not a one-way street.

Our marriage exists in name and outward appearance only. We have both known for a long time there is no marriage. And we both share responsibility for the causes of that.

I can no longer live in a relationship that doesn't exist. I will be seeking a divorce as soon as is practical. I am truly sorry it's over, but it must end. We must accept our joint responsibility and get on with our individual lives.

Peter

It is always painful for the therapist to preside over the death of a marriage, especially a long one, as in the case of this couple. And obviously, it is excruciating to be both bearer and receiver of these tidings. However, not to facilitate a divorce when people's individual lives clearly are falling apart is irresponsible at best and inhumane at worst. In this instance, Peter's having learned how to understand and accept responsibility for his contribution to the demise of his marriage softened the blow to them both and allowed them to leave the marriage with a much greater degree of understanding than they ever would have acquired had they stayed stuck in their endless feedback loop of shared depression, blame, and retribution.

*Helps Clients Empower Selves in Family of Origin.* Often, the most excruciating kind of pain is the feeling of being unloved and unworthy going back to childhood. Because of how they were—or perceived that they were—treated, people will behave in all manner of craziness because they experienced then and believe to be true now that they are unlovable as human beings. Needless to say, this daily compromises their functioning in subtle and not so subtle ways. Sometimes finding a partner in their current life who loves and values them is itself an emotionally corrective experience. And sometimes therapist and client together can correct this perception just by their mutual exploration of these disabling experiences. But sometimes, no amount of talking about those feelings will ameliorate their usually well-hidden anguish. Only speaking directly with the people who hurt them inaugurates a healing process.

Oliver, a thrice-married man in his middle 40s, provides us with an example. He had been abandoned by his father at the time of his parents' divorce when Oliver was 12, and the two men had not seen each other since the day the father moved out. Believing that the father's actions were a statement about his unworthiness,

Oliver had proceeded to earn the designation of unworthy. Although he had always managed to succeed in business, his personal relationships were a tangled mess. He was very adept at finding women to have sex with him, but every time they indicated any ongoing interest in him, he would flee to the next relationship. As a father himself, he was virtually absent, even though much of the time his children lived with him. When his third marriage began to falter, he gave in to my relentless suggestions that he begin to search for his father. Although he had professed no interest in hearing of his father, when he finally conceded the need to make contact, he knew exactly where he would find him. The following is an excerpt from the second half of an extended family of origin session that Oliver did with his wife and father after many months of cajoling and weeks of preparation.

*Oliver:* (To his father) I feel discomfort with you. I'm overwhelmed, and I want you to go away, because I'm sure this is going to end. It's too good to be true that you're here. All the time I was angry with you, I had you on a pedestal. I just can't believe I can have it! I'm sorry I put this off for months, no, years.

*Dad:* (In tears) You've missed part of life because of my inappropriateness.

*Oliver:* But I don't hold you responsible anymore. (Starting to sob) Dad, I'm not angry anymore. . . . It's hard to say, but I think you really did the best you knew how, and Mom even tried to undo some of that. For 30 years, I've had an image of you which dates back to when I was a boy, because of what my mother told me which I never bothered to check out. And now you come out here, and it's unreal and overwhelming. I have all these years to try to undo. I now can see that what mother said and did was the way to add security to her by turning me against my dad. . . . I'm so glad you came out here now. Everything makes a lot more sense now. I'm sorry I felt you were such a shit all these years, and for not at least giving you a chance. I'm so glad I finally decided to give you a chance.

*Dad:* So am I!

*Oliver:* Gallons of tears wash out many years of unhappiness!

*Dad:* This has brought up an awful lot of feelings for me. A helluva lot more than you can imagine! I have a lot of things to do. I should've done something else. . . . You've brought up a lot of things that have triggered feelings for me. And I've listened. You have said some things that have made me stop and think. I'm now going to get everything squared away.

*Therapist:* And now that the lines of communication are open, this is not the last moment. Rather, it's a special moment.

*Oliver:* I think you want to be different. It's overwhelming. It's all so hard
to believe. I don't remember you this way, but it's partly because of
what my mother said. I don't think my life—or our lives—will ever
be the same again!

It is certainly not Oliver's fault that his father abandoned him
when he was a child. The culpability for that lies with his parents.
And because the relationship between father and son was not all
that strong when they lived together, surely it could not tolerate the
twin nemeses of isolation and undermining by Oliver's mother.
However, what Oliver is responsible for is perpetuating the estrangement because of his defensiveness and self-protection. Once he
could be helped to assess his childhood situation and gain objectivity, he could begin to take responsibility for his own actions as
an adult. Then he could begin to see that he was accountable for
continuing to isolate himself as long as he failed to attempt to
speak with his father before he died.

It should be noted that just making contact with an estranged
relative does not guarantee a willing respondent. Indeed, sometimes people who perpetuate a cutoff have their own reasons for
cultivating it. However, as Bowen (1978) suggests, emotional cutoffs almost surely bode disastrous consequences. Conversely, identifying and rectifying the developmental logjams created by those
cutoffs usually has an enormously curative effect. And the best way
to prepare clients for that outcome is to help them identify and
prepare to remedy the ways in which they unknowingly may be
contributing to their ongoing misery in the face of these old hurts.


## How a Systems Perspective Is Essential
## in the Treatment of Men

Although my bias is that a systems perspective is preferable for
any psychotherapy, it is particularly useful in the treatment of
men. The following summarizes the factors that have been discussed throughout the chapter that detail why this perspective is
particularly efficacious with this population.

## Advantages to Therapists

1. Increases the therapist's access to clients' core issues because it does not engage their defenses.
2. Helps her mobilize people to change themselves and their situations.
3. Helps her activate family members to change, because they are not so fearful of being blamed for the dysfunction of the identified patient.
4. Helps her understand client resistance when it happens and plan interventions accordingly.
5. Helps minimize her natural tendency to blame one person and side with the other.
6. Helps monitor her own impact on and influence in the system, because it acknowledges that she, too, is a part of the therapy system.
7. Gives her leverage to interrupt clients' tendency to blame self and others for their plight.
8. Helps foster and then amplify the multiple ripple effects of change because it increases client cooperation with this nonadversarial process and enhances their motivation to change.

## Advantages to Men and to Others in Their Intimate Networks

1. Ends the counterproductive cycle of blame of self and others and helps people learn to take responsibility for their actions, wants, and needs.
2. Gives clients hope that they can affect their situations.
3. Helps people empower themselves to change their lives and their situations, because they are not consigned to wait for someone else to change before they can.
4. By redirecting people's natural tendency to project blame on others for their difficulties, helps clients take hold of their own lives because they truly can see that it is their responsibility to get themselves happy.
5. Helps neutralize the negative tone and feel of conflictual relationships because of ending the cycle of shame and blame.
6. Helps clients break anachronistic family of origin patterns of relating that are perpetuated unknowingly and that beget dysfunction.
7. Increases clients' acceptance of self and others.

## A Caveat

By the perspective I advance in this chapter, I do not mean to suggest that by sheer dint of will, people can accomplish anything they dream of doing. Sometimes there are truly factors outside people's control. And not to make that clear can seem to imply blame on those individuals for their difficult circumstances. For example, single people both male and female cannot simply make eligible and appropriate partners materialize out of thin air. However, those people can learn to understand their own part in not finding a satisfying relationship, in the event that a block of their own unknowingly impedes them. Furthermore, in the absence of a significant relationship, they can learn multiple avenues to a satisfying single life. The therapist must be careful not to assess blame for situations or to allow clients to do this, but she must also beware of this perspective being misused to blame the victim of unfortunate circumstances.

## A Final Word

In this chapter, we have discussed the basic elements of systems thinking and the clinical advantages to both clients and therapist when treatment is conducted from this philosophical stance. Then we applied these theoretical advantages specifically to psychotherapy with men. This approach promotes greater growth and change not only for men, but also for the significant people in their lives.

## References

Bateson, G. (1972). *Steps toward an ecology of the mind.* New York: Ballantine.

Bowen, M. (1978). *Family therapy in clinical practice.* New York: Jason Aronson.

Kelly, K., & Hall, A. (1992). Toward a developmental model of counseling men. *Journal of Mental Health Counseling, 14*(3), 257-273.

Kramer, C. (1980). *Becoming a family therapist: Developing an integrated approach to working with families.* New York: Human Sciences Press.

Marano, H. (1992). The reinvention of marriage. *Psychology Today, 25*(1), 48-53, 85.

McGoldrick, M., Pearce, J., & Giordano, J. (1982). *Ethnicity and family therapy.* New York: Guilford.

Meth, R. (1992, April). *Understanding the male experience.* Symposium conducted for Family Resources Institute, Edina, MN.

Meth, R., & Pasick, R. (1990). *Men in therapy: The challenge of change.* New York: Guilford.

Moore, R., & Gillette, D. (1990). *King, warrior, magician, lover: Rediscovering the archetypes of the mature masculine.* San Francisco: HarperSan Francisco.

Nichols, W., & Everett, C. (1986). *Systemic family therapy: An integrative approach.* New York: Guilford.

Pinsof, W. (1983). Integrative problem-centered therapy: Toward the synthesis of family and individual psychotherapies. *Journal of Marital and Family Therapy, 9*(1), 19-34.

Simon, F., Stierlin, H., & Wynne, L. (1985). *The language of family therapy: A systemic vocabulary and sourcebook.* New York: Family Process Press.

Tannen, D. (1990). *You just don't understand: Women and men in conversation.* New York: William Morrow.

Thoreau, H. (1962). Walden. In S. Bradley, R. Beatty, & E. Long (Eds.), *The American tradition in literature* (pp. 1152-1206). New York: Norton. (Original work published in 1854).

Walsh, F. (1982). Conceptualizations of normal family functioning. In *Normal family processes* (pp. 3-42). New York: Guilford.

Weiner-Davis, M. (1992). *Divorce-busting: A revolutionary and rapid program for staying together.* New York: Summit.

Welwood, J. (1990). *Journey of the heart: Intimate relationships and the path of love.* New York: HarperPerennial.

# Unresolved Loss: A Barrier to Intimacy

It is my firm conviction that loss is at the heart of much of what brings people into psychotherapists' and even into physicians' offices, whether the professionals or clients know or acknowledge it. Traumatic and life changing at the same time, loss has unique capabilities of arresting psychological development, thereby generating dysfunction of all kinds, both psychological and physical. This is because loss involves often severe reactions of both physiological and psychological systems.

## Loss and Men

Loss is difficult for all people, especially when it is unknown and unaddressed, but for men grief and bereavement have extra impact. This is in part due to their socialization against expression of emotions of any kind except anger. And it is also due to the centrality of grief in unlocking men's emotional lives. For as Robert Bly, the patriarch and poet laureate of the men's movement states, "Grief . . . is the doorway to a man's feelings. But men don't know what they are grieving about" (1989). Keen (1991) puts it another way when he says, "Men have much to mourn before they can be reborn" (p. 136). It is in the area of loss that men's socialization about emotions can become particularly insidious. This is because the adequate expression of feelings that accompanies a loss is a prime prerequisite for moving through a bereavement experience and emerging healed and whole, with a new definition of self that incorporates the loss and the meaning of the loss for the individual.

This chapter is about helping men to open doors they have closed long ago. These doors have protected them from emotionally knowing and feeling the losses they experienced in life. Peter, quoted in the previous chapter, capsulized his newfound realizations regarding his wholly ineffectual way of trying to cope with his unresolved losses when he said,

*Peter:* I've been the wall trying to climb myself, and I couldn't do it.

It is readily apparent from this succinct description that denial had become his primary way of coping with loss, and eventually, with everything.

Although savvy therapists readily may see men's emotional constriction, many clinicians are reluctant to acknowledge the centrality of loss in generating this condition, because this could mean reckoning with the impact of losses in their own life. Added to this is the reluctance of most clients themselves to adopt this perspective, even at the cost of staying dysfunctional. Why? Because to open those doors that people have long ago sealed shut is to reexperience—or for many, to actually experience for the first time—the pain that accompanied the loss. And yet, if they do not, they are likely to remain emotionally atrophied for the rest of their life, and the therapy that clients have a right to expect will be less effectual at best or impeded at worst.

## Loss and Intimacy

Loss in the acute phase, such as recent divorce or dismemberment, itself can jeopardize men's subsequent ability to be intimate, depending on how they, their intimate others, and even their therapists respond to the event. But even more disastrous is chronic and unresolved loss, such as accompanies childhood abuse or abandonment. This plagues current relationships because to keep such painful experiences outside their awareness, people must build up layer on layer of defenses. To add another complication, this whole process is usually done totally outside people's awareness. In actuality, clients cannot do otherwise, even though this way of coping serves only to make the situation worse.

## Loss, Intimacy, and Men

Time and again, I have worked with men who are struggling to experience genuine intimacy. This struggle is formidable even without unresolved losses to complicate matters. And with their socialization making it already a significant struggle to express emotions, individuals' responses to unresolved losses can become calcified into a pattern characterized by avoidance of intimacy as a means of self-protection. Although men are defending themselves from their own internal experience, they end up defending themselves from everyone else as well. This means that their willingness to risk trusting and being vulnerable—staples in any intimate relationship—are compromised. Mark, a client in his late 30s, described the dilemma about relating he had created for himself in this way:

*Mark:* My trademark has always been to reduce my window of vulnerability by minimizing the risks I took. I want to do it differently now, but I don't know how. And it's so hard to learn!

An unfortunate and unexpected outcome happens when people avoid losses in the belief that they can prevent more hurt. These defenses also cause them inherently to avoid intimacy. Thus, the relationships that men who are in these situations seek and form will be imperiled in ways that are totally outside the awareness of most couples, and alas, even of many therapists. And thus, couples are hurt anyway, by the dysfunction that is generated and all too often ends in divorce.

## Chapter Overview

Ironically, the only hope people have to free themselves from the grips of unresolved loss is to allow that painful material to reemerge into their consciousness so that it can be resolved, once and for all. Easier said than done, you say? Of course. But it is necessary. Clarifying the need for it, the process for doing it, and the role of the therapist in facilitating it is the focus of this chapter. Specifically, I will discuss the diagnostic considerations in discerning whether loss is a part of the presenting problem for clients. Next, I will discuss family of origin factors such as rules, precedents set by unresolved losses in previous generations, and ethnicity that further can complicate the resolution of loss. Then I will move on to discuss the relatively recent but epidemic phenomenon of the disappearing father and the resulting father hunger. Three specific aspects of father absence will be considered: (a) in the wake of divorce, (b) after a father's death, and (c) as experienced with traditional fathers. Next, the impact on the treatment of the therapist's own experience with loss will be discussed. Rounding out the chapter will be some guidelines for readers to use in identifying unresolved loss in clients and for dealing effectively with their own countertransference reactions to loss.

## Three Diagnostic Considerations

In diagnosing the multiple effects of loss, there are three levels of scrutiny the therapist must conduct simultaneously.

### 1. Is Loss Part of the Presenting Issue?

People rarely present for therapy stating that they are having trouble resolving a loss, particularly an old loss. If they have spent years denying the reality of a loss or ignoring its multiple impacts, they likely will abhor our uncovering it. And yet, if loss is a latent part of the dysfunction and it is never diagnosed, obviously it will not be treated. And then the dysfunction it creates will continue, often into subsequent generations.

If the therapist senses that there is a loss, she must discern if it is a discrete instance or a series of happenings that the client experienced as a loss. For example, in a divorce, people experience more than just the noncustodial parent's absence; there is the loss of day-to-day contact, even when the absent parent stays actively involved. And many children of divorce are not so fortunate. In one survey, the finding was that only 20% of the children of divorce saw their father once a week or more (Osherson, 1986). And even if a child is one of that lucky 20%, he or she loses much more than just daily contact with the noncustodial parent, but at the very least, the family as it was. Additional losses are idiosyncratic to each individual's situation and need to be named, explored, and grieved over.

*Case Example.* It should be noted that what an individual experiences as a loss is a loss, whether or not others see it that way. For example, at a recent presentation I made in another city on loss, a woman from the audience talked about the death of a favorite cat that occurred when the woman was a child. When she had attempted to discuss her pain about this, her mother did not even remember the cat's existence. The woman reported having seen this as a statement about the attention her mother paid to her needs in general, as well as to this trauma. Thus, in that one event, she experienced two losses: her beloved pet, and being left alone by her mother to deal with it.

One further note: I do not assume that there has to be an unresolved loss in the client's history. But I do not rule it out until I have thoroughly checked for the presence of one. Given that grief is the doorway to a man's feelings, and that he is socialized against emotions that would allow him to grieve adequately, I check especially carefully with men.

## 2. How Has Loss Affected Clients' Ability to Be Intimate?

Unresolved loss jeopardizes intimate relationships of men in two primary ways. As I have said, it tends to restrict individuals who usually already are emotionally constricted. And two, loss has a heavy influence, however unconscious, on marital choice. People who are chronically grieving typically pick individuals to marry who will perpetuate the emotional distance they have kept from themselves. And yet, as we have seen, this same protection becomes highly toxic to intimate relationships. Such couples arrive in therapists' offices seeking help to mend fractured relationships, largely unaware of the roots of the dysfunction. If the therapist herself is equally unaware, the dysfunction is perpetuated, even if it takes a different, apparently more benign form after treatment.

*Case Example.* Only once has a couple presented for treatment identifying that loss might be related to their current problem, which was sexual dysfunction. The couple, both in their late 30s, had struggled with all forms of intimacy their entire relationship. However, the most conflictual and painful area of contention for them was their sexual relationship.

In the intake session, after they laid out the problem as both saw it, the wife, a therapist herself, wondered aloud whether their trouble with intimacy may have something to do with her inability to come to terms with her father's death 20 years earlier. And then, as soon as she tentatively advanced her hypothesis, she retracted it herself, reassuring all three of us that surely this had nothing to do with their struggles with intimacy. She eventually did work with and resolve the loss, but even when people think they see a connection, it can take a long time for them fully to acknowledge it.

## 3. How Emotionally Distant Was the Man From His Father?

The third diagnostic consideration that relates specifically to men concerns assessing for father loss, an experience that most men have had whether their father lived with them or not. The loss of fathers through death or divorce are obvious losses, and the impact of these will be discussed in depth later in the chapter. But the losses that come from a traditional father who still lives in the home are more subtle, and in some ways, more insidious. Because of the significance of each of these for men's development, they will be discussed in more depth below.

If a man has experienced a great deal of emotional distance in his relationship with his father, that is a loss. Thus, even if his father is alive and well, he may have a relationship he needs to grieve over. "It is important to remember that we are dealing with a transitional generation of men who have typically lacked models for an active father role" (Gordon, 1990, p. 254). It is this fact that allows me to hypothesize that there likely is a father loss for men, and I rule it out only when I find no shred of evidence to support my belief.

This has significant ramifications for treatment as well. "With all men, regardless of whether or not they are fathers, the crucial psychodynamic significance of their relationship with their own father should always be a major dimension of the therapeutic exploration" (Feldman, 1990, p. 104). Feldman advances a hypothesis to which I heartily subscribe: Identifying and treating father loss is essential for adequate therapy with men.

*Case Example.* Scott was an extremely sensitive, although at times emotionally volatile, chief executive officer of a small company. His 15-year-old daughter's acting out was the initial reason for seeking treatment 5 years prior to the experience with his father that I will describe below. When that presenting problem was resolved, but with Scott's father loss readily apparent to me, I could have agreed to termination with the family. Instead, I dismissed the children and suggested that in order truly to inoculate the family against problems occurring in another place in the family, Scott needed to deal directly with the father loss that his explosive temper and mercurial moods indicated to me. Scott's response was to reject my suggestion out of hand and abruptly terminate the therapy. Then, about 4 years later, I got a call from a rather sheepish Scott requesting to resume therapy, this time around his older son's depression and inability to get a direction for his life. I agreed, had the family come back into treatment, and once again suggested that Scott's unresolved father loss was affecting him and the family. Once again, Scott refused to accept my suggestion and withdrew from treatment, after I had worked around the issue, trying to lay tracks to get to it as best I could. Then, about 5 months later, his wife called for therapy, saying that if Scott did nothing about his explosive temper, she wanted a divorce. That got Scott's attention.

In the session after that call, I met with the couple, and Scott's wife laid it on he line: either he deal with his feelings about his father and find more appropriate ways to manage his emotions, or he would find himself divorced for his 50th birthday present. After stalling on deciding for almost a month, he finally called for an appointment and began a relatively brief (3-month) course of treatment. This was capped by an impromptu conversation he had with his 81-year-old father at 11:00 at night, catalyzed by Scott's spending an evening of finally facing his father loss and sobbing about it, triggered by the homework I gave him to rent and watch a videotape of *Field of Dreams*. It is worthy of note that Scott previously had seen this movie in a theater full of crying men and came out amazed about others' strong reactions to a movie that was just about baseball.

In his late-night conversation with his father, Scott for the first time told his father how much he loved and needed him. Prior to this conversation, he was literally unable to contemplate his father's death without disintegrating into deep sobs because, he came to believe, his father's death meant that he, too, would die, because his truncated relationship with his father was a major factor that jeopardized his separation and individuation processes. He describes in his termination session the impact on him of that longed-for, delicious conversation with his father.

*Scott:* I joined the club of men.
*Therapist:* The club of men?
*Scott:* Yes. The club of men who understand now, who had not had relationships with their fathers before, the club of men who long for a relationship with their fathers. I was very fortunate. I could still go back to my dad and get what I needed. And I gave him something, too.
*Therapist:* My suspicion is that you won't need to be so panicky about losing your father now, because you have a relationship with him now.
*Scott:* Yes. I used to think that if he were to die, I couldn't go on living, because we weren't separate. He was me. Now I'll be sad. And I'll miss him terribly. But I'll be all right. I cried real hard on my dad's shoulder and told him how much I needed him. I may have grown myself up as a kid, but you grew me up as an adult.

Although the hoped-for outcome of therapy may be reconnection of men with their fathers in new, and more supportive ways, it should be noted that not all clients experience the resounding success that Scott's example above provides. "It is not always possible for a man to establish constructive contact with his father, but valuable learning takes place in coming to terms with this reality" (Gordon, 1990, p. 246). Sometimes this means helping men face some very painful realities. However, it does not mean that our task is to help men bury fathers who are still alive; that would generate an emotional cutoff and have very deleterious effects. Rather, we need to help them "free themselves from the emotional residue of the dysfunction in their relationships with their fathers—the anger, guilt, sadness, etc." (Gordon, 1990, pp. 238-239).

## Family of Origin Factors

In this section, I will discuss three notable family of origin factors that can complicate a man's already difficult task with grieving: family rules, precedents set by unresolved losses in previous generations, and ethnicity. Each of these can have a significant impact on how clients grieve and indeed on whether they grieve.

### Family Rules

All families have rules. As discussed in the previous chapter, this concept is one of those basic to systemic thinking. Rules govern day-to-day life in a family and thereby help to protect its integrity and stability by maintaining its preferred homeostasis. However, when families adhere to rules that are too restricting, a great deal of rigidity can result. This is particularly problematic with rules that govern the expression of affect. In this case, to adapt and fit into the family, people are covertly expected to give up who they are in the service of the family. And then when a loss comes along, they are all the more hamstrung in effectively grieving and coping.

A key in understanding the effects of family rules on individuals is that the rules only rarely actually are verbalized. Yet, conformance to them is silently decreed. I often tell clients that many people would have been better off if their family had posted the rules on the refrigerator for all to see, but none does. Unfortunately, often the only way people know the rules is when they break them. Then the sanctions are swift and can be severe. Just how severe the consequences, I take as a marker of the rigidity and precariousness of living in a given family.

*Case Example.* Jeremy provides an example of this. The youngest of three children, his mother died when he was 5 years old of an excruciatingly painful case of cancer. His father, a mental health professional whose personal style of functioning emphasized cognition and competence, took care of Jeremy's instrumental needs but left him and his siblings on their own for everything else. Knowing of my emphasis on grief and loss, Jeremy, also a mental health professional, sought me out for therapy. However, just because he could identify that loss was at the source of his dysfunction did not mean that he could deal with it at the drop of a hat. The process of preparing people to face their losses is the bulk of the work; actually dealing with it and resolving it is relatively simple by comparison.

One day, after struggling for untolled sessions trying to help Jeremy approach any of his emotions about any facet of his childhood, it occurred to me that doing so would probably be breaking some family rules. That would account for both his difficulty in finding his feelings and in appropriately resolving them. So together we made the following list of his family of origin rules. The reader is encouraged to read this list with loss as a backdrop, keeping in mind their extra restrictiveness when it comes to facing a trauma.

1. It is not OK to express strong emotions, or to express emotions strongly.
2. Competency should be the way of life.
3. You've got to be competent.
4. You've got to achieve.
5. Put someone else's needs first.
6. Only put someone else's needs in front of your needs when you think they're worthwhile people or you value them.
7. Give conditionally.
8. If you have a medical pain or problem, it's cause for alarm.
9. Emotional pain is cause for concern, but the concern will be expressed aloofly and intellectually.
10. Problems and concerns are to be met with a problem-solving, intellectual approach.
11. Subtle forms of elation and happiness are pretty good, but loud elation and screams are not.
12. Don't be extreme or overt. Restrict your range [of responses].
13. Be strong and independent.

Growing up in a family whose rules so tightly govern the expression of affect would be difficult for anyone regardless of the circumstances of his or her life. Add to that a male's gender socialization, compound this with the multiple impacts of his unresolved loss, and there is a recipe for sure emotional disaster. For treatment to proceed on any of these issues, a family's rules need to be understood and individuals need help to decide to rewrite them for their own lives.

### Family of Origin Precedents About Loss From Previous Generations

Often, how an individual deals with loss—or does not deal with it—is related to precedents set in generations above. Those become blueprints that are totally outside the awareness of the individual. When this is the case, these militate against the adequate resolution of losses because they form a template for the rules that govern how losses—or emotions of any kind—are dealt with for generations to come. These must be identified and reckoned with for clients to be able to deal effectively with their own losses; these precedents serve the same function as rules that govern people's behavior.

*Case Example.* Alan was a 40-year-old man referred to me by his female friend, who knew of my work with men. An extremely quiet, reserved, highly intellectual but still warm lawyer, he immersed himself vocationally and avocationally in social action and good causes. He was so emotionally constricted that sometimes it was difficult even to hear his voice as he spoke in sessions. Although mystified about the roots of his depression and generalized dissatisfaction with life, he was committed to understanding those and himself.

In the intake session, I sensed an unresolved loss in his history, so I inquired about his history with losses. Indeed, his mother had died of a cancer when he was 7 that had been diagnosed when he was 2. However, after he cried briefly in that session, I remained unable to get him back to any emotional expression for months. Finally, after trying technique after technique, approach after approach aimed at thawing his denial, I intuited that his lack of affect may have to do not just with him or with his sincerity about wanting to comply with therapy. I sensed a history of losses in his extended family that served as a precedent that he felt compelled to follow, however unconsciously. To test my hypothesis, I asked, "What messages did your father give you about loss?" The reply was a shrug of the shoulders and "I dunno." I probed again. "What were your father's own experiences with loss even before your mother's death?" Again he drew a total blank. So we began to construct a genogram of his family, going back to his grandparents' generation (see Figure 7.1). This was all the farther we needed to go to find our answer.

Scrutiny of Alan's genogram yields evidence of profound losses of significant people in four generations. Two generations above him on both sides, Alan's grandparents emigrated to the United States in flight from the pogroms in northern Europe. This meant the loss of home, country, and extended family in one fell swoop. One generation above him, the mother of each of Alan's parents abandoned their children, one in childbirth bearing Alan's father, the other by disowning her children and leaving home when Alan's mother was 4 or 5 years old. In addition, Alan's oldest sibling was a stillborn boy whose birth and death never were acknowledged. And finally, Alan had married a divorced woman with a child, and stepfamilies are born of loss. So everywhere we looked, for four generations, there was unresolved loss. No wonder Alan had so much difficulty feeling anything, but especially emotions related to loss.

The upshot of all of this is that these multigenerational precedents with loss undoubtedly became silent directives for what that family considered appropriate management of trauma. When Alan began to understand that, he also was able to grasp, for the first time, that his parents' virtually total silence around his mother's illness and subsequent death had much more to do with their own emotional impasses than with his worthiness as a person. His beginning to be unhooked from these crippling beliefs was evidenced in his comments during the session following the one in which we drew his genogram. I open the session by inquiring about his reflections since the previous session:

*Therapist:* I'm curious about what last session kicked up for you?
*Alan:* Utter surprise! I was utterly surprised at what we did there. I was totally surprised! All my life, I have wondered about everyone, but

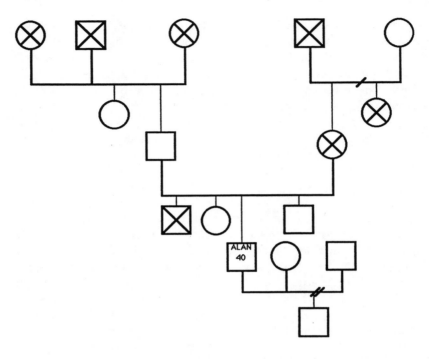

**Figure 7.1.** Multigenerational Losses Illustrated by Alan's Genogram. Used with permission.

was afraid to ask. To put the whole thing together and realize what I *didn't* know was shocking. Although I always kinda [sensed] this stuff. Speaking for my own need to feel connected to people (pause), and then getting slapped in the face with what I didn't know (pause) it was shocking.

*Therapist:* What's your understanding of why you didn't know any of this stuff? I mean, you knew it, but you didn't know you knew it.

*Alan:* My father had the reputation of being the best professor at the college, and I had to try to be the same way, a walking encyclopedia.... There always was an expectation that I should be the same way, and to act like I understood, even if I didn't. I was pretend-acting. And the other part was that [my parents'] marriage was such a wonderful marriage and such a loss, that he wouldn't want to talk about it.

*Therapist:* Why wouldn't he want to discuss it?

*Alan:* He went through a lot of stuff in his childhood, and he probably thought he had to be Superman (pause) or Steelman.

Later in the session:

*Therapist:* So what does figuring all this out mean to you? Or was it just an interesting intellectual exercise?

*Alan:* I was trying to get an emotional reaction. I've been trying to filter that through. Obviously, looking up at that board and seeing that I didn't know who I was, or had no identity profoundly disturbs me. But I'm having trouble feeling it. But I was mean and withdrawn all week. But my defenses are breaking down miserably.

*Therapist:* No, your defenses are breaking down wonderfully! It's your father who would say miserably.

*Alan:* Do you understand the frustration that I feel [because] I've always known perfectly well inside what I've been wanting and needing, but I just couldn't let myself really know?

*Therapist:* Yes, I understand. I think I've understood that even better than you have.

As we see in Alan's comments in the follow-up session, just doing the genogram alone did not unlock the door of his hidden feelings. However, we see evidence of his acknowledgment of steady thawing of his denial, and that this was a significant tool toward accomplishing that end. My therapeutic strategy was to continue to chip away at his denial bit by bit, until his emotions could be surfaced, worked with, and resolved.

## Ethnicity

Sometimes people's ethnic group adds yet another layer of complication to their successfully dealing with a loss. Our ethnicity patterns our thinking in both obvious and subtle ways, and therefore, has a great deal to do with what we think of as normal, acceptable behavior. Watzlawick (1976) reminds us that we see the world through our own "cultural filters," often persisting in established views despite even clear evidence to the contrary. Related specifically to the issue of grief, McGoldrick (1982) offer us some examples of different responses to and ways of expressing grief. She explains how throwing oneself onto or into the grave of a dead person, which is common to Italians, or the keening that is common to Irish and East Asians would seem virtually psychotic to WASPs, Germans, or Norwegians. Therefore, we are all culturally bound by the messages we received from our ethnic backgrounds on both conscious and unconscious levels that tell us how much grief, or if any grief, is acceptable. The wise therapist takes these factors into account in assessing the contributions of her clients' ethnic backgrounds to the current dysfunction. This can be especially crucial when clients' ethnic backgrounds vary markedly from one another's and from the therapist's. Then those differences can seem really discordant.

*Case Example.* Janet came into therapy to work on her anger which seemed constant and particularly distressing because it usually was aimed at her older son. In the course of our initial work, it became apparent that she experienced deep, old psychic wounds from her very distant relationship with her mother. Janet was the 39-year-old daughter of a mother who is a first-generation 100% German immigrant to the United States. According to Winawer-Steiner and Wetzel (1982), a characteristic German trait is emotional restraint. "Affection, anger, and emotion in general do not get expressed easily. People seem to contain what they might experience as too explosive. . . . In the German tradition people are not encouraged to show emotions openly or to display affection, grief, or anger in public. Passions get repressed or sublimated in work or art" (p. 255). All of these factors were operative in Janet's mother, outside the awareness of either woman. So Janet blamed herself for the lack of connection between her and any of her family members, but particularly her mother.

A middle child in a sibship of seven, Janet's only memories of attention from either parent revolved around the multiple surgeries she endured to correct a congenital foot condition that left her unable to walk for the first 5 years of her life. Other than that, she remembers a tenuous connection with her father, and virtually none with her mother. As most children do, she blamed herself for this situation, carrying on into her adult life the crippling belief that her parents' lack of responsiveness to her was due to her inherent unworthiness of it. This rendered her shy, withdrawn, and chronically grieving. She was so distressed and depressed at 19 that she dropped out of college and psychiatrically hospitalized herself for nearly 2 months.

In the course of that hospitalization, Janet and an attending psychiatrist called her parents in for a 1-hour session in which

Janet timidly asked her parents directly if they loved her. An argument then ensued between her mother and her. Janet's memory of that session 20 years earlier was of her sobbing, her mother shouting, and her father sitting off to the side silently crying. As she recollects it, her mother steadfastly refused even to say she loved her daughter no matter how much Janet begged and cried. And so the session ended with Janet's being even more convinced that she was unloved, unlovable, and unworthy. The following excerpt illustrates her discovery that there may have been other factors outside her and even of her mother's awareness that blocked the mother's empathic responses to her—or to anyone.

*Janet:* I remember my mother saying a lot "She's not strong. She cries." She prided herself for not even crying at my Dad's funeral! I know she prides herself for not crying. Crying is weak. I don't ever think I saw her cry. (Pause) Oh, one time. One time! I saw her cry when she was mad at my dad. That's the only time I ever saw her cry!

*Therapist:* What message did that give you?

*Janet:* I dunno.

*Therapist:* Think about it.

*Janet:* [Mad] is the only thing you could feel. (Pause) Yes, that's what I was taught.

*Therapist:* Now you tell me why you've been angry so much of the time.

*Janet:* Yeah. 'Cause that's the only thing I could feel.

*Therapist:* What's the feeling you get when you recognize that?

*Janet:* Sad.

*Therapist:* Tell me about it.

*Janet:* I'm sad that she couldn't have done more than that.

*Therapist:* Who are you sad for?

*Janet:* I think I'm sad for both of us. I don't remember a lot. (Pause) I just remember her giving orders. And being busy, too.

*Therapist:* And that's very German, too. (Pause) So she was just doing what she was taught. (Pause) What does it feel like to contemplate that?

*Janet:* Why the hell couldn't she have tried to do something different?

*Therapist:* You answer that.

*Janet:* I can't.

*Therapist:* How would your mother answer that?

*Janet:* That's just how it was.

*Therapist:* And that's very German, too.

*Janet:* (Pleased with herself) That's just how she'd answer that!

*Therapist:* What does it feel like, um, do you feel anything different at all after contemplating these factors?

*Janet:* I guess I just feel that there was nothing different I could do to change it. (Sobbing) It wasn't my fault! I think I always thought it was.

*Therapist:* And it wasn't. And technically, it wasn't even your mother's fault. She was just doing what she was taught.

*Janet:* But she doesn't understand that.

*Therapist:* No, but you can. You can understand it so it doesn't have to keep hurting you (pause), so you don't have to keep personalizing your mother's behavior. 'Cause it isn't about you, and it never was.

The preceding excerpt illustrates several aspects of ethnicity. One is how it dictates outside most people's awareness expectations for normal and expected behavior. Two is how it prescribes and proscribes certain behaviors. And three is how all too often those ethnically determined covert directives have disastrous consequences for people's emotional lives.

It also leads us to another key concept related to loss. Janet's case is clearly one of ambiguous loss, a concept advanced by Boss (1977). This relates to significant people being there physically but unavailable emotionally. An extreme example of this is the MIA or the POW, people who are still a presence in the life of the family but simultaneously gone for who knows how long. In discussing this concept, Luepnitz (1988) states,

> It is, in fact, quite probable that [parents'] *emotional* absence may be more difficult to contend with than their physical absence, since, like all ambiguous losses, it cannot be easily acknowledged and grieved. . . . In this, as in many other situations, human beings cannot come to grips with absence that masquerades as presence. (p. 182)

The follow-up therapeutic work with Janet was aimed in three directions. First, of course, was to help Janet resolve her loss from her emotional abandonment by her parents. Second was to help Janet redefine herself as being worthy and lovable, as believing she was not either of these was her inevitable conclusion prior to her recent discoveries. And third was to help her acknowledge her parents' limitations as adequate nurturers due to factors totally beyond their awareness and for which neither she nor they is to blame. Then she could free herself of these archaic thought patterns.

## Summary

Often, multiple influences from a client's family of origin operate totally outside conscious awareness; and yet, they still function as commands for certain behaviors. When those covert messages are raised to the level of consciousness, then people have the ability to choose to continue to live by them or not. However, when people do not consciously comprehend these dictates, they are consigned to live by them. It is our job to help them bring these mandates to the surface so they can make new, presumably more functional choices about those antiquated dictates.

## Factors That Contribute to Father Hunger

In this section, we will discuss father hunger. Sometimes, its etiology is a literal father absence such as from death, which because of its unambiguity, may be relatively easily solved. After all, dead is dead. Other times, the loss is more subtle, as in a divorce, desertion, or the ambiguous loss involved with a traditional father.

Although father loss of course can have serious consequences for women because of the emptiness they experience and the void they have for a model for healthy intimate relationships with men, the consequences can be devastating for men who need fathers for models about how to be men. Many men, because of their father's absence, experience a deep pool of father hunger that itself sets up a situation ripe for a chronic unresolved grief reaction. Thus, an otherwise difficult grief reaction is made even more treacherous and fraught with long-term consequences for their roles as both spouse and parent. Then they have only negative or nonexistent models for what men are and do. In this section, I will consider the impact of father loss on men from the vantage point of the different types of dynamics that this void can set up in adult male children. Grief reactions from divorce or desertion, from father's death, and absence in the traditional father will be considered.

### Divorce Which the Child Experiences as Desertion

After 21-year-old Mark was in psychotherapy for 5 months, I met for a time with his father, partly to get some clues about the nature of Mark's extreme stuckness in his life, partly to help the highly enmeshed father and son get more appropriate emotional separation, and partly to help the father do his part to meet Mark halfway on developing an affective connection. The parents had been divorced when Mark was 1 year old, and he had seen his father in the standard custody arrangement. Even though the father moved to within blocks of Mark every time he and his mother moved, this attempt to be near Mark had minimal effect: Mark acutely felt his father's absence. This was due, in large part, to the father's still behaving as a socialized father: taking care of Mark's instrumental needs with little attention to developing a nurturing, emotional connection. So, even though his father lived only blocks away, Mark was unable to feel connected with him. As a result, Mark had been depressed and suicidal his entire adolescence.

The first example illustrates the father's dawning realization of how off target he was with what his son needed.

*Dad:* I'm a Mensa member, and I can't for the life of me think of what I could've done to help my kids!

*Therapist:* That's just it. You've been thinking your feelings for years. It's time to feel your feelings and to learn that it is possible to think and feel at the same time.

*Dad:* I know that now. And I feel relaxed, for the first time in 20 years, because I'm beginning to realize that my telling my children to calm down and shhhh has been part of the problem. I had no idea how much I was hurting them! A lot of what I perceived to be the right thing was totally wrong. I did not look at things from a child's perspective. I intellectualized. But I honest to God did what I thought was right.

*Therapist:* I have no doubt that you did. And you all have been carrying around this sack of rocks of your unresolved grief about the divorce long enough. It's time to set it down! And I intend to help you do that.

Three weeks after the session in which the father began facing his grief, Mark spontaneously began to reflect on the changes he was perceiving in his father. Here he articulates how those have cleared the way for them to develop both a different quality to their relationship, as well as was creating the space for Mark to grow in some new and different ways.

*Mark:* The more I understand him, the more I understand me, because I've never really dealt with him as my father. It's starting to be that we're having more connections with our lives. I always thought I was so different from my family—and I am. But it feels good to see some similarities.

*Therapist:* Why is that?

*Mark:* It gives me a better sense of belonging. I'm molding myself a little better. I see more of a spark of being from my family, instead of just being.

*Therapist:* Can you say some more about why that's helping?

*Mark:* I've always been disgusted with my family, and I've been disgusted with myself. I've been alienating myself from myself. Finding my family is finding what I have to work with, what I am, where I am not.

*Therapist:* Would it be any different if you were doing this exploration with your mom?

*Mark:* Yes! It's a male thing. I've needed my father. He didn't give to me because he wasn't there. But I always thought he didn't give to me because he wasn't capable of it. But I'm learning it's different now. I'm getting to know him more. I've never understood his fathering, because I saw him on weekends. As far as I was concerned, he was on the moon. I feel a stronger connection now. The more he tells me about his past, the more I can associate with him.

*Therapist:* And that's extra significant, now that you have a father who's listening.

*Mark:* Yeah! It's a male thing. There's just this extra umph or extra bit of spirit, having my dad be behind me. He's always been behind me, but it's always been an outside thing. Now he's there.

In this example, we see the effects both of Mark's experience of father absence and of the foundation for developmental growth that reconnecting with his father can provide.

### Father Death: The Impact on the Male Child and on His Relationship With His Mother

Another way father absence can have serious consequences is that often these men become physically and emotionally overburdened by their overburdened mothers, as is illustrated in the following excerpt. Bob is a 41-year-old always single man, although he had had a series of long relationships with women to whom he has been unwilling to become emotionally intimate or to commit. He is the oldest of six children whose father died when Bob was 8 years old. This excerpt reflects a combination of sequelae that can have deadly effects on intimate relationships: the negative role model he had from his father who first emotionally and then actually abandoned him, and his fear of being trapped to repeat his smothering relationship with his mother. And yet, prior to the beginning of therapy, replicating his experience from both parents is exactly what he had done. Here, we see him articulate his new understandings about those patterns and about his fears.

*Bob:* I've been thinking about these caretaking, fixing issues which you keep pointing out. I never considered myself a caretaker, but now I see that I was trying to caretake something I couldn't do anything about. After my father left, my mother put too much responsibility on me. And I considered myself a failure, when it really wasn't something I could do anything about!

*Therapist:* Wow!

*Bob:* (Obviously pleased with himself and his new realization) Isn't that something! Now I can be free not to caretake so much, because I don't have to feel guilty. I understand now where a lot of that comes from, and that I don't have to do those things. I won't immediately jump into someone else's morass. And I can distinguish what's possible and what I can never do.

*Therapist:* How do you think that's going to influence you with the next woman you fall in love with? How do you think that will influence the quality of that relationship?

*Bob:* If someone wants me to take care of everything, I won't get involved. I need someone who has a quiet sense of herself. Someone who has a quiet inner confidence, which I now think I do, but it sometimes still gets annihilated by wanting to take care of someone else. I assassinate myself when I do that! I felt exploited in the last relationship. She was someone who valued me for what I could do for her, and not for how we could join forces. We need to be able to take the strengths and creativity of each and find a way for it to fit together so we're not bouncing off each other. A large part of why it has bounced off me is because I haven't let anyone help me, so the cogs don't mesh. So I have to clear the clogs out of the cogs, so I can mesh. I've been thinking there is somebody out there, but I just haven't let myself mesh.

*Therapist:* What does it feel like to hear yourself say all that?

*Bob:* It feels like Bob is talking, is being able to express himself. I hear my inner self talking. But it's also kind of a sad feeling. For so much time I've been someone who's held hostage by himself. And I feel pissed off and sad at all the time I held myself hostage. And another part is scared. It's a scary feeling. Now I am really out there in the world, so I'm more vulnerable than I was. And part of it is a relief that I haven't lost my inner self. I don't think as I did, even a month ago!

Here we see the etiology of one of the classic dynamics that make men fearful to commit in intimate relationships. And we also see that once the losses have been dealt with, the man comes to a qualitatively different place with himself that prepares him to be intimate with a partner who emotionally can meet him there. These comments indicated a readiness for termination of treatment, so follow-up work was to help him prepare for that.

## Losses With Traditional Fathers

The traditional father role has been defined by Feldman (1990, p. 88) as having two characteristics: (a) being a good economic provider, and (b) being a firm disciplinarian. He goes on to state that the nurturant role has been defined as the mother's domain and therefore has been left up to her. It would seem only logical that these bifurcated role structures likely would have a negative psychological impact on boy children. But he goes on to make a stark and unequivocal assertion: "The traditional father role also impedes the psychological development of fathers" (Feldman, 1990, p. 88). This means that both the psychological development of the men who currently are our clients and the psychological development of their children are negatively impacted by the socialization of men, because the quality of parenting that most traditional men were expected to provide often was very distanced because of the father being emotionally absent. It is precisely this situation that makes for an ambiguous loss.

The following clinical vignette illustrates the experience of an adult child who convened a family of origin session, a technique discussed later in the family of origin chapter. It illustrates the power of direct expression of feelings when that has been a taboo because of a family rigidly locking into silence about physical abuse.

Although I had begun suggesting within the first couple of months of treatment that we would probably need to do such a session, Mick would panic and strongly resist all my efforts in this

direction. Because the presenting problem was marital dysfunction, the initial work was on attempting to heal their marriage.
When his wife would have nothing more to do with couples
therapy, he requested to continue in individual treatment. I once
again nudged him in the direction of facing his parents. To no
avail. Then, I invited him to participate in my men's group, which
he did with more emotional availability resulting. But still something was missing. Finally, with all other options exhausted, he
acknowledged the need to face his fears and his father and agreed
to invite his parents to an extended session. He was surprised that
they immediately agreed to come, even though this meant traveling halfway across the country to get here. His reluctance was
precisely because of his resistance to dealing directly with the
father loss he had experienced from the deadly combination of a
traditional father who was abusive. But doing so catalyzed a
turning point for both men in relating with each other. The excerpt
included here occurred approximately 30 minutes into the first
half of the two-day session.

**Mick:** (to his father) It's a fear. . . . It's looking for love. It's an 8-year-old kid
looking for love. The fear and the love are closely intertwined. . . . I'm
so caught up in trying to please that I can't (Pause) I'm so afraid
somebody's not going to like me, that I'll do anything. (Tears stream
down his face.) It's not a conscious thing; it's stuck so deep inside of
me. I want your help getting back to that 8-year-old kid and letting
him know there wasn't anything he did to deserve being hit or yelled
at. I'm wrestling with that.

**Dad:** (Defensive at first) I don't think what I did was abuse. (Pause) But
it sounds like you think it was. It wasn't what you did, it was the way
I reacted to it. And that's *my* problem. It was instantaneous rage. . . .
You've got to understand what I'm saying. . . . There is no one in the
world I am prouder of! (In tears) I wasn't going to do this!

**Therapist:** Why not?

**Dad:** Because it's not like me.

**Therapist:** (To Mick) What's it like seeing your Daddy's tears?

**Mick:** It's really nice. (Crying harder) It makes me know you cared. . . . It
wasn't like I never felt loved. But what's confusing is that [abuse and
love] came from the same person. What I want to do here is disconnect
the two. I want to know that I didn't *deserve* what happened.

*Dad:* I don't think there's *any* question [of that]! It wasn't you, it was me. My stepdad beat me with everything he could. He just graduated. When razor straps didn't make me cry anymore, he graduated to a baseball bat. Planning to kill him until I was 16 was part of what I did to you. . . . I'm not making an excuse, please understand. I'm just trying to give you an explanation. . . . You've got to understand, that was *my* mentality. It had nothing to do with you. . . . I didn't know who my father was.

*Mick:* (Referring to his knowledge of transgenerational patterns) I realize that I'm a product, not only of what you went through, but what they went through, and what they went through. But I thought I was going to die!

*Dad:* I can understand how you'd take it that way. Especially when I think of it from the standpoint of an 8-year-old.

*Mom:* You wanted him to be strong.

*Dad:* Yes, I did. And he is. He's stronger than hell! We didn't recognize pain in our household, because if you are tough, you just rub it off. . . .

*Mick:* But I was so afraid of you, I would do anything! I remember time after time being pulled off kids who were bigger and older than me.

*Mom:* Did you [fight] because you thought he wanted you to?

*Mick:* Yes! I wanted to be tough! . . .

*Dad:* In the past few years, I've sensed there was a wall between us. . . . I would have done anything in the world to keep from hurting you! . . . What you never understood is that I'd have given up my life in 2 seconds for you. (Sobbing) What you've got to understand is that you're the pride of my life! (Dad initiates a hug, the two men standing in the center of the room.) I love my family more than life itself!

*Mick:* I know, I know. But it helps to hear. . . . I love you so much! I'm so glad you're still here to do this with!

*Mom:* That's the truth!

*Dad:* They say you can't go back. But when you do this, you do.

*Mick:* I know you love me!

*Dad:* I hope you do!

At this point, the two men were sobbing, locked in a hug that lasted for 4 delicious minutes, illustrating that the healing that comes from dealing directly with loss can be profound. In these precious moments, Mick had a chance to begin healing his chronic ache from his father loss born of the combination of his dad playing the role of a traditional father and from his avoidance of contact with his father to protect himself from any chance of further abuse.

## Concluding Thoughts on Father Hunger

Mick's journey to finding his father began with his painstaking realization that his father was simply not available to him, in any way, shape, or form, except as a figurehead, the occupant of a role. However, even men whose father spends hours with them can still feel a longing, a gap that obstructs their ability to know and be intimate with self or other. This is because of their inability to bridge the emotional gulf that developed between them. A well-respected family therapy colleague of mine wrote a moving piece on his own experience of emotionally finding the father with whom he had spent countless hours playing and working as a child. He wrote,

> And despite it all, I searched for my father for much of my youth and young adulthood. It was a source of increasing sadness to me that although he could talk about trees for hours, or about Indians, or about deer, he didn't know how to talk with me about feelings, and he didn't seem to be interested in them: my mother's, his own, or mine. Finally, . . . . I confronted him with my unhappiness. . . . Slowly, [he said], "But I thought you knew I loved you. You know how proud of you I am." "But I need to hear it once in a while, Dad," I said. (Sargent, 1990, p. 34)

In all of these examples, there is obvious a hunger for a father with whom to be emotionally intimate. These excerpts illustrate many different types of situations that all led, sadly, to the same void. The man whose father had died, the man whose parents divorced but whose father never lived more than blocks away, the man whose father played a traditional role that kept him the disciplinarian or riveted on his work, and the man who spent many hours working and playing with his father each had a central experience in common: father hunger. It is my belief that this hunger is central, particularly for men. It is the single most important loss with which nearly all men have to come to terms. In addition to the concrete losses that are brought about by untoward life events such as death, divorce, or desertion, there is the everyday loss that people experience when their traditional father lives in the same house with them but is emotionally unavailable.

Father hunger affects not only daughters and sons; it also can place a heavy burden on the women who try to love these emotionally deprived men. Often, the needs the men have for a loving father get transferred into expectations of the woman that she be for them what their father was not. This, of course, places an intolerable burden on her and on the marriage. Luepnitz (1988) again offers a cogent comment: "Many men without loving fathers grow up expecting women to give them all the warmth and limit-setting they were denied—and then hating women for not succeeding in what was, after all, an impossible task" (p. 183). When we as therapists see this happening, on behalf of both members of the couple and the marriage, our task is to help the man point his needs in the direction they need to go: his father. For help in doing this, the extended family of origin session, which is discussed in Chapter 11, or some Bowenian coaching to help the client go back to the family of origin and be different would be indicated. This can be expected to go a long way to de-stress a beleaguered marriage while attempting to help the man heal his grief.

With men, both unresolved grief and fear of intimacy compound the impact of their socialization as males. They then perpetuate with their children, as with their spouse, their fear of being hurt again. Thus, they play out the void with their children that their father did with them. Or they smother their children, either by doing a role reversal to get the child to do the parenting or by putting the child in a spousal role, because it can seem so much safer to get emotional needs met by a child than by a spouse.

### Summary

Instead of verbally and emotionally beating men up for failing to do what they have never learned to do, and for doing what their fathers showed them to do, our role as therapists is to help them to learn more functional ways of relating to themselves, to their partners, and to their children.

## A Multigenerational Clinical Example

When a man has unresolved loss in his history, that fact con-spires with his socialization as a male, with his family's rules and ethnicity, and with the intimacy fears that he has developed as a result of all of these to create an emotionally bound up individual. Those factors all braid together and compound the man's emotional unavailability. Each strand of the braid needs to be addressed for a man to develop a different way of relating.

The following clinical vignette illustrates the enormous complexity and far-reaching effects that chronic, unresolved loss can have on the life of a family. Don, a 62-year-old cardiologist, is beginning to grasp and grapple with the profound impact of multiple unresolved losses for him. He now sees that not only was his own personal development impaired, but also, in perpetuating what he was taught in the imprint grief experience that he had as an adolescent, he inadvertently crippled his children as well. Further, he is beginning to glimpse how he has architected all his intimate relationships to protect himself from being abandoned again, thereby inadvertently ensuring abandonment by virtue of the relationship dysfunction that generates. We accessed this long-repressed material excerpted below as we discussed the roots of his chronic depression.

*Don:* It seems like I've always been depressed. I remember a heavy cloud over me, going back to when I was in high school.
*Therapist:* To when?
*Don:* To when my brothers were killed. They were killed in the Second World War, 9 months apart. I was 15 and away at military school for high school, for 4 years. I had a lot of responsibility there. We were kept busy from 6:30 in the morning until 10:00 at night. So there was just no time for emotional stuff. Because all the masters and professors knew my brothers, who also had gone there, I felt I always had to achieve. I remember being criticized by one of the professors because I was feeling sad for myself that I had lost a brother.
*Therapist:* What did you do then?
*Don:* I tried to straighten out, to stuff it. And then, 9 months later, my other brother was killed, a couple of months before the end of the war.
*Therapist:* How do you think that influenced your grief process?
*Don:* (With amazement) Seems like I'm feeling it more now, going back, than I did then!
*Therapist:* Tell me about that.
*Don:* (With profuse tears) I don't know of any event that affected the life of my entire family more!
*Therapist:* Tell me about your tears.
*Don:* I seem to have them every time I go back to when my brothers died.

*Therapist:* Good! Because that's where you got stuck. So you need to let yourself have them now, so you can grow yourself up. (Long pause as he sobs) Tell me more.

*Don:* (Going back even farther) I was 14, 1 year before my first brother was killed, when my grandfather died, I remember going to the funeral. But I guess I didn't really feel anything, like I did with my brothers. That was the first funeral I remember.

*Therapist:* What was it like for you?

*Don:* I don't know. I guess I didn't have much of an emotional reaction. I was never really close to him. But I remember that as being my first exposure to death.

*Therapist:* How did that as a first exposure influence you?

*Don:* I don't think it helped prepare me for the loss of my brothers.

*Therapist:* What are those tears?

*Don:* Thinking about my brothers, I guess.

Don then went on to describe the family's receiving the news of his first brother's death. It came in a telegram with a star on the envelope, the symbol that there had been a war death. His mother received the telegram and cried, and Don cried with her. Then, his father came home from work and told the family that they had to be strong, and that they were going to "get the family back to normal as soon as possible." That is, in fact, what the family did. No funeral or memorial service was held for either brother for 2 years because the bodies could not be located. So it was business as usual.

It was natural that when Don's 42-year-old first wife died instantaneously of a heart attack 25 years later, his words to his four young children were, "It's good that she died on a Friday. Then we can have this family back to normal by Monday." As he told me this story, he smiled ruefully and said, "And by golly, we did it!" And then, as if realizing for the first time the implications of what he was saying, he quietly added, "That was probably the worst mistake I made in the whole thing!"

In this vignette, we see how the messages he got about loss from his family and from male authority figures around him promoted some very dysfunctional ways of dealing with strong affect. This imprint experience then formed the blueprint for how he would handle all other losses. Those messages, plus his socialization as a male, combined to create atrophied feelings in him and emotional carnage in his family and in his subsequent marriages.

## Men's Typical Ways of Being Close

Men know much more about being silent and still being intimate than do women, who sometimes depend too heavily on
words to communicate feelings. Clearly, there is a nonverbal way
that men relate, particularly to other men. Men work in work-
shops, hunt, and attend scout meetings with their fathers. In each
of these instances, they can experience a great deal of intimacy,
such as the peaceful, silent walk a man experienced with his
father. But as we saw from my colleague's experience, there still
needs to be the indisputable affective connection that affectionate
words and touch give for this basic need to be satisfied.

Aaron, a 30-year-old man, in reflecting on his experience of
father loss, said:

*Aaron:* I wish I'd had more physical contact.
*Therapist:* Meaning?
*Aaron:* Just like walking somewhere with our arms around each other, or
    playing around. We used to do it a lot when I was a kid. But we don't
    touch now. I miss that. Hmm . . . I just never thought about it or
    remembered it until now.

If they cannot affectively connect with their fathers, men will be
hampered in connecting at a feeling, nonsexual level with their
partners. And then they will pass on this inability to another
generation by not affectively connecting with their sons, either.
There is another whole experience that constitutes a loss for men if
they don't have their father's hugs or words that say they are loved,
even when there is no apparent other relationship rupture such as
happens in divorce or desertion. To not have the words is to leave
them in doubt, just as not having physical affection leaves an ache.

## The Impact of the Therapist's Own Experience With Loss

As I have repeatedly stated, the single most significant therapeutic instrument we have is ourselves. Just as we can be a finely
tuned instrument for healing, not looking at our own losses can
leave us discordant, out of tune both with ourselves and with our
clients. Therapists who have not identified and worked with their
own losses can be expected to erect barriers to identifying their
clients' losses. And if this is nontherapeutic for clients in general,

and I believe it is, it can be anathema for men. It is futile to tell clients to do as we say, not as we do.

I am reminded of a conversation I had many years ago with a student in training with me whose description of his own process when his father died left a strong impression. When I indicated curiosity about how he handled that experience, his words were, "I went out for an afternoon and took care of it." When I inquired further, he stated succinctly that he had sat for a while, and cried for a while, "and that was it." Such a stereotypic male response! I can only speculate on the nature of his relationship with his father, but with a response like that, surely there was no strong emotional connection. So imagine that same therapist sitting with clients who are embroiled in a current loss. And then imagine what the chances are that he would go looking for an unrecognized and unresolved loss. Clearly, therapists must be aware of their own loss issues and have come to some resolution of them, in order to be therapeutic for their clients.

### How Therapists' Unresolved Losses Affect Treatment

Therapists whose own losses are unresolved will have a signif-icant blind spot that will hamper both diagnosis and treatment. Especially if we have chronic unresolved loss in our history, we will be loath to suggest that clients discuss theirs. In fact, most likely, we somehow will give them the message that they should keep such material to themselves. Further, when a client who needs to grieve begins to do that, however unconsciously, we will steer them away from working with such painful material. This is never helpful for any client who needs to work with loss, but it can have additional deleterious effects with men, serving to per-petuate the tendency they already have to intellectualize or simply to keep silent about emotional material. So it behooves us to examine ourselves and our own issues. To not do so, leaves us and our clients prey to our immense blind spot.

## Seven Guidelines for Working Effectively With Loss

In this final section, I propose seven guidelines for shepherding clients through the painful process of dealing with loss. The discerning reader will note that there are several processes that relate to the therapist herself. These are based on the belief that effectively doing this work requires a therapist who has identified and resolved her own losses.

1. Accept the reality that loss is a necessary part of life. Although of course, logically we know that this statement is true, emotionally accepting it can be a different matter. It is a natural tendency to deny losses as a way of coping with them. And yet, none of us is immune to losses. They cannot be prevented; they only can be dealt with effectively and thoroughly when they happen. When you have accepted this for yourself, it will be much more natural for you to help clients with the spiritual struggle that resolving a loss entails.

2. Examine yourself and your responses to clients. Do you diagnose for the presence of loss, or do you not even take that into account? And when you hear evidence of loss, do you approach it with clients or do you redirect them from the topic? How you respond when you hear evidence of a pattern of losses is directly related to two factors: (a) your own experience with losses, and (b) the extent to which you have faced those losses yourself. It is impossible appropriately to treat clients, female or male, for their losses if you have not examined and resolved your own.

3. Seek consultation, supervision, or therapy when your own wounds begin to ache when working with clients in this area. For people who have the requisite sensitivity to be effective therapists, it is nigh unto impossible to sit with clients working with the white-hot pain of resolving a loss without having responses yourself. When your own losses are resolved, these responses are likely to be more out of empathy than anything else. When they are not, clients' emotions likely will rub your own wounds raw. When that happens, two equally deleterious conditions result. Either the therapist redirects the client away from the painful material out of self-protection and self-interest, or she cues the client to come take care of her. This role reversal is particularly problematic for clients who were spousal or parental children, because once again we have perpetuated their being used by their caretakers. This is one kind of

abuse that the therapist could perpetrate. And worse yet, the situation opens up both therapist and client to the possibility of the client being sexually abused through this kind of extremely intimate interchange. Either way, it is to be strenuously avoided. The savvy therapist takes her wounds elsewhere for healing. Otherwise, she blunts herself as a therapeutic instrument and risks perpetrating abuse.

4. Diagnose carefully for the presence of losses in general and for the role of men's fathers in their lives specifically. Even when people acknowledge a loss but protest that they do not need to go back over it because they have already dealt with it, I check carefully. I want to know *how* they dealt with the loss. Intellectualizing the experience without also surfacing the painful affect will accomplish nothing except to paint on another layer of defenses. And just because a man grew up with his father in an intact family, do not assume that he experienced no losses. Probe thoroughly and carefully for father hunger.

5. Don't be fooled when clients say they know they were loved. Ask *how* they knew that. If they were left to infer it using logic but were never told or shown affection, it is likely they did not feel loved. By the same token, if they consistently were told they were loved, but their caregivers' actions did not match, they are unlikely to know they were loved at a basic enough level for it to effect positively their self-esteem. People typically experience both of these situations as losses, and yet it can be very confounding to understand why.

6. Because losses of all kinds predictably have such profound effects on intimate relationships, this is yet another reason to avoid doing individual therapy with someone who is in a significant, committed relationship. This is an especially important consideration for clients who are convinced that the loss affects only them. I explain my approach to clients from three angles: (a) that even though their spouse did not experience the loss, he or she certainly is affected by their own struggle with witnessing their partner's suffering; (b) that the clients will need the spouse for support as they get into the difficult parts of the process; and (c) that dealing with these issues will be such a moving experience that they ought not to miss the chance to participate for the bonding it makes possible.

This also gives me the opportunity to assess for relationship dysfunction spawned by the unresolved losses and to correct it, without engaging the couple's defenses about the health of their relationship.

7. Diagnose carefully for multigenerational factors that have affected a man's successful resolution of loss or dealing with emotions of any kind. As we saw with Alan above, until a client understands these influences, they can be more significant than a man's personal commitment to dealing thoroughly with losses. And even when he does comprehend them, they do not melt away with that insight. If they are more significant than his commitment to progress, they inevitably will obstruct his progress in effectively resolving them, no matter what techniques you try. Understanding this can minimize your frustration with what would otherwise seem like noncompliance. It also can diminish his predictable tendency to blame himself and feel inadequate in the face of what appears to be an inability to progress. For the sake of all concerned, this will lessen the risk of being swallowed up in hopelessness.

## A Final Word

When we understand ourselves and our own experiences with loss, not only is our therapy not compromised; its effectiveness is greatly increased. Now we have another whole dimension to our understanding. And this, more than any technical competence we may have acquired, makes us effective clinicians. In this way, we can be certain that our grief experiences can enhance the treatment we provide. As females, we obviously cannot say that we have "been there" as men. But we can have the special way of knowing that comes from being with ourselves on our own issues and in our own grief.

Our charge as therapists is to help men to become more emotionally available so that they are more active and adequate participants in intimate relationships of all kinds. Clearly, for men to do this, they need to come to terms with the losses they have sustained in their lives, particularly their father losses. Otherwise, these will present major blocks to progress.

One 33-year-old man spoke to the crux of how these unaddressed gaps affect him when he asked in the second session, "How do I learn to become a solid link in a broken chain?" Teaching clients this is the therapeutic task before us. We repair the broken chain by clarifying clients' place in it.

# References

Bly, R. (1989). *A gathering of men: With Bill Moyers and Robert Bly* [video]. New York: Mystic Fire Video.

Boss, P. (1977). A clarification of the concept of psychological father presence in families experiencing ambiguity of boundary. *Journal of Marital and Family Therapy, 39*(1), 141-151.

Feldman, L. (1990). Fathers and fathering. In R. Meth & R. Pasick (Eds.), *Men in therapy: The challenge of change* (pp. 88-107). New York: Guilford.

Gordon, B. (1990). Being a father. In R. Meth & R. Pasick (Eds.), *Men in therapy: The challenge of change* (pp. 247-260). New York: Guilford.

Keen, S. (1991). *Fire in the belly: On being a man.* New York: Bantam.

Luepnitz, D. (1988). *The family interpreted: Feminist theory in clinical practice.* New York: Basic Books.

McGoldrick, M. (1982). Ethnicity and family therapy: An overview. In M. McGoldrick, J. Pearce, & J. Giordano (Eds.), *Ethnicity and family therapy* (pp. 3-30). New York: Guilford.

Osherson, S. (1986). *Finding our fathers: The unfinished business of manhood.* New York: Free Press.

Sargent, G. (1990, Fall). The men's institute. *AFTA Newsletter*, pp. 33-34.

Watzlawick, P. (1976). *How real is real?* New York: Random House.

Winawer-Steiner, H., & Wetzel, N. (1982). German families. In M. McGoldrick, J. Pearce, & J. Giordano (Eds.), *Ethnicity and family therapy* (pp. 247-268). New York: Guilford.

# Part IV

# GUIDELINES FOR
# TREATMENT PLANNING

# Training Wheels for Better
# Relationships:
# Individual Therapy

Individual therapy provides a powerful experience for men. Especially when the therapy is provided by a woman, many for the first time in their lives come to know the healing power of a safe, emotionally intimate bond. Here, rather than talking *about* relationships, they can practice relating to a woman who is a mentor who can guide. Sadly, all too often, the relationship with the therapist is the first time many men have experienced this or have been able to plumb their often frightening internal depths or explore the thrill and the terror of being intimate with another. And yet, most who do, report a truly liberating experience.

This chapter is about one-to-one therapy between female therapist and male client. Although this dyad will be the focus, this is not to say that only women can treat men. Male and female therapists both clearly can competently provide individual therapy; men simply provide clients access to a different set of transference reactions than a female therapist would. However, what a woman can offer a male client just by her presence is access to the client's reactions to the women in his past (mother, stepmother, grandmother, sister, wife) that still without his conscious knowledge may be overshadowing and hindering his present-day relationships with women, whether at home or at work.

Many female clients, of course, have similar needs and issues, and they also require sensitive and caring help. And much could be written about the salutary effects of their receiving therapy either from a female or male therapist. But that topic is beyond the purview of this chapter or this book. And perhaps because their socialization does not prohibit either intimacy or asking for help in the same ways men's does, women come to treatment with relative frequency, and engaging them in the process of change is not so treacherous as it is with men.

## Chapter Overview

In this chapter, I will discuss the noteworthy curative effects available to clients, and the specific therapeutic tools available to therapists when a woman who is clear on the special therapy needs of men does individual treatment with them. The primary focus of the chapter will be on identifying the predictable issues and the background for those motifs that naturally surface when women treat men.

Individual therapy gets its unique curative power because it provides the client with a genuine and presumably healthy relationship with the therapist on which the man actually gets to practice. This primary potency for helping men change must not be overlooked or minimized. And yet, there are some special pitfalls of which the female therapist needs to be knowledgeable and wary in working with men. In addition, although there is only one client in the room for this therapy modality, the therapy proposed here still is definitely systemic. By that I mean that the therapist is working constantly with an eye on the man's relationship networks, both to gauge the effects of the treatment and to ascertain the factors contributing to his problems. Both of these highly significant ideas have been discussed in great detail earlier in the book. So rather than being redundant, this chapter will assume those bases of knowledge and instead will focus solely on the issues involved in creating the healing effects of individual therapy provided by female therapists for male clients.

## Clinical Example

The words of a divorced 45-year-old lawyer and father of three describe his discovery of the healing that can begin when this kind of experience is possible. This is an excerpt from his 11th session, the first 5 of which were with the woman he has been dating for 8 years, in an effort to help them determine both the solidarity of their relationship and the seriousness of its dysfunction.

*Ted:* I left here last time feeling, for the first time, that I'd been really, deeply understood.

*Therapist:* What was that like for you?

*Ted:* It was liberating. I felt hopeful.

*Therapist:* What was liberating?

*Ted:* It was liberating because now I can shed that skin, and you can help me make the necessary adjustments for my life.

*Therapist:* But what do you think was so liberating?

*Ted:* That I got [to say] what the rational world would say is idiotic.

*Therapist:* And I didn't say it was idiotic.

*Ted:* Yes! Those are hurts that maybe have had a more profound impact on me than I would like to admit.

*Therapist:* What do you mean?

*Ted:* I've been hurt very deeply, more deeply than I've ever let on. I've just let it eat my guts out in the middle of the night. And that handicaps me with women.

*Therapist:* Exactly! And that handicaps you in dealing with life! And that's what we're working on. (Pause) You were very clear when you talked about how you felt about having been able to share last week. Can you say something about how you felt about me and about us, for having been able to do that?

*Ted:* I respect you because of your qualifications. But you behaved like a friend. You're not going to hurt me, or think less of me, or make fun of me. And now I've told somebody who has the qualifications to help me. When I left here, I said to myself, "Now maybe I can get to the bottom of this!"

*Therapist:* It sounds like you never had the luxury of having someone you could need or really open up to.

*Ted:* Probably. I always thought I'd pick someone who was dependent on me.

*Therapist:* Now what do you think about that?

*Ted:* Now I realize how nice it would be to be able to call someone and say, "I need some reassurance. I'm scared." Somebody like you, for instance. Somebody who I knew would have my best interests at heart, who wouldn't take advantage of me.

*Therapist:* So how does it feel to let yourself in on needing me?

*Ted:*  It's fine!
*Therapist:*  Is there any part that's scary?
*Ted:*  No! I have this conviction that, if I can let myself need you, that you'll help me.
*Therapist:*  And you're not scared that you'll get too dependent?
*Ted:*  You won't let me. You're not going to want me to call you on Saturday morning and tell you how my date was or how the hockey game was.
*Therapist:*  You're right. You did take a quantum leap last week!
*Ted:*  I don't know. All I know is that I feel different.

And so begins Ted's journey inward that will equip him to move toward others in new and exciting ways.

## Call to Action

How do men learn what Napier (1991) calls "a new map for masculinity" (p. 15) that allows and encourages them to take the often frightening, heroic journey inward? How do they become what Doherty (1991) augurs: "men with the confidence to share power, to nurture, and to be full partners in the human journey?" (p. 31). Although these questions have significant implications for our culture at large, finding answers to them has special import for family therapists. It is we who are in the business of exploring avenues for family change. And yet, "Family therapists for decades have acted as if we thought men were too fragile to treat; we would merely have them sit in and watch while we bashed their wives and mothers" (Pittman, 1991 p. 22).

Here I will consider how men in individual treatment with a female therapist can experience a powerful resolution of important issues that can provide what Braverman (1991) calls for: "substantive changes in the character of men's lives with their families" (p. 25). The kind of therapy described here takes place when men are not in a committed, ongoing relationship such as a marriage. For those who are, the treatment I provide is in joint sessions with their partners, sometimes with individual sessions for both partners interspersed with conjoint meetings. Unlike their successfully committed counterparts, the men who are represented by the voices below have been unsuccessful in relationships up to now; it is this frustration and pain that bring them into my office.

# Predictable Issues

There is a plethora of idiosyncratic issues that people bring to therapy, hoping for our help to resolve. And then in addition, several topics surface for men in individual therapy with a female therapist. Many of these issues converge into predictable themes, which will be highlighted below. The resolution of all of these is central to a client's successful completion of a course of treatment, as well as to his ability to be intimate in life. But before we turn our attention to the specific concerns that naturally surface for men in therapy, some general comments need to be made, which serve as a backdrop for this section.

## Background

Two ingredients are necessary for healthy male functioning. First, a man must be able to tolerate dependence, with the security that he will not be shamed, overwhelmed, or swallowed up if he allows himself to feel this. And second, he also must be able to tolerate separation, with the security that the people he loves will not turn their back if they are away from him. These dynamics probably get the most direct and concentrated attention in individual sessions with a female therapist. With a therapist who understands this tension, and who has no emotional needs of her own tied up in him that would cause her to act out of self-interest, he gets the opportunity to practice learning this balance. Successfully working through it makes the male client a candidate for better, more intimate relationships with others.

In the language of the mythopoetic movement, Napier (1991), a prime spokesman, writes:

> At the nadir of the hero's journey, he faces fearsome creatures; and if he overcomes or defeats them, he is often . . . united with a powerful female figure, a Goddess. . . . Woman represents the totality of what can be known. This reunification with mother, of the female principle, is a necessity for many men who missed emotional support from their own mothers, and who have denied their own feminine, creative energies. . . . Often it will be a good woman therapist who represents this redeeming figure in the literal life of the male sojourner. (pp. 13-14)

In guiding men on their modern hero's journey inward and away from their "narcissism of self-focus" (Napier, 1991, p. 12), perhaps the greatest therapeutic resource we have in working with men—or with anyone, for that matter—is our relationship with them. And the greatest opportunity to focus on and develop that is in individual therapy.

## Two Caveats

Just because we have been trained as therapists or counselors, it is easy to be lulled into thinking that we are immune from difficulty with these issues, that our lives *should* go better than the average person's, and that we automatically will know how to handle these difficult issues. And our clients naively will expect that of us. And yet, if we have not paid special attention to understanding these quandaries, we can expect to have difficulty treating clients around them. So two special requisites need to be noted before we launch into a discussion of how to treat clients with these issues.

*Therapists Are Not Immune From Unresolved Conflicts.* An obvious question for the therapist in helping clients of whatever sex with these issues emerges. How successfully has she identified, faced, and resolved them in her own life? If she still has unaddressed struggles in any of these areas, her ability to guide another, even her willingness to diagnose the issues, will be severely jeopardized. I hasten to add that this is not to imply an expectation that she have these concerns all worked out once and for all, because I sincerely believe there is no such a thing. However, she needs to have examined them and be willing to work with them when they resurface for her. Otherwise, her issues will bleed into the treatment she provides.

If the therapy she provides seems to stall, perhaps the first place she might look to dislodge the logjam in the therapy system is at her own old conflicts. Issues from either her family of origin or her current relationships may be getting in the way. If she is unable to make progress with this on her own, consultation and possibly therapy is crucial for both her and her clients.

*Females in General Are Not Exempt From These Issues.* It is also important to state that it is not just male clients or men who are plagued by these issues. Women, especially those of our generation who have invested in actualizing their potentials in their careers, may also have great difficulty in attending to the vulnerable, relationship aspects of their lives. An excerpt from a session with a divorced 41-year-old female physician reflects this struggle, which parallels most men's.

*Mary:* I have the feeling I'm going to be alone for a long time.
*Therapist:* Why's that? Tell me about that.
*Mary:* I don't fit your typical picture of a typical female. And, of course, I've got children. And nobody'll ever cross my doorstep who doesn't like children! So there's a lot of pretty hefty strikes against me! But there's lots of stuff I can do to enjoy myself with just myself. (Pause) But it would be awfully nice to have somebody to do things with. And maybe I have to learn how to be dependent on somebody. But I have a lot of resistance to that. It's kind of hard!
*Therapist:* What's hard? Can you say some more?
*Mary:* Finding the right way, where independence has to stop.
*Therapist:* Yup!
*Mary:* Because there are some things you can't really do yourself.
*Therapist:* Yup!
*Mary:* But it'd be really hard to learn. Now, I'm so independent, that the guys [other physicians] are really afraid of me!

As we have seen, males' typical way of operating, which is to be totally independent and aloof from acknowledging their needs, can afflict women also. If Mary were a therapist, one could easily predict a different course of treatment for her patients than the one I am proposing. Here we see the same denial of needs and neediness with which men typically present for treatment. The conflict that surfaces for my female client when these feelings emerge is readily apparent and very similar to men's. In these cases, treatment proceeds in much the same way as it does with men. However, there are two additional layers that need therapeutic attention: (a) the issues with which a woman struggles by virtue of her being a woman, and (b) how her being a professional woman exacerbates these conflicts internally for her and for those around her.

### General Therapeutic Issues for Men
### in Therapy With Female Therapists

Perhaps the main issues with which clients must reckon are: dependence, needs, and neediness; sex, sexuality, and sexualizing relationships; family of origin rules and precedents; and echoes of previous relationships. Although these issues would be present regardless of the sex of the therapist, they take on special dynamics when women treat men. And this is by no means an exhaustive list. However, it proffers some common denominators for where to begin with most men.

*Dependence, Needs, and Neediness.* Most men fear dependence, and because of this, they fear any powerful feelings that may make them dependent and render them needy. The prohibition against showing feeling is strong for men with their fathers, but being vulnerable with their mothers can be enormously prohibitive for different reasons. And yet, it is with their mothers that men learn an unconscious blueprint for male-female relationships.

> Dispensing love and affection gives a woman power and makes her a powerful figure to boys in that respect. A man can feel very fragile at the threat of loss of love from a woman, and since he is not supposed to need it, feelings of anger and rage and the need to control women can build up inside him. (Allen, 1990, p. 226)

This illustrates how "The roots of closedness for men are found in insecurity, not in a feeling of being in control" (Gordon & Allen, 1990, p. 202). Although this basic insecurity may, of course, spring from many sources, those germane to this chapter relate to a man's early experiences with women, particularly his mother. Allen (1990) articulates what most of us likely would accept as common sense: "The early relationship with his mother can shape a man's relationship with female partners later on in his life" (p. 225). I believe that this relationship forms the blueprint for *all* other male-female relationships, as do females' relationships with their fathers. That is, either people seek to build relationships that are identical to the ones they had with their opposite-sex parents, using that as a gauge for what is right and good, or they seek the opposite, having unconsciously promised themselves never again to live the way they did. In either case, they build current relationships with that relationship as their template—and often that blueprint must be changed for a man to enter into genuinely healthy relationships.

Whether we recognize it or not, male clients will use the same blueprint with us, going to one extreme or the other. This transference reaction can be used therapeutically to help them examine their choices, making certain that perpetuating this unconscious choice they made in the past remains in their best interests now. Thus an early therapeutic task is for both of us to understand their association to us with their parent, and discern whether it was a hostile or holy alliance. This allows us to help them restructure their relationship grid if necessary.

Most men have difficulty admitting a need for others in general. Over the years, I have concluded that until people, men in particular, admit to a need for therapy and for the therapist, both they and the therapy progress at no more than a snail's pace. With all appropriate means are at her disposal, the therapist must persist with this theme to gain the requisite therapeutic contract to facilitate relationship growth for a man.

*Clinical Example.* Josh is a 33-year-old highly eligible bachelor. He admits to a great deal of loneliness and pain, stating that he greatly desires to have someone in his life to make a commitment to. But he is so skittish about, and therefore controlling in, relationships that even though he says he wants one desperately, he has had only one significant relationship in his life. And he walked out on that one 7½ years before seeking treatment for his relationship problems. In this excerpt I open our eighth meeting in the way that is my custom with most sessions:

*Therapist:* What do you need to work with today?
*Josh: Need* to? Nothing.
*Therapist:* What do you mean?
*Josh:* I don't *need* to work on anything. I'll survive without it. So I don't *need* to work on anything. But I might *want* to work on the ski trip I'm going on with some friends next week.

Depending on one's perspective, one might perceive this as either friendly or hostile banter as both people settle into a therapy session. One also can see here the covert announcement to me that he still sees therapy and the therapist as dispensable. This is a replication of how he related to adults when he was a child. His parents divorced and his father abandoned the family, moving across the country when Josh was 6 years old. By the age of 7, Josh was taking himself and his younger brother downtown from the suburbs on a bus to meet their mother, even though they lived in a major metropolitan area. When his mother remarried a short time later, he describes engaging with his stepfather in endless battles for "who was in control of the family." I see his repartee as telegraphing that he is still working on control by making me and this process optional. Diagnostically, it is apparent to me that we have not progressed past the delicate first stage of therapy to even begin the depth work of middle-phase treatment.

The central therapeutic task, then, is to allow and to facilitate a man's willingness to experience dependence on the therapist, to make a situation in which it is safe for him to know these feelings and to work to examine his prohibitions against them. This allows for two therapeutic benefits: (a) he can have a corrective emotional experience (Yalom, 1985) that he can then replicate in his relationships outside the therapy, and (b) at the same time he can examine those feelings and the root causes for his conflicts about them. Together, therapist and client can parcel out which elements of his feelings derive from his socialization as a man and which derive from his early life experiences. The goal is to help him master feelings that, by inhibiting his ability to trust, ban dependence. Then, he can work toward functional dependence in his relationship to a significant other.

*Clinical Example.* The words of a 28-year-old man whose fiancée has just ended their relationship illustrate extreme prohibitions against dependent, needy feelings for men. They also indicate the progress he has made in several areas. First, he could acknowledge his feelings. Second, he could talk about how vulnerable and hurt he felt because his fiancée chose not to honor his needs any longer. And third, he was willing to risk being needy again by asking me for help. These are big steps for many men, for which credit is due them, and the prognosis is good for those who can make these steps.

*Bart:* It's a real shameful thing for a guy to need someone. If you're a guy, that means you're weak. A part of me knows that everyone needs someone, but it's a real shameful thing. So I need you to help me with that. (With profuse tears) All I'm aware of is that I feel shame for needing someone so bad. It's hard for a guy!

The therapeutic task now is threefold: (a) to help him experience his vulnerability with a trustworthy person both to help him avoid devastation and also for healing; (b) to help him examine the roots and the present-day reality of his fears; and (c) to help him translate the skills he learns in his encounters with the therapist into preparing himself for a healthy intimate relationship with someone outside the therapist's office.

As I stated above, when the client acknowledges and owns his need for the therapist, that is a key signal that the real therapeutic work has begun. I see this as the vehicle for learning to depend on a partner. However, sometimes it is easier to acknowledge his need for someone other than the therapist as practice for the vulnerability involved in allowing a here-and-now experience. Reflections from 29-year-old Aaron, whose words we hear throughout the book, illustrate this. He speaks of his ache to tell his father of his need for him, despite the strained and episodic relationship they have had since the parents' divorce when Aaron was 11.

*Aaron:* I want to go talk to my father. This week! I think I could tell him now how I've missed him, and how I need him in my life, and how he has to be more than he's been for me to respect him. (With profuse tears) I think we just need to cry in each other's arms and to tell each other we love each other.

*Therapist:* What are your tears?

*Aaron:* (Pause) I need to cry in front of him. It's something I haven't done since I was a child. See, I like him so much. And I really, really, really want to be with him. I just feel like walking into his house and sitting down with him and sobbing.

*Therapist:* And what would you be sobbing about?

*Aaron:* I would be sobbing because I would be pleading and begging him . . .

*Therapist:* To what?

*Aaron:* To be my father. (Pause) I miss him, and it's been too long! God! I feel like a kid! (He winces in pain as tears stream down his face)

*Therapist:* In many ways, you are. Emotionally. (Long pause) So what are you going to do?

*Aaron:* I'm going to go see him. Tomorrow. And I'm going to have a heart-to-heart talk. (Pause) I'll certainly be making myself vulnerable!

Illustrating the positive effects of a man's being able to acknowledge his need for someone, Aaron began the following session
with these words:

*Aaron:* I'm appreciating people more and more now. And I'm realizing
that I do want to marry [his girlfriend] now.
*Therapist:* How does it feel to see that?
*Aaron:* Relieved! So relieved! I've realized what good friends she and I
are. Sure, I love her. But I wanted to make sure she and I are friends
first. I see my future being a lot brighter now. I cry a lot when I'm
with her now. They're just little cries, but they're brought about by
happiness and love. My feelings are so intense, and that's the only
way I can express them. And it feels good to do that. Wow!

Regardless of whom the client admits he needs, doing so is a
significant first step, particularly in the treatment of men. Their
experiencing, let alone admitting, these feelings breaks a cultural
taboo. And regardless of with whom they start, to make substantial headway, they need also to acknowledge the need for the
therapist in much the same way Ted did at the opening of this
chapter. This signals that they are ready to begin building an
intimate relationship, rather than merely talking *about* it.

### Sex, Sexuality, and Sexualizing Relationships

Men are socialized to believe that intimacy *equals* sex. I have seen
this and the effects of it in both heterosexual and homosexual
relationships. That equation and most men's already considerable
inability to communicate feelings can together conspire to generate much pain in themselves and in their relationships. So to be
able to develop an emotionally intimate relationship that does not
center on or even include sex can transform a man's entire way of
relating to partners. Hence, "one of the clinician's tasks is to help men
discover how restrictive and limiting messages about sexuality have
been for them" (Meth, 1990, p. 219).

Men need to learn two very important notions when it comes to
sex and sexuality: (a) not to sexualize relationships, even those
where sex is permissible, and (b) that sexual feelings and responses are a very natural and acceptable part of relationships.
When they have begun to learn these premises with their female

therapist, they can move on to explore how and why they sexualize other relationships and learn not to do this.

Keeping the many facets of this issue clear and therapeutic is perhaps the greatest challenge a woman faces when working with men, especially in this intimate context. Here, sexual feelings, which are usually just under the surface whenever men and women work together, can become compelling for one or both. Although they are natural, they can become quite uncomfortable, at least for the client if not for the therapist. Part of the discomfort is in thinking that such powerful feelings cannot or should not be shared. And yet, when we do not recognize them, at least to ourselves, we blind and bind ourselves, thereby missing a great opportunity for therapeutic mileage. If we can keep our boundaries clear—and we must—clients can experience a relationship with a woman, perhaps for the first time, that is genuinely intimate without the risk of becoming sexual or sexualized. Being able to develop an emotionally intimate relationship that does not include sex can transform a man's whole way of relating to women.

*Clinical Examples.* The words of several men speaking in a men's group address different dimensions of this issue. For each, the need to acknowledge his feelings freed him to do the therapeutic work of learning to relate intimately. Once these feelings were admitted, they were out of the way, and each could begin to see the therapist as a person, not as a sexual being. What all these excerpts have in common is that each man's response to me as a woman was, at least initially, an issue for him in the therapy. How that affected their therapeutic work, until it was acknowledged at least to themselves, is the key point.

### Oren

At the start of individual treatment, Oren was a self-proclaimed philanderer whose search for intimacy and security was being undermined by his sexual "solution" to all his relationship needs. I sensed in the first session the sincerity of his request for help. But I also knew that he would, consciously or unconsciously, operate out of this pattern with me until he could learn a new one, thereby unwittingly keeping himself stuck. This is why, about 20 minutes into the first session, I simply announced that we are not going to have an affair. The following excerpt from a group session that took place many months later illustrates how putting the subject on the table and firmly drawing a limit early in the therapy began to free him from his habitual pattern.

*Oren:* (Age 49) You are probably the third or fourth woman in my life that I haven't thought of as a sexual person, as opposed to a woman I can respect for nonsexual reasons. And I think it's because—we talked about that right from the beginning, when you made it clear in the first session that we weren't going to have an affair. I've already admitted that I'm guilty of thinking of women as sexual persons. But [not doing that] was not hard with you. I just got it sorted out early on, that this is not a sexual person. This is a woman I deal with in counseling.

### Gary

Gary entered treatment for help in recovering from the devastation of the divorce his wife initiated because of her affair after a 27-year marriage. Here he reports having to steel himself against my being a woman, a defensive move that remained unconscious until I brought up the subject of his response to me. Had I not done that, I suspect his work in therapy would have been significantly compromised by his need to deny his very natural response to me as a woman.

Gary: (Age 47) I put up a wall when I came in here. I thought to myself, "This is the therapist that I'm going to try to work with, and that's it." It wasn't until I acknowledged that this is a human being across from me that I found physically attractive that you became real, became a person. And you are also a competent therapist. It's a mix. Now I don't have any trouble working with you. That's just part of who you are.

The actual physical attractiveness of the female therapist is less relevant than is understanding the twin concepts of men's socialization about women and transference reactions. I refer you back to the example cited earlier in the book of a 41-year-old men's group participant's response to my nearly 70-year-old portly cotherapist that he would like to see her in a hot pink bikini. Sexual feelings are part of the transference reaction that happens without regard to the therapist's actual appearance. When present, they provide a rich vein to mine about how clients view women and intimacy, provided the therapist is clear and confident about her issues in this area.

I confess that I still sometimes struggle not to feel as awkward as a seventh grader when I raise this issue with my clients. And when I do, I must be sure that I am not self-aggrandizing, seeking compliments myself. But the alternative is to miss an opportunity. For such conversations can be very helpful for men to discover more about themselves and about how they relate in intimate relationships. To avoid these conversations is to invite an unspeakable issue to take on the proportions of a secret. Our own timidity or self-consciousness then can become a major pitfall in our work. To guard against this, we must learn to raise the issues even if we blush while speaking.

### Affection Is Not Sex

Both therapist and client need to keep clearly in mind that affection is not sex. For a man to learn this usually makes a marked improvement in his relationship with his significant other. And because there is no way he can have sex with you, he is in an ideal situation to learn the distinction between affection and sex in individual therapy. Most women know, and struggle to make their significant others understand, that a pleasurable sexual experience begins long before two persons take their clothes off. Further, it is commonly accepted that if a man and a woman are having a dispute or there are hurt feelings, he will feel more connected to her if he can have sex first. For her, it is just the opposite. She needs to talk first to feel connected. Herein lies much of what strains the sexual relationship between a man and a woman. Yet, because of his socialization, this can be a very difficult concept for a man to grasp. So being able to be affectionate and not just sexual can add a very satisfying dimension to a relationship between a man and a woman. Therefore, while they have us as their training wheels, men can learn to make this very important distinction. For example, although sexual expression in our office or in our therapeutic relationships is strictly forbidden—as well it should be—nothing precludes the expression of affection, provided it is within the confines of acceptable, appropriate interaction. Here, the therapist can model that affection is not sex by being affectionate while still maintaining appropriate boundaries.

Why does a man sexualize his relationships with women? Of course, there is not a unitary explanation. However, in addition to his socialization, the core of it probably relates to his needs to establish control as a means of chasing away his fears. Men who can uncover the causes and practice experiencing a different way of relating in a safe place can then parlay their knowledge into improved intimate relationships with their significant others.

*Clinical Example.* An excerpt form note I received in the mail from Aaron as a follow-up to a session illustrates his sudden clarity about these differences: "Driving back Monday after session, I thought of how I didn't need to chase those women looking for love, especially the kind my mother gave, because I've found it in you. Monday in your office, I felt as if a search was over, at least for a while. I hope I can hold on to that feeling between visits."

How can men learn that sex is just a part of intimacy, rather than a substitute for it? By having a powerful, intimate encounter where sex is not a part of the equation at all.

## Family of Origin Precedents

A client in individual therapy has perhaps the greatest opportunity for concentrated, focused attention free of distractions or someone else's needs. Now he can concentrate on articulating and understanding his family of origin patterns and their impact on him. These then also become standard themes for exploration in individual therapy. Using techniques such as those from Bowenian theory or preparation for extended family of origin sessions as discussed in Chapter 11, he can, for example, learn about how his family's rules and myths pervade all facets of his life. Thus, he can come to understand the transgenerational precedents that are at work today and their deleterious effects on his ability to be intimate. The other area relates to exploring how he projects onto others—the therapist included—unfinished material from significant relationships in his family of origin. Both can be explored in depth and without distraction in individual therapy. Both of these are avenues for changing the patterns that are outside his awareness but that compel his behavior nonetheless.

For example, as I have said in the chapter on loss, often without their knowledge or conscious assent, people stick loyally to their family of origin rules, and sometimes those rules can have disastrous effects on their relationships. To remain unaware is to be impotent to change the rules. It goes without saying that both men and woman can be negatively influenced by their family of origin rules. I suspect that the families who become part of a clinical population arrive in our offices, at least in part because of the crippling effects of these rules and precedents on them and on their relationships. And yet, often even therapists remain blinded to them.

*Clinical Example.* Suzanne illustrates that it is not just men who have proscriptions against intimacy that have been handed down the generations to them. She is a 41-year-old corporate executive who comes from an ethnic group whose watchword is stoicism. Divorced 10 years, she has been in a relationship with Ted, whom we met at the beginning of the chapter, for almost 8 years. Their relationship has been characterized by a roller coaster of emotional highs and lows, times of intense loving followed by sometimes weeks or even months of not seeing each other. At those times, the relationship is supposedly over. Then one or the other initiates contact, and the cycle starts again. When Suzanne began treatment, although she frequently wept spontaneously and profusely during sessions, the only word which she knew to identify her feelings was "frustrated."

What prompted me to explore her family of origin rules was a persistent sense that she literally was bound and gagged in the expression of emotions—hers and Ted's. This, of course, bound the therapy as well. I explained to her that we all have a set of implicit rules that govern our behavior. We learned them growing up, and we carry them with us in our heads today. I asked whether she would mind our figuring out her family's rules. She hesitated,

which I interpreted for her as protection of both herself and her
family of origin, but finally agreed. We then together generated
the following list:

### "S" Family Rules

1. Be hardworking.
2. Be caring for other people.
3. Be strong, strong-willed, and strong on the outside.
4. Show that you can deal with things externally even if you have
   feelings internally.
5. It's preferable if people get along.
6. Getting angry isn't getting along.
7. Keep hurt, sadness, etc., way inside.
8. It's OK to show good feelings.
9. But showing good feelings in an obvious way is never done; it has
   to be done subtly.

Before we could finish making the list, quiet tears began to well
up in her eyes. When I asked her to tell me about her tears, the
following conversation took place.

*Suzanne:* (With profuse tears) It's not always easy to be that way!
*Therapist:* Can you tell me about that?
*Suzanne:* It's difficult to be strong on the outside when you don't feel that
   way on the inside. And when I do let my feelings show, it doesn't
   often come out right. It's not perceived the way I'd like it.
*Therapist:* It sounds very lonely.
*Suzanne:* I never think of it in those terms.
*Therapist:* What happens if you think of it that way now?
*Suzanne:* I don't feel that way.
*Therapist:* What do you feel, then?
*Suzanne:* More sadness than anything.
*Therapist:* Tell me.
*Suzanne:* (With more tears) I'd like to express my sadness in a way that
   I'm understood.
*Therapist:* I know how painful and isolating it is not to feel understood.
   Do you think you have any fear of reprisal if you live your life
   different from those rules?
*Suzanne:* Yes, I suppose. My father would be judgmental. I still want to
   please them, I guess.

With such a list of prescriptions and proscriptions in her head, little wonder she has such an approach/avoidance reaction to intimacy! And little wonder that Ted has been fearful of sharing his hurts and fear. The therapeutic task, now that she is aware of these implicit injunctions, is to help her examine which of them she wants to continue to use as guideposts for her life, and which she wants to consciously work to counteract or change. For her not to do so would be to continue to live under the spell of her family's ethnicity and of its silent decrees.

*Echoes of Previous Relationships.* Intergenerational family therapists accept as a given that whatever patterns people have been unable or unwilling to address and resolve from their past will replay like broken records in the present. Strong feelings in men that surface especially in individual therapy often can be traced back to childhood experiences. And yet, it is almost without these men's knowledge that they are living in the shadow of the past. Because these unconscious grooves are so well worn and outside of awareness, gaining access to them can be difficult. Exploration of memories often leads to the dead end of intellectualized, empty insight that does nothing but reinforce defenses. Resolution of unconscious conflicts requires insight plus catharsis, a marriage of cognition and emotion. Therapists need strategies for gaining access to this long-repressed, highly charged material. Working in men's relationships with us with echoes of previous or other relationships allows them real, unintellectualized access to potentially salient material. Working through this material enables clients to have a corrective emotional experience (Yalom, 1985) that can be used to help break the power of very old patterns. Then they are able to construct new pathways to intimacy with a partner. The content of this work is looking for evidence, particularly in their relationships to us, of family of origin issues that are braided through their present lives and replay again and again. Once those are located, then the strategy is to isolate and discharge feelings about them.

*Clinical Example.* Mark, from whom we heard earlier, has been in individual therapy for a year. Now 21 years old, he has been in four other therapies since his early adolescence, when he was actively suicidal. After his parents' divorce when he was 1, he lived with his highly narcissistic mother. His relationship with her was characterized by cycles of absence alternating with intrusive affection that he describes as feeling like rape, both responses being peppered with unpredictable outbursts of her abusive anger. For example, in the midst of an angry confrontation between them when he was 15, she forbade him to participate in the school play, in which he had earned a starring role. He walked out and moved in with his father and recalls no further conversation with either parent regarding either this event or his feelings about it.

The excerpt below is from a session a year into individual treatment, 1 week after he failed an appointment. Because of his tendency to intellectualize and to wallow in his depression, I decide to use some heavy confrontational artillery. I tell him point-blank how weary I am of his going over and over the same material in a detached, cerebral way. I tell him how transparent his sabotaging himself is when he fails to make the appointment immediately after a good one, despite all my supposed therapeutic magic tricks to prevent that. I label his transference reaction to me, suspecting aloud that he is blocking me the same way he did his mother, unconsciously attempting to recapitulate his relationship with her. By doing this, he can experience a kind of ersatz familiar closeness with her and retrace the steps in the dance he knows all too well, rather than learn new ones.

*Therapist:* What does it feel like to hear me say that I am considering stopping therapy with you, if you keep missing appointments and keep going over the same stuff all the time?

*Mark:* I'm scared of needing somebody.

*Therapist:* I'm not somebody.

*Mark:* I know. (Pause) I'm scared of needing you—'cause I know my pattern.

*Therapist:* You're doing your intellectual bullshit again!

*Mark:* OK. (Long pause) I know I'm real scared of being responsible.

*Therapist:* (Tracking) You were talking about needing.

*Mark:* I think needing has to do with responsibility. Or vice versa.

*Therapist:* If you're going to give me an intellectual treatise, spare me!

*Mark:* I know (pause) that most of the time, I (pause) feel I'm not good enough (pause) to be (pause) I don't know if this makes any sense, but sometimes I don't feel good enough to be trusted by anybody. (Pause)

*Therapist:* How do you play that out with me?

*Mark:* It's kinda obvious. Because I don't allow any trust . . .

*Therapist:* You're bullshittin' again!

*Mark:* How is that bullshit?

*Therapist:* I can hear it in the sound of your voice and see it by the look on your face. Ten minutes ago when you were crying, I was very impressed. Now, I am singularly unimpressed.

*Mark:* (Pause) I don't want to leave, Beth, 'cause I need you. You're the first person who's seen through me and has confronted me with it, so I can learn to start confronting myself.

*Therapist:* What's it like to say that?

*Mark:* I feel like I need you. I feel like I trust you.

*Therapist:* What's it like to say that?

*Mark:* Real scary.

*Therapist:* Can you say some more about that?

*Mark:* I'm not sure I have words for that.

*Therapist:* Will you work on getting words?

*Mark:* I'm not sure I ever have.

*Therapist:* Um hum. 'Cause what do you do when you get scared?

*Mark:* I climb up in my head and hide. I've never not done that. I don't think I've cried uncontrollably since I was 9. 'Cause I never let my mom get to me like that. I was so angry at her, that I'd never let her see that. Angry that she was so preoccupied with her own emotions, that I never could get that way. Sometimes, I really want to fall to pieces and have someone help me with it and tell me it's OK.

*Therapist:* That's what we're working on, Mark.

Therapists are given many clues to track that suggest a transference reaction is happening. Some examples are: when both client and therapist can see that clients' feelings are out of proportion to the present situation; when clients' prior experience and feelings are having a pronounced effect on the client's present life; when the therapy stalls; when we start having our own countertransference reactions; when clients' make pronouncements like "I don't trust anyone but myself." Each of these indicates to me that people are responding to a previous, unresolved experience. These anachronistic reactions then become the subject of the therapeutic exploration.

*Clinical Example.* Mick, from whom we heard in the previous chapter, had been episodically abused by his father when he was a child. And now he was married to a woman whom he experienced as being like his father in her constant verbal and sometimes physical abusiveness. They had been involved in a stormy on-again, off-again relationship for several years. Although he had previously decided to end the relationship, he resumed it, struck by remorse and fear that he would not know how to live differently. Fearing and expecting rejection, he hesitated to bring that decision into therapy, despite my repeated reassurances and constancy over the course of treatment. When he finally divulged his decision, I happily surprised him with my response, saying, "I hate to break it to you, Mick, but it's too late. I already care about you, and that's not going to change just because you felt you had to make a decision for yourself." After his sobs of fear mixed with relief subsided, we went on to explore his reaction. He was able to articulate his feelings in the here and now. And he also was able to understand how he expected to feel the same inadequate feelings he had felt whenever he had contemplated crossing his father and his wife. Finally, he was able to experience a qualitatively different response from what he expected. For him not to have been able to bring up his expectations and his apprehensions would have left him continuing to operate in his father's shadow, which he had replicated with his wife, without his even knowing it. And it would have meant that he missed the very powerful, healing experience of knowing unconditional positive regard. This is an example of being able to capitalize on a transference reaction, so that a client could see and feel a different outcome from the one he repetitively predicted and dreaded.

*Messages From Severely Dysfunctional Families.* Severely dysfunctional families are characterized by rigidity and lack of nurturance. Men who grow up in these families have whatever messages a man in our culture receives, with the extra unfortunate factor of rigidity to complicate his struggle. Even men who sincerely want to learn to express and understand the mysterious world of feelings and relationships are hampered in their quest for this if they came from these types of families. Therefore, there is an extra dimension of therapy that must go on simultaneously with—and sometimes before—the gender work can continue.

It is important that the therapist work in two ways with a man from this unfortunate circumstance. First, she must keep the degree of his family of origin dysfunction in mind in making her diagnosis. Not only must she assess what it was, she must assess how his current relationships have been affected by growing up in this sort of environment. Second, there are implications for treatment planning. Although the therapist still needs to treat the man for his gender issues, she also must take into account how these are exacerbated and overshadowed by his family's extreme dysfunction.

*Clinical Example.* Brett is a 30-year-old child of two highly abusive, intrusive, manipulative parents and whose mother had several psychotic breaks. A therapist himself, he came to treatment because intrusive thoughts about his past were starting to affect both his current relationship and his work. Below we see how his ordinary struggles as a male in our culture are confounded by his leftover material about his parents. Work with him proceeds along the same ultimate course, but much more slowly.

*Brett:* When I think about really needing someone, . . . I think I'm helpless. And that's a real scary feeling!
*Therapist:* Why's that?
*Brett:* Because I don't want to get hurt again.
*Therapist:* You seem to make an equation, which I can understand that you'd make: If I'm helpless, I'm automatically going to get hurt. That's what we're trying to disconnect.
*Brett:* (Pause) What are the feelings? Yeah. It's not a cognitive thing. Yeah. And then (pause) if I (pause) do get what I need (pause) parts of me feel ashamed.
*Therapist:* There. We gotta talk about that.
*Brett:* I don't know. All I am aware of right now is that I want to leave. (Turning toward the door)
*Therapist:* Can you tell me what that's about?
*Brett:* All I'm aware of is, I don't want to be blasted. And even as I'm saying that, I feel like I'm being hit or thrown around. (Pause)
*Therapist:* Who's throwing you around?
*Brett:* First thing that came to my mind is my dad.
*Therapist:* What's he throwing you around for?
*Brett:* 'Cause he's angry.
*Therapist*: Do you think there's any chance he's throwing you around 'cause it's not manly to say you need?
*Brett:* I don't know. The connection isn't there yet. I just know I'm real scared. And I feel ashamed 'cause I'm scared.

The direction of this therapy periodically needs to switch away from the generic concepts of treatment—the client's gender and relationship issues—to a more specific focus on traumatic memories. This, in a nutshell, is why progress in these kinds of cases usually is so slow: a unitary direction for the treatment is virtually impossible.

Before we leave this section, I offer a postscript. After Brett finished working with the piece that he remembered that day, I asked whether he thought his parents would have had the same response to his being scared if he had been a female. His response was immediate and definitive. "No! I notice them being a lot more empathic with my sister even now." With this question, I am laying tracks back to gender-based issues whenever he is ready to move back to them.

**Summary**

This chapter has provided a discussion of some of the standard themes and issues that typically emerge when a woman does individual therapy with a man. Although many of these issues might emerge in treatment done by a male, there are certain transference considerations with a female therapist that can both augment the client's learnings and jumble the treatment. Female therapists who wish to work confidently and comfortably with male clients would do well to clarify their thoughts and approaches on these very important considerations before they begin the enterprise of specializing in this sort of treatment.

## Five Guidelines for Working With Men in Individual Therapy

The following is a list of suggestions that the female therapist may keep in mind to help her effectively manage this highly intimate and uniquely potent therapy modality:

1. Remember that affection is not sex. Helping men learn the difference between affection and sex can have a very positive impact on their relationship with their significant other. And if they can learn that distinction with you, where there is no chance of sex, they will have a better chance that the learning positively will influence their relationship with their spouse or significant other.
2. It is your responsibility to be clear about how much affection and how much aggression are acceptable in your office. If you

yourself are struggling to keep the boundary between you and your client, seek consultation, supervision, or even therapy.

3. For men to be willing to accept their feelings, therapists need to help them name, identify the roots of, and validate these emotional reactions. What better venue is there for their learning these processes in a concentrated way than in individual therapy with a woman?

4. If you are going to help clients work out, for example, their dependency needs, it is essential that you have at least a working knowledge of your own. Without awareness, you will have difficulty providing leadership to your clients in these emotionally charged, difficult areas. In fact, it is likely that you inadvertently will obstruct therapy by either disallowing their functional dependence on you or by eclipsing their autonomy in favor of your own needs.

5. In the intimacy of individual therapy, sexual attraction between therapist and client likely will be the strongest, if it is going to be there at all. There are several ways to handle sexual attraction. It is not always necessarily talked about in the therapy; when and whether remain the therapist's clinical judgment. However, she must be mindful, particularly with clients who are approximately her age, that strong transference reactions to her sexuality or to her gender are very real and natural possibilities. She must also be willing to admit at least to herself if she experiences a strong countertransference reaction to a male client, so that this does not impair her judgment as a therapist. At the very least, she needs to keep track of her own responses and to watch for signs of his. If she senses that these reactions may be obstructing the therapy process, she needs to err on the side of caution and raise the issue for their mutual consideration.

## A Final Word

It is in individual therapy that the most intimate therapeutic connection is possible, and consequently, it is here that there is the greatest chance for transference and countertransference reactions. It is imperative, therefore, that women who work individually with men be clear about their own issues. They must be able to know and draw their own boundaries. They must be able to handle their clients' sexual attention to them in a way that becomes therapeutic for their clients without leaving them feeling rejected for having the feelings or defensively making themselves eunuchs. They must be able to be intimate and to nurture without being engulfing or feeling engulfed by the man's neediness themselves. They must be able to encourage dependence that is not ultimately crippling, fostering independence when it is time. They must offer nonpossessive love. They must be able to help men find and respect their own ways of being intimate, based on a masculine model, not on a feminine one. They must "Be willing to forcefully confront [men with] the consequences of their behavior, [without] protecting and caretaking [them]" (Napier, 1991, p. 11).

## References

Allen, J. (1990). Men and mothers. In R. Meth & R. Pasick (Eds.), *Men in therapy: The challenge of change* (pp. 224-233). New York: Guilford.

Braverman, L. (1991). The dilemma of housework: A feminist response to Gottman, Napier, and Pittman. *Journal of Marital and Family Therapy, 17*(1), 25-28.

Doherty, W. (1991). Beyond reactivity and the deficit model of manhood: A commentary on articles by Napier, Pittman, and Gottman. *Journal of Marital and Family Therapy, 17*(1), 29-32.

Gordon, B., & Allen, J. (1990). Helping men in couple relationships. In R. Meth & R. Pasick (Eds.), *Men in therapy: The challenge of change* (pp. 181-208). New York: Guilford.

Meth, R. (1990). Men and sexuality. In R. Meth & R. Pasick (Eds.), *Men in therapy: The challenge of change.* New York: Guilford.

Napier, A. (1991). Heroism, men and marriage. *Journal of Marital and Family Therapy, 17*(1), 9-16.

Pittman, F. (1991). The secret passions of men. *Journal of Marital and Family Therapy, 17*(1), 17-23.

Yalom, I. (1985). *The theory and practice of group psychotherapy.* New York: Basic Books.

# It Takes Two to Tango:
# Couples Therapy

What is intimacy, and how does one find it? Every year in our culture, people spend billions of dollars on deodorant and cologne in an attempt to ensure that others will want to be close to them. Intimacy is an experience all humans want; those rejecting the need for connections do so out of defensiveness and self-protection. And yet, as much as we want togetherness, it is the human condition to be terrified of it. Why? How is this push-pull woven into relationships? How is this dread manifested? How is this already-felt tension exacerbated by women's and men's gender socialization? This chapter deals with the interconnectedness of men's and women's experience and how we as therapists can help couples cultivate pleasure and success in relationships. It does so by providing an evolving psychodynamic approach, rather than a pre-scribed methodology for enhancing couple relationships.

## Chapter Overview

The first segment of this chapter will provide a context for why couple, particularly male-female, relationships are so tricky. To do this, we will consider the cultural context in which these relationships exist, the impact that feminism and a feminist perspective sometimes can have on relationships, and what Doherty (1991) calls the "deficit model of manhood" (p. 29). Before we consider how to help couples attain intimacy, we need to know how each sex defines it. With that understanding, we will be in a better position to become interpreters of women's and men's experience to each other. This also will enable us to help couples to change their relationship paradigm, rather than simply reversing the power imbalance—as some contemporary thinkers are wont to do—that traditionally has pervaded male-female relationships. Then, roadblocks to intimacy in both men and women will be discussed. Specifically, I will discuss an experience common to all significant relationships: the struggle over finding the desired amount of intimacy and distance. Other concerns are the problem-maintaining cycle that happens in relationships; the messages that couples give each other to change and then change back; and finally, the ways in which these contradictory messages are fueled by people's catastrophic expectations about intimacy. Rounding out the chapter will be guidelines that therapists can use in structuring gender-sensitive treatment of couples.

## Disclaimers

This chapter is about parlaying concepts related to gender into the couples arena. Although the bulk of my work with couples is with people who are married or in other types of ongoing committed relationships, these same ideas can be utilized for work with premarital, separated, postdivorce, and same-sex couples. Obviously, depending on the specifics of the case, the stage of the relationship, and the exact nature of the relationship contract between people, there are variations in approach. But my experience tells me that the basics are the same in working in each of these circumstances.

When doing couples work, it is the therapist's primary responsibility to diagnose for the likelihood that a relationship can be salvaged legitimately, and not merely be preserved by the weight of homeostasis or habit. Although many marriages can be saved by bubble gum and Band-Aids, the next question is: Should they be? Not all relationships should be saved. Some marriages need to become divorces. Which outcome will generate more health for those involved: the preservation of the marriage or the commencement of a divorce? This additional layer of assessing is critical to the success of marital therapy, because therapy that conserves the marriage but totally compromises the development of the individuals within it is not therapy at all. It is co-optation by the marital system.

Despite what I just said, my biases make me an unabashed marriage saver. That means that when there is an ongoing relationship, I approach couples work looking to preserve and improve the relationship. My initial assessment is for redeeming factors on which all three of us can build to repair—and sometimes even resuscitate—the marriage. My conscience dictates that this is my strongest responsibility when children are involved. Even so, therapists do not have the right, nor should they assume the responsibility, to decide or direct what couples ought to do with their relationships. That is the purview of the couple.

## Current Cultural Milieu

Many societal strictures have been loosened in the last few decades, giving both women and men what appears to be much more freedom in many arenas. However, lest we think that this automatically makes male-female relationships easier and better, we might consider an observation offered by Goldberg (1987):

> In retrospect, defining the nature of relationship problems was simpler before. The issues and the "enemies" were more clearly defined. The solutions and proper direction seemed more clear. Women needed economic, sexual and personal liberation, while men simply needed to overcome sexist ways and develop their intimate, sensitive side. Then, we thought, everything would start to work out and a new world would be created. (p. 63)

Alas, in some ways, these changes may have been just an illusion of progress. Although on the surface there appears to be a loosening of role prescriptions that allows greater freedom on one level, the undercurrent that pervades intimate relationships suggests that they remain as polarized as ever. Even in the midst of the apparent changes, many women and men experience increased tension and confusion between the sexes and desperation about ever developing good relationships.

This increase in pressure comes from many sources. Perhaps most worthy of note is the profound shift that has been made possible in the 20th century. Our culture now provides for most of us a level of prosperity of which most of our grandparents could only dream. Because the basic survival needs of much of the Western world have been met sufficiently, many people can turn their attention to what Maslow (1968) called self-actualization. As this new industrialized epoch affords people the luxury of the requisite time and attention to pursue their inner worlds and to seek satisfaction in relationships, what one sociologist labeled "the revolution of rising expectations" has begun. In the context of relationships, that means that people have begun regularly to expect what Maslow (1968) called peak experiences.

We are living at a hinge of history. And yet, relative to the precedents stamped into our nervous systems over the millennia, a few decades is not much time to change the sex role stereotyping for which we are all socialized. In 1965, Fred Hoyle (quoted in Hillman, 1967) wrote:

> Our special problem today is just this: we are essentially primitive creatures struggling desperately to adjust ourselves to a way of life that is alien to almost the whole past history of our species. . . . Today we are living at a unique moment, neither in the long primitive era nor in the better-adjusted prosperous future. It is our century, our millennium, that must perforce take the maximum strain, for it is our fate to live during the transitional phase. And because we live in this special phase, we find social difficulties, pressures, situations that defy even the simplest logical processes. We find ourselves in no real contact with the forces that are shaping the future. (p. 4)

These comments were made over 25 years ago, but little has changed to ease the tension that accompanies the struggle to make these transitions. It is this new, bewildering, and yet exciting era that provides the context for the male-female struggle out of which we as therapists are expected to midwife mutually beneficial change. Perhaps this accounts for much of the perplexity for therapist and client alike when it comes to engaging couples in family change.

## The Threads That Connect

The words of 10 different clients illustrate the interdependence of men's and women's experience. Each articulates some of the multiple facets of the disappointment, fear, and hurt that come from being unsuccessful in getting relationships to work. Whereas men's challenge is that emotional intimacy is so unprecedented as to be unheard of for most, women's dilemma is that we are socialized to think it is a prerequisite for success for us. We want it. We strive for it. We struggle to attain it. Then, when it eludes women for whatever reason, the failure to find intimacy can be onerous indeed. The words of the following women speaking in group, individual, and couples sessions illustrate some common relationship motifs for females.

*Margaret:* (a 41-year-old divorced woman) I spent all this energy for 16 years trying to do everything for Bob, and I never got anything back for me.
*Shirley:* (a 60-year-old woman married for 41 years) I was so oppressed, I couldn't see it. I didn't know what was happening. I suppose it was easier for me to take it than to learn how to stop it. I'm angry because I don't know what I could've been in my life because of this. I didn't realize I had any potential. Now I feel cheated. I'm starting to have a part of me that's angry and resentful that [my husband] won't come with me to therapy anymore. I told him it's very difficult and can be very painful. But he thinks therapy is bullshit. He's really afraid to find things out about himself. He says it isn't manly.
*Deanne:* (a 37-year-old always single woman) In all my relationships [with men], I felt I was vulnerable. And when I got hurt, I felt I got what I deserved. But now I believe I deserve to be loved, and I want to be loved. And I'm ready for a relationship. Now I just have to find one.
*Nanine:* (a 29-year-old always single woman) I feel like I'm keeping myself really busy, in order not to have to try to get close to people.

*Marne:* (a 50-year-old woman married for 25 years) I guess I think intimacy has to be on both sides, and a lot of the stuff I was doing was pretending, playing a game. And I don't think anybody can be truly intimate with another person without being truly open. It's a two-way street. I had been blaming a lot on [my husband]. Now I'm seeing that—a lot of things got stopped because I was afraid.

It would not surprise most clinicians that women, with their socialization toward relationships, experience a great deal of distress from relationship quandaries. But I wonder how many realize that men suffer as well. This is especially true for the men who are attempting to engage in a new type of male-female relationship despite their socialization training them away from personal connection and relating. The words of some of my male clients give voice to the emotional mayhem that they, too, experience when they cannot get relationships to work in new, more mutually satisfying ways than those for which they were socialized.

*Sean:* (a 42-year-old divorced man) Usually, I have to get a relationship totally in control, or else I'm in pain. And I'm in such pain, such agony now, because I now realize that I can't be in total control. I'm so afraid of losing her, that it's eating me up. I've—always been able to conquer and then discard, throw [the relationship] back. I didn't realize how manipulative that was! I did that until I was secure. But I've never felt like this before. Not like this! This morning I walked around at work looking at the clock, waiting for her to call. I got several things started, but nothing done. So I ask myself, "Why can't you do this? You always have before. Why can't you this time?" (Bursting into tears) It hurts so much! I've never felt out of control like this. It's so painful! [I feel] despair, frustration [about] not being able to handle it, [about] not being stronger. And I feel loneliness and emptiness, too.

*Pat:* (a 62-year-old separated man) I was trying to find a formula, but I'm finding out it doesn't work. I've tried to solve problems that way all my life, and I'm finding that it doesn't work with emotions. I finally realized that I can't find the formula I want. I'm asking myself, "What the hell is love?" And I'm starting to learn what love *isn't*, rather than what it is. And what I'm also learning is that the ones I love, I reject, because that's what happened to me. [Now] I'm putting a different definition on it so I'm not running from it, so I can deal with loving.

*Jonathan:* (a 33-year-old always single man) I hate to say it, but I feel like I'm nothing without a date. I feel like I stick out like a sore thumb. That's why, on New Year's Eve, I went to the office and cleaned out my desk. It was easier. Then I didn't have to be reminded that there's nobody who's there for me.

*Ollie:* (51-year-old remarried man) [My wife] occasionally tells me to stop being so wimpy. And the great temptation is to throw myself right back to what I learned: big boys don't cry. Well, if I get wimpy and kind of puppy-dog around, . . . what do I do, you know, if that's what I feel like doing right then? The alternative is to say, "Well, screw you!" and walk out the door. I guess I get really confused about that. And I worked so damned hard to learn how to cry in front of women!

*Sam:* (a 28-year-old gay man in a primary, monogamous relationship for 3 years) It's OK as long as [my lover] and I are getting along. But when we're not, it can be really bad. But it seems to help when I can think of some way to reassure myself. When I needed reassurance at home growing up, I knew just what to do. I'd go to work on a merit badge or get better grades. Now at least I've gone to my room and cried. But I still have to get better at doing it in front of [my lover].

## Central Premises

Central to understanding the concepts in this chapter is accepting three premises. One is that both men and women suffer distress when the relationship aspect of their life is unfulfilled. As more and more men are beginning to listen to their hurts and their pain, it is increasingly apparent that women do not have a corner on the misery and loneliness markets. Another is that not all relationship problems are caused by men. As systemic thinkers know, women contribute their part to relationship impasses and dysfunction as well. And last is that the distortion of gender defenses makes it seem as though men are responsible for relationships not working. Feelings are the primary legal tender of relationships, and men are socialized to conceal and control feelings. Thus, they can appear to be the culprits because of their need to distance and intellectualize to avoid the powerful inner core of themselves against which they have been taught they must defend.

## Marriage: A Feminine Institution

Intimate relationships are constrained by socially created gender prescriptions. What seems to be easy or obvious to one sex is actually foreign, painful, and frightening for the other to contemplate. According to Goldberg (1987), "In the way that it is constructed, marriage is essentially a feminine institution. The requirements for success are heavily weighted toward qualities more highly developed in the feminine sphere of consciousness" (p. 59).

That is, the skills and abilities required to be in this new male-female relationship play to women's relationship-oriented strengths and competencies and are not usually attributes of traditional males. This leaves men at a distinct disadvantage.

It is almost inevitable that because of men's socialization, it is the male who appears at first blush to be the cause of the problems that lead to the breakup of relationships. This is because men generally defend themselves by withdrawing and breaking contact, whereas women defend themselves by making contact and seeking reassurance about the relationship. Men's typical style of distancing is what is so threatening to most women and what makes men appear to be responsible for relationship disharmony. But it is essential for the reader to grasp that women and men in tandem, not just men, contribute to the fragility of the human connection. Understanding this and guarding against blaming men or allowing them to be blamed will help to prevent the perpetuation of the gender polarization that compromises our treatment and pervades so much of our society today. It also will temper our tendency as female therapists to advocate for women and not for relationships, for when we advocate only for women, our objectivity is compromised, our effectiveness is blunted, and relationships are unnecessarily jeopardized.

## Impact of a Feminist Perspective

Both contemporary intimate relationships and psychotherapy have been profoundly affected by feminism. Although in many ways this has been good, certain aspects and interpretations of this perspective, whether intentionally or not, have given rise to an antimale bias. A feminist perspective on relationships, according to Farrell (1991), has become like fluoride in water—we drink it without being aware of its presence. The complaints about men, the idea that "men are jerks," have become so integrated into our unconscious that even advertisers have caught on. After analyzing 1,000 commercials in 1987, researcher Fred Hayward found that when an ad called for a negative portrayal in a male-female interaction, an astonishing 100% of the time the "bad guy" was the man (p. 81).

Clearly, not all feminists believe or tout that men are jerks who are to blame for all problems. Likewise, not all of them accuse men of being infected by "testosterone poisoning," to use Keen's (1992) phrase. However, some appear to. It is particularly distressing when comments of some leaders of the feminist family therapy movement reveal this antimale bias, because as systems thinkers, we are supposed to understand the interlocking nature of problems between people. However, many seem to have a blind spot in this area, subtly or not so subtly laying the cause of relationship dysfunction and political quagmires at the feet of men. One explanation for this is that a feminist perspective often looks at and decries the socialization of men without considering what is underneath that socialization to see how to help men break through the constraints placed there by societal expectations of them.

Thus, a feminist perspective can give rise to a sometimes faint, sometimes blatant, but still insidious alliance of female therapists with women against men. According to Lipchik (1991), this aligning with women has roots in the feminist movement of the 1960s, "whose mission . . . gradually became the implicit mandate for feminist therapists, who automatically advocated for the woman, thus becoming adversaries of men" (p. 60). This, more than anything, will compromise treatment of couples and hamper successfully engaging men in family change. As Moore and Gillette (1990) state, "The feminist critique, *when it is not wise enough*, actually further wounds an already besieged *authentic* masculinity [italics added]" (p. xviii).

Further, we must resist three misconceptions that female therapists, whether feminist or not, can hold. One is that maleness itself, and not political realities, is responsible for the exploitation of women. Two, that maleness and masculinity are synonymous with the male mystique. Three, that all males are exploiters. It behooves the female therapist to examine her biases about men so that she can adequately treat them. According to Kimbrell (1991),

For men who are sensitive to feminist thinking, this view of masculinity creates a confusing and debilitating double bind. We view ourselves as oppressors yet experience victimization on the personal and social level. *Instead of blaming maleness, we must challenge the defective mythology of the male mystique.* Neither the male mystique nor the denigration of maleness offers hope for the future [italics added]. (p. 70)

What is the male mystique? It teaches that mean are and should be competitive, uncaring, and unloving. It goes far beyond autonomy, creating isolation, turning men permanently against each other in the dog-eat-dog world of earning a living, and segregating them from those whom they are supposed to love. Far too often, men have been seen only as the power elite. But they pay a high price for a life of entitlement and privilege.

The assumption that men only benefit from their positions of power and do not pay a price poses a danger against which, to be effective, the female therapist must guard. This bias blinds us to clearly assessing a couple's situation and makes our interventions so one sided as to be dangerous. Further, as Pittman (1991) says, "We have to keep in mind that men display excessive masculinity when they are afraid. They have been taught that masculinity will ward off evil spirits" (p. 22). To do this work effectively, the therapist, even if she considers herself a feminist, must remember the full range of men's situations and advocate for the relationship, not siding with one for the defeat of the other, for victories won thusly are in fact losses for the people involved and our society as a whole, further tearing at the already fraying fabric of the family.

## Deficit Model of Manhood

Pittman (1991), in a presentation before a national family therapy conference, asks,

> What happened to us [men]? How did we become the monsters of feminist nightmares? The answer of course is that we underwent a careful and deliberate process of gender training, sometimes brutal, always dehumanizing, cutting away large chunks or ourselves. Little girls went through something similarly crippling. If the gender training were successful, we all ended up being half persons. (p. 18)

Doherty (1991) puts out a call to action that may help mollify the tendency to blame men for all relationship woes. He names this new gender trap "the deficit model of manhood":

> The old patriarchal model made men the measuring stick for the human; women were men with deficits. Feminists have effectively

challenged this model of womanhood in family therapy. . . . Men had
to be brought off the pedestal, and women out of the mud. . . . We have
a long way to go to overcome the deficit model of womanhood, but
this distorted view has been identified as crippling to women and
therapy, and alternatives are being actively pursued. . . . What I fear
is happening among men who have embraced many tenets of feminism . . . is that we have moved manhood from the pedestal to the
mud, from an idealized model to a deficit model. (pp. 29-30)

Doherty goes on to state that therapists and their male clients need
to take a lesson from the feminists who effectively learned to
challenge the deficit model of womanhood. It is time we do the
same for manhood. Neither sex can be glorified or denigrated if
there are to be genuinely equitable relationships between people.
In truth, each sex and the socialization it has experienced brings
both strengths and weaknesses to the table when it comes to
relating. Rather than disparaging men for who they are and what
they have been, Napier (1991) calls for the therapeutic community
to contribute to the creation of "a new map for masculinity" (p.
15), which seems like a much more worthy and promising endeavor.
Once this map is drawn, we will approach an answer to the question
posed by Braverman (1991): Does all the talk about men and relationships "lead us further down the path to substantive changes in the
character of men's lives with their families?" (p. 25).

## Definitions of Intimacy

To reiterate, the creation and enhancement of intimacy are goals
that are sought extensively in the contemporary Western world, even
though they have been regarded as a rarity and an option in other
times and places. Yet, they seem to elude many people, much to their
chagrin and pain. To many couples and therapists, seeking the intimate encounter is such a given that few efforts are made even to
define it. But unless people are fortunate enough to grow up in a
family where intimacy was commonplace, few know what it is or how
to find it. And even when they do, most experience regret that more
close encounters of the personal kind seem to be militated against by
the press of the routines of ordinary life and the dust of daily battle.
    But perhaps another reason intimacy seems to elude couples is
that people's definition of intimacy is gender based, and therefore

what could be seen as an intimate encounter by one is not necessarily experienced that way by the other. And yet, what is intimate is taken for granted because so much of how we experience and define intimacy depends on our gender. Therapists' grasping this is yet another way we can become interpreters of men's and women's uniquenesses so that they can be helped to build bridges to each other to replace the walls with which they usually enter treatment. Then it can become clear that there are advantages and disadvantages to men's and women's styles of intimacy on which couples can capitalize.

### Researchers' Definitions of Intimacy

To many researchers and clinicians, intimacy is equated with sharing of emotions and self-disclosing. Whole books are written on this subject, many of them leaving out a more masculine form of intimacy: doing for others and sharing activities. In fact, Swain (1989) states, "Researchers concerned with intimacy have assumed that verbal self-disclosure is the definitive referent for intimacy and have thus interpreted alternative styles that involve instrumental action as less intimate, or non-intimate behavior" (p. 72). To illustrate this, notice the emphasis on personal self-disclosure by family therapists Wynne and Wynne (1986) as they seek to define this all too elusive concept and experience: "Intimacy is a subjective relational experience in which the core components are trusting self-disclosure to which the response is communicated empathy" (p. 384). Another well-known family researcher, Lewis (1979), discusses what constitutes a healthy family. To him, intimacy is so central a concept for healthy family functioning that he devotes an entire chapter to the topic, in which he says,

> [Intimacy] describes those moments when there has occurred a disclosure of deep and private feelings and thoughts. It implies a reciprocal process in which each person can share deeply from within and accept a similar disclosure from the other. Intimacy is usually a peak experience rather than a stable, constantly present state. (p. 74)

Still another researcher, Waring (1988), defines intimacy as a composite of (a) affection, (b) expressiveness, (c) compatibility, (d) cohesion, (e) sexuality, (f) conflict resolution, (g) autonomy, and

(h) identity. Waring's conceptualization hints at two ingredients that to a man would foster intimacy: compatibility, which he goes on to define as the ability of the couple to work and play together comfortably, and autonomy, or the couple's degree of positive connectedness to other family and friends. Finally, Swain (1989) offers perhaps the most general definition of intimacy that is readily applicable to both men's and women's styles of friendship and intimacy. He defines intimacy as "behavior in the context of a friendship that connotes a positive and mutual sense of meaning and importance to the participants" (p. 72).

The last definition allows people to determine what behaviors are meaningful and intimate to them and assumes that there may be several avenues that can result in experiencing closeness. The third definition hints that alternatives to deep personal self- disclosure may be acceptable. The first two definitions overlook entirely that men express their caring through direct action whereas women express their caring verbally.

## Women's and Men's Styles of Intimacy

In her landmark work on women's development, Gilligan (1982) discusses at great length the gender differences that shape our views on intimacy and our roles in relationships. According to her and others, women's primary focus has been on establishing related-ness (Miller, 1986). Because of this, most have developed and pruned relational skills to a fine art. This enables us to be highly responsive to emotion, which to women is the legal tender of relationships. They have refined their aptitude in verbal persua-sion and responsiveness to others and to nonverbal cues. This positions us to create and to seek to sustain a sense of connected-ness and community that are the ingredients of strong attach-ments and bonds. It is women's giving priority to these needs that makes us such competent caregivers. As a result, we expect to attain higher levels of development by affiliation and tend to view autonomy rather than closeness as dangerous and unattractive.

In contrast to women's goal of establishing and maintaining relatedness, men's focus typically is to achieve separation. This results from a mix of their own internal developmental imper-atives and their introjection of societal messages. According to Letich (1991), "Our society's ideal man is not supposed to have any emotional needs" (p. 86). Typically, men believe they can achieve their most fully developed self by individuation and autonomy. As Gilligan points out, men tend to view attachment as a paralyzing entrapment and caring as an inevitable precursor to entrapment. She further points out that there has come to be an assumption that attachment and caregiving are seen by many men as at best way stations for those who have not achieved "mature" goals of separateness and independence. Looked at like this, it is little wonder that emotional closeness is not often sought by men if they are left to their own devices. They experience closeness by doing, by shared interests and activities. Herein lies the crux of much of men's internal conflicts about engaging in what women call intimate experiences. Men need to feel certain that to do so will not thoroughly compromise the primary element that makes them male, their need for autonomy.

Furthermore, for most men, it truly does appear that actions speak louder than words and are the vehicle for communicating their caring and concern. They view talking as only one option for expressing caring. This speaks both to men's belief that to fix situations for their loved ones is intimate and to their activity-oriented style of being together. For example, one couple I worked with decided through the course of the therapy to divorce, whereupon the man's first act was to change the oil in his wife's car before she left. To the woman, this represented a callous disregard for the feelings of both of them. But for the man, it signaled caring and continued regard for her welfare despite their decision to divorce. Believing my role as interpreter was critical here, I intervened to explain the gender-based differences in ways of experiencing and expressing caring. This helped them both head off yet another cycle of blame and recrimination.

Generalizing about men, Swain (1989) states,

> From his activity-oriented perspective, he actually views women as restricted by a lack of alternatives to verbal expressiveness. These expressive alternatives are available to men . . . by sharing and understanding common activities. Nonverbal cues, expressed in active settings, contribute to private, covert, and in general sex-specific styles of intimacy. (p. 78)

This perspective certainly provides a more useful and affirming outlook on men than merely disparaging them as inexpressive. If we broaden our definition of intimacy, surely more of males' actions can qualify.

### Comparing Men's and Women's Styles of Intimacy

Men and women have different styles of intimacy that reflect the often separate realms in which they express it. Many expressions mean something different to him than to her. According to Goldberg (1987),

> A good relationship [to him] means the freedom to be left alone while they are together, without feeling guilty. To her it means achieving a fantasy of deep, intertwined closeness, a melting together that he couldn't possibly be capable of. The end result is that she feels herself to be in great pain over being distanced by him; he is tense and raw over feeling pursued and pressured for a closeness he can't give. In his psyche, she is *everywhere* (even when she isn't there) and threatening to engulf him. In hers, he is *never really there*. (p. 25)

The overall concept here is that women and men may place a similar value on friendship and closeness but have different ways of expressing it. And the deficit model of manhood seems to imply that men's active style of intimacy needs to be totally replaced by skills that are usually thought of as feminine. This negation or denial of men's active style of intimacy threatens to demotivate men from taking up the challenge of a more emotionally based expression of intimacy that is the legal tender of strong relationships. Yet, if no respect or credit is given for the ways in which they do show their caring, there will be little or no incentive for them to learn to meet their partners emotionally. For example, in one couple I worked with, the man's fondest, closest memories from childhood involved his family playing golf together and then coming home to pitch in and prepare the evening meal. The wife, herself a therapist, rejected his repeated request that she and their children learn to do some activity like this together, discounting that this could qualify as intimacy. The couple fought, in essence, over whose definition of intimacy was "right." When I detected the brewing power struggle that would ensure that nobody's intimacy needs would be met, I explained the gender bases of definitions of intimacy. Then I asked the man to explain in a way that did not simply sound like another run-of-the-mill request on his part what family activities would mean to him. Then the wife explained that she had never realized before that such activities were so significant to him emotionally. This allowed him to feel recognized and validated for his preferred style, and the process of elaborating on his wonderful childhood memories of these family outings set off profuse tears over the fact that those times would never happen again because his father was dead. This understandably touched his wife deeply because he shared emotions that he had never let her in on before. And of course, it accommodated her definition of intimacy and therefore was deeply satisfying to her. Thus, they both had the opportunity to experience getting their needs met in their preferred style while learning about the other's. This obviously deepened their relationship while giving them additional pathways for intimacy.

Both clinician and client need to keep in mind that there are advantages and disadvantages to both feminine and masculine styles of intimacy. Feminine styles of intimacy are useful for acknowledging and sharing vulnerable material such as fear, disappointment, and sadness. Admitting and expressing emotions like these greatly enhances the problem-solving process because it deepens the trust and security in a relationship. Likewise, masculine styles of intimacy are productive for confronting precarious situations, for facing times of feeling weak, and for just plain having fun. His style can empower them both to action, to deal creatively and constructively with their difficulties. Both styles are necessary for a balanced approach to life.

The challenge for therapists and for couples is to find ways to capitalize on and integrate the different styles into a workable unified approach that facilitates a balanced and productive life for both persons. Thus, instead of their continuing to coexist in two separate worlds, respecting and capitalizing on their differences assists each in giving meaning and voice to inner worlds in individual but shared ways.

## Roadblocks to Intimacy

As a way to work on dismantling the barriers to intimacy that clients erect, it is helpful to understand for ourselves and then teach them to grasp the etiology of common scuffles that occur between women and men. The aim of this section will be to explicate this undertow that exists outside people's conscious awareness that pulls them into unconstructive ways of relating and burdens relationships. As each sex expects the other to meet their defensive needs, either conflict or stony silence typically ensue. This is usually because of the tug of war that often happens when women, because of their gender socialization, want more closeness and men, because of theirs, want more distance. The four primary factors that fuel this ongoing struggle between couples will be discussed separately. We will start by discussing the struggle over regulating the amount of intimacy and distance that makes relationships run amuck. Then we will move on to consider the problem-maintaining cycle that happens when couple relationships become dysfunctional. Next, we will consider the messages that people give each other to change, and then to change back when they become frightened by alterations in their comfortable and familiar homeostasis. And finally, we will see how those messages are fueled by the catastrophic expectations of each member of the couple. As these ideas form the central constructs of the gender-sensitive couples work I am proposing, it is important that the reader grasp them. Doing so not only will maximize her movement with both members of the couple, but also it will help to mute the easy tendency to align against the person, usually the man, whose behavior appears to be creating the greatest problem.

The overall goal is to sensitize the reader to some of the multiple and complex difficulties that make arriving at a truly intimate connection so arduous. By contrast, the experience of falling in love that pervades the initial stages of any relationship is simple. And as discussed in Chapter 5, learning only behavior change that typifies a content approach to therapy is much too facile for understanding the undertow that plagues couples.

## The Struggle Over Intimacy and Distance

Two primary factors contribute to the struggle men and women have in attaining intimacy: their socialization and their unconscious anxiety.

*Socialization.* Femininity teaches women that what counts is relationships and that they are to mold themselves to a man's identity. Masculinity teaches men to be what Goldberg refers to as "enclosed men" and that relating in personal ways is threatening, frustrating, and unsatisfying. These societal imperatives carry with them different, often mutually contradictory expectations that are usually poorly understood and that silently create pressures and undercurrents:

> When such expectations are not made clear, they lead to conflicts that are difficult to resolve because they are not understood by either party. Men and women are less able to be distinct individuals, i.e., to be differentiated in a relationship, when expectations are unstated or inappropriate. (Meth & Pasick, 1990, p. 182)

But even when expectations can be articulated, neither sex automatically can relate differently by fiat or by sheer dint of will, even if they want to earnestly. And most people want to when they become aware that they are having problems. For example, although it makes logical sense to a woman that letting go of demanding that her husband be her whole life might actually produce more of the love she craves, emotionally she can encounter a great deal of difficulty in doing this. Conversely, a man might want desperately to acknowledge his emotional pain, alienation, and despair, but because this skill is so underdeveloped in him, he likely will feel thwarted in his attempts to do so. The proscriptions that each has internalized from society's messages will militate against their attempts to change. At this juncture, if their often desperate attempts to find a bridge fail, for many all that seems to remain is to leave the relationship and begin fresh somewhere else or give up on relating altogether. We therapists must be that bridge until they can learn to build one themselves.

*Unconscious Anxiety.* It is because of unconscious anxiety that intimacy is something we all want and yet about which we have a great deal of fear. According to Feldman (1992), "In marital and family systems, anxiety generally takes one of two forms: fear of interpersonal closeness or fear of interpersonal distance. . . . In distressed families, this type of fear leads to dysfunctional distancing in marital or parent/child relationships" (p. 5).

Relationships have to contend with the existence of this dimension—whether couples and therapists want to acknowledge it or not. And in fact, this dynamic forms the primary fuel for the push-pull in relationships. That is, although everyone wants an intimate connection so as not to be bereft and alone, everyone also has fears of being hurt by it. In addition, it is highly unlikely that both members of a couple will experience spontaneous synchrony in their preferred amount of closeness and distance. In fact, in light of the impact of gender socialization on preferences for closeness and distance as modes for reassurance, it is most likely that at least in the beginning, they will not. This is another reason why the first 2 to 3 years of a relationship are usually so stormy. People are attempting to find and to regulate their mutually acceptable style for seeking closeness and distance. And couples who become part of a clinical population are undoubtedly experiencing dysfunction on that level. To attempt to teach them skills for greater intimacy without also attending to blockages on this dimension is ingenuous, for even though people may nod assent, they will be unable to attain genuine closeness without truly understanding this depth dimension. They will continue their dance away from each other just as soon as they begin to get close, fueling rather than extinguishing conflict.

## The Problem-Maintaining Cycle

Understanding the recursive, interlocking nature of human interaction allows the therapist to be aware of what is happening on another dimension than the conscious one, for clients' underlying processes and the degree of their gender-based defensiveness determine the limits of their capacity to relate personally, regardless of their intentions or the priorities they place on communicating. Conceptualizing this gives the therapist much leverage to help people work through and move past their logjams internally and with each other.

These concepts are based on the premises advanced by Feldman (1979, 1982, 1992), Pinsof (1983, 1991), and Feldman and Pinsof (1982). Feldman (1992) states, "Individual and family interactional problems are maintained by multilevel feedback loops. In order to interrupt these feedback loops, both intrapsychic and behavioral changes are needed" (p. 105). The assumption is that change at one level will lead directly or indirectly to change at another. For example, when a man begins to reclaim his feelings and respond sensitively to his partner, this can become mutually reinforcing as both experience new levels of closeness and positive feelings. Often, however, change at one level is blocked by the lack of movement or a negative response to change at another. For example, although many women enter treatment complaining that their spouse is insensitive and unapproachable, sometimes when changes begin to take place, they have a negative reaction such as Ollie reported from his wife at the beginning of the chapter. Rather than blame the spouse for her natural change back message, it is important that the couples therapist know how to identify this response for what it is and effectively learn to intervene with it.

## Change and Change Back Messages

Lerner, in her two highly acclaimed books *The Dance of Anger* (1985) and *The Dance of Intimacy* (1989), labeled this very common and baffling clinical phenomenon. Why in the world would people come to therapy; invest the considerable time, money, and energy it takes to do it; and then want to change back just when they begin to get what they came for? Puzzling as this spectacle is, the couples therapist needs to be aware of this covert dimension of interaction in order to intervene therapeutically.

Why would people obstruct the very changes they are seeking when they come to therapy? The answer to this question rests on the principle of mutual regulation advanced by Watzlawick, Weakland, and Fisch (1974). They posit that each family member regulates and is regulated by the other family members. This relates to a important concept that is central to family systems thinking: that symptoms serve a very important function in families. Surely, this makes no logical sense. Why would people want to continue to be plagued by the very problems they come to us to fix? It is because, on an unconscious level, these symptoms are important in maintaining individuals' or families' equilibrium. That is, they keep people out of emotional mischief. By that I mean that although the problem vexes those involved, it also acts like a pressure cooker valve; it allows people to let off the steam of their unconscious anxiety, brought to too high a level by constructive, usually intimacy-seeking, behavior. Eventually, the level of symptomatic behavior exceeds the system's permissible deviation limits, signaling members to begin seeking constructive alternatives. As Feldman and Pinsof (1982) state, "We conceptualize family systems as oscillating between a state in which problem behavior is in the foreground and a state in which non-problem behavior or 'constructive alternative' behavior is in the foreground. These states are not necessarily of equal duration or intensity" (p. 299). This accounts for the recursive interaction cycle that we see with couples in treatment. These concepts are useful in helping the therapist to understand and explain such puzzling clinical phenomena as a resurgence of problem behavior just when the couple begins to enjoy the intimacy they seek. Once systems of all kinds get regulated, it is as though they develop the grooves of a well-calibrated machine. This means that although people enter treatment begging for change, on a covert, unconscious level, there is a resistance to it. This element of avoidance must be taken into account in structuring and pacing interventions.

How does the couples therapist proceed in light of this covert dimension, without being extruded by a couple's self-protective homeostatic mechanisms? She first must identify for herself the messages that people give to change and then change back. The more rigid and dysfunctional the system, the more of those messages she will detect. This is particularly the case when couples get the modifications that on a conscious level were the desired effect of the treatment. She must expect this, alert the couple to anticipate it, and plan strategies to avoid the treatment's being sidetracked by this natural human tendency. And as soon as she sees that the couple is ready, she carefully must articulate what she sees. She must proceed with caution on this operation, however, because the more rigidly dysfunctional the system, the more resistant the people will be to this assessment and interpretation. Their refusal to see or accept this premise often serves the function of the ultimate protection of the homeostasis of the system. When systems are not so unyielding, she may proceed with her interpretation and intervention less gingerly; this, too, is an important aspect of ongoing assessment as the treatment progresses. Whenever she deduces it is safe to do so, she must intervene to prevent and explore the obstruction of the changes; otherwise, what the people say they want and need will continue to be canceled out and they may eventually leave treatment as the ultimate protection of their dysfunctional system.

### Catastrophic Fears or Expectations

Perhaps the most useful notion to explain what fuels the resurgence of symptoms is the psychodynamic concept of catastrophic fears or expectations. This concept has its origins in Freud's work on anxiety-producing situations that people experience as dangerous. Pinsof (1983) defines catastrophic expectations as:

> individual and/or collective fantasies about the catastrophic consequences of feared thoughts, feelings or behaviors. They are conscious or unconscious and concern self and others. . . . Catastrophic expectations and the anxiety with which they are associated constitute the driving force behind most psychological problem-solving blocks. (p. 29)

Triggering catastrophic expectations serves to ward off the anxieties generated by intimacy-producing experiences. The system becomes incapable of implementing a constructive alternative to this behavior, because at that moment, this problematic behavior is serving a survival function.

Catastrophic expectations may or may not be rational or appropriate; clinical experience shows that most are irrational and inappropriate *in the present context.* But it is important to grasp that they were a rational survival mechanism at the time they were developed. For example, if a parent dies when a child is very young, it is a sure bet that the child will have a catastrophic fear of abandonment. That seems a rational fear, but being plagued by it in adult life despite promises and reassurances of loyalty is irrational. Likewise, if a man were abused as a child, it is a safe prediction that he will fear his own destructive impulses in ways that will obstruct the constructive expression of anger. And therapists know how corrosive the inability to express anger can become to individuals and relationships over time. So the key point here is to help people realize that catastrophic fears and the anxieties that they generate are antiques from their past. Then we can help them learn different, more functional ways to take care of themselves now.

It is likely that catastrophic fears form the basis for clients' transference reactions to us, and so those, too, should be explored when they occur. Further, they can be seen as a vehicle for helping couples explore their transference reactions to others as well.

Because catastrophic fears were developed and now operate outside people's conscious awareness, they can be difficult to identify and articulate. However, with experience, the therapist can cultivate a sensitivity that allows her to hear them even when she is not asking directly about them. This will come through especially clearly when people describe their attempts at intimacy. Pinsof (1983) assumes that every nonbiological block is directly associated with one or more catastrophic expectations. In fact, he states that those fears and the anxiety associated with them constitute the driving force behind most psychological problem-solving blocks.

When articulated, catastrophic expectations assume an if-then form. It should be remembered that they were developed in the service of the family and the individual involved and as such acted as protectors from intense anxiety—irrational as these relics sound now, they served a survival function. I listed common fears in the first chapter, but they bear repetition and elaboration here, inasmuch as they are key concepts for gender-sensitive couples work. These are the five fears that Feldman (1979) articulated, along with an elaboration I have added to explain each:

*Catastrophic fear of abandonment* (being left bereft) "If I open myself to people and let myself love them and then they leave, I will feel abandoned and bereft again as I did before. So I won't really let people in, because they inevitably will leave anyway. And then it won't hurt so much when they do."

*Catastrophic fear of merger* (being swallowed up) "If I let people in, they will engulf me, swallow me up, and I won't have a life of my own ever again. So I'll just not ever let anybody close."

*Catastrophic fear of exposure* (sharing too much and then being rejected) "If I show people who I really am and they don't like what they see, they will reject me and I will be devastated. So I will just keep all my feelings and most of my thoughts to myself."

*Catastrophic fear of one's own destructive impulses* (rage) "If I let people close to me, eventually they will do something to get me angry. So since I can't trust what I'll do, I'll protect them from getting hurt and myself from the humiliation I would feel if I did hurt them by keeping everyone at arm's length."

*Catastrophic fear of attack* (persecutory attack and annihilation) "If I let people close enough to make them angry, I'll be destroyed by them. So I'll control every relationship by keeping everyone far away from me. Then I won't ever get hurt again."

One can see the weight of people's fears and the urgency that they can feel to avoid them. However, what most people do not realize is that when they protect themselves like this, warding off catastrophes in the ways suggested above, they virtually guarantee that disasters will happen. The strain caused by the distance that comes when people protect themselves in these ways generates much relationship dysfunction and pain that eventually can become unbearable.

Over many years of working with this concept, I have developed the following generalizations about catastrophic fears: (a) People have at least one. (b) The problems for a couple when either has more than one catastrophic fear are compounded exponentially. (c) A couple's catastrophic fears usually fit like hand and glove, because what quiets one person's anxiety spikes the other's, such as abandonment and merger. (d) When both people have the same fear, it can be especially immobilizing, for example, a fear of exposure such that neither is willing to risk sharing anything of substance. (e) If you cannot discern clearly what a woman's worst fear is, abandonment is a safe bet, because she seldom gets the degree of closeness with a man she is programmed to seek—but he is socialized to avoid. (f) If you are not sure what catastrophe a man fears, merger is a good guess, because he is socialized for autonomy and therefore often experiences being crowded in an intimate relationship with a woman who likely wants a great deal of closeness.

Our job as therapists is threefold: (a) to help clients identify when their fears are being set off, (b) to help them learn what sets their partner's fears off, and (c) to help them find constructive alternatives for the shared management of these fears. Doing this will enhance the quality and the degree of intimacy between people. Needless to say, it is impossible to eradicate these fears from people's lives, but it is very feasible to help them manage these otherwise compelling motivators propelling them apart so they can use their understandings as tools for increasing connection.

Two ideas about how to work with these concepts are important to note. One, I do not mean to imply that I discuss these concepts in an invariant order; I wait for cues offered by my clients to tell me when and in what order to work with them. And two, because uncovering catastrophic fears often unearths highly charged unconscious material, the reader is advised to do this clinical intervention circumspectly. Over the years, I have noted several classes of reactions. For some, understanding immediately gives them a potent key for changing their destructive pattern. Others flatly deny that they even have fears such as these, despite behavior and words that display them. Still others, the first time or two the issue is discussed may literally forget it was ever even talked about. I assume that this is their unconscious protecting them from threatening material and preparing them to grapple with it in bits at a time. So in fact, I often paradox clients, inviting them to forget by the time they get to the elevator. Still others experience heightened emotionality of all kinds, almost as if a cork has been popped. I prepare clients for all of these reactions, which have become standard to me but often are experienced as frighteningly unpredictable by clients.

A final word on the treatment of couples' catastrophic expectations is in order. People often ask how long therapy will take. The therapist can hazard a response to that question based on her assessment of several factors: (a) how resistant the couple is about naming and owning their catastrophic fears, (b) how adroit they are at managing their catastrophic fears rather than continuing to allow their fears to manage them, (c) how involved and intractable the problem-maintaining cycle is, and (d) the depth and duration of the symptoms generated. Treating some people is like cutting with a warm knife through butter; with little effort, their defenses melt and can be restructured. Others seem to require a chisel, a jackhammer, or even dynamite to blast away their defenses and the problem-maintaining cycle they spawn. The therapist's assessment of these key variables will give her a relatively accurate "guesstimate" of the length of treatment.

*Clinical Example.* Katherine and Sam, from whom we heard in Chapter 1, provide an example of how to translate these abstract concepts into a series of clinical interventions. In their late 30s and 8 years into the first marriage for both of them, they have three children. Although Katherine has a master's degree, she stays home to care for the children. Sam is a consultant to small businesses, an occupation that takes him out of town at least half the time. Both are oldest children in sibships of four.

When they presented for treatment, Katherine was an extremely socialized, dependent woman who believed herself incapable of doing even the smallest task without Sam. This would be burden-some to both people in any relationship, but it was particularly problematic in light of Sam's heavy travel schedule and the formi-dable demands of parenting three children. The more we worked, the more it became apparent that Katherine's helplessness was less incapacity than a strategy for getting attention from Sam. In fact, as treatment progressed, she continually was delighted to discover just how capable she was. The first stage of therapy was devoted to helping Sam to see that he, too, had contributed to the problem between them; that it was not up to Katherine to fix it as she had attempted to do in three other individual therapies. As Sam began to be convinced, both agreed to participate in group psychotherapy as an adjunct to the couples therapy, she in a women's group and he in a men's group.

Once both people genuinely bought into the notion that their conflict was a problem *between* them and not just one that resided *within* one or the other of them, we settled down to work on understanding their pattern for seeking intimacy and distance. That is, I first explained the concept of the intimacy-distance regulation cycle, how it functions in relationships, and that this could be observed in all couple relationships. I then helped them articulate theirs so they could see the pattern and begin to bring it under conscious control. Following that, I moved on to helping them answer the question: What is the fuel for this pattern?

The following excerpts are from three consecutive sessions. In the first, I guided them both to begin to understand and articulate their own and each other's contributions to the pattern between them. When they could grasp and articulate this, I took my cue to help them describe the circle of their entire dance. And then, I helped them verbalize their long-repressed catastrophic fears. To reiterate, the point in vocalizing these unconscious thoughts and fears is for clients to bring the behaviors that they engender under conscious control, rather than continuing to be controlled by them.

*Katherine:* (To the therapist) What you said last week about my anger being bogus must have really been true, because after saying I was sorry to Sam, it dissolved. So it must've been bogus.

*Therapist:* So what must the anger have been for, then? What we have to figure out is, what is the function of the anger between you?

*Katherine:* It creates the distance at home that we have when he is on the road.

I see this statement as my opportunity to explain the concept of the intimacy-distance regulation cycle, and we proceed to articulate the pattern that they have developed to regulate the degree of closeness and distance. Several observations can be made about their dance, which is diagrammed in Figure 9.1. One very good sign is that this couple has more pathways back toward each other (five) than they do away from each other (three). When I discover the opposite in doing this diagram with couples, my heart sinks, because diagnostically this augurs a greater degree of dysfunction and distance—graphic evidence of the nature and the degree of problems between them. Such diagrams can give therapist and client alike a focus for structuring the couples work. In addition, this diagram gives graphic proof that neither one of them is to blame for the problem, that it really does take two to tango. And finally, seeing this makes concrete for couples that they both have choice points throughout the circle where either one of them can behave differently and thus generate a different outcome. When they both can see and act on their choice points, they are in an extremely favorable position to alter their unproductive cycles.

In the next session, the following discussion takes place, in which as they are both acknowledging their progress at breaking their hindering cycle, I see my opportunity to help them take even greater control of their pattern by isolating the catastrophic fears that fuel the dance. The reader is encouraged to label the fears as she reads their words describing those fears. As each of them begins using the knowledge they gained in understanding their repetitive, circular pattern, they can begin to take hold and change the pattern of their responses to each other.

*Katherine:* I realized sitting here last week that I didn't know how to ask for what I need. And so he didn't tell me, and I didn't tell me, either. There were a few times where he tried to make me feel good, and I tried to recognize that.

*Therapist:* (To Sam) Did you notice her doing that?

*Sam:* (To Katherine) Yes, we were calmer. I just noticed things were better between us.

*Therapist:* That you both interrupted the cycle accounted for that. That's what made for the better day.

*Sam:* For my part, I decided not to be so pissy about everything.

*Katherine:* And I decided not to be a victim and let the outside define what I was feeling on the inside. And I chose to recognize Sam's actions,

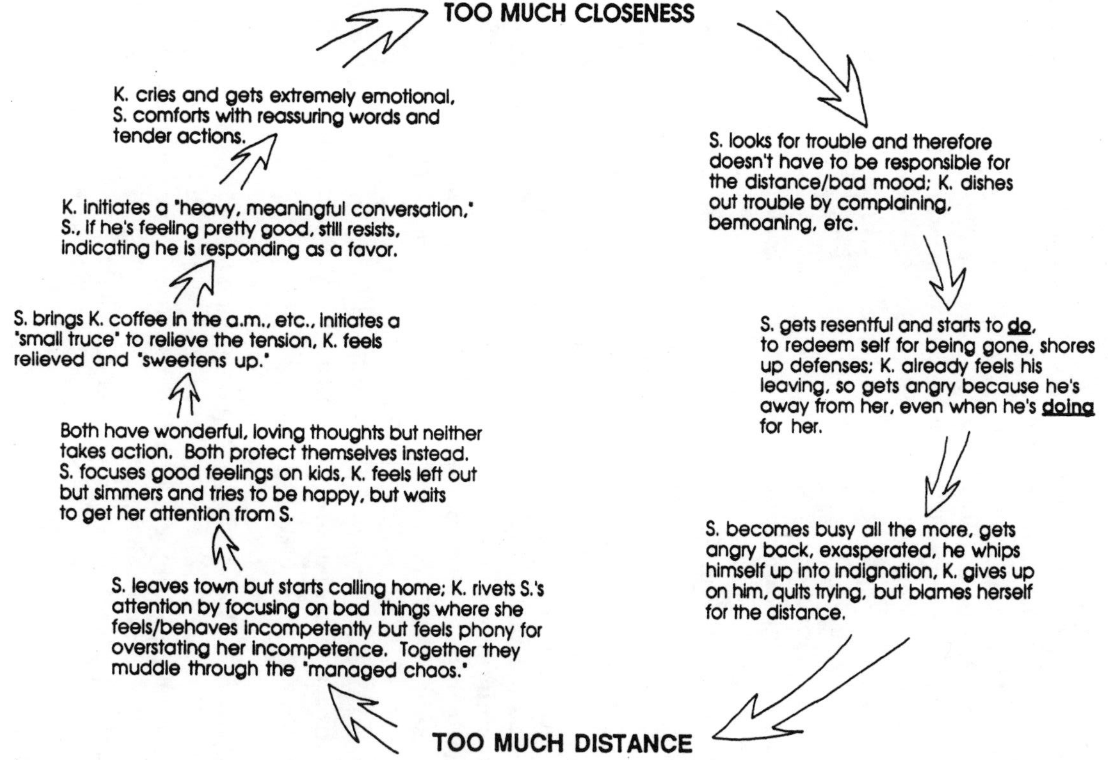

**TOO MUCH CLOSENESS**

K. cries and gets extremely emotional.
S. comforts with reassuring words and
tender actions.

K. initiates a "heavy, meaningful conversation."
S., if he's feeling pretty good, still resists,
indicating he is responding as a favor.

S. brings K. coffee in the a.m., etc., initiates a
"small truce" to relieve the tension. K. feels
relieved and "sweetens up."

Both have wonderful, loving thoughts but neither
takes action. Both protect themselves instead.
S. focuses good feelings on kids. K. feels left out
but simmers and tries to be happy, but waits
to get her attention from S.

S. leaves town but starts calling home: K. rivets S.'s
attention by focusing on bad things where she
feels/behaves incompetently but feels phony for
overstating her incompetence. Together they
muddle through the "managed chaos."

**TOO MUCH DISTANCE**

S. looks for trouble and therefore
doesn't have to be responsible for
the distance/bad mood; K. dishes
out trouble by complaining,
bemoaning, etc.

S. gets resentful and starts to **do**,
to redeem self for being gone, shores
up defenses; K. already feels his
leaving, so gets angry because he's
away from her, even when he's **doing**
for her.

S. becomes busy all the more, gets
angry back, exasperated, he whips
himself up into indignation, K. gives up
on him, quits trying, but blames herself
for the distance.

**Figure 9.1** Katherine and Sam's Intimacy-Distance Regulation Cycle.

the positive actions. He was trying to be more sensitive to my needs, and I decided to acknowledge it. That was all positive.

*Therapist:* Good stuff, you guys. You can feel very proud of yourselves. And now we need to figure out what is the fuel for this cycle. (After explaining the concept of catastrophic expectations) What do each of you imagine scares you the very most about being intimate with each other?

*Sam:* One option for me is the loss of individuality.

*Therapist:* Can you say more?

*Sam:* Intimacy is a blending of two people. That means a loss of self. Hmmm. But now maybe that means a loss of my aloneness.

*Therapist:* (Still probing) What would that be like?

*Sam:* It has been hard won. I know it has been hard won.

*Therapist:* But what would that be like? What's so scary about that? What would be the worst part of that?

*Sam:* I don't know. (Pause) There's a submissiveness or subjugation with that. I don't know why. (Pause) It's almost like a surrender. It requires trust, and I don't have that much trust. And it makes me vulnerable, and I don't like sharing power over me.

*Therapist:* How does being vulnerable mean others have power over you?

*Sam:* If I leave myself vulnerable, then others can take advantage of me. I don't really trust anybody.

*Katherine:* I know.

*Therapist:* Sam, what's it like for you to say that?

*Sam:* (Pause) I think people are really frail, and if you rely on them too much, they're going to disappoint you. It's as if they can't help themselves. You can't rely on them.

*Therapist:* You keep making statements about "those people." Can you make it personal?

*Sam:* I haven't found anybody I can rely on. (Pause) But I may have found a self-defeating situation.

*Therapist:* I think you have. You certainly have with Katherine.

*Sam:* I feel very vulnerable about everything!

*Therapist:* The key, then, is how do you manage your vulnerability?

*Sam:* I make a big buffer zone between me and everybody else. It's a void, an empty space. I'm even talking about the people who are on my side, the people I'm supposed to have a personal relationship with. I still maintain a distance.

*Therapist:* (To Katherine) And what do you think scares you the most about getting intimate?

*Katherine:* The rejection. Getting truly close, letting my guard down, and getting told that I'm not what he thought and he doesn't want me anymore.

*Therapist:* So you hide.

*Katherine:* Um hum.

*Therapist:* So Sam has been perfect for you. There's been no chance of
having to expose yourself to him.
*Katherine:* And that is what this [dance] has always done. It always
allows me to stay knocking at the wrong door.
*Therapist:* Because if you stay knocking at the wrong door, then there's
no risk of exposure.
*Katherine:* Yes. And that's just what I did with my mother.
*Therapist:* And Sam, Katherine has been perfect for you, too. Because then
you could stay behind your buffer zone and never know your fears
were even there.

The discerning reader probably has determined that the catastrophic fear we isolated for Katherine was her fear of exposure;
for Sam, it was a fear of merger. It should be noted that these were
not labels unilaterally affixed to them by me; they were agreed to
by the couple.

In a follow-up session to the one in which we completed the circular
diagram detailing their intimacy-distance regulation cycle and uncovered their catastrophic fears, the ensuing dialogue occurred.

*Katherine:* I feel we've been working through things a lot better. I'm
finding a way to say what's bothering me in a way he can understand.
And when I do, he seems more receptive, and so I feel better. And
even when I've said my piece and it's not resolved, a part of having
it resolved is just being heard.
*Therapist:* Sam, what's your perspective on the week?
*Sam:* When we last met, you said we might have a tendency to get double
crabby this week. And we talked about how you'd said that.
*Katherine:* And by the time we talked about it, I decided I was wrong to
be angry, because I couldn't figure out why. So I decided it must be
just my reaction to last session. And I was so relieved that Sam spotted
it. It just felt like more of a connection—that we could hold on to the
deeper level we had gotten to in session last week.
*Therapist:* What made for the deeper level?
*Sam:* Katherine said she was about ready to scram, to get a divorce, and
you concurred. So it made me more real and made me more motivated.
*Katherine:* (In tears) He told me he loved me twice that day! And he never
says that unless I initiate it.
*Sam:* It didn't take a lot to make that chart usable!

Over the coming weeks, we wove these discoveries into our sessions as Katherine and Sam braided them into their interactions at

home. By then, it was easy for them to see that small changes in the attitude and behavior of one of them could lead to an amplification of those changes by the responses of the other, provided they could manage the fears that those small, positive changes can beget.

Because there is so much meat in the example above, detailed analysis of it can help the reader translate these concepts into clinical practice. This will be discussed from three angles: (a) how the couple operationalized the concept of the circularity of their interactional patterns by noting choice points and capitalizing on them to generate a different quality to their interactions during the week, (b) how I helped the couple identify and acknowledge the catastrophic expectations that are telegraphed by their words, and (c) the specific therapeutic interventions that were being made in this excerpt.

*Seeing and Capitalizing on Choice Points.* All three excerpts illustrate two basic systemic premises. One is that very great changes can result from a relatively small modification in the pattern of behavior between people. And the other is that both can do their part to amplify those changes. For example, at the beginning of the first excerpt, both Katherine and Sam talked about the realization that sometimes their anger was not a genuine expression of emotion but instead functioned as a distancer. When they realized that, they could also see how in those instances it kept them stuck. When they saw this, they could begin immediately to change their behavior. The net effect of these changes in attitude and behavior clearly was felt by both as they described a calmer feeling between them as each began to act with greater sensitivity to the needs of both. These changes are underscored by Sam's closing comment in the third excerpt.

*The Articulation of Their Catastrophic Expectations.* In the middle excerpt, I spotted my opportunity to explain their catastrophic fears when they began to see that they could make choices about their behavior, thereby exercising a great deal of influence on the quality of interactions between them. The next logical question that I asked myself, which is what led me to focus them on figuring out their worst fears, was a version of "If they are enjoying their increasing closeness so much, what stops them from having more of it?" This led directly to a consideration of catastrophic expectations.

I signaled this by my question, "What do each of you imagine scares you the most about being intimate?" Sam indicated his fear of merger in his first sentence when he said that to him intimacy means a loss of individuality. Although he elaborated, thereby providing corroboration of my initial conclusion, his opening salvo was sufficient to substantiate my hypothesis. Likewise, Katherine's first sentence gave away her fear of exposure, when she talked about expecting and fearing rejection.

*The Therapist's Interventions.* In the first excerpt, when I queried about the function of anger for them, I was reasonably certain that much of it served as a distancer between them. Katherine's acknowledgment of this positioned me to challenge them to think about the repetitive pattern between them. It should be noted that not all of their anger is spurious; sometimes they are angry appropriately. And it is our job also to help couples discern one from the other, so that anger that genuinely needs to be expressed to keep accounts clear between them does not get minimized by a mere interpretation of it. But any recurrent emotion can be misused to distance rather than connect people when it acts as a homeostat for a disturbed system. So we need to help clients learn to discern the times their emotions serve a system-maintaining function so that they can make other choices. Otherwise, they will never be able to attain any except the most superficial closeness. And worse yet, when the toxicity that constant counterfeit emotionality generates is consistently pumped into the marriage, it pollutes the life-sustaining elements between them.

In the second excerpt, where the couple's catastrophic expectations are uncovered, there were several interventions that led to that unearthing. The first was to amplify the couple's successes in the intervening week and to help them do the same. This was done by asking Sam if he noticed Katherine's different behavior and by underscoring that the better week was no coincidence. If people have a part in what is not working, they also contribute to the better functioning. It is important that those factors be known and acknowledged; otherwise, people may think that the changes were happenstance or coincidence. Having established that when I heard the opening to explore catastrophic fears, I went with it, as discussed above.

In the third excerpt, once again I ask them to name and elaborate on their successes due both to the ongoing choices they each were making and to their newfound understanding of their heretofore subterranean fears. In addition, I ask them to reflect on the meaning of the experience that both reported having due to these novel skills and understandings. Then, over the coming weeks, we wove these concepts into their increasing understanding of the pattern between them and the choices they could continue to make to interrupt it.

## Twenty Guidelines for Therapists

The following is a list of guidelines that the therapist can use in structuring gender-sensitive treatment of couples. It is in no way intended to be definitive, and the reader is invited to add her own items.

1. Remember that you are the relationship's therapist, not the man's or the woman's. As has been reiterated throughout the book, it is essential that the therapist not "know" in advance who is to blame for the relationship dysfunction, because in truth, both parties are. You are hired for your skill *and* your objectivity. Maintaining your neutrality will empower you to heal the relationship and the people in it.

2. Remember that good couples therapy is very complex and demanding. It is far more intricate than merely doing what passes for couples therapy in all too many cases: conducting individual therapy with the partner in the room. Doing this work effectively requires another whole subset of skills that allow for assessment of and intervention into the couple's relationship system, as was discussed in Chapter 6. To not know how to do this is to be rendered ineffective at best, and to risk doing harm to individuals and their families at worst.

3. Even if you are bullish on preserving relationships, remember that there may be a time to quit trying and to help clients to do the same. Sometimes when you have to work doggedly to preserve a relationship that was dead on arrival, the most humane approach is to help people end the relationship with as much dignity as possible. For couples evidencing extreme

gridlock, stating that ending the relationship appears to be
what each wants without saying it often breaks their inertia
and jars the couple into getting to work on the marriage, rather
than protecting their own turf. Discerning when to call for the
question is perhaps the key diagnostic task in couples work.
But even when you are persuaded that a relationship is beyond hope, I firmly believe that you still are working on behalf
of the relationship. The goals then are to help the couple
disconnect from each other in ways that do not ignore or
negate that their lives touched in the past, and to promote
their leaving with their self-respect intact. This is especially
important when there are children involved. Usually, it means
helping people to see and to own that both had a part in the
demise of the relationship, rather than allowing them to fixate
on the facile tendency to blame one or the other. Alas, you
need to expect that sometimes you will not be given the
opportunity to do this by clients who are too angry to be
constructive. In that event, it is likely that one of the couple
will exit the therapy, leaving you to do with the other one what
they were unwilling to do: help pick up the pieces.

4. Even while you are working on behalf of the relationship,
strive to promote the individual development of those in it.
The aim of psychotherapy is to generate development, and
this approach has the greatest chance of perpetuating growth
for the relationship, for the individuals in it after therapy, and
for any children involved. For example, my assessment of Katherine in the case described above was that she first needed to
learn how to have a sense of herself as a competent human being.
This was the case regardless of whether she stayed married or
got divorced, even though if she did not develop herself, her
marriage surely would remain in jeopardy. Therefore, one of the
explicit goals of therapy was to help her develop a more clearly
defined sense of herself. This would serve the triple function of
enhancing her self-esteem, removing the burden of caring for her
from Sam's shoulders, and improving the marriage. One of the
many ways she worked on this was participating in one of my
women's groups as an adjunct to the couples work. Similarly,
Sam eventually agreed to participate in a men's group that
also coincided with their couples work. Here, the specific
purpose was to help him develop himself by learning how to

affiliate. So the same intervention was done with different goals in mind. In addition to these larger interventions, the therapist must be alert to any instances where the development of one person or the other is compromised and intervene appropriately. Not to do this is to damage the relationship as well as the individuals in it. For as Ackerman (1958), who is widely recognized as the grandfather of family therapy, believed that the only true autonomy is in togetherness. And I would add, "The only true togetherness is in autonomy." That is, unless people are well-defined, separate individuals, their relationship eventually will become stifling and unfulfilling. But the best opportunity to learn who one is comes in the context of relationships.

5. Maintain a balanced alliance with both members of the couple. This is the cardinal rule of good couples therapy, but it is particularly critical if you are hired because of your gender. Then both partners likely will expect you to take sides, although this is an expectation that is rarely expressed or even acknowledged. The man will expect you to side with the woman because you are a woman; the woman will expect you to side with the man because it is for your gender that they came to you.

6. The exception to the rule of balance is when you deliberately choose to align with one member of the couple to disrupt a rigid homeostatic balance in the couple. This is a common strategy employed by systemic therapists to shift dysfunctional systems. This is done to shake up a rigid system enough to make it possible for resistant couples to learn new responses. Although it can help refractory systems yield to the therapy, it is a precarious clinical intervention, so do it deliberately and carefully. When you are first learning how to do this, consult with a colleague or supervisor. In any case, rebalance your relationship with both persons as soon as this tactic nets the desired shift.

7. Even when the couples system is not rigid, shift your alliances often. This will allow you maximum movement within the system while preserving your role as both individuals' therapist, as well as reinforcing your position as therapist for the relationship.

8. If your relationship with clients becomes unbalanced without deliberate choice on your part, act immediately to correct this

situation. First, discern the nature of the imbalance. Perhaps it has happened because one member of the couple has attempted to triangulate you into the couple system in much the same way that an affair would stabilize and preserve an unhealthy balance in all relationships. Sometimes the couple will attempt to triangulate you out of the system, thereby preserving their homeostasis by closing the system to all outside inputs. In either case, corrective action might be to discuss that dynamic carefully at the next session to see if it can be corrected. If that seems ineffective, suggest an individual session with each to restore your alliance with both. If both are ineffective, it is likely that the couple is colluding to undermine the therapy and likely will unilaterally terminate treatment.

9. If the precipitant for the imbalance is your own behavior, such as consistently disliking or siding with one member of the couple, search your own responses to discern what in you has gotten hooked positively or negatively. This is an indicator of a countertransference reaction of which you may not be aware. But beware, because it has the potential to obstruct the entire therapy. If you are not sure or cannot work through this response, consult with a colleague. To correct this with the couple, particularly if you find yourself not liking one member of the couple, also ask for separate sessions. This will allow the best opportunity to establish an empathic connection with the person with whom you are experiencing difficulty. However, be careful to equalize any individual sessions you have by meeting with each. Otherwise, you inadvertently will undermine your efforts to rebalance.

10. Sometimes, despite your best efforts, clients retreat behind a dysfunctional united front and eject you to preserve their unhealthy equilibrium. If you spot this trend early enough, taking some or all of the corrective actions suggested above may be effective. However, people in a rigidly dysfunctional system may opt for maintaining the status quo rather than giving up their symptoms and learning how to become functional. In this case, sadly, you must prepare for the event that you will be rendered impotent in your efforts to stem the tide even while you continue working to do so.

11. Be on the lookout for unconscious motivators undermining the couple relationship and the treatment. Your job here is fourfold: helping people to identify this undertow; helping them to make other, more functional choices; avoiding blaming people for their unconscious material; and keeping them from blaming each other.

12. Be aware of how your own socialization influences your actions as a therapist. It would be nice if we all could eradicate the negative parts of our socialization and keep the rest. But we cannot. Learn to identify when your socialization is intruding into the therapy inappropriately, and capitalize on it when it is useful.

13. Don't apologize for being a woman or expect a man to apologize for being a man. Simplistic as this sounds, too often gender-based therapy seems to imply that being one sex or the other is inappropriate or wrong. By the same token, as stated throughout the book, do not attempt to gain acceptance from men by becoming an honorary man.

14. Keep in mind that emotionality does not necessarily equal openness or intimacy. Simply expressing effusive emotion does not inherently mean that people are accessible for intimate connections. In fact, it may mean just the opposite. Words and emotional expressiveness can get in the way when they are used as distancers and not connectors. It is the therapist's job to discern which is which and to help clients to do the same. In sum, don't be fooled by excessive displays of emotion.

15. Remember that men and women have different ways of expressing feelings and behaving intimately. Give men credit for the ways in which they do express their caring and behave intimately. This will enable you to join them much sooner and will motivate them to learn other more emotional ways of connecting as well. Further, it will enrich the couple relationship to help the woman broaden her definition of intimacy to include a more action-oriented approach as well.

16. Help both partners learn to develop their short suit. That is, help women, who are socialized to nurture and to seek relationships, learn to stand on their own. And help men, who are programmed for self-sufficiency and fixing problems, learn to be

genuine givers and receivers of nurturance. This will enhance the quality of the connection between them. And it will help both of them to further their own personal development by exploring what would otherwise likely remain their shadow sides. And this will give them many more and new dimensions for the development of intimacy between them.

17. Remember that men display masculinity when they are afraid. Knowing this likely will help you to feel less frightened when you see it so that you can help the man to learn new, more effective and dignified ways of handling fear. Appropriately channeled, his fear can generate intimacy instead of obstructing it. And maybe he can experience genuine support and nurturance when he is vulnerable, instead of the criticism and humiliation he expects for not being a "real man."

18. Stay focused on the relationship and on individuals' internal processes, rather than being distracted by requests or demands for quick fixes. As discussed elsewhere in the book, the greatest, most long-lasting change will come from a qualitative shift in the process between couples and in individuals' internal processes; it is our job to facilitate that.

19. When the therapy seems stymied, stop and identify whether the catastrophic fears of one or both members of the couple—or even your own—may have been triggered. This will allow you to readily recognize and work to remove the stumbling block not only to intimacy but probably even to the whole of the therapy.

20. Remember, it takes two to tango. No one person is responsible for the problems in or demise of a relationship. It took both people to create the problem-maintaining cycle that developed between them. It takes both people to maintain it. And it will take both people assuming responsibility for their part in the problems to change it. Thus, the behavior of both can either preclude more effective action and better feelings between them or create them.

## A Final Word

If it is important to maintain the balanced perspective that systemic thinking offers us in working with men in general, it is of critical importance that we do so in working with couples. This will minimize the tendency to blame one or the other of them for their problems—it usually ends up to be the man for reasons stated above. And it will empower them to work *together* to face life's challenges.

## References

Ackerman, N. (1958). *The psychodynamics of family life*. New York: Basic Books.

Braverman, L. (1991). The dilemma of housework: A feminist response to Gottman, Napier, and Pittman. *Journal of Marital and Family Therapy, 17*(1), 25-28.

Doherty, W. (1991). Beyond reactivity and the deficit model of manhood: A commentary on articles by Napier, Pittman, and Gottman. *Journal of Marital and Family Therapy, 17*(1), 29-32.

Erickson, B. (1992) Feminist fundamentalism: Reactions to Avis, Kaufman, and Bograd. *Journal of Marital and Family Therapy, 18*(3), 263-267.

Farrell, W. (1991, May/June). Men as success objects. *Utne Reader*, pp. 81-84.

Feldman, L. (1979). Marital conflict and marital intimacy: An integrative psycho-dynamic-behavioral-systemic model. *Family Process, 18*(3), 69-78.

Feldman, L. (1982). Dysfunctional marital conflict: An integrative interpersonal-intrapsychic model. *Journal of Marital and Family Therapy, 8*, 412-428.

Feldman, L. (1992). *Integrating individual and family therapy*. New York: Brunner/Mazel.

Feldman, L., & Pinsof, W. (1982). Problem maintenance in family systems: An integrative model. *Journal of Marital and Family Therapy, 8*(3), 295-308.

Gilligan, C. (1982). *In a different voice: Psychological theory and women's development*. Cambridge, MA: Harvard University Press.

Goldberg, H. (1987) *The inner male: Overcoming roadblocks to intimacy*. New York: Signet.

Hillman, J. (1967). Senex and Puer. In J. Hillman, H. Murray, T. Moore, J. Baird, T. Cowan, & R. Stevenson (Eds.), *Puer Papers*. Irving, TX: Spring.

Keen, S. (1992, June). *Can we end the battle between the sexes?* Lecture presented at the annual meeting of the American Family Therapy Academy, Amelia Island, FL.

Kimbrell, A. (1991, May/June). A time for men to pull together: A manifesto for the new politics of masculinity. *Utne Reader*, pp. 66-74.

Lerner, H. (1985). *The dance of anger*. New York: Harper & Row.

Lerner, H. (1989). *The dance of intimacy*. New York: Harper & Row.

Letich, L. (1991, May/June). Do you know who your friends are? Why most men over 30 don't have friends and what they can do about it. *Utne Reader*, pp. 85-87.

Lewis, J. (1979). *How's your family? A guide to identifying your family's strengths and weaknesses*. New York: Brunner/Mazel.

Lipchik, E. (1991). Spouse abuse: Challenging the party line. *Family Therapy Networker, 15*(3), 59-63.

Maslow, A. (1968). *Toward a psychology of being*. New York: Van Nostrand Reinhold.

Meth, R., & Pasick, R. (1990). *Men in therapy: The challenge of change*. New York: Guilford.

Miller, J. (1986). *Toward a new psychology of women.* Boston: Beacon.

Moore, R., & Gillette, D. (1990). *King, warrior, magician, lover: Rediscovering the archetypes of the mature masculine.* San Francisco: HarperSanFrancisco.

Napier, A. (1991). Heroism, men and marriage. *Journal of Marital and Family Therapy, 17*(1), 9-16.

Pinsof, W. (1983). Integrative problem-centered therapy: Toward the synthesis of family and individual psychotherapies. *Journal of Marital and Family Therapy, 9*(1), 19-35.

Pinsof, W. (1991, June). *Rediscovering the individual: A step forward or back?* Plenary presentation for the American Family Therapy Academy annual meeting, San Diego, CA.

Pittman, F. (1991). The secret passions of men. *Journal of Marital and Family Therapy, 17*(1), 17-23.

Swain, S. (1989). Covert intimacy: Closeness in men's friendships. In B. Risman & P. Schwartz (Eds.), *Gender in intimate relationships: A microstructural approach* (pp. 71-86). Belmont, CA: Wadsworth.

Waring, E. (1988). *Enhancing marital intimacy through facilitating cognitive self-disclosure.* New York: Brunner/Mazel.

Watzlawick, P., Weakland, J., & Fisch, R. (1974). *Change: Principles of problem formation and problem resolution.* New York: Norton.

Wynne, L., & Wynne, A. (1986). The quest for intimacy. *Journal of Marital and Family Therapy, 12*(4), 383-394.

# Sitting in a Roomful of Fathers:
# Men's Group Therapy

We live in an age of the waning of belonging.

People today must go to great lengths to feel the belonging that was a given a few generations ago. This increasingly fragmentary sense of community likely is due to a complex of factors: our mobile society, distancing from extended family, divorce, desertion, and the general fraying of the fabric of the family. Some of the ways people adapt in order to feel that essential sense of belonging are commendable and comforting; others are not so salutary or satisfying. One thing is certain, however: Those who are unable to find their elusive place suffer great pain.

More and more, it seems that the role as anchor once filled by extended families, communities, or churches has fallen to psychotherapists. It now seems that it is part of our charge to nurture a feeling of fellowship and to build an awareness of community. Of all the psychotherapeutic modalities that can help build an expansive sense of belonging and provide people a safe place to practice the reparative skills necessary to live successfully in families, group therapy is perhaps the most natural candidate.

## Chapter Overview

As before, this chapter will combine the theoretical with the practical. It will be divided into five major parts. The first part will address the unique benefits of group psychotherapy. I will answer the conceptual question of whether group psychotherapy can be seen legitimately as an adjunct to family systems therapy or whether each must be seen as an end and a modality unto itself. The question of how cofacilitators can manage potential disharmony that can arise from these differing orientations is also a part of this discussion.

In the second part, I will offer an abbreviated version of the process I went through in developing the model I am proposing here so that the reader can get the flavor of its evolutionary process. When I began doing men's groups in 1987, I knew of no other women doing this. As an aid to developing and refining my thoughts, I conducted a pilot study to test my tentative hypotheses and methodology. My findings, which will be described briefly, helped empower me to do more men's groups. Those wishing to learn about this study in depth and how it formed the backbone for the development of the model that is merely summarized here are encouraged to watch for a journal article entitled "The Development of a Model for Women Leading Men's Groups" (Erickson, unpublished manuscript).

My main research question was to explore the advisability of a woman running a men's group. Of interest to the reader likely will be the conclusions I reached about what I learned from that maiden voyage, which continue to significantly influence my thinking even now with all the groups I conduct. This section will be rounded out by a brief discussion of the four approaches to group leadership that I have used to date.

In the third part, I will provide an overview of the model I have developed with the help of my several cofacilitators and the many men who have participated. I will answer the following questions: Can women really effectively work with men in groups? What are the typical logistics of a men's group? What are the curative factors available to males who participate in men's groups? What are the unique features of two women leading a men's group? What is similar or different when a man and a woman colead a men's group, compared with two women? What are the curative factors available to men with female group therapists? How is the remainder of treatment structured? What are recommended selection criteria?

What are some contraindications for a man's participation in these groups? What are some typical issues that can be expected to surface? Are there particular hazards when women run men's groups? What are some clinical advantages and disadvantages to men's participating in these groups, compared with mixed-gender groups?

The fourth part will be a brief discussion of predictable issues that can be expected to surface when women facilitate men's groups, and the final part will offer guidelines for women facilitating men's groups.

## A Disclaimer

This chapter is not written for the uninitiated in group psychotherapy. It is beyond my purview here to delineate the basic principles of group therapy while at the same time I answer the lengthy and ambitious list of questions specific to women running men's groups. Readers who are unfamiliar with principles and procedures of group psychotherapy are encouraged to read some basic group literature, such as Yalom's (1985) classic text, and to obtain some good supervision in group psychotherapy before attempting to put these ideas into practice. Although it is imperative that group leaders be highly sensitive and knowledgeable for facilitating any group, it is fundamental for women running men's groups because of the extra layers of issues and dynamics when men meet in groups that are led by women. For all concerned, supervised study is the safest and most efficacious way to begin this enterprise.

## Unique Benefits of Group Psychotherapy

Participating in groups can be seen as a somewhat natural transition for many men to make, because of their experiences since childhood with team sports. In playing sports, they were participating in groups, and well-functioning psychotherapy groups work like teams. Good coaches teach the team the rules of the game and then sit back and let them play, calling in occasional directions from the sidelines. And with some shaping on the part of the facilitator/coach and some monitoring for the deleterious effects of becoming competitive, this experience, so common for most men, can be translated readily to a psychotherapy group experience. Here, too, some coaching and coaxing are needed from the facilitator on how to build the team. And in addition to building a team among the leaders and then helping the members build their own team, we then can help them translate those learnings to other significant relationships, such as those with spouses, children, parents, and friends. Then a natural translation can be made.

Of course, participating in the kind of team experience centered on sharing and being, rather than playing and doing, can be unprecedented and even frightening for most men. Their learning to face this new confusion is our clinical challenge. Thus, the leader has another task: coaching the group members on how to overcome these fears, just as they learned to overcome their fear of a 250-pound lineman coming at them.

## Limitations of Treatment Modalities When Applied Alone

Although some therapists act as if their approach was The Way for everyone, no one treatment modality is a one-size-fits-all proposition. It is up to the wisdom and the clinical acumen of the therapist to know when to apply which modalities, in what order, and in what combinations. To make those clinical judgments effectively, the therapist must be cognizant of the limitations of each of the major modalities when used alone.

### Limitations of Individual Therapy Alone

Although individual psychotherapy has its uses, it also has significant limitations. Clients are consigned to *talking about* how to relate, with the only actual relationship on which they can safely practice being with the therapist. And as we need to remind ourselves, therapy is not life! Although I strongly advocate individual therapy as training wheels for better relationships (see Chapter 8), the association with the therapist is not a lasting and permanent one, and many clients are poignantly aware of that, as they face risking learning to trust someone who eventually will disappear. This relationship is only for practice. If we are doing our job, like good parents, we must work toward launching our clients and celebrate their graduation.

## Limitations of Group Therapy Alone

Like the other modalities discussed, group psychotherapy has many advantages. However, there are three disadvantages to this approach. One is that because of the sheer number of people involved in a group, it is impossible for each participant to experience the same depth of attention to his or her personal and family issues that is natural in either individual or family therapy. Although from time to time one person's concerns do receive in-depth attention, it is more common for discussions to relate to how a given issue is more generally applicable to everyone. Another limitation of group therapy alone is that like individual therapy, it precludes participants working out their issues directly with the people in their lives; it only provides them the opportunity to *talk about* those concerns, gaining practice and perspective on how to work with them. The third significant disadvantage is that when a client who is coupled participates in group therapy alone, there is a risk of that experience significantly tipping the equilibrium between the couple. And if the therapist is not also continuing at least periodic couples sessions, she will have no way of monitoring and titrating the amount of change that is infused into the relationship or of helping the couple deal with that. A group experience can be powerful for the individual participating, but it can have a potent and sometimes negative effect on the couple or family relationships of that group member. It is our job to help monitor those homeostatic mechanisms so that what could be a potent tool for change does not unnecessarily become the undoing of significant relationships. The same caution needs to be exercised in doing individual therapy with a coupled client.

## Limitations of Family Therapy Alone

Family therapy at least provides a vehicle for actually learning *how* to relate, rather than *talking about* relating, as in individual therapy. However, family therapy, too, has a significant limitation. No matter how robust, there are certain central ingredients essential to good group therapy that are still missing. Compared to group therapy in the hands of a highly skilled and sensitive group therapist, there are at least three benefits that are absent in family therapy alone. One is that unlike group therapy where participants have the opportunity to learn by trial and error, practicing relating in a laboratory where they can make all the mistakes they need to while they learn the vicissitudes of relating intimately, in family therapy it's the real thing. People they love are witnesses or guinea pigs as participants work to master those elusive basic skills of intimacy. Two, in a group setting, another reason the price of mistakes is extremely low is that others are experimenting as well. Because they are usually novices themselves, making mistakes is expected, and therefore, it is not devastating when they happen. In family therapy, those natural mistakes can have painful effects. And three, if the group facilitator has set optimal group norms, there need be no concerns over being judged for saying something stupid or hurtful. In fact, one of the standard ground rules for all my groups is that there is no such thing as a stupid comment or useless idea; we just have not learned how to use that thought yet. But if a couple or family is still polarized, it will be very easy to criticize and blame as they learn.

## Group Therapy as an Adjunct to Family Systems Therapy?

What the therapist decides about which of these two treatment approaches is primary and which is adjunctive is a critical theoretical decision. Which modality one decides to emphasize can have significant effects on at least two issues. The first is whether group needs or individuals' desires receive primary preference when the therapist is making clinical interventions on a minute-to-minute basis. The second is how cofacilitators reconcile potential discrepancies between their approaches and biases, if they have differences—and if they are to work together effectively, this reconciliation is a must.

### Which Treatment Modality Is Primary, and Which is the Adjunct?

I firmly believe that family therapy is the most robust approach that therapists have at their disposal for broad-sweeping, long-lasting changes that can influence the quality of life in families for generations. I have come to see group psychotherapy as a powerful ancillary to a family systems practice. But I see groups as supporting and not as the primary treatment modality, a view that has significant implications when I arrive at a juncture where clinical judgment is required as to which direction to follow, which lead to pursue in group.

Because a family systems approach is the camera angle from which I see all clinical situations, I usually tend to opt to help a group participant better understand himself or herself, rather than first emphasizing a group process issue. That is, I opt for a focus on individuals' concerns first and focus on the group's needs second. I suspect that this judgment call would be the opposite for a therapist whose primary identification is as a group, rather than a family systems, therapist. This is not to say that group process needs are irrelevant or that I do not attend to them; rather, they tend not to be my first emphasis, because of my family systems orientation.

*Clinical Example.* In a particularly moving session in the most recent men's group my cofacilitator and I ran, a group member shared for the first time an unusually abusive childhood experience and the total lack of response to it on the part of his mother when he summoned the courage to disclose it to her. The entire group was transfixed and moved, many of them to tears. To this point in the life of the group, my cofacilitator and I were of like mind in the direction we needed to go with this particular man and with facilitating the group in general. Our difference came the following session.

She was operating on the basis of a rule of thumb of group work that suggests that in a meeting following an intense session, the group is likely to distance to protect itself from the vulnerability and intimacy of the previous one. Therefore, she was in no way bothered that everyone, including the man whose disclosure the previous week had galvanized such a powerful response throughout the group, spoke of what had happened in the previous session only as if something interesting and curious had happened. In fact, none of them was willing to disclose more personal responses. I, on the other hand, would have preferred to see if we could deepen the newfound understandings of the man who had shared by at least encouraging him explore the group's potentially curative responses to him and crystalize what Yalom (1985) calls a corrective emotional experience. He would have nothing of it; he had retreated. Further, I would have preferred to use that intense, heavy-duty experience as a vehicle to facilitate everyone's having an experience with a new level of depth, intimacy, and connectedness that was apt to be a rarity in their lives. Three times, I tried to bring the group back to the experience of the previous week. On the third try, I gave up, choosing not to be the "heavy" with the group. However, as a family *plus* group therapist, I have seen countless instances of one degree of intimacy begetting another, and so I was deeply disappointed. That day's debriefing after group with my cofacilitator, where we clarified our differences in interpretation of the situation and in our approach, was critically important, though heated, for both of us.

This incident illustrates two significant issues for which cofacilitators must be on the lookout. One is that when the leaders have a major difference in approach, if they are not vigilant, there could be an unnecessary breach in the relationship that would be very deleterious for the group. And the other is that regular debriefing after sessions is critical, so that no feelings between the two leaders build into resentment and pulling in opposite directions.

To summarize, I underscore two points. First, each facilitator must believe that both approaches offer salutary advantages; it is simply a matter of which gets emphasized first when a split-second clinical decision is required. Second is that it is important to be willing to let the other facilitator's approach prevail as readily as one advocates for one's own.

### Summary

The primary benefit of group therapy is that it offers the ultimate in permissive experimentation while providing a structured and safe environment. These conditions maximize growth and minimize threat and form what is known in the psychoanalytic literature as a holding environment. The development of this milieu is essential to effective group therapy—or any therapy, for that matter.

### How Do Cofacilitators Manage Differences in Emphasis? Or Can They?

Perhaps it would have been easier for both my cofacilitator and me if we were either both group or family therapists in primary orientation. But we are not, and we continue to affirm that this difference adds a dimension of richness to which neither the groups nor we as professionals would have access if we had identical orientations. And besides, it adds freshness, an antidote for the staleness that can plague even the most highly motivated clinician. So we remain adamant that there are many ways to put the two orientations together, reconciling them to the benefit of all concerned.

Exactly how do we manage our differences? As any group leader knows, disagreements and unresolved conflicts between coleaders are sure to invite insurgence or at least counterproductive effort among group members. And then several untoward reactions happen in the group, for example, the group mirroring the leaders' conflict by squabbling among themselves, or choosing sides with one of the facilitators. Any of these reactions reduces the cohesion of the group. Eventually if this situation is allowed to continue, the outcome of the entire group experience is jeopardized.

Perhaps another personal example will illustrate. My female cofacilitator has been a leader in the group psychotherapy movement since the days when she was a student of Kurt Lewin as he and his followers were developing and refining their ideas about the workings of groups. I am a thorough-going family systems thinker and therapist. Although our approaches have some significant differences, we have both been adamant that we will not allow ourselves to become competitive or let our conversations deteriorate into right/wrong positions.

Practically speaking, our approach to reconciling this philosophical difference has been fivefold. First, she was my supervisor when I was learning group therapy. Although I took a group work course many years ago in my master's program, at base, our ideas about how groups operate converge because she taught me most of what I know about them. Second, we have spent many hours sharing our philosophies, looking for similarities rather than just emphasizing our differences. This allows us to know that we can see when and how it is possible to aim in the same direction at a given juncture in a session, even though we might define that juncture differently. Third, we have a shared orientation of a psychodynamic theoretical base. This allows us to know that even though we might make a different intervention on a process level, there is virtually total overlap on the content on which a participant needs to work. Fourth, we have made a very simple verbal agreement. If one of us seems to be taking the discussion in a direction different from that in which the other wishes to go, we simply state in group something like, "I'd like to explore this a bit further, if I may, before we shift the process." As simple a statement as this sounds, it helps us avoid fruitless competitive clashes, tugs in opposite directions, or stony silences of capitulation. It reminds us that, after all, we are headed toward the same overall goal. And fifth and probably most important, we are good friends, having worked to fertilize that friendship by lunching together every week after group, by spending other social time either alone or with our spouses, by serving together on professional committees, and the like. This keeps us communicating. And this experience also makes us better able to model to group participants how to weather storms and still stay connected.

## The Genesis of the Idea

I first got the idea of doing a men's group in 1987. I was doing a conjoint session with a remarrying couple that had been seeing me for premarital therapy. Over and over, I sensed the man's father being a specter, overshadowing and criticizing rather than comforting and encouraging him. My client had grown up the only son and namesake of a father whom he adored but who had a capricious and frighteningly explosive temper that spilled out in torrents of either self-denunciation or diatribes at my client.

Every time I tried to suggest that perhaps he had some conflicted feelings about his father and that he, and his fiancée, and their children might benefit from his working on those issues, an explosion resulted. Once, he even threw a box of tissues across the room and stomped out, threatening never to come back, incensed that I even would suggest he might have some unfinished business with his father. This performance, of course, convinced me even more that my clinical hunch likely was accurate. In one particularly difficult session, fearing that the therapy and therefore the couple's relationship would stall completely and nearing my wits' end, I asked whether he would ever consider participating in a men's group. His response was surprising and immediate. "Only if you ran it!"

His idea was a fascinating one. Immediately, I began to ponder whether this was clinically appropriate, to say nothing of therapeutically efficacious. Not wishing to seem gender insensitive to men or presumptuous about them or to assume that I as a woman understood them, after mulling over his suggestion for quite some time, I contacted some of my male family therapy colleagues in the men's movement, asking their opinions. Their responses were unanimous. Not only were they not offended; they were encouraging.

So I decided to try a pilot group. And because it was a pilot group, which meant I had no idea about how it would turn out, I decided I would facilitate it alone. That way, I would have no one else to blame if it did not work and no one else looking on if I fell flat on my face. And further, it would help me minimize the variables in the group, a motif that became a rule of thumb on which I will elaborate below in planning that maiden voyage. The results were so enthusiastically endorsed by the six men who participated in that first group that this treatment modality is now the cornerstone of much of the family treatment I provide. Groups now being a staple in my practice, I run men's, mixed-gender, and women's groups. I will discuss later, in the section on selection criteria, how I make the clinical judgment about whether clients best can benefit from same-sex or cross-gender groups.

## A Thumbnail Sketch of That First Group

This section will discuss my multiple deliberations as I planned that first men's group.

*How the Participants Were Chosen.* That first group was composed of 6 participants who responded to a personal letter I had sent to 11 men inviting them to participate. In each man's letter, I tailored at least one paragraph specifically to his clinical needs, stating how I thought this experience might be a help for his particular issues, in addition to the general comments I made to everyone about the clinical advantages of group participation. All men either were currently in treatment with me or had completed therapy with me within the previous year. Now I merely verbally invite participants, and we discuss the pros and cons of their participation.

*Demographics of the Participants.* Because this pilot study was the first men's group for me, and I knew of no other women at that time who were doing men's groups, I decided to minimize the variables as much as I could. Hence, I chose men who despite their chronological ages, developmentally were working on accomplishing what Levinson (1978) calls the mid-life transition, which he says occurs typically between the ages of 40 and 45; their ages ranged from 30 to 50. All were in relationships with women. At the start of the group, three were married; one got married during the group; one had been divorced and had been in an on-again, off-again relationship for 3 years; and one was in a relatively new relationship, exploring with his partner whether to make a commitment. Thus, only 4 spouses filled out the pre and post measures, with those in the uncommitted relationships opting not to respond.

Only one man did not have at least one master's degree. One had completed postdoctoral work. One had completed a law degree, had partially completed a doctorate, and was a certified public accountant as well. The annual income of one participant was just under $75,000. The others earned between $100,000 and $200,000 annually. So clearly, I played it safe in choosing a group whose life-style allowed them the luxury of time to introspect, as none of them was worried about the next meal. However, busy life-styles themselves became a therapeutic issue, in that it suggested philosophies of life that perhaps needed questioning, if not changing. Further, consistent group attendance was an issue with these high-powered executives. Since that group, I have learned many strategies to minimize absences.

*Demographics of the Spouses/Significant Others.* The significant others, all women, ranged in age from 30 to 50. One had a master's degree. Two had bachelor's degrees. One had a nursing diploma plus a master's degree in nursing. One was taking undergraduate courses at the time of the group. Five of them worked outside the home; the sixth, who was college educated, had never worked outside the home. The income of those employed ranged from $20,000 to $150,000.

*Pre/Post Measures Administered.* All the measures I designed and administered were qualitative, rather than quantitative. Although both pre and post measures for both participants and significant others contained items that required Likert-scale types of responses, the richness of the data was in the open-ended questions. Thorough analysis of these data will be reserved for the article I am writing (Erickson, 1992). Suffice it to say that based on both participants' and spouses' responses to these questionnaires, I felt not only confident but compelled to continue offering such groups. Therefore, a summary of the conclusions I drew from their responses will be included here. It is my hope that in reading the discussion below, this chapter, and my forthcoming article, the reader can be empowered to begin experimenting with men's groups such as these herself.

*Discussion.* Several conclusions emerge that I will deliver in the form of three lists: (a) my summation of the men's reactions to the fact that the group was led by a woman, (b) my conclusions about their thoughts regarding men's groups in general, and (c) a synopsis of the wives' responses to their husbands' experiences.

### Conclusions About Groups Led by a Woman

1. Women can lead men's groups, individually or with cofacilitators.
2. Women, at least in the beginning, seemed to be less threatening men's group facilitators than men.
3. Some men found it easier to trust a female facilitator.
4. Some men expected male facilitators to be more critical and less accepting of them.
5. Some men were very fearful about expressing vulnerability in the presence of a male facilitator.
6. Some men acknowledged an unabashed need to work with a woman to get at their underlying issues.
7. Most men reported improvements in their relationship with their spouse, which they attributed to the group experience.
8. There was a higher probability of success, because of existing trust levels, when groups were composed of selected current or recent clients of the facilitator.
9. To feel safe enough to do hard emotional work, men who were in groups with a woman needed to feel that they were in the presence of a strong woman.

*Conclusions About Men's Responses to Being in a Men's Group*

1. Most were anxious about participating, though they expressed having decided to do so because of their confidence in the leader.
2. Most men were at least initially extremely frightened about being vulnerable in the presence of other men.
3. Most men expected to be judged by the other men as less manly men when they began to risk vulnerability.
4. As the group proceeded, most expressed less reticence about being vulnerable in the presence of other men.
5. Most men expressed more freedom to be vulnerable in the presence of women than with men.
6. Their previous relationship with the facilitator made a big difference in the trust factor.

*Conclusions of the Wives About Their Husband's Experience*

1. Spouses were not only not threatened by their significant other's experience, they expressed gratitude for it.
2. Many expressed high hopes that this experience would remove roadblocks of one kind or another for their husband.
3. All could see obvious changes in their husband.
4. Most mentioned appreciating their husband's being in the hands of a sensitive and competent facilitator.

## The Importance of Monitoring Spouses' Responses to a Men's Group Experience

Before we leave this section, a comment needs to be made about the need to monitor the spouses' reactions carefully. Good family systems therapists have developed a healthy respect for the concept of homeostasis, a vital concept discussed in Chapter 6. I had no idea to what extent either the participants or their significant others would become threatened by the experiences the men were having, and then either consciously or unconsciously work to sabotage the very process they said they so heartily endorsed. The job of the therapist was to keep an eye on this kind of situation, to keep it from developing, and to nip it in the bud if she saw it happening.

My particular fear, which fortunately turned out to be unfounded, was that the women might feel jealous or threatened from their husband sharing intimacies with another woman without their being present. Unlike couples therapy, when both parties are aware of everything that is being said, here I was worried that they might feel left out. And my worst fear was that this would come to feel to them as if their husband was having an affair, even though, of course, nothing inappropriate was happening. In my experience after 6 years of doing men's groups, these fears are unfounded. But they need to be monitored carefully nonetheless. In two instances, this sort of situation might have developed, but my cotherapist and I did what we could to prevent this red herring between the couple from becoming a group problem. These issues are internal to the couple, but sometimes couples prefer to triangulate the therapists into their conflict. In other words, we resisted allowing the couple's conflict to be about us or about the group.

To summarize, I am happy to report in the pilot study, as has been the case with all but two members of subsequent groups, the women's responses were thoroughly enthusiastic. For most, at no time did I sense jealousy or threat or see signs of obstruction. Quite the contrary. I received from time to time notes such as the following. "Thanks for the opportunity to complete this survey, I hope [my husband] finds [the group] to be a great experience in opening doors." Another said simply, "I feel very pleased that [my husband] has chosen to participate in this group." And yet another, "I am expecting this will be a tremendously important experience in the continuation of [my husband's] process of 'coming alive.'"

In short, although I worried that the wives might feel jealous of their husband's learning intimacy skills with another woman or might feel frightened of the changes they saw taking place, that did not turn out to be the case. Quite the contrary. All indicated gratitude.


## The Overview of the Model

In this section, I will detail the unique features of the model I use.


### Can Women Really Work Effectively With Men?

It has been assumed since the days of Freud that men can work as effectively with women as they can with men, but I have seen little evidence of wide acceptance of the corollary of that assumption. In fact, if the truth be known, when I began to work in the men's movement with men's groups, I did so very gingerly at first. For example, because he knew I was contemplating starting a men's group, a well-known family therapy colleague of mine, an author and active spokesman on men's issues, asked a fellow male presenter at a conference on men whether he thought a woman could lead men's groups. Without a moment's hesitation, the other presenter shot back, "Well, then it wouldn't be a men's group, would it?"

Both women and men ought to be asking ourselves why, when a man runs a women's group is it still a women's group, but the reverse is not true when a woman runs a men's group? That made no sense to me then, and after 6 years' experience, it makes even less sense now. Clearly, my experience with running men's groups contradicts this sexist belief. But the more important point is that this sexist assumption remains unchallenged in all too many circles, even among some women. I encourage all of us to question this illogic and the way it limits all of us.

## What Are Typical Group Logistics?

Having not yet found a female cofacilitator whom I could respect and trust, I conducted my first three men's groups alone. When I facilitate groups alone, I usually do not accept more than six members, although sometimes I end up with seven. With a cofacilitator, I prefer eight but will accept nine participants.

Since those first three groups, I have coled men's groups with Dr. Pearl Rosenberg, 22 years my senior and a venerable practitioner in the group therapy field. In addition to weekly men's groups, I have conducted one men's intensive therapy weekend for eight of my clients with a male cofacilitator and colleague well known in the men's movement, Richard Meth. Further, I have conducted one mixed-gender therapy group with a practicum student and doctoral candidate, Michele Gargan, and several by myself. I have facilitated my women's therapy groups by myself. Currently, I also run a mixed-gender therapy group specifically for therapists, with one of the themes being the difficulty in navigating the interface between their personal and professional lives. I have plans for continuing all of these types of groups on an ongoing basis.

All groups except two for women were time-limited. Two of the women's groups were open-ended; the others were limited to either

15 or 20 weeks. All the weekly groups meet for 1½ hours. The weekend intensive group ran for 10 hours, on a Friday evening and Saturday, with Friday evening's dinner and Saturday's lunch part of the process of the experience and therefore included in the cost.

To date, all the groups I have facilitated have been composed of clients from my current marriage and family therapy practice, with two exceptions. My female cotherapist has brought two men from her primarily individual psychotherapy practice into our most recent men's group. Our goal is to constitute groups composed of half her existing clients and half mine as her practice expands to include enough men that this would be possible.

## What Are the Curative Factors Available When Men Participate in a Group Facilitated by Women?

There are numerous healing agents at work when a man participates in a men's group, especially one facilitated by women. Each of those factors will be discussed below.

*Access to Transference Reactions in Vivo.* I always have butterflies in my stomach at the start of each new group. I am both eager and curious about what the experience that we are all about to have will hold. In one of my early men's groups, I became particularly anxious when Bill sat mute the entire first session, except when he introduced himself. Did I blunder in choosing him for the group? Although I knew he was shy, would he be too overwhelmed to gain anything from the group? The most disturbing question I was asking myself was: Would the group experience harm him somehow?

My anxieties were allayed at the beginning of the following group. Bill, the first to speak, explained his silence the previous week, stating that he had been bowled over. His experience of sitting in that men's group was both intense and compelling for him. Now 40, he was abandoned by his father after his parents' divorce when he was 8. It had been a long time since he had been with any adult male except for occasional contact with uncles and colleagues— he even managed to work surrounded entirely by females. Now he was surrounded by men. A man of few words, he gave an explanation that was elegantly simple and characteristically to the point: "I felt like I was sitting in a roomful of fathers last time. That's why I couldn't talk!"

This is a graphic example of the transference reactions that can become very authentic, as opposed to the intellectualized conversation *about* them that dominates countless psychotherapy hours. With few exceptions, clients who have participated in men's groups have found them to be a profoundly evocative, positive experience that vivifies transference reactions so that they can be worked with, rather than merely talked about.

*Repair of Archaic Views of Family of Origin Members.* As stated above, perhaps the greatest advantage of group psychotherapy for people of either sex is the transference reaction that it virtually certainly catalyzes. The ability of this type of group experience to stimulate both father and brother transference with the other men, and mother, sister, and lover transference with the women facilitators, is the core of what makes this application of group therapy unique. These transference reactions can assist men in repairing their archaic views of their family members, particularly their parents, which often affect and infect their perceptions of their spouse, children, and all authority figures.

There has been considerable discussion of the benefits accruing to men who participate in any men's group, regardless of the sex of the leader. Gordon (1990) explains why men's repairing their view of and relationship with their fathers is central when he says,

> Men measure themselves . . . unconsciously not only by what they saw in their fathers, but also by what they thought their fathers saw in them. A silent or distant father may well have unintentionally conveyed the message . . . that he did not care that much or that other things were more important. (p. 238)

Emotional access to this compelling historical material is easily catalyzed in men's group therapy, where a man is no longer *talking about* his relationships; he is living them. Therefore, he can surface and heal his pain about the type of ruptured alliances that form the template for his current relationships with important persons.

*Relief From Existential and Actual Isolation.* As with all group therapy, a primary curative factor is realizing and feeling at an incontrovertible, visceral level that one is not alone. This can be a particularly compelling need and poignant experience for most men, because they have been socialized to go it alone. Meth (1990) writes,

> Men [do not] lack emotions; rather, they learn to express a narrow range of emotions and deny others considered unmanly. Competitive feelings are permitted, but vulnerability, pain, compassion, fear and weakness are avoided. Boys learn to deny feelings that may leave them open to ridicule. This process of denial begins from a very young age, where men learn to conceal feelings from others and, eventually, from themselves. (p. 214)

The result, as men in these groups come to acknowledge, is that this sense of isolation indeed can be crippling.

Of course, women, too, can feel a sense of alienation and loneliness that they also experience as gripping. However, because women are trained *toward* intimacy and relationships their whole lives, they often have an easier time of finding places for and having intuitive knowledge about how to seek connections. Because for so many men emotionally connecting with both self and others remains problematic, it is experienced by most men as an unbelievable blessing that they have found a place where they can experience togetherness.

It is especially difficult for modern men to find opportunities to experience a sense of community, and especially painful when they cannot, in light of their internalized socialized messages prohibiting connection and the external social messages that label them sissies for seeking it. One of the places where they receive covert threats prohibiting personal bonds is the workplace. Oh, yes, they get messages about being part of the team in order to sell a new product or to beat out a competitor. But this is different from establishing personal relationships. The sub rosa text often is that to get ahead, it is a given that it be at someone else's expense—that when men are vulnerable in the workplace, others will go for their jugular. For example, a senior-level executive of a huge company arrived for therapy one day in blue jeans. After I joked that I hadn't thought he owned any, I noted that this meant that he obviously had not gone to work. When I teased that he must really have been sick not to have gone to work, he replied that in fact he was. And then with great pride, he said this was the first sick day he had taken in his 25-year career. What previously would have been impossible for him to do and still maintain his image of himself as a man was now a marker of progress to him.

*Clinical Example.* In group, when participants do begin to share vulnerabilities with other men, they are validated even with their fears and anxieties. Only another man truly can affirm men's masculinity and reassure them of their normality. Bill, who earlier articulated the experience of sitting in a roomful of fathers, describes his new perspective after participating in a 15-week men's group coupled with brief individual and premarital couples therapy:

**Bill:** It's that horrible loneliness. But it's hard for me to realize that loneliness is what's going on.
**Therapist:** What do you mean?
**Bill:** I was often so out of touch, I just couldn't tell what was going on. So all I knew was that I was miserable. And when you don't know what you feel, then you can't take steps to correct it. It's like when something is wrong physically, you can't do anything about it. Once you know, you can start doing something about it. So I'm not so afraid of my loneliness now. Remember when I used to wish a doctor would tell me I had cancer, and what a relief that would be? Now I think of having a future!

This man, whose abject loneliness generated so profound a wish to escape that he prayed for death from a dreaded, grotesque disease, tells us here how he found a new lease on life when he discovered at a visceral level that he was not alone.

*Support for Vulnerability From Other Men.* For some, the idea of participating in a men's group—already overwhelming—is inconceivable if it is *not* facilitated by a woman. This is especially true if the man had a contentious or critical relationship with his father. It would have been inconceivable for the man whose comment sparked my first men's group to have had his first group experience facilitated by a man. Because of his expectation that he would never measure up as he felt he never had with his father, and because of his doubt that any male authority figure would treat him differently, he literally would have been unable to take that risk without first being in a group facilitated by a woman. The fact that there was a female leader enabled him to feel confident about sharing vulnerabilities with other men. This made for the positive, less threatening experience that helped him change. When he expressed confidence and readiness to be in a group led by a man, each of us saw that shift as evidence of understandable growth.

Most men begin the group finding it incredible that other men have similar insecurities, frustrations, and vulnerabilities. Through the group experience, they come to know that they are not alone, and they begin to see that there is something synergistic and healing in openness and vulnerability, rather than these being deplorable signs of weakness and personal flaws.

*Opportunity to Be Dysfunctional in a Nonthreatening Setting.* In a safe, well-functioning group, participants can begin to disclose what they have long considered to be shameful or despicable actions and critique themselves without feeling excessive humiliation or fear about it. Hearing themselves, they can make their own decisions to change their behavior or attitudes. The leader must be aware that this happens in the later, working phase of a group after group cohesion has been created. Although the facilitators can aim the group toward this working stage, encouraging, facilitating, and rewarding risk taking, they cannot push for it prematurely or they will obstruct the group's progress toward this very significant stage of group development.

*Access to Different and Better Male Role Models.* Direct access to positive role models is another curative factor, even though this is almost never consciously or verbally acknowledged. However, it is as commonplace to the ambience of a good group as wallpaper. Brad, who typically sat silent but listening intently during most group meetings, said the following:

**Brad:** [The group] allows you to take a quantum leap, by seeing yourself in others.

Another example comes from the youngest member in a group whose age range spanned 21 to 48. Here, he talks about finally being able to see how others do their lives and to learn from it.

**Mark:** It is more than just my personal battle with me. It was kind of a symbol of my future—if I'm starting now, when I'm my age, how much farther will I be when I'm their age. It's very hopeful! I think

I'll be much better adjusted. Group is good for me to open up, to be that accepting, sensitive man we're creating in the group. On the other hand, it is a kind of role model, even though I hate to admit I'm looking for fathers! I don't feel like I want to waste any more time not being the way [I want to be].

This example would be poignant enough. But it comes from a man whose parents were divorced when he was a toddler, and so he felt abandoned by his father. His void for adequate, sensitive male role models was a gaping hole that began to be filled by his group experience.

*Decreasing Dependency on Significant Others as Men's Only Source of Intimacy.* All too often, men expect women to meet all their needs for intimacy. This even can extend to the expectation that women feel men's feelings for them, which is not the same as empathically feeling with them. The former is so that they do not have to learn how to deal with the messiness that feeling, rather than thinking, can sometimes involve. When that happens, obviously a great deal of marital dysfunction results, because the woman feels suffocated and the man feels cut off and alone. And then the couple turns in on itself, often fighting to come up for air, which they get from the distance created by the conflict. The following excerpt was spoken by a man who was highly successful in his professional life, but very emotionally constricted at the beginning of treatment.

*Jack:* If Sally leaves, this person whom I like a lot will leave with my emotions! That's how I solved the problem of my inability to feel. She was supposed to be there to take care of my levelness.
*Therapist:* How do you feel, being so dependent on her?
*Jack:* That's new for me to realize. I hadn't thought about that before. That part [feeling my own feelings]. I wouldn't be able to do.
*Therapist:* How do you see yourself then?
*Jack:* If she's not there, I'm dead. She's my source. Without her, I'm nothing!

Many men for the first time learn the exhilaration of having men as intimates, not just drinking buddies or sports buffs, when they have participated in either a men's or a mixed-gender group. By learning to meet their own needs, they have more verve with which to infuse their relationships with their significant others.

*Opportunity to Learn More Functional Ways to Relate to Women.* With female facilitators serving in the transitional role, men can have the experience of intimacy with participants as well as with other men. One of the facilitators' primary roles is to offer nonpossessive love. The leaders must be women neither to be taken care of nor to be feared. This decreases men's dysfunctional dependence and enhances their autonomy in ways that are not stereotypically counterdependent. Thus, they are better prepared to be in more equitable relationships. At the same time, they have the opportunity to explore new facets of functional dependence on others in a way that helps them give up the rigid self-reliance that men are often socialized to expect of themselves.

In addition to seeing themselves differently in relation to women, men can come to see women differently as persons to whom to relate. Typically, men see relationships with women as sources of engulfment. Hence, they often develop a style by which they keep a great emotional distance from others. Being able to have an experience with women on whom they can be dependent without being engulfed, with whom they can be emotional and not explode, allows them to remake many of their ingrained preconceptions about what to expect in relationships. Presumably, this enables them to be less skittish when it comes to participating in relationships outside therapy.

*Opportunity to Relate to, and Not Compete With, Men.* The issues that typify most male interactions (power, competition, achievement, isolation) become less prominent for men in these groups as they progress. Growth on these dimensions comes from the combination of the group experience plus participation in either individual or couples therapy. Hence, they encounter an uncharacteristic opportunity to be functionally dependent on the female leaders in a way that they report is nonthreatening. They can grow through their dependency and become independent and interdependent. They get to experience coming to depend on other men as well, so the entire group experience is aimed at lessening this typical competitive male way of relating.

*Learn Greater Emotional Range.* When Wilcox and Forrest (1992) write about men's groups, they say, "Men's groups provide an environment for addressing the many issues that have interpersonal implications for men. Restrictive emotionality, maintaining control and independence, fears of acting feminine in the presence of other men, can be identified and changed within a group" (p. 294). Learning about these, and many more issues, is a potential benefit for men participating in men's group therapy.

Other writers extol the virtues of men having access to other men. And of course, a ready venue for that kind of access is men's groups. Moore and Gillette (1990) write,

> What is missing [for men] is not . . . what many depth psychologists assume is missing: adequate connection with the inner *feminine*. In many cases, these men seeking help, had been, and were continuing to be *overwhelmed* by the feminine. What they were missing was an adequate connection to the deep and instinctual *masculine* energies, the potentials of mature masculinity. They were being blocked from connection to these potentials by patriarchy itself, and by the feminist critique upon what little masculinity they could still hold onto for themselves. (p. xviii)

Another writer, Gordon (1990), advocates men's groups as an antidote to men's measuring themselves not only by what they saw in their fathers, but also by what they thought their fathers saw in them. "A silent or distant father may well have unintentionally conveyed messages" (p. 238). If this is the case, sitting in a roomful of different fathers can serve to mollify those messages and become a balm for a man. Being there can help each man to answer the question of how he heals the wounded child within.

*Opportunity to Be Mentored.* Perhaps the final reason that a group of men sitting together can be so healing, almost without regard to the specific content that is being discussed, relates to Jungian archetypes, as discussed in Moore and Gillette (1990). "[These] provide the very foundations of our behaviors and our thinking, our feeling and our characteristic human reactions" (p. 9). Simply sitting in the presence of the ritual elder or mentor is healing. Although there are natural leaders in any group, each participant is at the same basic place in his life, struggling to make sense of it with the help of the other men and the facilitators. Still, each participant in turn, using his own accumulated wisdom, is able to perform the function of the ritual elder for the others from time to time. This experience—one that modern men are sadly lacking—can itself be extremely healing both for the one whose turn it is to play that role and for those who are the benefactors of that man's accumulated wisdom. "The ritual elder is the man who knows the secret wisdom, who knows the ways of the tribe, and the closely guarded men's myths. He is the one who lives out a vision of mature masculinity" (p. 7). It is the job of the facilitator of whatever sex to help to call out that ability that each participant has at one time or another to lead or mentor, based on his own accumulated wisdom.

## What Are Some Unique Features When Two Women Lead a Men's Group?

Allen (1990) explains why examining and repairing a man's relationship with his mother is central both to his healing and to his being able to develop healthy relationships with women. It only stands to reason that the more conflicted he is about his relationship with his mother, the less able he will be to develop a clear and healthy one with a spouse or significant other. However, too many young lovers seem blind to that. Allen writes,

> As a man gains a more realistic perspective about his mother and his relationship with her over the years, he is freed from some of the disabling feelings associated with this powerful woman. When he becomes able to understand his mother in her many dimensions . . . he is able to project his new understanding to the women in his current life. The present is no longer the arena in which to play out conflicts, fears, and hurts from the past. (p. 227)

Sometimes for reasons out of men's control, such as their mother's death, dementia, personality disorder, and the like, men are unable to work out a healthy intimate relationship with their own mother. This would seem to doom them to a life of conflict and unfulfillment in their relationships with their spouse or significant others. Although this fact makes developing a more workable, healthy relationship more difficult, it is by no means impossible. That is where an alliance with a healthy female therapist can be an invaluable substitute. A men's group facilitated by women offers participants unique opportunities to resolve leftover issues from both parents, but especially from mothers.

### What Are the Curative Factors Available
### to Men With Female Therapists?

What are the curative factors that are present when women lead men's groups? Of course men's groups can effectively be led by two men or one woman and one man, but the emphasis here will be on the special benefits when two women lead men's groups. I will discuss psychological factors and social factors separately; the reader will recognize some of my comments restating what has been said throughout the book.

*Psychological Factors.* First and foremost, having two women lead a men's group provides very rich psychodynamic material. This potent content comes from of the potential for groups to generate regressive affect and functioning that then can become grist for the therapeutic mill as the participants learn to rework the feelings emerging as markers of early experiences on which they are stuck. Successfully doing this helps them grow themselves up.

It is commonly accepted that the effectiveness of a group revolves around participants' replicating what they learned in their family of origin in the group, at least unconsciously if not in their behavior and feelings. Then, when they isomorphically recapitulate in their other relationships these same behaviors and feelings, they can learn to understand and do otherwise. With the other men, they can play out their issues with father, brother, friend, and boss. With the women facilitators, they can surface their latent issues with mother, wife, girlfriend, sister, and friend. Uncovering these repetitive patterns gives participants the opportunity to acknowledge, work through, and resolve their outmoded transference reactions.

Another element that makes for potency in men's groups facilitated by women relates to the fact that women have traditionally been the source of nurturance for men and women alike. In men's groups with women facilitators, participants can experience a greater degree of safety, which makes it more conceivable to risk the possibility of narcissistic injury. Thus men can experience a very special and safe holding environment for containing both their aggressive and their wounded feelings. This is so because the women provide sources of nurturance while the other men provide allies and an additional safety net for aggression and regression.

All of these factors provide men the opportunity to reexperience and become more realistic and less reactive about their issues with both men and women in the same experience. These elements make this experience uniquely healing.

*Social Factors.* The second category of reasons relates to men's and women's socialization. Here there are benefits on which to capitalize from our socialization as women, as well as potential liabilities that must be taken into account. Just as men have been trained to perform task-focused and productive roles in our culture, women have been socialized toward intimacy. We therefore acquired many tools for enhancing emotional expressiveness and relationships that most men simply do not have. However, as has been stated throughout the book, a female therapist who wants to work effectively with men, especially as a men's group leader, also must be capable of leadership functions that have been typically associated with men. That is, she must unequivocally be able to indicate that she is strong enough to tolerate his aggression and to set limits on it so that he does not become unduly frightened of himself and the therapy does not derail.

Without a doubt, women holding positions of authority are still unusual for most people. One might well expect that it would not be uncommon for women in authority to produce some degree of anxiety and generate some regressive reactions in men. And this is not all bad. In fact, in the hands of a skillful therapist, the man can have a uniquely reparative experience. However, if the therapist has her own ax to grind, is unnecessarily fearful, or otherwise bungles the situation, or if, as Rosenberg (in press) says, "As long as males equate power with self-esteem, the loss of power will become a real threat to the male with a female group leader," then the situation can be precarious indeed.

*Clinical Example.* Doug is a 38-year-old man who had been separated from his wife of 13 years. He freely admitted at the outset of therapy that he had used his horrible temper to scare and control his wife. Their separation had been catalyzed by yet another outburst of temper that had scared her one too many times. So she finally, appropriately, asked him to leave.

After approximately 4 months of living apart and doing marital therapy, Doug and Janine decided they were ready to try living together again. But this generated a great deal of anxiety for both, because understandably Doug did not trust his ability to manage his temper appropriately, and Janine commendably did not want to become terrorized again. The method Doug had used during the separation to manage his anger was simply to refuse to get angry. But he recognized that back in the pressure cooker of living in the marriage with their three adopted children, this might not be so easy to do.

In the session previous to the one excerpted below, Doug discussed his fear that someday if he got angry enough, he might "buy an Uzi and take it to a shopping center." He further directly requested of his wife that if she sensed that he was at all threatening, she was to take the kids and leave immediately. My response to that was immediate and twofold. First, I told him that I appreciated that although he might be afraid of himself and had convinced Janine to be afraid of him over the years, I was not. And then I laid out exactly what would happen (hospitalization, that they should list my consulting psychiatrist as the attending physician, the hospital emergency room they were to go to, how long he could expect to be hospitalized, etc.) should there be any doubt in the mind of either of them that this might be necessary for anyone's protection, including Doug's.

The following dialogue occurred as Doug began the marital session just after the threats of his getting violent were discussed. He stated that he had something that he wanted to confess to me after the previous week's session.

*Doug:* I wanted to find out who was stronger here; could I chase you out of your own office? I was manipulating you. And I don't want to do unreasonable, unfair things anymore. I've done a lot of that in my time. And I knew I wasn't gonna win if I did that again.

*Therapist:* But how did you know you weren't gonna win? This was a test of me, wasn't it?

*Doug:* Yeah, it (pause), it was a test of you. And I really feel bad about it because it's unfair of me.

*Therapist:* Why?

*Doug:* Because I've already committed [to this therapy], and I shouldn't need to test you. I decided a long time ago that I was here to get help, and you were here to provide help.

*Therapist:* But this was different. I think you had something very important to find out last session.

*Doug:* I had to find out if I was gonna *accept* help.

*Therapist:* And I think there was something else. I think there was another thing. I think you had to find out if I'm strong enough to meet you and to tell you to cut the crap. Does that register?

*Doug:* Yeah, but I came into that session with a lot of confidence that no matter what I said, you'd have a counter.

*Therapist:* So once again, you found out I was strong enough to take care of you.

*Doug:* I don't like admitting that, but I have to. I would be crazy in *every* sense of the word not to.

*Therapist:* You got a ton of stuff figured out last week. A ton! And I'm glad you did [the testing], every bit of it.

*Doug:* Thanks!

*Janine:* And what I've seen in the last week from you is that you've been more initiatory with me than you've ever been.

*Therapist:* My guess, Doug, is that you've been less afraid of yourself and your anger in the last week, am I right?

*Doug:* Yeah. 'Cause the anger isn't me. It's just a game I play. I see that now.

*Janine:* And it covers up all your stuff.

*Doug:* Right. I see that now.

Having women in authority in a group of men affords the opportunity to surface and disrupt the early socialization that acts as a limitation to genuine intimacy and equitable relationships with women. According to Rosenberg (in press) this primarily means that the woman facilitator:

1. Must be able to demonstrate both competence and leadership ability while she also offers warmth and nurturance
2. Must be capable of demonstrating in a nondefensive way that she can take care of herself
3. Must be able to offer nurturance and support
4. Must be able to confront without being intimidated and without coldness
5. Must be able to tolerate the group's anxieties without helplessness and without being inappropriately helpful
6. Must be capable of not personalizing the group's transference reactions
7. Must be capable of nonreactivity and objectivity
8. Must be "firmly benevolent"

With female therapists as models and midwives for these changes, men can be helped to modify their basic attitudes and

find a new set of pathways for relating more intimately as partners, fathers, sons, friends, and colleagues.

## When Is Group Therapy Indicated?

There are several markers that I watch for now that tell me that
group therapy is indicated. Once I discern the presence of enough
of these markers, then it is up to me to decide whether the client
could benefit more from a mixed-gender or a same-sex group.

1. When clients indicate feeling isolated.
2. When clients are stuck in one of the other therapy modalities and
   seeing modeling from other group members could provide a vision
   of another way to be or to work out their problems, or could thaw
   their denial.
3. When clients repeatedly respond defensively to feedback from the
   therapist, and hearing similar input from peers neutralizes defensiveness, thus making it more possible for to hear ego-alien, threatening ideas.
4. When being in a group could be reparative of the voids of significant relationships clients experienced early in their life (e.g., men
   with father loss or whose only experiences with women have been
   negative).
5. When clients continue to blame their partner for all the problems in
   their relationship.
6. When men have learned how to feel and then realize how lonely
   they have been throughout their life.
7. When men are ready to learn how to make friends with others,
   rather than just compete as they have always done.
8. When clients begin to acknowledge needing others but feel they
   have nowhere to turn in getting those needs met.
9. When clients can be open enough with their experiences that they
   can learn to share and to enjoy vulnerability.
10. When clients have learned to acknowledge that they need help, that
    they cannot do it all.
11. When clients can acknowledge their fear at the prospect of being in
    a group.
12. When a client's experience with family is so fragmentary that the
    capacity of a group to offer a replacement family experience can be
    reparative in ways that endless talking *about* family experiences and
    their resulting voids cannot.

13. When a client has gone far enough on his inward journey to reevaluate his relationships and begins to realize that many have to be left behind for him to continue to grow, but is bewildered about how to form healthier ones.

Although there are others that could be added to this list, those are prime markers that get me thinking that the individual has progressed far enough in therapy that participating in even one group series could be beneficial.

## How Are Group Members Selected?

In group therapy, client selection is a perennially thorny issue. With men's groups, that consideration takes on even more significance, because for most men, the idea of entering a therapy group, especially one composed only of men, is extremely threatening. If being vulnerable is frightening anyway, visions of not measuring up, as many men felt they did not in junior high school locker rooms, strike terror in them. Hence, selection of appropriate members is especially critical here.

The key struggle the therapist must balance is: Will this configuration of men be able to develop a culture of supportiveness and at the same time be willing to learn to confront one another constructively? Although caring is critical to participants' feeling safe enough to risk, the yeast of any group is its members' willingness to challenge and be challenged. And the leader must be committed to defining and demonstrating that both are how a group demonstrates caring. This, too, can sometimes be difficult for women to do who have been socialized to "make nice," to be too good for their own good.

Perhaps the biggest stumbling block for many men is their difficulty with believing that they are part of the problem because of the socialized messages they received that they need to be in charge and able to fix anything. Admitting this vulnerability makes for several difficulties for a man to own. One is that he cannot fix every situation himself. Another is that if he needs anything, especially help, to many this indicates there is something seriously wrong with him. So most men deny recognizing that they need help. And because of these destructive messages that muzzle men from acknowledging the need for help, many wait too long to seek therapy and then find themselves in significantly worse messes by the time they finally give in and admit what they need.

*Clinical Example.* Harry is a 46-year-old man who was invited to participate in my first men's group 1½ years before he actually decided to do so. When I first asked him to participate, he was in couples therapy working on his marriage; when he finally decided to participate, he was emotionally separated, just waiting for his last child to leave home so that he could honorably divorce.

In an individual session the week after the first group meeting in which Harry actually participated, he both articulated and valued a central attitude that indicates a man's readiness to constructively participate in a group. He also indicated how his responses to his socialization have markedly changed.

*Harry:* As intimidated as I was for so long about being in a group, I'm really enjoying it. The idea that there's a group of men who are serious about what's going on in our lives, and that there is a group of men who can be supportive (pause), I'm not used to it. I've never joined a group to be part of a group; I've always joined a group for a purpose.
*Therapist:* You sound kind of amazed that you're both in it and enjoying it.
*Harry:* I'm surprised that I'm enjoying it! I don't need to tear this group up. I'm far more comfortable now with what I can do and who I am not. I don't have to prove anything to anybody. I don't have to show off.

To summarize, the most important factor in group selection is that participants must be willing to at least consider acknowledging the need for help. This, of course, eventually will likely amount to a change in worldview. Obviously, many men do not enter therapy with that attitude, and so it is our job to help them change that. However, men who remain so resistant as to be polarized with either their partner or their therapist in their wish to protect the status quo are not good candidates for men's groups.

*Clinical Example.* One 58-year-old woman describes her husband's basic attitude that makes him a poor candidate for group—or any other—therapy. It is this central mind-set for which to screen in deciding against his being a potential group member.

*Sharlene:* He doesn't think he needs any help. He doesn't want to know or think that he's any part of my problems.— He doesn't think he has any problems.

Needless to say, he was not considered for a men's group, although if he ever could allow himself, he might benefit immensely. The caveat is that if these types of characters can have a dampening effect on groups in general, they can have a disastrous effect on a men's group, as vulnerability traditionally has been strictly forbidden for men. Hence, men who would prefer to continue to replicate in the therapy their dominance in the world are not good candidates for men's groups until or unless their attitudes can be addressed and they begin to change through either individual or couples therapy.

Sometimes putting one man in a group who has a less strident version of the view just articulated can be workable, because this man can soften as he experiences the fellowship of the other men and learns that changing does not mean he is sick or a sissy. In fact, maybe that is the only way for some men to catch the vision that change is both possible and not so terrifying. I usually end up with one such participant in each of my groups because I have seen over and over that even though their verbal participation is usually constricted and very limited for a long time, through a process of osmosis, the group gets to them in ways that neither their spouse nor I alone can. A word of caution is obvious here, however. More than one of these per group likely will mobilize everyone's resistance to being vulnerable, and a fiasco probably will result.

By contrast, men who are good candidates for groups are those who are willing to consider revising their standard definition of what makes for success. This usually means being willing to revamp it to such an extent that it includes having and nurturing satisfying relationships. This attitude change need not have been completed before a man enters a group; otherwise, why would he need a group experience? But he must be willing to reconsider what he has always thought constitutes achievement and success.

One point is important to underscore. Although a man needs to be in the process of revising his yardstick for success, he need not have adapted this new measure wholesale for him to have a constructive group experience and to be an addition to the group.

However, he needs to have developed an openness to recalibrat-
ing his traditional measure of success; otherwise his attitude may
pose a block for his or for others' willingness or ability to be
vulnerable in the group. Further, this does not necessarily mean
that a man must come in knowing that he will or even should
change what he does for a living; but spontaneously many begin
to examine the meaning and the place of work in their lives, and
if need be, to contemplate making some changes. Otherwise, as
Levinson (1978, 1990) points out and as I discussed in Chapter 4,
masses of men will continue to have a life of quiet desperation to
look forward to if the life structures on which they have built their
life are faulty. In other words, although they may keep the same
occupation, they may find themselves needing to change the ways
in which they think about it and do it to make room and time for
vulnerability, genuine intimacy, and satisfaction.

*Clinical Example.* One man speaks to this point when he comments
on the changes he is beginning to see in himself and in his definition of success. This evolving attitude makes him a very good
candidate for a group therapy experience.

*Sam:* I'm paid $50,000 a year to do my job, and wear certain garb, and
make phone calls. But I think about the isolation and the unreality of
that. There's another world going on out there. And now I see there
is another world going on in me that I don't usually get to get in touch
with. I think that repressing and not dealing with things on my job
makes me repress and deny in my life. It is nice for me to make a clear
identification between "This is my job" and "This is my life." It makes
me feel good about doing something about it.
*Therapist:* What you're saying is that doing therapy now will help ensure
that you have a life and a job.
*Sam:* Yes. And it will help me see also how my life impacts my job. And
it helps me when I interrupt my workday to have these sessions,
because it forces me to think about this in ways I wouldn't if we met
in the evening or on Saturdays. I can see now that it isn't worth it to
me now to stay at work until 7:30 or 10:00 on Saturdays or Sundays.

There are many clinical considerations to group selection, and
these will be summarized at the end of this section.

## How Does Participation in Men's Groups Compare With Mixed-Gender Groups?

There is no question that both types of group experiences can be very robust interventions. It is only a matter of deciding where the emphasis needs to be for each participant. And as usual, this is not a unilateral decision I foist on clients. By this phase of therapy, it is one we consider and decide together.

I have established two central deciding factors that help me discern which group experience likely would be more advantageous for a given man at a particular time. On the one hand, if a man's central dysfunction seems to relate primarily to unresolved historical factors, particularly those with his father, I recommend participation in a men's group. The multiple transference reactions that become vivified in the ways detailed above make those obsolete feelings more real and easier to get at in that venue. On the other hand, if a man's dysfunction seems to be localized in his inability to develop an intimate relationship with a woman in his current life, even though of course there are roots for that inability in his past, I will opt to encourage his participation in a mixed-gender group. There he can—and is forced to—practice relating with women as well as still having the opportunity for transference reactions to surface about his fathering or mothering that interfere in his current life, made possible because of the presence of other men and of female facilitator(s).

Though I have my own considerations in steering a man toward either a men's or a mixed-gender group, in reality, I usually leave the decision up to him. It should be noted that participation in one type of group does not preclude participation in the other at another time if the needs and the goals for that man change. Both are very robust tools for change; it is simply a matter of deciding which is indicated at what time.

## How Is the Remainder of Treatment Structured?

No one who wishes to participate in any of my groups—men's, women's, or mixed-gender groups—is invited to do so without first beginning a course of either individual or couples therapy with me or my cofacilitator. This is for three reasons: (a) to check for compatibility between potential members as well as with the leaders; (b) so that they and we can develop a working familiarity with their own personal issues, ensuring that those needs do not get lost in the group's dynamics and processes; and (c) to make sure that the level of sophistication is at least in the same ballpark with the other participants, so that the group is not held back. It is a well-accepted group therapy shibboleth that a group can go only as fast as its slowest member. Careful screening saves frustration, wasted energy, and sometimes even hurt.

Experiencing intimacy, developing affective competencies, and increasing personal awareness are goals of all the therapy I provide. Exactly where in the treatment process a man's participation in group comes is not particularly relevant as long as he has completed enough treatment to be open to learning about feelings and being intimate. With some clients, when the decision is made to participate in group, that is the only psychotherapy in which they participate. Others may still need intensive work to change their personality structure so that intimacy is possible. These people may choose to participate in both separate individual or couples appointments plus group therapy weekly. Still others may combine weekly groups with separate appointments on a periodic basis, such as every 2 to 3 weeks. And others will have group be their main psychotherapy focus, but will request separate appointments on an as-needed basis.

Who else is involved in separate sessions is dictated by the needs of the case. For some men, their separate sessions are with their spouse or significant other. Some are with their sons or father. Others meet only individually in those sessions. For those who are not in a significant, committed, ongoing relationship, their separate appointments usually are individual sessions, unless they are working directly with family of origin members. It is up to the therapist's clinical judgment to discern the best structure of treatment regarding who should be involved when. As with all family therapy, who is in the office at what time is a critically important decision. However, as was stated in Chapter 6, family therapy can go on with only one person in the room. The therapist needs to clarify her own decision rules to avoid working at cross-purposes with herself.

*A Caveat.* As with all group therapy, to protect the integrity of the group, the facilitator must be wary of working with group issues in separate sessions. For example, clients must not be allowed to express their anger at another group member or the other facilitator in these separate sessions. As we discussed in Chapter 6, this would be triangulation, and this dysfunctional communication itself has the probability to undermine the group because the anger expressed only individually to one therapist becomes a secret between them. And as systems thinkers know, secrets make systems unhealthy. Participants who feel emotions such as these are to be encouraged and helped to bring them up in group. However, it is permissible for group members to work on highly charged personal issues that were stirred up in group. For example, the first discussion of a client's sexual abuse is often held in separate sessions.

## What Are Some Contraindications for Participation in Men's Group Therapy?

I recommend that men *not* participate in a men's group while they continue in couples or individual therapy with another therapist. I rely on the old adage that too many cooks spoil the broth, and as family systems therapists know, the risk of triangulation is high. The client may experience working with two therapists who are strangers too much like having an affair or take the opportunity to replicate childhood experiences of pitting one parent against the other. In either instance, little or nothing therapeutic is accomplished, and worse, clients are often hurt by well-intentioned but ingenuous therapists. Thus both therapies are compromised.

It is quite different when two therapists who are facilitating the same group meet weekly. Because each can observe participants' behavior in vivo, they enjoy a golden opportunity to work with and resolve dysfunctional patterns. But an outside therapist, unaware of the influence of the group, may encourage the replication of a disruptive pattern, which then usually becomes even more ingrained.

## Conclusion

Men who are good candidates for men's or mixed-gender groups must be willing to have intimacy and vulnerability become as important as coming out on top has always been. They must also begin to be able to grasp the value of nurturing personal relationships as well as careers.

### Summary of Selection Criteria

The following is a summary of the selection criteria that my female cotherapist and I have found to be significant in selecting men to participate in these men's groups. Obviously, some, like nonpsychotic behavior, apply to any group participation. Others are specific considerations in choosing men to participate in such groups.

- History of at least one close relationship
- Willingness to examine current goals and priorities in life
- Sufficient prior treatment so that defenses are decreased
- Some insight about their own issues and contributions to problems
- Some ability to gain access to emotions
- Desire and intent to express feelings
- Sufficient degree of ego strength
- Spouse/significant other unlikely to be threatened excessively by man's participation
- Relationship equilibrium with partner unlikely to be excessively tipped by man's participation
- Nonpsychotic

It is likely that the experienced group therapist could add her own criteria to the list.

## Typical Issues That Surface in Men's or Mixed-Gender Groups

After doing many of these groups, I now see the issues that surface in two categories. One category is idiosyncratic issues, which each man struggles with depending on the specifics of his situation. The other kinds of issues that surface for any men in a group are more general and will be discussed separately below.

## Idiosyncratic Issues

One man may struggle with recovering from a divorce even as another questions whether or not to get divorced. One man may wrestle with how to open a meaningful dialogue with his father so that he can grow himself up, and another man may long to create a more connected way of relating to a son. One man may agonize with the depression resulting from being fired, as another man battles the anxiety of being a successful entrepreneur. Sometimes one of these forms the focus of the content of a given session or a part of a session; other times, the more generic issues, such as those discussed briefly below, form the bulk of the work for that day. Which topic is featured and for how long depends on the developmental stage of the group, on the ability of the leaders to integrate individual and group dynamics, and on the leaders' clinical judgment of where the group is on a given day.

## Generic Issues

Whatever the specific personal issue a man brings to the group to get help solving, there also is another set of issues that undergird all men's groups. Although issues such as these are common denominators in any therapy group, some are especially apparent in men's groups because of men's socialization. Still others are more prominent because these men are in groups led by women, this tending to bring out other facets of these often latent themes.

In the groups I have done over the years with men, the most significant and precarious issues that emerge are competition, power, control and being controlled, fear of anger, fear of intimacy, and sex and sexuality. Further, each of these can generate additional anxieties in men's groups that are facilitated by women because of the participants having to and being able to surface these in our presence. When any of these motifs surface, that is the work of the therapy.

The limits of space preclude a detailed discussion of how to handle each of these issues. Furthermore, the most lively therapy does not happen in a paint-by-numbers fashion. The reader is encouraged first to clarify these issues for herself, so that she is able to use her creativity in eliciting healing revelations from her male clients.

## Competition

Competition is ingrained in our culture. It is what made America great. And men have received an extra dose of competitiveness. Because of their socialization, men will and do compete about almost anything! And participants in men's groups—even though they are there to become less competitive and more affiliative—are no exception.

On a positive note, because of this ingrained mind-set of competition, group facilitators have a tool to use in working with men's groups that they can either use or abuse. For example, especially in the early meetings, my cofacilitator and I capitalize on this tendency to compete. When we do, we reframe what men have typically thought of as women's purview—risking emotionally—into a more male way of thinking by asking questions such as, "Who has the guts to share his feelings on that topic?" We reinforce a man's willingness to risk emotional material in his typical language, making statements like, "Being vulnerable is only for the strong."

Group leaders must be careful in using this intervention. Applying it too frequently may push men's competition buttons in such a way that we begin to perpetuate their already strong tendency toward competition. When this happens, they likely will have difficulty in developing the norm necessary for and conducive to mutual helpfulness. Then a negative culture develops. Once this infects a group, it can be deadly and difficult to eradicate. Further, because men are very sensitive to this issue of competition, justifiably they may begin to complain that the facilitators are perpetuating the very tendency they say they have joined the group to learn to avoid. Hence, this technique, like garlic, enhances but must be used judiciously. However, even if the men complain, the response can be used to help the men understand at a visceral level, not just at a cognitive level, how competitiveness permeates their lives and what a strong pull they experience to engage in it. One marker that a group is working especially well is that all the men are able to capitalize on the team spirit for which they have been socialized. When they can do this, they can cooperate to help each man reach his individual goals, rather than competing with one another. When that culture of mutual investment is apparent, the group has attained the optimal working climate.

A final note here is to point out how differently women and men are socialized about competition. Women have been taught that competition is not nice, and so typically our competitiveness is more covert, and in that sense, can be more insidious. Therefore, a female therapist needs to monitor her own competitive feelings both with the other facilitator and with male participants so that her tendency to deny those very natural feelings does not undermine the group's dynamics by bleeding into the process.

## Power, Control, and Being Controlling

People often confuse power with control and with being controlling. Yet, there are worlds of differences among these three concepts. First, I will offer some simple definitions, and then elaborate.

*Power* is internal strength and the ability to achieve your goals, which involves taking responsibility to ask for and seek what you need. Doing so increases the likelihood that your needs will be met. *Control* is a disowned need for power because of the fear of the threat to one's survival. That apprehension usually means giving up one's power or not claiming it, so means of need satisfaction are indirect, such as Doug's destructive style of attempting to meet his needs prior to therapy. When people operate this way, their needs are virtually guaranteed to be frustrated. *Being controlling* uses indirect tactics such as manipulation, intimidation, passive aggression, withdrawal, and other types of relationship terrorism to get what one wants.

People who are exercising their power come at life from a base of personal strength. They are assertive, ask for what they need, are grounded and centered in a clear, healthy sense of self, and in general value themselves well enough to take responsibility for themselves and for their own feelings and needs. By contrast, people who are controlling come at life from a base of weakness. That is why they become controlling: to try to acquire some strength while hiding their weakness. But their ways of going about it doom them to more frustration and ineffectuality. Often anger results from the powerlessness they feel, as we also saw above with Doug. In sum, genuine power is a manifestation of strength; being controlling is a manifestation of weakness.

Contrary to what some might believe, both women and men can have issues with power and control; it is not just men who run amuck in these areas. Both sexes tend to get controlling when they do not own their own power and when they feel afraid. Even though it seems that this fear of vulnerability usually is attributed to men, women can be afflicted by it, too.

This makes power a central issue to be addressed in groups. Regardless of the individual manifestation or the sex of the person who is doing it, the misuse of power and being controlling permeate participants' ways of working in the group and in life. It is those disruptive patterns that they come to us for our help in changing.

In addition, there are some specific ways this is a particular struggle for men, who are socialized to be in control of situations and to fix problems. This is the way to be considered "real men." So there is a societal injunction that men be in control that many men need our help in learning how to change, rather than our castigation for being that way. Our job is to teach clients two elegant paradoxes of human relationships. One, the more we try to be controlling, the more out of control we get. Two, the more we take our personal power by taking responsibility for ourselves, the more in control of our lives we get. When people think they are showing their power by controlling, they have not learned how to separate power from control, or even that there is a clear difference. They have not learned that one can be powerful without being controlling. It is the desired outcome of therapy that people are able to begin to give up this antiquated notion by learning to separate the two.

Obviously, men who need to learn to separate these two often-fused notions will have great difficulty if they experience their therapists being unable to do this. And all too many women, because of their socialization, do not know how to exercise power without being controlling. Yet, failing to do this precludes equal and equitable relating, because to be strong, one must assume one's personal power. And equitable relating is possible only if *both* people are allowed and encouraged to be strong, much like the principle Doug learned in the dialogue quoted above. The best way to help our male clients with this highly charged issue is to be certain that we are being clear and therapeutic ourselves.

## Fear of Anger

It is widely accepted that the primary emotion that men are socialized to believe is acceptable for them is anger. And yet, many are fearful of expressing their anger, lest they become rageful and violent. In fact, one of the primary factors in men's emotional constriction may be that very fear. Research conducted by Gottman and his associates (1991) found that the single best predictor of divorce in couples is whether the husband withdraws during conflict. According to their findings, although this may look to the wife like lacking interest, it is quite the opposite. He retreats because he is feeling strongly, and it frightens him, so he stonewalls, emotionally withdrawing from the fight. And yet, understandably, "The husband's stonewalling is very aversive for the wife and leads to her physiological arousal. She responds by trying to re-engage the husband" (p. 5). As one might predict, this can become an ever-deepening cycle of distance between them as the husband either totally withdraws farther, leaving them both lonely, or erupts as he feared, leaving them both bruised literally or figuratively.

In order to contain such a powerful and feared emotion as anger, many men see no choice but to rigidify and constrict all emotion. Then, by the time they come to acknowledge the need for feeling and expressing emotion, even if they are not presently engaged in a fight, it is no surprise that they sometimes become emotionally explosive or at least fearful that they will be.

*Clinical Example.* George, age 36, offers us an example of one man's extreme fear of his own anger. The following dialogue occurred in a session where he and I were preparing him for the extended family of origin session that was to take place 2 weeks later. After experiencing perpetual isolation in his family, through individual and group therapy, he had come to realize how hurt and angry he was about his situation. Although he acknowledged that he knew he must expose these extremely vulnerable feelings to his parents and brothers, he also expressed always having been extremely fearful of his anger. So as a way to cope, he learned to withdraw totally, which further reinforced his isolation in the family and once again fueled his anger. My primary goal with him during that preparatory session was to help him titrate his expression of anger so that he neither deadened himself by withdrawing to avoid his anger, nor exploded in unconstructive, effusive rage at his family.

*George:* When my anger gets mixed up with my feelings, it bends them out of shape. And then [my feelings] come at people like spooks.

*Therapist:* So you're very afraid of your own anger.

*George:* Yes. I find that people shy away from feelings. And because I've got so much anger, it scares the hell out of people. And it kinda scares me, too. And then the anger is like a pain. (Pause) And I feel like it's because expressing the feelings then is so new, that when they come out, [they're] like hellions. That's why I just decide that the only way I can handle things is just by not talking.

*Therapist:* But aren't there any other options to either exploding or just not talking to people?

*George:* That's the big one! You even told me that I'm an isolate. I've been painting. That's the way I communicate. But it came to me that the paintings don't have any people in them.

*Therapist:* So our job is going to be to help you express your anger in a way that it's not going to be the hellion you're afraid of, but so that you don't have to isolate yourself, either. (Pause) How would you go about doing that? (Seeing his tears) What are you feeling?

*George:* Just sadness. But it's true; when I let myself feel other feelings, then the anger *does* go away!

*Therapist:* Yes! That's how it goes!

*George:* If I start with anger, it's because I'm not dealin' with the rest of my feelings. But if I start with the rest of my feelings, that doesn't happen.

*Therapist:* Good stuff, George!

Female leaders must first establish a holding environment so that the group can tolerate, work with, and contain participants' anger without excessive fear of it going out of control. Then the men can learn to do so themselves. I start by stating directly that it is my responsibility as the one in control in my office to see that the man, the others, myself, and my office will be safe. And I *will* see to that. I talk contingency plans, such as temporary hospital-ization, with both the man and significant others if his fears of going out of control are extreme, as I did with Doug above. I offer appointments on an as-needed basis until a client can develop the requisite confidence that his anger will not make him the hellion George feared he would become. And then the group and I help him learn to trust himself so that others can trust him. This is where the presence of other men can be reassuring, to both the angry man and the facilitators alike. Between the leaders who take charge and the other men who are backups, there is the requisite reassurance that there will be bounds on the expression of anger.

The important factor to know about men's rage is that perhaps more than anything else, it is what has kept them from intimacy with others, out of protection and love for the others, as well as out of avoidance of the shame they anticipate if they exploded or became violent. When the therapist has this perspective firmly in mind and does not have residual and undue fear of men's anger of her own with which to contend, their rage is much less frightening for all involved. And then he can be helped to learn constructive expression of anger with his partner so that they do not become one of the statistics Gottman (1991) described.

## Fear of Intimacy

Because fear of intimacy has been a theme that has pervaded much of the book, not much more of a theoretical nature needs to be said about it. But a clinical example will speak eloquently to this fear that we all have, but to which men in particular can fall prey.

Don is a man from whom we have heard in two other spots in the book. He is the 40-year-old always single man who became terrified of any relationship with a woman because of the reaction formation he developed in response to how incested he felt because of the intrusive, sexualized relationship he had with his mother.

At the time he spoke the words reproduced below, he had been in individual therapy for approximately 14 months and had participated in a 20-week mixed-gender therapy group facilitated by another woman and me. Here he describes his discovery that he really is lonely, that he needs a woman in his life, and that he no longer wants to defend himself by being alone. His words speak eloquently of his fear, his need, and the progress he has made toward accomplishing his primary treatment goal.

*Don:* (With tears in his eyes) I'm just now acknowledging my need for a woman. For a long time, I thought, "Why would I need someone to make me happy?"

*Therapist:* And now?

*Don:* Now it's important. Now it's (pause) it's (pause) I don't want to say I'd be miserable without it. But I can say it's an important component of living. The desire to have someone to hold that I love seems overwhelming now!

*Therapist:* Does that make you sad?

*Don:* Yeah!

*Therapist:* Can you tell me about that?

*Don:* The sadness has to do with some of the other things I was feeling about (pause) living such a (pause) scared life, in a way. The sadness has to do not only with lost opportunities, but also with not fully taking advantage of relationships I did have, or feelings I did have at the time. Sometimes why I stuffed my feelings was feeling the loss that had to go with recognizing that I hadn't had [feelings] before.

Don's realization that he no longer wants his fear of intimacy to propel him away from relationships with women puts him in an ideal position to be able to change this. Until now, he had been mystified about his blandness, was lethargic and unmotivated about doing anything about it, and was so well defended that closeness with anyone was precluded.

Female leaders, to avoid covertly hampering men in their quest for intimacy, must have some positive experiences with it themselves and must believe that it is not just men who obstruct the process of attaining intimacy. Optimally, the female therapist will have an understanding about how she, too, obstructs intimacy in her close relationships. This will give her an inside-out perspective on the struggles involved in developing good communication.

## Sex and Sexuality

As has been repeatedly stated throughout the book, sex and sexuality are a part of any female-male interaction. Thus, it is no surprise that these issues lurk just beneath the surface in men's groups that are led by women. Sometimes it is this fact that is talked about in group. Other times, different aspects of the topic of sex are discussed, such as men's early messages about sex, early experiences with masturbation, whether or not they felt/feel they measure up to other men sexually, and what pleases a woman sexually and with intimacy in general. All of these are highly personal topics. The important idea to remember about sexual discussions is that somehow being able to have them, whatever the specific content, seems to break the ice for people. This is probably because, unlike locker-room bravado, these conversations help them reach unprecedented levels of intimacy with each other, likely because of breaking a very primitive taboo. In our experience, this sort of openness has the potential to beget even greater sharing in group and even with their significant other. So in this instance, the particular content of the conversation is less important than that it is happening.

Optimally, the female therapist, regardless of her sexual preference, will have experience with satisfactory sexual relationships and will have attained a comfort level in being able to talk about this topic, in order not to hamper the growth of her male clients in these areas.

## Some Hazards When Women Run Men's Groups

Women without a clear understanding of their own issues about men are not good candidates for running men's groups. Because of the tendency for all of us to get our own issues caught up in our clients' struggles in general, then surely in a roomful of men, the potential that someone else's issues will be a flint for our own is great. Further, if we have unresolved issues about power, control, competition, intimacy, or anger, we will be especially susceptible to becoming nontherapeutic.

As with any good therapy, understanding one's own issues is critical to success with men's groups. Otherwise, we may join the men in competition and struggle for control. Not understanding our own issues also may cause us subtly to blame them for the difficulties in our lives. To work effectively with men, we must be neither intimidated by nor belligerent about men.

Another major hazard that a female men's group leader must overcome is suggested by the evidence offered by Correa et al. (1988) that people tend to view men as more appropriate than women for task leadership; they note that women had the most difficulty leading men, for these followers would not allow the leader readily to exercise her authority. They also note that the gender role expectations that many participants have can make the situations that women leaders confront less favorable. However, because the group model proposed here involves handpicked participants from our practice, this has not been the author's experience. And as Correa et al. (1988) further found, men in groups led by women learned the most.

Because women are socialized to nurture and to mother, another hazard is subtly discouraging group members' individuation because of our own needs to avoid losing them either from our groups or from our practice. Men can come to experience this as a

threat to the autonomy for which they were socialized and therefore reject the help many so desperately need. The therapist needs
to be constantly vigilant about the strong pull to become over-
involved emotionally with clients of either sex.

Another risk is subtly allowing and even encouraging the men
to compete for the attention of the leader, even for the leadership
of the group. This would perpetuate men's socialization as each
other's rivals, as well as short-circuit cooperation in the group.
This can be a particularly precarious issue for attractive women.
Although none of us would deliberately prompt such a response,
we must be vigilant about our own nonverbal messages and
hidden agendas that may invite such reactions.

## A Baker's Dozen Guidelines for
## Women Leading Men's Groups

After facilitating many men's groups, several with a female
cofacilitator, one with a male coleader, and some by myself, I can
offer the following recommendations.

1. Women need not be hesitant about leading men's groups.
   There are distinct advantages to women facilitating such groups.
   They can create a unique holding environment that allows the
   completion of unfinished family of origin business. This provides an experience that can build on the already strong tendency to replicate transference patterns.

2. Although groups led by women were considered more stressful than those led by men, participants of both genders felt
   that they learned more in groups led by women. This significant finding of Correa et al. (1988), although calling for us to be
   somewhat circumspect, also empowers us to know that men in
   our groups can expect to have a powerfully positive experience.
   That means that female leaders of groups with men can expect a
   greater level of stress for them personally but greater gains for
   the participants.

3. Know that men are capable of achieving deep levels of intimacy with each other, and that they will then be capable of
   parlaying that into their relationships with their significant
   others. Left to their own devices, men in the presence of men

tend to replicate the task focus that pervades their work life or hide in a topic focus. Pasick (1990) vastly undersells both group treatment and men's ability to engage in rigorous self-examination and to be truly intimate with each other, because of his prescribed format for men's groups. He lists week-by-week topics around which he centers the groups' discussions, which perpetuates the perception that men are capable of interacting with other men only around tasks or by a formula.

4. Men's groups facilitated by two women have distinct advantages over those run by either two men or a male-female leadership team. In these other combinations of leadership teams the chances are greater of the woman being in the one-down position in which she so often finds herself in society in general. According to the group therapy literature represented by Correa et al. (1988), the woman, who already is at a high risk of being the brunt of transference reactions, can be at an even greater risk for negative transference in those instances.

5. Remember that probably the best way to establish your credibility as a woman is by demonstrating that you can comfortably perform executive or agentic tasks as well as communal tasks in the group. Try to keep in mind that although the best way to join women is sensitivity, it works best to join men using sensibility. This will garner you the most respect and more readily will put the transference reactions to you that get stirred up exactly where they belong: with the clients.

6. There is a unique opportunity to finish family of origin business in a men's group led by women. The group would provide "mothers," "sisters," and "lovers," as well as "fathers" and "brothers," for transference objects. Understanding this makes risking intimacy easier, and participants have a golden opportunity for it in men's groups led by women.

7. If these groups are to be run by a cotherapy team, it is important that both facilitators have worked out a respectful, synergistic, cooperative relationship. Men's socialization for competitiveness may have the tendency to hook unresolved issues in the leaders' relationship. Plus, men who have had little experience with women in authority will tend to look to the male leader first. Thus, the group will become counterproductive and

HELPING MEN CHANGE

nontherapeutic, and obviously the leaders' relationship will be compromised.

8. Although it certainly is possible to do, depending on the level of trust and mutual respect of the cofacilitators, male-female coleadership teams for groups *tend to be more precarious than same-sex leadership teams.* According to the research of Correa et al. (1988), "Both men and women view men in positions of authority more positively" (p. 223). Thus, the woman in this situation may end up with extraneous issues to overcome to be allowed to be an effective, respected group leader.

9. If you are working with a male cofacilitator and find yourself in a one-down position, take steps immediately to correct this situation. My first suggestion is that you bring this to your cofacilitator's attention at your first available private opportunity. And then, even if the two of you solve it, bring it to the group, as a way for the participants to learn how they may do this. It could be a chance to help them understand and stop this insidious tendency.

10. If you find yourself not receiving the credibility you are due, work to achieve it without becoming hostile. The group therapy literature suggests that groups are unforgiving of male leaders who are too soft, just as they are merciless with female leaders who are too brash or antagonistic (Correa et. al, 1988). Seize the opportunity to model that it is preferable that people be capable of both strong and soft styles of functioning. Also be prepared to deal with these with group participants and to get some supervision on these painful and confusing issues if you are unable to extricate yourself on your own.

11. Remember that, according to Correa et al. (1988), "Women trainers and therapists more frequently become targets of negative transference than do their male counterparts" (p. 223). Inure yourself to being a ready receptacle of projections and transference reactions so that you do not so readily personalize such reactions. Examine your behavior to see if there is any truth to the allegation, and then if you conclude that there is not, chalk it up to transference, and resolve to help the client understand his outdated reactions. If you stay stuck in

your own responses to the attack, seek supervision or consultation from your cotherapist or another trusted colleague.

12. Remember that neither you nor participants can create massive changes with everyone in every group. Just as important, however, is that people's ability to observe and participate in others' changes can provide a powerful impetus for their own growth at a later date. Often, therapists are no longer even in the picture when the seeds that were planted long ago bear fruit in individual metamorphoses.

13. Trust the process. Individuals and groups have an intuitive sense of what they need to do if they and we get out of their way. Remember, as I discussed in Chapter 5, development is an invariant process once the factors that have arrested it have been removed. So do the best you can, and then get out of the way.

## A Final Word

My experience has shown that the best work with men proceeds with a dynamic and affective focus. And psychotherapy groups are no exception. Depth understanding of themselves and of others is where the greatest intimacy can be developed and the greatest basic change can be fostered in all their relationships.

## References

Allen, J. (1990). Men and mothers. In R. Meth & R. Pasick (Eds.), *Men in therapy: The challenge of change* (pp. 224-233). New York: Guilford.

Correa, M., Klein, E., Stone, W., Astrachan, J., Kossek, E., & Komarraju, M. (1988). Reactions to women in authority: The impact of gender on learning in group relations conferences. *Journal of Applied Behavioral Science, 24*(4), 219-233.

Erickson, B. (1992). *The development of a model for women leading men's groups.* Unpublished manuscript.

Gordon, B. (1990). Men and their fathers. In R. Meth & R. Pasick (Eds.), *Men in therapy: The challenge of change* (pp. 234-258). New York: Guilford.

Gordon, B. , & Pasick, R. (1990). Changing the nature of friendship between men. In R. Meth & R. Pasick (Eds.), *Men in therapy: The challenge of change* (pp. 261-278). New York: Guilford.

Gottman, J. (1991). Predicting the longitudinal course of marriages. *Journal of Marital and Family Therapy, 17*(1), 3-7.

Levinson, D. (1978). *The seasons of a man's life.* New York: Knopf.

Levinson, D. (1990, July). *Adult development of women and men.* The Cape Cod Summer Symposium, Eastham, MA.

Meth, R. (1990). Men and sexuality. In R. Meth & R. Pasick (Eds.), *Men in Therapy: The challenge of change* (pp. 209-223). New York: Guilford.

Moore, R., & Gillette, D. (1990). *King, warrior, magician, lover: Rediscovering the archetypes of the mature masculine.* San Francisco: HarperSanFrancisco.

Rosenberg, P. (in press). Comparative leadership styles of male and female therapists. In B. DeChant (Ed.), *Women, gender, and group psychotherapy.* New York: Guilford.

Wilcox, D., & Forrest, L. (1992). The problems of men and counseling: Gender bias as a gender truth? *Journal of Mental Health Counseling, 14*(3), 291-304.

Yalom, I. (1985). *The theory and practice of group psychotherapy.* New York: Basic Books.

# The Major Surgery of Psychotherapy: The Extended Family of Origin Session

In the course of therapy, people often come face to face with unresolved issues from their past. With very little effort, most therapists can probably list case after case where people's progress in therapy—and in life!—has been stymied by their inability to work through an event or period in their past. And yet, we are often unable to get the therapeutic leverage required to help clients to move through that moment or era. We have tried the more standard experiential techniques for resolving old hurts, such as open-chair dialogues, letter-writing campaigns, family sculptures, and hitting or hugging stuffed figures. Yet clients continue to be mired, languishing on one end or the other of the continuum from intellectualized detachment from the experience to profuse, unrelenting affect about it. This inability to resolve emotion-laden events can be problematic for anyone, but may particularly plague men who because of their socialization, already tend to deal with feelings by intellectualization and rationalization.

This chapter first appeared as an article in the *Journal of Family Psychotherapy*, 3(1), 19-44 (1992). Reprinted with permission.

When this situation goes unchecked, isomorphism takes effect. This is the systemic concept that identifies the tendency people have to repeat in every system in which they operate the interaction patterns they learned in their original system, their family of origin. To interrupt their repetitive, dysfunctional interaction cycles, often we must help them by going to the source. Sometimes insight and "arm chairing" simply are not enough to unfreeze the developmental arrests that have taken place around repressed material and unexpressed feelings about it.

When clients reach this therapeutic impasse, we need to be able to help—and sometimes propel—them to work directly with their feelings in the presence of key family members. Anything less calcifies and memorializes "analysis paralysis." In these instances, only being able to talk face to face can finish unfinished business and dislodge developmental logjams so that psychological growth can resume. This face-to-face resolution of issues directly with the family of origin perhaps best distinguishes the contributions to our field of Framo and Napier and Whitaker.

There is a common misconception among family systems therapists that an approach cannot be systemic if it is psychodynamic, that the two are somehow mutually exclusive categories. This breaks the field into artificial categories and at the same time dismisses the seminal contributions of such psychodynamic thinkers as Ackerman (1958) and Paul and Paul (1986). Moreover, it ignores the more recent movement toward rediscovering the individual within the family system. This is represented by such voices as Schwartz (1987, 1988), Watanabe-Hammond (1987), and Nichols (1987).

As the field of family therapy moves past its adolescence, the time has come to reconcile the once-rejected ideas of individual therapy with a systemic perspective. Rather than further polarizing, the technique offered here relies on an integrative framework that combines an emphasis on both the individual and the system.

## Definition

### What Is an Extended Family of Origin Session?

Over the past 12 years, I have experimented with and arrived at what I now consider to be the optimal format for these sessions. I prefer to schedule two 2-hour segments that occur roughly 24 hours apart.

I intentionally schedule no more than 4 hours for these sessions. I keep them brief, intense, and pointed, so that people can no longer avoid dealing with each other and with their logjams. And yet, it is important to offer sufficient time so that issues not only can be identified but also worked through. I also allow just enough time for people to explore, directly or indirectly, how they would like their relationships to change after this experience.

Often concern is expressed about the short length of time. I have found that if the time is too short, people will intellectualize, talking *about* their feelings when they need to surface, explore, and resolve them. What already feels risky seems too unsafe for exposing real vulnerabilities. If the time is too long, people will avoid, procrastinating dealing with their feelings until the eleventh hour. Then, the anxiety unnecessarily and inappropriately builds, and people risk leaving each other in the middle of an issue at session's end.

Further, I have discovered that approximately 24 hours between segments is also useful, for several reasons. People need time, literally and figuratively, to sleep on the first piece. One of two eventualities usually happens in the first day. Either people spill the material they dread the most, and then they and the family spend the balance of the sessions working through it, or they start with easier, though still significant, material in an effort to lay groundwork. The time between segments is critical in either case, for clients and their family to have time to digest what they have heard, working with responses to and implications of this material, or to screw up their courage to spit out their most feared secrets.

Even though I have found 4 hours to be optimal, in recent years, I have done some innovating on this structure, usually because some client contingency needs to be accommodated. Sometimes I will do two 1½ hour sessions, particularly if one of the family members is frail and lacking in stamina, such as those sessions I have conducted with an aging or ailing family member. Occasionally, I have done the entire session on the same day. In one instance, I facilitated a session convened by two parents with their four remaining adult children to talk about the unresolved death 2 years previously of their son who was killed in a motorcycle accident. Their surviving son, a medical resident, simply was unable to arrange for 2 consecutive days out of the hospital, and

I believed that excluding him would have serious consequences. So we did one 3-hour session with a brief break in the middle. In another instance, I conducted a 4-hour session in 1 day, with a 2-hour lunch break in the middle because one of the adult children was home on a 3-day pass from the military. As with any good therapy, it is up to therapists to exercise their best clinical judgment in arriving at both an appropriate and workable structure on a case-by-case basis.

## Clinical Advantages

### What Are the Curative Factors in Direct Conversation With Family Members?

Fear, perhaps more than any other reason, is why people get stuck on an experience. Fear can have many different roots. One is actual terror repressed at the moment of a critical experience, such as when a child is abused. Another is fear of loss of love if one confesses an early experience. For example, I once helped a client disclose in an extended session to her horrified parents her shame and self-blame because when she was a child, her older brother had raped her. Another form is fear of the parent's anger at the child who says how he or she really feels and has felt on any subject. An example is the recent session in which an extremely ingratiating client shared with his mother how terrified he was at even the thought of angering her. Another form of fear is that of social incest if the child allows any emotional closeness with the parent, such as the session in which a man disclosed to his mother how his phobia about closeness with his fiancée had developed out of how incested he felt because she was smotheringly affectionate and emotionally effusive. Whatever the specifics of the situation, fear is a primary motivator for silence in families. And this silence keeps adults emotional children.

Whatever the specifics that generated the logjam originally and perpetuate it now, talking face to face can eliminate it in a way that talking endlessly *about* it cannot. And yet clients tend to avoid such conversations in silent allegiance to their family's rules, established long ago, unquestioned and still in force today. And therapists inadvertently may perpetuate this. It is very difficult for people fully to become adults if they remain in the role of children in their family of origin.

In addition, in the confines of the therapist's office with 4 hours stretching ahead of them, both clients and their family seem to intuit that there is no escaping each other; that it is time to clear some accounts. There, if the therapist can create a therapeutic ambience, people can feel free to air their dirty laundry, cleaning it up once and for all.

## When Are These Sessions Indicated?

After countless sessions of talking and even catharting, some clients remain immobilized, unable to free themselves of the paralyzing effects of early experiences. Often these clients have had many previous therapies but are still languishing in their symptoms. In many instances, they have talked about these events ad nauseam, but they still feel stuck. And I believe they will remain so until they can work directly with these feelings and experiences with key family members. These discussions provide the seminal moments that are possible when family members talk. Speaking directly with those involved helps to extricate people from unproductive patterns and helps both families and individuals to move on developmentally.

## Why Is It Important to Have These Conversations in the Presence of a Therapist?

Any family of origin work can break a family's conspiracy of silence, and the reader might well ask: Why do clients have to bring family members to the therapist's office to do that? Do all clients have to do this? How can the therapist tell when these sessions are indicated? It should be underscored that these sessions are the psychological equivalent of a surgical procedure in terms of time, energy, and expense. Thus, they are not appropriate for everyone in all situations.

Sometimes I coach clients, strategizing with them on ways to go back into their family and individuate, as Bowen (1978) suggested. This methodology needs to be used carefully for two reasons. First, to send clients back to their family alone can sometimes be to send them into the lion's den. Second, particularly for men, it

is easy to intellectualize feelings. People assume they have resolved an experience and should be ready to move on, when what
they have really done is add another layer of defenses. In those
instances, doing the work in the presence of the therapist is essential, so that this tendency to only cognitively grapple with an
experience that must be felt to be resolved does not continue to
compromise clients' further growth.

I begin to advocate strongly for such sessions when other more
conservative and traditional interventions have been of minimal
benefit, when I suspect that both fear and the family's conspiracy
of silence (Bowen, 1978) are so great that a client would be unable
to have a corrective emotional experience (Yalom, 1985) without
the therapist's help. Some clients' and families' desire to analyze,
intellectualize, and rationalize an experience can be so strong that
even if they do meet on their own, it would be more of the same.
I also suggest these sessions when the therapeutic agenda would
be simply too overwhelming and difficult for the client to accomplish successfully alone.

## What Are Some Predictable Outcomes of These Sessions?

Ideally, every family of origin session ends with a major reconciliation after some sensitive revelations. And most do; in my
experience, that is by far the most common outcome. However,
not all end with this optimal result.

But even when they do not end optimally, I consider the sessions
a success, because of the ego strength that clients accrue from
facing—and sometimes facing off with—their family. When the
client has a basis in a reality for seeing family members accurately
instead of just defensively, even what appears at the time to be an
untoward or even minimally successful outcome can be liberating.
For then, although the client's only recourse is to grieve over the
fantasy family, doing this provides freedom to move on. The client
no longer languishes in anger or pining about the family that
never was. It can also be a self-esteem builder to know that the
family, too, has some complicity in one's logjam; it is not merely
the client who is responsible.

Occasionally, but the end of the 4 hours, people seem even more
at odds than they did before the session started, pulling farther away
from each other. Although that is an outcome that is somewhat

uncomfortable for me as the therapist, I have learned not to be overly alarmed. In those few instances, particularly if the entire family was so enmeshed in repetitive struggles that individuation seemed impossible, I consider lessening of their pseudomutuality a success. Given that convening a family session is deliberately breaking the family's rules and ending the conspiracy of silence, even if it yields apparently limited success in terms of the original goals and provides no dramatic reconciliation, it can be a great tool for individuation for both clients and family members.

The following is an example of this. Approximately 2 months after an extended session, a father in an extremely enmeshed family spoke of his experience in the time since the session that I had thought at the time bore only a modest amount of fruit.

*Hal:* I was too involved in my children's lives before. So I've told them now that I'm going to back off. In the old days, I would've said, "Oh oh!" and would have moved back in. It's not easy for me to do this, even though I now know this is what I should do. But I know I'm on the right track.

My client and I can capitalize on the differentiation made possible by the sessions, and his infantilized adult children can also be benefactors.

Rarely, the outcome serves to increase the amount of disengagement in the family, at least temporarily. This occurs in families whose rigid distance protects some very significant pathology in their entire way of interacting, in one or both of the parents, in the parents' marriage, or in all three. Tragically, in those cases the parents have such a high stake in perpetuating the emotional distance and the scapegoating that has so pervaded the adult child's lifetime, that it means sacrificing the child and their relationship to him or her. It is my role to help the parents grasp the significance and the consequences of their untoward response to the adult child's request in an effort to redirect them all to more constructive responses. But as systems thinkers, we know that sometimes a family is too severely dysfunctional and its homeostasis is simply too formidable and rigid for a qualitatively different response, no matter how legitimate the request.

Forty-one-year-old Sara's meeting with her parents was an example of this unfortunate outcome. The focus of what she wished to address was how isolated and lonely she had always felt as a child, having clear, conscious memories, going back to age 4, of being either ignored or blatantly rejected by her parents. The session was difficult and disappointing from start to finish, despite our best and repeated attempts to generate a different outcome. Near the end of the 4 hours, in desperation to get something nurturing from them, Sara made what seemed to both of us to be a simple, straightforward request. She asked both of her parents to affirm that they loved her. One parent refused to answer. The other begrudgingly said yes, but hastened to add that Sara's question was resented because it sounded like a request that they show favoritism to her over their other children. This was despite repeated attempts to reassure them that this was not Sara's intent. In subsequent sessions over many weeks, I helped Sara to grieve, to accept her parents' limitations and her own powerlessness to change them, and to stop blaming herself for their inability to come through for her. In the face of this kind of profoundly disappointing response, the only option therapist and client have afterward is to grieve for the family that never was and never will be, now that it is clear that this is clearly the case. It should be underscored that this does not mean cutting the family off. It only means attempting to stay connected with them in workable ways, while being fully in touch with the reality of what they are and what they are not.

One point is important to underscore. If people have not sincerely tried to inaugurate a new and better way of relating, such as these sessions can provide, giving up and grieving are premature. However, when they have, it is the only recourse left. Even in those instances, an important distinction must be made. One does not help them bury their live parents, but rather helps them grieve for the parents they did not and will not have.

Often clients will protest that they have tried everything to talk to their family. But my experience says that it behooves us to be skeptical until we have seen with our own eyes that significant change is impossible, at least at this time. Families' homeostasis can be formidable, and our clients, caught in rigid roles, may themselves be acting as homeostats. Although we have some predictors that can help us anticipate families' responses in advance, it is important that we not, based on our clients' descriptions, sell their family short. It is impossible to know in advance which families will allow a shift and which will further rigidity, so it is a risk that both therapist and clients have to take to have the chance that the situation could improve. But an adverse outcome is a possibility for which clients need to be prepared.

## Technical Considerations

### How Does the Therapist Deal With Client Resistance?

Clients who need to do these sorts of sessions have emotion-laden material that they have kept hidden from their family members— and even from themselves—for a long time. And most, at least initially, prefer to keep it just where it is. So the question of how one broaches this subject with clients is critical. Further, timing this intervention is integral to its success.

Timing has three dimensions: (a) when to first bring up the idea of such a session, (b) how to tell when a client is far enough along in the therapy to begin planning such a session, and (c) when a client is ready to do such a session. Each of these will be explored below.

When I first broach the subject that I have begun thinking that the client may need to do a family of origin session, predictably I am met with resistance. This may come in the form of discounting the suggestion, flat-out refusal to even think about it, or panic at the thought. If people and their family have had a high stake in denying, they initially will be loath to face themselves and their pivotal experiences. Often it takes many months of laying tracks again and again, looping their current problem to this source experience from their past, to help them to see that the benefits from facing their fear and their family would outweigh the cost. And sometimes even if people are willing to examine their own pain, they are very resistant to asking family members to face them. In most instances, clients need to be shown over and over that such a session potentially can be to everyone's benefit.

In the beginning, I take an indirect hypnotic approach, relying heavily on paradoxical suggestions (Palazzoli, Checchin, Prata, & Boscolo, 1978) so that clients resist themselves rather than resisting my suggestion. I might say something like, "You're probably going to think this is a dumb idea, but as you know, I have lots of them. Lately, I've been thinking how helpful it could be for you to be able to say these things directly to your parents, rather than imagining important conversations with them. But I also know that doing that would be really hard, so you're probably not going to want to even think about it." And if clients resist my suggestion, as they most often initially do, I don't worry, because I have planted the seed. From then on, whenever I hear an instance where having a live conversation would help, I point it out, either directly or using another paradoxical injunction.

When I make direct interventions, I say things like, "It makes sense to me that you have such trouble feeling strong about being directly angry with your spouse, when you are still that scared little girl who never owned her anger at her parents. Maybe together we could do something about that." The point is to demonstrate the advantages, over and over in whatever ways clients present opportunities, facing family members directly.

### When Is a Client Ready to Plan an Extended Session?

Several markers tell both the client and me that it is time to begin planning the session. One is that all other interventions have been exhausted, and still the problem persists. When such a session is a last resort, clients usually no longer resist. In fact, they actively embrace this as the next and perhaps only remaining step. That is not to say that there is no longer any anxiety or fear about doing the session; there is. However, the fear is no longer strenuous. Or when it is, it is openly identified by the client, explored, and then given up.

In general, these sessions occur in the middle phase of therapy, when the client's presenting problem has been resolved, but discomfort still exists. In fact, because of the need for careful preparation in order to maximize its effects, I would recommend against doing such a session until the middle phase. Only those who have the insight and investment to go beyond simple symptom resolution become candidates for this procedure. Because so much groundwork must be laid in order to maximize this once-in-a-lifetime opportunity, I do nothing more than lay tracks early in treatment. Because of this, not all clients for whom I think such a session is indicated convene one.

Another reason for these occurring in the middle phase of therapy is that a cooperative relationship between therapist and client(s) needs to have been clearly established. There needs to be a sense of teamwork and joint effort both in planning and executing this very delicate intervention to maximize its effects.

## When Is the Client Ready to Do an Extended Session?

A client's readiness is somewhat more difficult to discern, but it is perhaps the most critical dimension of the timing question. I believe that these few hours offer an unique opportunity. For clients not to squander this chance, they must be carefully prepared by the therapist.

Perhaps the first and hardest hurdle for most clients is admitting that they need help from people who have been very hurtful in the past. They must be ready to both identify where they need help, plus be willing to risk sharing their feelings about that nexus. Clients must have a clear understanding of the issues that make up the crux of their developmental logjams. They must have emotional access to both that nexus and to the implications of it. And they must be willing to share their emotions, rather than sterile intellectual descriptions about it. Until clients are ready to do each of these, the preparatory work continues. This is why it can take months, and occasionally even years, for such a session to actually occur. It should be noted that the focus of the preparatory work is not directly on planning for these sessions during this entire time. Regular couples or individual exploration is groundwork that is also crucial to the success of the intervention.

## How Can the Therapist Help a Client Prepare for the Session?

Over the 12 years since I began developing these sessions, I have concluded that fully three quarters of the work of the sessions is done before family members ever enter my office. That work is to help clients flesh out the issues, surface their feelings about them, and get key family members to participate. Sometimes it takes months to enlist family members' participation; sometimes to clients' surprise, it can take seconds. Once both client and therapist are convinced that the session is needed, both must be prepared not to take no for an answer.

The astute reader may have noticed by now that I have not used the word "confront." I do not conceptualize these sessions as a confrontation of family members. I see them more as opportunities for clients to confront themselves and their fears and begin to take corrective action. Besides, if family members expect to walk into a lion's den in the therapist's office, they understandably will be highly resistant to cooperating. And I don't blame them for not wanting to be blamed! But my clients will have missed a great opportunity. The key here is for clients to take responsibility for what they need and to ask all family members to take responsibility for what they did or did not do, or at least for the fact that the client has felt hurt. This is not to say that anger is not expressed; sometimes it needs to be and it is. In fact, denied or repressed anger is itself sometimes the crux of the logjam. In those instances, it must be dealt with. However, if clients' mind-sets are only to angrily confront without being prepared also to resolve, then they are not yet ready to convene the session.

A note of caution: The therapist should help clients prepare for the session just enough that their affect is on the surface and available, but not so expressed that the session becomes like cold oatmeal. Exactly when the session should occur is another dimension of the timing issue and is a matter of the therapist's clinical judgment.

### Who Invites Family Members?

Sometimes just getting our clients to ask and the family to agree to attend is the bulk of the therapeutic work. This is especially true, for instance, for clients whose needs were never really addressed or who developed a highly counterdependent interpersonal style. For example, getting narcissistic parents to meet the needs of the client for a change is in and of itself therapeutic.

In general, I help clients strategize to get the requisite people to attend, rather than doing it for them. This helps them make a statement both to themselves and to family members that their needs are valid and that attention must be paid to them. However, I must be ready to support and cajole my clients, particularly when family members are extremely resistant to doing the session. For example, in one instance, it took 6 months to get a father to fly into town for a session, even though he was a world traveler in his personal and business life. I assumed this was due to mutual resistance in both father and son. What finally turned the key was when my client could say simply, "Dad, I need you to come." Hearing his son's direct and impassioned request, the father relented and scheduled the trip. On a follow-up note, ever since that session took place 6 years ago, that client reports that he and his father take annual vacations by themselves, in addition to the time they spend with each other during my client's regular visits home.

Sometimes family members will not agree to come for such a session without speaking with me first. Honoring this request allows them to get a sense of who I am and what my approach will be. But I often suspect the hidden agenda for these contacts is to assess whether I believe they are to blame for all of their child's woes. Such calls can be blatant campaigns to triangulate, attempting to get me to see what a terrible, misguided, ungrateful, and so on person my client is, to illustrate how innocent family members are of whatever they imagine my client will accuse them, or to establish their own power position in advance of the session. These presession calls, sometimes necessary to enlist the participation of family members, can be precarious for the therapist. The only advice I can offer is to be wary of being triangulated while taking this opportunity to join with family members as you solicit their aid.

In extreme instances, I will initiate a call to family members myself. This is when they remain resistant to the client's request and I believe that this experience has singular potential to break up emotional and developmental logjams. I will do ethically whatever it takes when I am convinced that to not have this experience would be to have clients languishing in the purgatory of not knowing their place in or feelings about their family.

## Who Should Be Included?

In any family therapy, the question of structuring treatment is critical to the intervention's success. Having the wrong people or not having the right people in the office can make or break therapy. And given that this is a time-limited intervention, this question is perhaps more critical.

The first and easiest question to settle regarding inclusion is whether or not the client's partner, if there is one, should attend. In my experience, these sessions are so powerful, that to solidify the couple bond, I prefer to do them in the partner's presence.

Further, as there will suddenly be many people involved in the therapy with whom I do not have a prior relationship, the partner can often act as a kind of cotherapist, a perception check for me, and a bridge between client and family.

However, there are some exceptions and some caveats to this. For example, where spouses themselves have become controversial for the in-laws, their inclusion could inadvertently provide a scape-goat as a continued distractor for the family. Nonetheless, sometimes having them there can help to extricate them from that role. It is up to the therapist and the clients to discern which is more advisable. In these instances, I talk openly with clients about the pros and cons and make recommendations, but I leave it to them to decide.

In instances where a spouse intuits that the session will uncomfortably shift the dynamics in the marriage, although he or she may sabotage the session, his or her absence can itself be a worse sabotage. In those instances, it probably is less precarious if the spouse attends the session with the client. However, timing of the session is critical. Much groundwork needs to be laid with the couple so that potency of the session is not undermined.

Another instance where spouses' participation needs to be considered carefully is if their family of origin issues strongly parallel the clients', but they have not yet resolved theirs. Then attending the session will be very painful for them. If they choose to attend, triaging their responses periodically during the session is critical, as well as being available afterward if too much overpowering material of their own surfaces.

As to whether to meet with just the client's parents or entire family, the therapist must carefully assess the locus of the client's blockage. If it appears that the presence of siblings could help and they would have a limited stake in operating homeostatically, then I encourage the client to include them. However, if their presence would in any way dilute the effect of clients' getting their needs met by the parents, then I discourage siblings' attending. Developing separate relationships with family members is the key to individuation. In most instances, I leave it up to the client to make the final decision, although I will make strong recommendations. These sessions occur in the middle phase of treatment when a highly collaborative relationship between therapist and client has been forged, and by now we are operating as a team. At this point, I trust them as they trust me.

## What Are Some Ways to Engage Reluctant Family Members?

It is important that both client and family members know that the purpose of these sessions is not to blame parents for what is wrong in the client's life. The expectation of being condemned understandably causes people to shy away from participating at first. That makes it essential, in order to enlist others' participation, that clients be capable of approaching family members, communicating that the purpose is not to blame. Until clients can develop that attitude, they are not ready to convene such a session. When they are, family members usually are willing to help.

Men often have a particularly difficult time saying they need family members' participation, because of their socialization against dependency. Thus, getting clients to be vulnerable enough to acknowledge and then to state their need is often another matter. This is the cornerstone of the preparatory work. When they do, they usually can enlist cooperation.

## What Is the Flow of a Typical Session?

To establish the hierarchy, my credibility, and that I will be in charge of the session, I begin both segments. This also allows me the opportunity to join the family and to help these new people begin to get comfortable enough to make good use of such a compressed amount of time. First, I thank all attending for making themselves available to do this work, stating how important doing this is for the client. Sometimes I spend several minutes joining people who seem very tense; sometimes my introduction is only brief. This depends on my assessment of the level of anxiety in the room. I then explain the structure of our time together. In an attempt to generate a shared investment, I state that the time limitation will make it important that each of them take responsibility for getting something for themselves from the experience, that although it is primarily for the benefit of my client, I firmly believe that each of them will get something out if it. I then turn the meeting over to my client, who is primed and ready.

Prepared clients are a major secret to success of these sessions. In preparing, I have suggested that my client consider two primary questions: What do you need to say to your family? What do you need to hear from them? Once that is clarified, I then suggest that they plan only a starting place and let the session flow from there, rather than having a set agenda that could become stultifying. Early on, after the client has made an initial disclosure, I facilitate an opening of the dialogue by inviting family members to respond to what they have heard so far. I further facilitate dialoguing by opening the second segment with asking everyone to share some of the reflections they had overnight. This invites more mutual self-disclosure and helps me to assess the system, looking for homeostatic mechanisms that may have already kicked in to obstruct change or compromise the ongoing progress.

The session then is spent either working up to the major disclosure that clients often feel they must make, or working with the implications of what has already been shared. In the process of doing this, everyone's part in the maintenance of the system's unhealthy balance can be examined, so that the equilibrium can then begin to shift toward a different, presumably more functional, stability.

Usually people spontaneously end their time together considering how they want to relate postsession. If, however, that does not emerge or become apparent by inference, I will invite people to discuss this. At this point in the session, I am attempting to help the family rewrite its rules so that a more appropriate, satisfying way of relating can be fostered.

Even if we have only a few minutes left, I try to end these sessions with an opportunity to process the experience. I invite everyone to respond to open-ended questions such as: What was this experience like for you? or What was the best part of this experience? This allows both for closure and for people to make statements that eliminate any residual doubt that might be lurking about whether this was a good idea. This also helps me gauge the extent to which the family's homeostatic mechanisms might be a factor for my client in follow-up work.

### Are There Some Special Techniques or Skills Required to Do These Sessions?

By the time of the actual session, my clients are primed and ready. My role after establishing my place in the hierarchy by starting each segment is twofold: to facilitate, and to make certain that participants are getting to the crux of the matter for my client.

First and foremost, the therapist must be adept at joining. Important in any therapy, it is critical here so that family members can feel safe enough to do the work clients so desperately need in so short a time. Then, I steer if I see people avoiding salient topics. I gatekeep if I see that someone's needs are going unnoticed. I act as a sounding board if my client seems lost or muddled in the family's typical ways of interacting. And I even confront, if I have to. If needed confrontation could result in my client being emotionally orphaned, I usually do it myself. This protects the client's place in the family, and opens the family long enough for people to take in the very emotionally charged information that the client needs to share.

The issue of how actively to be involved in the session is probably the single most critical clinical decision the therapist must make on a minute-to-minute basis during the actual session. On the whole, if the session is going along as hoped, very little direct intervention is required. However, the therapist must stand ready to intervene and probe or redirect based on the client's previously clarified goals for the experience. Just how active one must be needs to be assessed on a case-by-case, minute-to-minute basis.

Probably the other most challenging skill is knowing when to rheostat up or down the level of intensity and emotionality in the session. For families that tend to intellectualize and keep their emotional distance, part of the therapist's task is to heighten the intensity so that emotions are surfaced and dealt with. On the other hand, with families that deal with emotions effusively and never understand or resolve any issue, it can be important to rheostat down the level of emotionality so that people are able to take an issue or an experience and work it through to completion. Again, the therapist's clinical judgment must be the guide.

## Clinical Example

The following example illustrates the power of direct expression of feelings. Jerry, a 39-year-old man, invited his 43-year-old brother and their parents, both in their 70s, to an extended session. Although I had begun suggesting within the first couple of months of treatment 4 years previously that we would probably need to do such a session, he strongly resisted all of my efforts in this direction.

Because the presenting problem was a marital rupture, the initial work was on resolving that crisis and on healing that marital breach. And still his emotional constriction plagued both him and his wife. So when he returned for individual therapy some time after completing that first course of treatment with his wife, I once again nudged him in the direction of facing his parents. To no avail. Then I invited him to participate in my men's group, which he did with many apparent changes resulting, according to both him and his wife. But still something was missing. Finally, with all other options exhausted, he gave in to my relentless suggestions and invited his parents to a session so that he could finally face his father. Doing this catalyzed a turning point for him. It should be noted that the father hunger that he talks about stems not from an actual absence, but rather from the emotional unavailability of a traditional father.

The following excerpt is the climax of approximately 2½ hours of struggling. First, the son had to be cajoled and helped to say what truly was on his mind. Then it took the father seemingly an eternity to even grasp the meaning of the questions his son was asking. And third, the father needed to be helped to comprehend and proffer the kind of response his son needed from him. This is an actual transcript, but it is cut to spare the reader the tedium of the false starts and drudgery it took to get them to this point.

*Therapist:* (To Jerry) Do you know what I think part of this (referring to his fist which he has clenched during most of the session) has been? I think it's anger.

*Jerry:* Yeah, probably.

*Therapist:* And I think a lot of it's about your Dad, at your Dad.

*Jerry:* Yeah (sighing). I mean, that's what I've been trying to let go of.

*Therapist:* Yeah, but you've not told him directly, "Dad, I've been angry."

*Jerry:* No. I s'pose that's true. I guess that's true. (To his father) I talked a little bit yesterday about the feelings I remember. And I think they're the ones that I hold old anger about, and they're the reason I hold you apart or push you away. And that's . . . it's anger at your not being there.

*Therapist:* Tell him about that.

*Jerry:* You just weren't there. All the important stuff that you had to do, and those people at work were more important than me.

*Therapist:* How did that make you feel?

*Jerry:* All alone! All alone, even with the family around, and in the house, and with stuff to do, all alone, because those people at work were more important than me. And that's where the anger comes from.

*Therapist:* Because it hurts.

*Jerry:* Yeah, it hurts! And right around behind that anger is fear, that just goes along and makes it even worse. It's fear for your reaction if I tell you how I feel.

*Dad:* Well, I feel badly about that.

*Mom:* Say, "I love you, Jerry!"

*Dad:* I do love you, Jerry! You know that!

*Jerry:* (Almost inaudibly) I don't know if I know that.

*Dad:* Huh?

*Jerry:* (Crying softly) I don't know if I know that!

*Dad:* Well, I'll tell you! And I'll show you!

*Therapist:* (To Jerry, attempting to heighten the intensity so that a catharsis could take place) Tell him what your tears are, Jerry.

*Jerry:* That's the first real time I've heard "I will!" instead of saying, "We'll work on it." You said, "I will!" and I believe you.

*Dad:* Yes, I will!

*Jerry:* (Crying harder) But don't let me down. Don't let me down!

*Therapist:* Tell him about it, Jerry

*Jerry:* Just don't, . . . you just can't stop. You know, I've got a process started, and I got this far, and we got this far, and I want you to know that I just can't have you back away. (Sobbing) Don't leave! Don't disappear!

*Dad:* (Coming over and putting his arms around Jerry) You know I won't.

*Jerry:* No, I don't know that you won't! And that's what I need. I don't know that you won't.

*Dad:* Well, I'll show it to you!

*Jerry:* That's what I have to have! I don't know that you won't. We've gone this far, and I've gotta trust that you'll be there. That's what I need. I just need you to be there. The words are fine now. But when we walk out of this room, and when we're at the table or on the phone, I just need you to be there.

*Dad:* It's the follow through that counts.

*Therapist:* 'Cause it's so scary to let yourself count on his being there, and risk disappointment again.

*Jerry:* Yeah, 'cause I'll fold. That's how important it is, Dad.

*Therapist:* That's how important you are, Dad!

*Jerry:* That's how important it is that you're there.

*Dad:* I'll be there!


*Two follow-up notes.* First, the weekend following the extended session, at the parents' anniversary celebration, Jerry and his wife had a huge argument. It seems that his surfacing his anger uncorked hers, and she sped away from the restaurant at which they were celebrating, leaving Jerry to walk the short distance back to the hotel where the family was staying in honor of the occasion.

About a block from the hotel, Jerry's father appeared out of the darkness and asked if there was anything he could do. Jerry reported that his response was, "No, just walk with me." So the two men walked in a companionable silence, now that each of them had a blueprint for how to be different with each other. Each now knows that just being together can be the height of comfort and intimacy if it is not a silence born of fear and ambivalence. Second, about 6 months after the extended session, Jerry's 21-year-old son, with his parents' knowledge and permission, called me to request that I facilitate a session between them, himself, and his younger sister. The issue he wanted to discuss? His anger at his father's not having been emotionally available for him when he was growing up. The father responded in the same way his father had had to, only without the defensiveness. He apologized profusely for his absence and his ignorance of his children's needs, and resolved to be much more available. He gave profusely and willingly to his children in 1 hour what it had taken him 3 hours to wrestle from his father.

That this excerpted interchange occurred in the second half of the second segment underscores the degree of fear that Jerry experienced in honestly approaching his father. Reading the excerpt, the struggle Jerry had in getting his father to hear and to address his needs is apparent. To have expected that he would have been able to even broach the subject on his own, to say nothing of resolve the feelings, would have been expecting too much. Hence, dealing with the subject with the therapist's help was the only real option for him to address this very painful, anxiety-provoking topic.

## Conclusions

### What Are Some Types of Situations Where This Technique May Be Indicated?

The situations where this technique may be therapeutic are as varied as clients' issues. Some examples may illustrate the multiple possibilities. Perhaps the most typical theme that cuts across session after session is the need to reconcile alienated relationships. A frequent use is to ask parents to make amends for childhood abuse.

Another is emotionally finishing a chronically unresolved divorce or death of a family member. Some more specific examples of the varied kinds of applications that I have made of this technique follow. I have facilitated the "coming out" of a gay man in his mid-30s. I have assisted a client's resignation from his job as a parental and spousal child, a role that he took when his parents divorced when he was 11 and his mother became suicidal. I have fostered adolescent children's learning the truth of their parents' divorce, so that they are no longer gripped by unknowable and unspeakable secrets. I have insisted that longtime divorced couples achieve the emotional divorce that can end their ongoing conflict. I have helped a sibship of three adult children confront their parents with their recently recovered memories that they had been physically and sexually abused by their father. I have encouraged a family of eight to prepare for the imminent death from leukemia of the youngest child. I have assisted a business partnership that had previously also been an extramarital affair to dissolve when the romance ended. The actual uses of this type of session are limited only by the creativity of the therapist.

I have not found socioeconomic factors or levels of intelligence or achievement to be key issues in deciding for whom this technique is appropriate. What is far more salient is people's willingness to be involved and to help. It should be noted that parents who agree to attend have a singular advantage. They get to do now what their children would have wanted them to do before, thereby getting the chance to make up for lost time and missed opportunity.

## Are There Any Contraindications for Family Members' Participation?

The difficulty for the therapist is that in advance of the session she has only the clients' eyes through which to see the other family members and assess people's strength. And yet that consideration is essential. For it will profit the client nothing if relatives either in the session or only hearing about it have the perception that the session is being held in callous disregard for anyone else's needs. This could understandably trigger a massive negative feedback loop alienating the client and the family even more.

The issue of family members' strength has two facets: (a) ego strength and (b) physical stamina. Each will be discussed below.

Ego strength is perhaps the most difficult to assess without meeting family members. It can be gauged by considering such issues as: the extent to which they have social supports to help them with their own anxiety before and after the session; how involved in or reclusive from life have they been, as a way to infer how much strength they could be expected to have from life experiences; evidence through vignettes shared of family members' experiences both inside and outside the family that would demonstrate a certain amount of flexibility and resilience. These sorts of indicators lead me to identify families that are good candidates for this intervention. It should be noted that I have found ego strength to be a far more significant variable than socioeconomic status, education, or intellectual level.

Physical stamina is at once easier and harder to assess without seeing the people involved. The therapist's task is to discern if there is any substance to health concerns, or whether people are being their own homeostats, particularly if they resist involvement for reasons of physical health. This is particularly germane in families where there was an unspoken rule that to speak certain concerns is to make someone sick. In those instances, after a careful assessment is made, the sessions can become even more important as a way to disabuse people of that notion. All the same, people with recent hospitalizations or life-threatening illnesses in the acute phase could likely be sufficiently stressed by the session to compromise their health. For usually, at least initially, these sessions are as stressful for family members as they are for clients. All of this needs to be carefully assessed.

Jerry's family again provides an example. For years, every time I suggested that his best route to helping himself was probably dealing directly with his parents, he discarded the suggestion, mumbling something about it being irrelevant, protesting that he should be able to work this out for himself. As all other options were exhausted and he still remained emotionally unavailable to his wife, who was getting angrier and angrier, he finally began to seriously consider the wisdom of my suggestion. In the meantime, his father, in his late 70s, had a stroke. So I began to have grave doubts about the father's stamina and began to relent on my suggestion. Was it already too late? Had my client missed his chance? As I had no right to violate the father's privilege of confidentiality by contacting his physician, instead I chose to request a consultation with my client and his brother, who also would attend the session, as a way to help me make my determination. In that consultation, I explored with the brothers their concerns for the father's health. At that time, it became clear that the stroke had impaired the father's physical movement but not his speech or his thought processes. Although he was certainly weakened, he was functioning optimally for a stroke victim. I then asked the brother his view on his father's ability to tolerate any additional stress such a session might place on him in his condition. His response was immediate. He had no doubt that the father could tolerate the additional exertion. Thus, I decided it was both reasonably safe and very possible to proceed with the session as hoped.

If it emerges in the session that any family member or subsystem could be at psychological risk afterward due to the session, I spend some time before the end identifying family therapy resources in their hometown, using my professional association directories as a guide. I also help them identify distress signals that could indicate that therapy back home might be helpful. This both provides a comfort level for family members and helps alleviate undue responsibility or caretaking for them on the part of client. I myself generally do not follow up with family members, for that would seem to defeat the purpose of attempting to have short, intense contact that clearly highlights heretofore latent issues. Nevertheless, in two instances, after approximately 1 year, I did begin therapy with extended family members in two different families.

## A Final Word

Family of origin extended sessions offer a unique, reparative experience for both our clients and their family members who participate. They offer an opportunity to remake seminal moments that have shaped clients' lives and families' interactions for decades. The possibilities are limited only by people's courage and therapists' creativity. As daunting as these sessions are for therapist and participants alike, they can be a significant source of healing with the potential to positively shape the course of family life for generations.

# References

Ackerman, N. (1958). *The psychodynamics of family life: Diagnosis and treatment of family relationships.* New York: Basic Books.

Bowen, M. (1978). *Family therapy in clinical practice.* New York: Jason Aronson.

Nichols, M. (1987, March-April). The individual in the system. *Family Therapy Networker, 11*(2), 32-38; 85.

Palazzoli, M., Checchin, G., Prata, G., & Boscolo, L. (1978). *Paradox and counterparadox.* New York: Jason Aronson.

Paul, N., & Paul, B. (1986). *The marital puzzle: Transgenerational analysis in marriage counseling.* New York: Gardner.

Schwartz, R. (1987, March-April). Our multiple selves. *Family Therapy Networker, 11*(2), 24-31; 80-83.

Schwartz, R. (1988, November-December). Know thy selves. *Family Therapy Networker, 12*(6), 20-29.

Watanabe-Hammond, S. (1987, March-April) The many faces of Paul and Dora. *Family Therapy Networker, 4*(2), 54-55; 87-89.

Yalom, I. (1985). *The theory and practice of group psychotherapy.* New York: Basic Books.

# Part V

# EPILOGUE

# Some Treatment Disappointments

It is human nature to abhor the feeling that one has failed. This experience is probably especially difficult for us as therapists. And that is not merely owing to grandiosity or perfectionism. When we miss the mark, we leave families with the pain they brought to us in the first place, sometimes even intensified by our shared sense of not being able to do what was needed. The days I drive home from the office feeling as if I have bungled a case or have been blocked from doing in one instance what I have been able to do in countless others are hard. When I cannot do the job for which I was hired, it is more than being unable to accomplish a given task or sell a product. I have been unable to help relieve human suffering—a privilege and a responsibility I take very seriously.

But even if I have not blundered, I still sometimes experience disappointment. The character portrayed by Kevin Costner in the movie about fathers and sons, *Field of Dreams*, speaks to this dilemma. Despite others' disbelief and even ridicule, he felt he simply had to "go the distance" in fulfilling his dream of finding his father. I am afflicted by a similar wish to go the therapeutic distance, in the hope that clients can deeply and significantly alter

their lives in the process of therapy. When for one reason or
another, I am unable to inspire clients to go the distance in this
quest, rather than settling for mere abatement of symptoms, I am
always disappointed. I believe—and my experience bears it out—
that in most cases a qualitatively different life is possible for people
who have the requisite help and motivation to strive for it.

Perhaps my greatest struggle is in separating what part of the
unsatisfactory outcome of a case is mine, and what part belongs to
the client. I also sometimes have a different view of what constitutes
a satisfactory outcome than clients do, and this discrepancy can
result in disappointment for me even if clients report satisfaction.

## Chapter Overview

This chapter will provide a framework for sorting out what can
account for those therapies that stop short of the mark, as well as
identifying some factors that might explain these unsatisfying
outcomes. Two central questions will be addressed: How does the
therapist cope when she feels as though she has failed to do the
job for which she was hired? What are some factors that account
for treatment disappointments?

When I try to understand this complex issue, I come up with
four major categories of disappointing outcomes. One set of factors
is attributable to the lack of chemistry between therapist and clients.
Another set clusters around incompatibility between therapists' and
clients' goals for therapy; that is, either clients unilaterally decide to
terminate therapy, or the therapist, based on her clinical judgment,
recommends it. Both such instances will be discussed. Still another
set of factors relates to clients' undermining the integrity of the
therapy, whether consciously or not. And the final category relates
to the therapist's clinical misjudgments.

## Four Types of Treatment Disappointments

Each of the main types of treatment flops I have experienced,
whether foisted on me by clients or catalyzed by my own clinical
errors, will be discussed in the sections below.

## Lack of Chemistry

When I was in my postdoctoral training learning family therapy, one of my favorite teachers, Dr. Chuck Kramer (1979) of The Family Institute of Chicago, had a deceptively simple phrase to describe what goes on between two partners that is a significant factor in their bonding and gets couples through when all else fails. He calls it a spark and says that couples who have it can weather even the roughest storms in their relationships. I see the relationship between therapist and client as needing some of that same ingredient. There must be a kind of spark between us and our clients, too.

It is very difficult, if not impossible, for me to work honestly with and invest in the healing of people with whom I do not feel a spark and whom I sincerely do not like. In my youth and folly, I had the grandiose notion that I could and probably should like everyone who came into my office. And as if this weren't enough, I will confess believing that all clients should like me as well. After all, I saw myself as both competent and nice, so surely I could charm or cajole or bamboozle people into changing. Now, in my age and wisdom, I recognize that clients have to want to change, and they have to buy my approach to helping them. I cannot make them either like me or want to metamorphose. That is up to them. I can be a very significant change agent. I can help them find hope, if they will search for it. I can offer them the benefit of my training and many years of clinical experience. I can share with them some of my own personal struggles, which I do freely where appropriate. But the rest is up to them. Now I can honestly say that if the spark is not there, it simply is not there. In those instances, I cheerfully refer them on to someone who might be more compatible with their needs. In both the short and the long run, this saves both me and my clients much frustration and disappointment.

And I am getting better and better at sensing by the end of the first session who will be back and who will not. I am especially attuned to clients who are only shopping and probably are not ready to engage with me—or with anyone—in the hard work of change. In fact, my final question in the intake interview is: "Do you have a sense about whether or not you can do the work you need to do here, with me?" This allows both of us to explicitly address the questions of personal chemistry and compatibility.

But I still confess a smidgen of disappointment when they don't return, for I have been able to help in many instances where other therapists have been stonewalled by clients who languished in misery for years. How do I as the therapist and the person deal with that? I remind myself that there are many other people I do connect with and help; that it's impossible for me to help everybody; that I only have so many hours in a day, and if I keep plugging at trying to help those where the spark does not exist, I am shortchanging them, myself, and the prospective clients with whom I could connect. To be unable to put this situation in this perspective is to risk doing clients harm and burning myself out. Both they and I are better off that they not see me. And then I move on to the next clinical challenge, for surely there will be many more to come.

### Incompatibility of Treatment Goals

Sometimes therapists and clients have irreconcilable differences and want different processes and outcomes of therapy. As I repeatedly have stated, my personal bias is that rather than opt for simple problem solution, I prefer to take a crack at resolving the underlying issues that fuel the symptoms. In most cases, I am able to work that way with clients, either because my reputation has preceded me and people know this is how I work, or because I am able to show them the multiple advantages of this more thorough approach. However, this is not always the case.

In some cases, I am unable to demonstrate the benefits of my approach clearly enough or convincingly enough to generate the requisite commitment on clients' part to look beyond simple and immediate pain relief. In those instances, clients usually decide to terminate treatment. In other cases, where I believe that due to numerous idiosyncratic considerations such as motivation, money, or time available they cannot undergo long-term treatment, I get them to a reasonable stopping place and then recommend that they terminate treatment.

*Clients Unilaterally Deciding to Terminate Treatment.* Clients' unilateral decision to terminate treatment usually constitutes a significant treatment disappointment for me, especially if I have invested in and with them. I am concerned that this choice means that they will recycle their issues. Perhaps they will manifest in a different guise, but there will be other symptoms nonetheless. Because of never cleaning out the emotional infection and straightening out the transgenerational patterns that are causing their pain, those clients likely will enter a revolving door of mental health treatment, generating emotional wreckage for themselves and for those who try to love them.

*Clinical Example.* A few years ago, I received a frantic call for help from a woman whose fiancé had called off their wedding 2 weeks before the event. Clearly, both felt wounded and needed help. In our first session, they both expressed goals related to symptom relief: resolution of their considerable anxiety and pain over whether to marry or not to marry—in a few weeks or ever. But particularly in light of each one's first marriage ending in divorce, I had an additional agenda. I hoped to help them explore the underpinnings of the whole issue of marital choice, as a way to help them inoculate themselves and others with whom they might become involved against yet another painful, poor choice.

Because of their crisis, I worked them into my schedule for an appointment as soon as I could, and we began the excruciating exploration of what had caused his bolt virtually from the altar. Early in the therapy, it became clear to all three of us that this couple had coupled for precarious reasons, and that this left them on very shaky ground for committing to marriage. Major reasons were that each had very naive concepts of what commitment and family mean, and each had virtually no ability for self-reflection and introspection. I bit my tongue and kept asking questions until they both saw that to marry would be to invite divorce. They then attempted to part as friends, a goal that both realized soon enough was a lofty ideal of which neither was capable. At that juncture, I was at least able to influence them enough that they did not cut each other to ribbons as they left.

Then I hoped that what I saw as the real stuff of therapy could begin, the work that would help them both in the long run. In individual sessions, I attempted to help each of them see that there were reasons in each of their psychic economies that they found each other. I predicted that they were likely to repeat those in their next relationships if they did not understand the dynamics. I wondered aloud about the function and the meaning of the fact that both had chosen to marry someone starkly different from themselves in every way. In fact, the only real commonalities that I could see were that each wanted to be married, and they both liked sex and money. I attempted to illustrate my concerns by family of origin exploration and by teaching skills for personal reflection and uncovering and sharing feelings in the few individual sessions I had with each.

They would have none of it. They both remained steadfast in the belief that were it not for the other's sickness, they and the relationship would have been just fine. Finally, after a total of eight sessions, both stated that now that their decision had been made not to marry, they saw no need to continue with any treatment. They wanted to "get on with their lives."

My primary goals at the end of treatment are always twofold regardless of the reasons for or the initiator of the decision to terminate. My first aim is based on the belief that people do not know what they have learned until they can articulate it. To be unable to do that means it will float around on the fringes of their awareness and use of the new information will happen on a hit-or-miss basis. So I try to help clients consolidate and articulate their gains and claim ownership both of their new tools and of the credit for what they have done. Second, I try to have them leave with a good enough taste in their mouths about therapy that they will ask for help again should they need to, from me or from another therapist.

At this point with the couple mentioned above, I was relegated to doing a termination session with each of them and turning them loose. In those sessions, I attempted to help them clarify for themselves what they had accomplished in the therapy. I also helped them articulate what I call "early warning signs" that they might be beginning to repeat the mistakes they made with this relationship. I predicted aloud the high probability of replicating those mistakes in their next relationships, and we said an awkward good-bye.

Sometimes I wish, as in this instance, that I could affix a warning label much like those on the sides of cigarette packages to the foreheads of clients who leave treatment refusing to understand what motivates them. It would say, "Warning: This Individual May Be Hazardous to Your Health." It is especially disappointing and worrisome for me when men precipitously leave treatment. It is these people who stigmatize well-meaning women and men. I believe people virtually inevitably will repeat their patterns, thereby hurting themselves again as well as damaging others who would try to love them. But alas, I was left only with the hope that they would not do too much damage.

Sometimes this sort of termination can turn out well in the end, if I am willing to be patient and supportive of people's need to try it on their own. In recent months, I received three calls from former clients, each of whom had made a unilateral decision to terminate treatment against my recommendations. In each case, in the final session I had done what I described above. When they called seeking to come back into treatment with me, each acknowledged that I had been accurate in my assessment that he or she would repeat the same mistakes. In fact, each had. In the first instance, the man reported that after he and his wife left treatment, they decided to get pregnant, believing that a child in their lives would cure the toxic feelings between them. Of course, it had not; it only intensified the dysfunction and conflict. In the second instance, the woman who called to reinitiate treatment had left after she and her husband had finally decided to divorce, stating that she now could see that it was time to explore the extremely painful family of origin issues that rendered her crippled about intimacy. In the 2 years since she left therapy and her marriage, she had been in and already ruined what she called "the relationship of her life." She finally was ready to get to the bottom of her need to perpetuate her own pain. In the third instance, the man who called to reinstate treatment had bolted 1 year before, immediately after a session in which he began to have feelings for the first time since they had become frozen when he was a toddler. In each instance, I stifled my urge to remind them that I had told them this would happen, and we carved out a new, more thorough working contract that none of the three of them resisted again.

In each of these instances, I had been disappointed and frankly worried when the client left treatment. Particularly in the first instance, I worried, and sought a case consultation about my part in the couple's leaving treatment before they had gone the distance. But I also know that it does no good for the therapist to want more for clients than they want for themselves. I had to turn them loose.

After I had parceled out responsibility, I was able to let the people go in my own mind. I helped myself do this by taking a long-range perspective that I base on two premises. First, I have a solid belief that people are doing what they feel they need to do at the time to survive, even if the wisdom of their choices escapes me—and sometimes even themselves. I remind myself that people have their own very reasonable, if illogical, reasons for doing what they do. It is just that on neither side is that truly discernible at this time. The second thought that comforts me is looking at treatment as a process that does not end when formal sessions end. When I take this perspective, I am able to put clients' needs and choices in a perspective that is helpful both to them and to me. In the final analysis, they are in charge of the decision to terminate treatment. Even if I disagree, I no longer fight them about it, and they are able then to launch themselves from the therapist in an adult fashion. This in itself can be an emotionally corrective experience (Yalom, 1985) for those whose launching from their family of origin was compromised for one reason or another. It may not be an ideal launching or provide a fully corrective experience that clients then can use as a springboard to grow themselves up, but it is preferable to sudden, unresolved, unilateral flights into health, ambiguous drifting away, or the fights with clients that risk shaming or infantilizing them that clients sometimes orchestrate and therapists often permit. Kramer (1980) offers a way to think about termination that can be particularly helpful in cases where we are disappointed: "Treatment literally is never terminated; . . . it goes on as a self-perpetuating process within the family after formal sessions have been discontinued; and . . . therapeutic progress, if it is to be successful in its deepest sense, must truly be interminable" (p. 211).

Although I feel disappointment over clients' unwillingness to go the distance, the predominant feeling I have for myself is relief. I am comforted in the knowledge that I have done what they will allow. To push for any more would be to set up a power struggle with clients that would net nothing for any of us. I simply need to turn them loose to go live and see if life induces them to learn the lessons that I was unable to inspire them to master.

*Therapist's Recommendation to Terminate Treatment.* Occasionally, I myself recommend termination of treatment before the client has been able to do the depth work that I have seen enables people to overhaul their life. In those instances, I do so because of contingencies that would impinge on the successful completion of their process if I were to push for or even to allow them to continue.

*Clinical Example.* For example, I saw 53-year-old Jared in therapy for about 5 months when I began to wonder whether he might be someone whom I should not nudge to go the distance. He had been making suicide attempts periodically since age 17. Many of them, like his first, went undetected. Although he had not been actively suicidal for approximately 1½ years, he requested treatment from me because he could see his old, familiar downward spiral beginning again, despite his years in therapy. Each of the two most recent times this had happened, he had been psychiatrically hospitalized for relatively long periods, followed by extensive outpatient psychotherapy with his two admitting psychiatrists.

I conceptualized the roots of Jared's suicidal ideation as reaching back into his childhood. He was the youngest of three children of a teenaged mother and an abusive, alcoholic father who abandoned the family when Jared was born. Already living in poverty, isolated from family, and with few marketable skills, the mother found that the birth of her third child left her unable to care for them and for herself. So periodically, she would put her children in an informally arranged foster home until once again she had collected the funds to support them and herself. This began when Jared was 5 years old and continued until early adolescence. Although these separations may have offered a feasible resolution to the mother's terrible dilemma, for the children, they were a disaster. The woman in whose home Jared lived was cruel and abusive to all of the "foster" children who lived with her. Despite these many strikes against him, Jared was able to educate himself through two master's degrees.

And then the lights went out. About 10 years before this therapy began, Jared developed a life-style-impairing case of multiple sclerosis. This severely limited his mobility, forced this previously counterdependent male to be totally dependent on everyone around him, virtually destroyed his work identity and performance, and understandably triggered periods of deep depression and suicidality. It also restimulated all of his old issues that had never been resolved. By the time he came to see me, he had been through two marriages and again was seriously questioning whether life was worth living.

In the initial phase of therapy, the goal obviously was to treat his suicidality and the depression that fueled it. Then, when it seemed safe to do so, we moved on to the underpinnings of this very precarious way of coping. It was that line of inquiry that led us to his relationship with his mother and how profoundly rejected and worthless he had always felt because of what he experienced as regularly being given away as a child. For as most children do, he had always blamed himself as being unworthy of being loved.

Perhaps the most startling revelation for Jared occurred in the session in which he allowed me to reframe his mother's actions as desperate acts to ensure everyone's survival, rather than loathing and rejection of him or of his siblings. Those realizations generated a crisis for him, only this time, it became the turning point. Later that day, he called me to describe the profoundly jolting experience seeing this had been for him. Even though this new perspective was overwhelmingly positive, it was shattering in that it required that he dismantle his former belief system. In the phone call, he described that session as the one in which he "found his heart."

The timing of that dramatic revelation could not have been more propitious. He was to travel to another state to see his mother within the week. During this visit, he initiated conversations with her the likes of which he had never had. And, for the first time since he could remember, they told each other of their mutual love. He came back from that visit vowing to "go home." With a job he hated, a second marriage that had just ended, and his only family and connections three states away, I saw no reason for him to stay. I saw every reason for him to want to live a life of connectedness with family, rather than the barren existence he was currently living. This was particularly significant in light of his disability, his increasing need for care, the limitations that his disability imposed, and his mother's unsolicited offer to help care for him if he were to move home. In that I could see no reason for him not to move, the goal then became to help him prepare to do that in 6 months.

I believe very strongly that assessment is an ongoing process, not one that happens in the first session with the therapist settling on a diagnostic category from the DSM-III-R and then forgetting it. The therapist needs constantly to refine her goals, objectives, and treatment interventions in light of her diagnosis of ongoing needs. Jared's rapprochement with his mother demanded a new assessment of his situation and introduced the question about what to do with therapy. I am firmly convinced that although therapy is a powerful tool for changing lives, it is not life. Therefore, therapy must enhance, not impinge on, life. This raised a poignant therapeutic dilemma for me, made even more critical in light of Jared's preexisting emotional fragility. As I have repeatedly stated, my bias is that depth psychotherapy is the surest way for clients to learn how not to recycle their issues again and again. Yet in this instance, his doing depth work had the potential to create the opposite outcome from the one desired. It could interfere with his being able to move on with his life, compromising his ability to functionally lead a handicapped person's life, distract from his need to attend to the myriad details involved in making the multiple life changes he was contemplating, and jeopardize his clarity and directionality.

After much personal pondering and openly discussing the options with Jared, I recommended that we tie together the pieces we had done, rather than start into further depth work. Therapy could hold him up from getting on with his life for many more months, if not years, and this would be the opposite outcome from the desired one. Sometimes, people initiate a change in location to take the "geographical cure" for their problems. But my assessment of Jared's situation was that in this instance, this was not the case. Adequately accomplishing major life changes takes an emotional toll. Thus, my therapeutic responsibility, as I conceptualized it, was to titrate the amount of emotional work Jared would have to do without his becoming distracted or overloaded. This would enable me to maintain a supportive role with him during this time of multiple transitions without unwrapping him and leaving him in the middle of his process, thereby rendering him extremely disadvantaged if not nonfunctional. This approach also helped to ensure that his nascent developmental growth would not be compromised or arrested again, which was the risk if he temporized and did not move.

However, when I raised the question of slowing the pace of therapy and preparing him to move, Jared had a reaction for which I was not prepared but perhaps should have been. Experiencing a strong transference reaction to me from his mother, Jared felt profoundly rejected by my suggestion. The day after we discussed doing no more depth work for the first time, he called to tell me of his feelings and was extremely relieved when I reassured him that I was in no way trying to get rid of him or send him somewhere else. Because he was able to identify what he felt and take responsibility for it by sharing it with me, even his painful reaction to my suggestion was therapeutic, because it gave him the opportunity to share his feelings, check his perception with me, and ask for what he needed. So even my oversight was therapeutic. It also gave us an opportunity to see that he had indeed reworked a major piece that had been a significant contributor to his long-standing depression, even though he had opted not to go the distance in therapy.

Although I must confess some dissatisfaction in instances such as these, it is easier for me to deal with these types of disappointments than with others. I believe that sometimes it is irresponsible and even unethical for therapists to open clients up when we cannot be available to help them work through what they uncover. This is particularly significant for therapists and counselors whose work contexts preclude their being able to work with clients for as long as it takes.

To summarize, the role of the therapist in this instance is to tie together the pieces that have been done in such a way that the client is able to take them with him or her, as well as to lay tracks for the client to seek treatment later from another therapist if there continues to be a felt need.

## When Clients Undermine the Integrity of Therapy

A third category of disappointments usually happens more suddenly than the two discussed above. These are the terminations that are both frustrating and shocking to me as the therapist. Although most therapists do not talk about it, it happens even to the best of us from time to time. Just when we think we are making headway with clients, they begin to balk. Perhaps appointments are canceled or are not rescheduled because of conflicts that clients insist are unavoidable. Or if people do come in as scheduled, they are evasive and distant. When we try to address what is happening in these instances, people refuse to discuss their feelings and reactions openly. But we can feel their sabotaging both themselves and us. Finally, we are notified of a sudden decision to leave treatment. Often a crisis between therapist and clients is created to justify their flight into health or away from treatment. These are

painful endings, because now we are being blamed for their flee-
ing. And perhaps, we blame ourselves.

Exactly what happened? Why does this happen? And how do
we deal with our own feelings of being hoodwinked in the process? What are we to do now with the personal investment we had
made in these clients?

Over the years, I have come to understand that this situation
usually happens when clients feel too threatened about the changes
they can envision they would need to make, should they continue
treatment. I have come to conclude that this is particularly a risk
in couples therapy, when one member of a couple recognizes that
the basic changes being made by his or her partner will also
require changes for the other. Perhaps it means bringing out into
the open and dealing honestly with long-repressed material. Perhaps it means a potential loss of power or leverage for the partner
who experiences the other's growth.

Whatever the reason, try as I might in these instances, I am able
to do nothing to stem the rising tide of sabotage of the therapy.
Therapy and I are about to be ambushed.

*Clinical Example.* For a year, I had worked intensely and apparently
successfully with Marlene and Bud. It was a second marriage with
children for both. They had had a stormy 8-year marriage marked
by constant, angry conflict that they managed to stop just short of
physical violence. Both had been abused in childhood by alcoholic
fathers while a fearful, ineffectual mother watched.

The initial phase of the treatment focused on stopping the constant, repetitive cycles of nonproductive conflict that always ended
in threats of divorce. These shouting matches so panicked Bud that
he would crawl back to Marlene begging to be forgiven (as if the
fights were all his fault), even if the apology were not really his to
make. In fact, Marlene was proud of the fact that she never apologized. The fights typically started over what a bad kid Bud's
younger son was in Marlene's eyes. The next task was to extricate
the 6-year-old boy from the middle of their marital conflict. Once
done, the way was cleared for family of origin exploration. Understanding the precedents for their painful style of seeking intimacy
would allow us to gain access to the roots of their conflict.

Initially, Marlene did a very powerful piece of work on her father's
death. As he had been an abusive drunk who eventually died on skid

row, it was very difficult to induce her to examine the impact of his life, death, and absence on her and on her marriage. She staunchly maintained in the beginning that she had always been better off without him. And with much effort and with her characteristic loquaciousness, she managed to continue to convince herself that she was fine.

Then it was Bud's turn, and this is where the problems began. As he began to examine the father he knew before the abuse and the alcoholism raged, he began to find ready access to his multiple and profound losses. Working extremely hard to do this, he was highly motivated to feel better and to change his life—and his commitment to working hard and to feeling better began to threaten Marlene. Because she was highly competitive, his progress was beginning to outshine hers. Also, she could feel changes were taking place that would necessitate commensurate changes from her. All of this took them into uncharted territory in the marriage and in themselves. It also meant that Marlene was losing control of Bud and of the marriage. Although I had inklings that she was feeling threatened, each time I asked her about it, she smiled and denied any discomfort. I offered to slow down the therapy, but Bud, eager to experience more of the peace and freedom he was coming to know, would have nothing of it.

At first when Bud started canceling appointments saying Marlene was suddenly called out of town on business, I thought nothing of it. She recently had secured a plum of a job and was low person on the totem pole, so it made sense to me that her work would draw her away. But when it happened for the 3rd week in a row, I became suspicious and irritated. When they finally did come in for an appointment, it was to announce, in true dysfunctional united front fashion, that her schedule simply would not permit her making herself available for any more sessions. Judging by the agony created for Bud by this pronouncement, I read it as a way to sabotage the changes that were beginning to take place within themselves and between them. It was a truly agonizing last session, at least for Bud and me, seeing them leave so precipitously. Try as I might, I was unable to help them get closure on the multiple issues we had opened, especially for Bud. Marlene simply had made up her mind, and I was impotent to inspire them to proceed further into the therapy. There was no stopping them or even slowing them down; their exit had already been orchestrated. And the "fault" for the ending of therapy clearly was to be mine.

How did I deal with my disappointment? This type of unfortunate situation usually takes some time to heal. As much as it is no
doubt difficult and painful for the client who leaves the therapy
reluctantly, as did Bud, it is also wounding for the therapist. I truly
believe that we were doing good work until Marlene's retreat. As
I was allowed to do nothing to wrap anything up for or with them,
I simply had to get closure myself. I did that by getting a case
consultation with a trusted colleague, by allowing myself to feel
my feelings of being bruised, let down, and frustrated, and by
experiencing my sadness and concern for them because of the way
they chose to deal with their pain and fear.

But the hurt and regret took a while to dissipate. And that is to
be expected, when one invests.

## The Therapist's Clinical Misjudgment

In each of the previous instances, I sincerely believe the clients
left treatment for reasons of their own, good or bad. And in all
instances except with Jared, they left therapy against my recommendation. In these cases, I believe that it would not have mat-
tered what I did or did not do. They had made up their minds.

I hasten to point out that not every time a therapist blunders is
the mistake terminal to the treatment. In fact, some of my most
productive sessions happen in processing my mistakes or what
clients perceive as my mistakes. In doing this, I provide a powerful
model for humility and for owning one's own behavior and errors.
And being able to work the problem out tends to forge an even
more solid working alliance between therapist and client as two
human beings doing the best they can in aiming toward a common, higher purpose.

However, occasionally I do not experience either of these re-
trievals of a clinical misjudgment. The times I have made a clinical
blunder I cannot recover from and that sidetrack the whole of therapy, I have a particularly sad struggle. Although I may know intellectually that none of us is perfect and that clients and I usually truly
have learned a great deal from my mistakes, it can take some time to
come to terms emotionally with what I know full well intellectually. Those are the times that careful but loving scrutiny of our
clinical decision points is essential. For then, as Beavers (1985)

reflects, "It seems to me that success and failure intertwine; they are not opposites but close kin" (p. 201). The task of all of us in these unfortunate instances is to use them as a springboard for our own growth. Again quoting Beavers (1985) as he discusses his own failed cases, "I will try (as all conscientious therapists do) to play my therapeutic cards the best I know how, and to learn from my failures" (p. 206).

What makes for these situations? Sometimes I blunder when I think people are ready to move to another, perhaps more difficult issue, and I attempt to lead them there before they are ready. Sometimes I time a particular intervention incorrectly, for example prematurely offering a negative reframe to a client who is denying a problem. Sometimes I read the natural ambivalence that comes in the late stage of long-term therapy (Pierce, 1990) as lack of interest or resistance, and I confront clients too strongly about it. Sometimes due to forces at work in my own personal life with which I am struggling, I appear to be uninterested, or critical, or somehow self-absorbed. There can be any number of reasons that therapists make clinical missteps, all of them unfortunate. And those of us who are honest know that it happens to the best of us from time to time, no matter how vigilant we are in trying to prevent this.

*Clinical Example.* Darcy and Dwight, in their late 30s, originally sought treatment when their 16-year-old daughter had become so unmanageable that the mother was insisting the daughter go into foster care. The initial phase of therapy was with the whole family. I focused on teaching the parents more effective behavior control methods and on helping them become a more functional united front in dealing with their daughter's verbal and sometimes physical assaults on them and on her three sisters. After a very tumultuous start with the identified patient acting like a thug both in and out of therapy, therapy progressed nicely, and the parents began to venture statements about their perennially unresolved arguments about differences in their family of origin. Hearing these latent conflicts that were embedded in the family's dynamics, I offered couples sessions to examine these struggles more closely. They happily accepted my offer, even though they already had tried marital therapy for over 2 years with another family therapist.

At first, to make sure that the parents' floundering toward more intimacy did not stress the family system too much, I suggested that we alternate couples sessions with family sessions. They accepted this suggestion, too, despite the identified patient daughter's grumblings now about being excluded, after she had protested strenuously about being included initially.

Work progressed nicely on family of origin issues. We dealt with finding the appropriate place for both mothers-in-law in the family. We resolved the death of Dwight's father, which Dwight had been openly forbidden to discuss with family members. We helped both parties understand why they had felt so abandoned and alone as children, even though their parents had been alive and well their entire childhood. And then it came time to examine directly their marital dynamics. When that led us to some potentially very frightening topics, such as the disparity of power and responsibility in the marriage, this was too much for them to bear. Although both said they wanted to feel and operate better, both strenuously resisted redefining the marital balance of power. It seemed apparent to me that the results of this could lead them to dare to wonder aloud what I believed each of them privately considered: whether divorce was possibly a healthy option both for them and for their children.

When one of them finally merely mentioned the word *divorce*, they both immediately became resistant to continuing treatment. Both stated flatly that they simply would not consider divorce as any kind of option. That was when I began making my mistakes. I tried to encourage them to face this question so that if they were to stay together, it would be for reasons of confidence rather than fear. I do agree with Ahrons and Rodgers's (1987) contention that divorce can be a healthy experience that can be better for all involved than languishing in a stagnant or highly conflictual relationship. I then confronted them for their retreat, rather than allowing and even paradoxically encouraging it. In short, I did not take my own advice and help them wrap up the piece they had done and send them on their way. Had I done this, they might have been able to recognize the benefit of proceeding further at some later date. Instead, I wanted more for them than they wanted for themselves. By now it was apparent to me that their marriage persisted more out of habit than out of genuine intimacy or even affection. And I saw each of them as potentially very capable of

finding more satisfaction in life if they had enough faith in themselves to try for it—either together or separately. But they still
would have none of it. By that time, I had already made my fatal
mistake. I had pushed people who on some level knew that to go
further probably would mean divorce and they were unwilling to
risk that possibility and believed that their life was good enough.
Clearly, they believed that my vision of what is possible in life and
in relationships was aiming too high for them. And to make
matters worse, they refused to come for even one more session so
that we could talk about either their decision or my mistake,
thereby getting some closure.

In those instances where there is nothing salvageable from our
mistakes because clients have become too fearful or have made up
their mind, how does the therapist deal with her disappointment?
Clearly, these sorts of situations make for the most pain.

The first action I take is to try to put this outcome in perspective.
If I am unable adequately to do this for myself, I seek the wise
counsel of a trusted colleague who can help me take an honest look
at where I made my mistakes so that I may learn from them. One
of the most helpful perspectives in looking at this troublesome
experience is offered by Kramer (1980):

> Both [therapist and clients] have to face up to the realization that the
> universal infantile wish for complete gratification can never be
> fulfilled. Just as the therapist is asking, "Did I help my patients
> enough?" . . . On the other side of the equation the family is asking,
> "Have we been helped enough to go on our own?" (p. 209)

In other words, there really is never enough, and there cannot be.
Both therapist and clients have to reckon with that and find some
closure all the same.

Just as putting our thoughts into proper perspective can be
helpful in getting us unhooked from our sense of failure, it is
important to attend to feelings as well. If we are to expect this of
clients, it is important that we do so as well. Otherwise, we risk
this single disappointment becoming contagious. Who of us has
not had the emotional reaction to a clinical misstep be the belief
that we really do not know what we are doing anyway? Our task
is to keep this momentary self-doubt from generalizing and becoming an assault on our self-esteem as clinicians or as people. I

try to turn the disappointment loose, rather than turning it in on myself. There is no doubt that these are the endings that hurt both therapist and clients the most, but when all is said and done, we must learn to learn from our mistakes and to forgive ourselves for making them. Only then can we be truly human so that we can model doing the same for our clients. The humiliation of mistakes and understanding them both makes us humble and allows us to go to the next challenge better prepared.

## A Final Word

Whatever the reason for the treatment disappointments we all have, each one is characterized by regrets over missed opportunities by both therapist and clients. Terminations that are mutually planned and mark the completion of a process have the best prognosis for clients and are the most rewarding for therapists. However, we are not always fortunate enough to be given the chance to experience this, sometimes due to our own gaffes, sometimes due to factors beyond our control. Whatever the cause, it is important that we find ways to help ourselves with the feelings that these endings generate for our clients as well as for ourselves. Not to do so leaves us at risk of canceling out all the good that had come of the experience. And it leaves us as therapists at risk of burnout, with an unwillingness to be touched by clients' struggles or to examine our own role in the therapy system.

Coleman has edited a courageous and touching book in which a host of family therapy luminaries addresses the concept of failures in family therapy. Liddle (1985) says, "Our traditional American response to failures is to reject them, to consign them, metaphorically or actually, to the refuse heap" (p. 152). He then goes on to call for the careful examination of them, just as L'Abate and Baggett (1985, p. 223) do when they assert, "Our therapeutic defeats keep us humble." In another article in that volume, Keith and Whitaker (1985) suggest that "grandiosity is a hidden danger" and "there is relief in the collapse of a delusion" (p. 22). Elsewhere in the book, Tomm (1985) confesses a time when "I had lost confidence in my own work and was losing hope" (p. 322). I will summarize my point by asking the question Kaslow (1985) poses: "Is this then a failure or the beginning journey and quest in which the final destination and results may remain unknown to the therapist?" (p. 298).

Failure—or even disappointment—is a relative phenomenon. It is important that we keep this in mind. It is also important that we remind ourselves that we can learn from our disappointments, and that we can never be certain what clients take with them from the therapy, no matter how optimal or murky the circumstances of their leaving. Above all, the way we talk to ourselves about these disappointments is important, as is what we learn from them, and I believe I have learned from each one. In this way, we can grow far more than simply doing therapy paint-by-numbers style will ever allow.

# References

Ahrons, C., & Rodgers, R. (1987). *Divorced families: A multidisciplinary developmental view.* New York: Norton.

Beavers, W. (1985). Systems therapy of a family presenting with a schizophrenic member. In S. Coleman (Ed.), *Failures in family therapy* (pp. 190-207). New York: Guilford.

Kaslow, F. (1985). Circumlocution and nonresolution. In S. Coleman (Ed.), *Failures in family therapy* (pp. 284-299). New York: Guilford.

Keith, D., & Whitaker, C. (1985). Failure: Our bold companion. In S. Coleman (Ed.), *Failures in family therapy* (pp. 8-23). New York: Guilford.

Kramer, C. (1979, September). *Introduction to family systems therapy.* Lecture presented at The Center for Family Studies/The Family Institute of Chicago, Chicago.

Kramer, C. (1980). *Becoming a family therapist: Developing an integrated approach to working with families.* New York: Human Sciences Press.

L'Abate, L., & Baggett, M. (1985). A failure to keep the father in family therapy. In S. Coleman (Ed.), *Failures in family therapy* (pp. 222-240). New York: Guilford.

Liddle, H. (1985). Five factors of failure in structural-strategic family therapy: A contextual construction. In S. Coleman (Ed.), *Failures in family therapy* (pp. 152-189). New York: Guilford.

Pierce, M. (1990). *Countertransference and loss of self: Barriers to therapeutic intimacy.* Seminar for The Family Institute Alumni Conference, Evanston, IL.

Tomm, K. (1985). Struggling with the threat of suicide. In S. Coleman (Ed.), *Failures in family therapy* (pp. 300-329). New York: Guilford.

Yalom, I. (1985). *The theory and practice of group psychotherapy.* New York: Basic Books.

# Shapers in a Social Revolution—or Reactors to It

Why is it so hard to inspire and induce men to change? Ask yourself that question, and I am sure that you will come up with many answers. Some are founded in stereotypes. Some are based on your own personal experiences with men. Still others are based on your satisfactory or not so satisfactory clinical experiences with them. And some detractors simply think it impossible to get men to change.

Yet, how many of us have sat quietly for a minute to take stock of the magnitude of what we as a clinical community and the women in men's lives are asking them to do? We are calling on them not merely to learn new skills and acquire affective competencies. Rather, we are enjoining them to change their entire worldview. And most of us would admit that this is a very tall order indeed!

Although many women made this change in worldview, starting nearly 3 decades ago, there was much more support among each other for doing so. Men are changing for many reasons. Some in reaction; some out of their own felt need. But by contrast, generally women changed because they saw the need to change, not because someone or some factors out of their control were demanding it.

Perhaps keeping this difference in mind will allow us to be more empathic, or at least sympathetic, with our male clients, and could save some wear and tear on us as well. Our compassionate understanding will maximize the chances of men's being willing to create the adjustments required to learn qualitatively different ways of being. This will allow the development of a wholly new set of skills to permit them to undergo basic changes in themselves, in their relationships, and in their values on such charged issues as work, sex, parenting, and friendship.

## Our Shared Woundedness

There can be no question that historically many men have humiliated and demeaned women. But not all men are villains. We as therapists may be more alerted to how women have suffered from the constriction of gender roles, but men have suffered, too. According to Keen (1991):

> When the powerful begin to feel their impotence, when the masters begin to feel their captivity, we have reached a point where we are finally becoming conscious that the social system we have all conspired to create victimizes us all. Men have begun to feel their unique form of the pain of victimization that has led to other liberation movements among women and minorities. (pp. 206-207)

Men who realize the ways that they, too, have been victims are going on now to discover their full potential, which has been hampered by their socialization.

It is important to underscore that dehumanizing ways of being have left their scars on both women and men. Welwood (1990) speaks to our shared woundedness:

> Centuries of imbalance between the masculine and feminine ways of being have left a deep wound in the human psyche. No one can escape the effects of this wound—which pervades both our inner and our outer lives. . . . Until human consciousness can transform the ancient antagonism between masculine and feminine into a creative alliance, we will remain fragmented and at war with our-

selves, as individuals, as couples, as societies, and as a race. Our personal struggles to develop a deeper level of intimacy are a primary vehicle for this critical move forward that humanity needs to make. As we begin to move in this direction, the man/woman relationship takes on a larger purpose, beyond just survival or security. It becomes an instrument for the evolution of human consciousness. When we look at our present difficulties with relationships in this light, they no longer seem so bewildering or overwhelming. (p. 3)

These thoughts activate several pivotal questions. How can women and men overcome the strife that has beleaguered us for thousands of years and go on to forge a new alliance? How can we learn to draw on who we uniquely are and what each sex has to give the other? What is the role of the therapist in mining these largely untapped resources that would contribute not only to increasing the quality of life of individual men and women but also to our society as a whole?

## Crisis in the Masculine Identity

In the late 20th century, we face a crisis of major proportions in the masculine identity. For men, the options for behaving in less traditional ways have vastly increased. But many still experience being caught. The price of breaking society's prescribed roles for men is still great. And yet, the cost of not moving beyond those strictures also can be exorbitant for men. The current generation of men lives at a unique moment in history that offers unprecedented challenges and opportunities. According to Kimbrell (1991):

Though often still trapped by economic coercion and psychological co-option [sic], we are beginning to see that there is a profound choice ahead. Will we choose to remain subservient tools of social and environmental destruction or to fight for rediscovery of the male as full partner and participant in family, community, and the earth? Will we remain mesmerized by the male mystique, or will we reclaim the meaning of our masculinity? (p. 74)

It is at this unique juncture that we as therapists have a singular opportunity either to midwife significant, people-affirming changes or to further the polarization between the sexes. It is time that men stopped accepting the blame for everything that is wrong in the world. And it is time that women stopped implying or saying that they should. This is no way to begin the dialogue that is required to establish a partnership between women and men to make the world a better place for everyone. I agree wholeheartedly with Welwood (1990) when he suggests what I consider an antidote to the "deficit model of manhood" (Doherty, 1991, p. 29):

> When a man can celebrate his maleness, he feels more at home in himself in a relationship. Most women will find such a man completely attractive. The more she celebrates the essential female in herself, the more powerful and attractive she becomes as well. . . . When the sexes honor their different qualities of spirit, instead of trying to convert each other to their own style as the "right way to be," their relationship develops greater power and depth. (p. 158)

The next obvious question the reader ought to be asking herself is what is the role of the therapist in teaching men and women how to do what all the authors quoted in this chapter describe?

## The Role of the Female Therapist

The need for men to change is clear, even among many men. How those changes can come about and whether female therapists can play a significant role in facilitating those changes are less clear. Some psychoanalysts and feminist therapists may have difficulty in accepting this premise. Traditionally, guiding change with men has been assumed to be the sole province of male therapists, particularly among the psychoanalytic community. It has been considered a given that although women can be treated just as effectively by either sex, only men can treat men.

With the advent of the feminist critique, gender sensitivity was assumed to be synonymous with understanding a woman's viewpoint, thereby excluding men either by default or design. It seems sometimes that the feminist critique of psychotherapy tilts in the direction of assuming that women's ways are somehow better, as if women truly can be empowered by now holding power over men.

The perspective of some feminist therapists is that men should do their own psychological work; wives and women should not have to help men along. They say that doing so perpetuates women's roles as caretakers in relationships. Likewise, the perspective of some males in the men's movement is that only men can work effectively with each other, that only they truly can understand the male experience and that what men need is "male mothers" (Bly, 1989). In the best of all worlds, perhaps both of these current voices are true. However, the field of psychology is experiencing a trend that is being labeled "feminization," with the number of male psychologists dropping even as the number of female psychologists is increasing. According to Julie Kohut, director of the American Psychological Association's Office of Demographic, Employment and Educational Research, "The end result is that about two-thirds of psychology students at all levels are women" (quoted in Adler, 1991, p. 12). If what is happening in the field of psychology is any indication of a trend across the board for all types of psychotherapists, more and more counseling services are being provided by women. Therefore, to polarize into positions that assume that clients should be treated only by same-sex therapists is shortsighted and misses an opportunity.

Further, a trend in the social order makes effort in this direction urgent. Increasingly, men are becoming aware of the need for change. There is a growing emphasis on changing institutions. Therapists, who first and foremost are change agents, are in an unparalleled position to help. Imagine the impact we could have, for instance, in decreasing the incidence of divorce or abuse or in humanizing corporations and institutions. To squander this opportunity is to be less effective than our clients and our society as a whole need us to be. On the one hand, if we miss this crossing, one can predict an increase in the polarization that seems to be fostering a new kind of self-righteous sexism. On the other hand, if we can capitalize on this chance, we can help deliberately to bridge the gender gap.

## The Opportunity Provided When Women Treat Men

As has been reiterated throughout this book, there are unique and unrepeatable opportunities in the therapy process when women treat men. Perhaps the most noteworthy element is that we can be their training wheels for better relationships. That is, by developing a genuine and equitable relationship with us, they can begin to learn the requisite skills to do the same in their personal and professional lives. Our offices can become laboratories that are safe places to practice these skills. Further, there are some unique aspects to this cross-gender treatment that allow us to capitalize on our socialization as women. In addition, there are some specific transference aspects to which both therapist and client have access when women treat men.

However, there is a significant hazard of which we as female therapists must be aware. Our socialization as women could combine with an attitude of political correctness about the "right" way for people, and men in particular, to think and to behave. And in fact, in some quarters in our field, a rigidity in the thinking of some feminists is stifling our field (Lipchik, 1991) and threatens to squelch men and strain relationships as well (Erickson, 1992). The female therapist who wishes to treat males effectively must be on the lookout for this tendency. As Meth and Pasick (1990) state, "Women must let men find their way, which requires accepting that it will be based on a masculine model, not a feminine one. Therapists, too, must operate from this perspective" (p. 206).

## Therapist as Guide

In ancient times, the shaman was the guide and companion on individuals' journeys into themselves. According to Moore and Gillette (1990), he was

> the healer, the one who restored life, who found lost souls, and who discovered the hidden causes of misfortune. He was the one who restored wholeness and fullness of being to both individuals and communities. . . . The shaman as his fullest human vessel, aims at fullness of being for all things, through compassionate application of knowledge and technology. (p. 110)

Just as in ancient times, our role today is to help people on their inward journey. It also is to be with them on their journey, as far as that is possible. What that requires of us is what Moore and Gillette (1990) call using our role as shaman or magician properly: "We will be adding to our professional and personal lives through a dimension of clear-sightedness, of deep understanding and reflection about ourselves and others, and technical skill in our outer work and in our inner handling of psychological forces" (p. 118).

This person, then, is the archetype of thoughtfulness and reflection that our clients need of us as therapists.

## A Final Word

Do we want to be shapers of this social revolution that inevitably is happening around us? Or are we mere reactors to it? As shapers, the point is not only to dwell on our gender differences, but also to search for confluences in men's and women's experiences.

Our clients and our society need us to use our skills as therapists/shamans to bridge the gender gap, rather than to perpetuate it.

## References

Adler, T. (1991). Will feminization spell decline for field? *APA Monitor, 22*(10), 12.

Bly, R. (1989). *A gathering of men: With Bill Moyers and Robert Bly* [video]. New York: Mystic Fire Video.

Doherty, W. (1991). Beyond reactivity and the deficit model of manhood: A commentary on articles by Napier, Pittman, and Gottman. *Journal of Marital and Family Therapy, 17*(1), 29-32.

Erickson, B. (1992). Feminist fundamentalism: Reactions to Avis, Kaufman and Bograd. *Journal of Marital and Family Therapy,*

Keen, S. (1991). *Fire in the belly: On being a man.* New York: Bantam.

Kimbrell, A. (1991, May/June). A time for men to pull together: A manifesto for the new politics of masculinity. *Utne Reader,* pp. 66-74.

Lipchik, E. (1991). Spouse abuse: Challenging the party line. *Family Therapy Networker, 15,* 59-63.

Meth, R., & Pasick, R. (1990). *Men in therapy: The challenge of change.* New York: Guilford.

Moore, R., & Gillette, D. (1990). *King, warrior, magician, lover: Rediscovering the archetypes of the mature masculine.* San Francisco: HarperSan Francisco.

Welwood, J. (1990). *Journey of the heart: Intimate relationship and the path of love.* New York: HarperPerennial.

# Appendix A:
# Guidelines for Clients in
# Reclaiming the Ability to Feel

A colleague once told me that there are 465 words for feelings in the English language. Never having checked a dictionary to verify this, I am not sure of the accuracy of that number, but I do know that for most people, there are only two such words at their disposal: good and bad. And yet, those two words technically are not even feelings; they are composites that sum up a global experience of a vague and usually unknown sense. And if people cannot identify the feeling they are currently having, obviously, they cannot share it.

Everyone is born with the capacity to feel. For many people, this capability becomes blocked along the way, due to circumstances that are as varied as people themselves. This ability to feel, like muscular dexterity, becomes atrophied if not used. A good analogy is that if your arm were in a cast for 6 months and then the cast were removed, your arm would feel lifeless and useless until you regained your previous level of muscular strength and agility. So it is with "feeling muscles" that go unused for years. It takes practice to recover the use of them.

The relearning process can be slow, tedious, and often painful. However, to have the material to transact at perhaps the most basic and bonding level in a relationship—the emotional level—attention must be paid to reclaiming and relearning how to use feelings. These pages will provide you with a description of the basic skills and processes involved in recovering the ability to feel.

## Guidelines for Relearning How to Feel

1. In order to know *what* you are feeling, you need to learn to identify *that* you are feeling. The best way to teach yourself that you are feeling is to learn how to read the physiological cues that your body gives you. Almost always, there is a physiological marker or body sensation that indicates that you are feeling something. For example, you may be aware of a pit or butterflies in your stomach, a tightening across your forehead, sweaty palms, and so on. Likewise, therapists often can detect when you are feeling by noting a change in such visible signs as a tightening or a lengthening in your facial muscles, a change in your eyes, a clenched fist, a raised or lowered voice. If you are unaware that you are feeling and draw a blank every time your therapist asks you about your emotions, signals such as these will be your first clues that you are experiencing a feeling to which you need to pay attention.

2. Now that you know that you are feeling, your next task is to figure out what the emotion is. Through the use of a feeling list, such as the one that follows in Appendix B, you can begin to decipher *what* you are feeling. Even though using this list is awkward at first, I encourage you to handle it like a crib sheet that you used for open-book tests in school. When your therapist asks what you are feeling or when you spot a physiological marker that tells you that you have an emotional reaction, turn to that sheet. The five words in boldface type at the top of the page are general category headings of common feelings. Underneath those headings are synonyms for those words, each with a different shade of meaning, that will help you name your feeling more precisely. For example, under the category of "happy," the words "exuberant" and "glad" have very different connotations or shades of meaning, even though in a general sense they both mean "happy." This exercise will seem cumbersome at first, but eventually you will

begin more and more precisely to label and articulate what you are feeling. The chief benefits of learning this skill are that you will begin to feel more understood by others while at the same time feeling more clear about yourself and your own internal experience.

3. It should be noted that not all feelings have to be shared with all people. Part of your task is to decipher with whom you want to share which feelings and what feelings you want and need to keep to yourself. For example, telling your boss that you think her most recent decision was stupid would probably be considered honesty to the point of foolishness. Remember, just because you have feelings, this does not give you the right to recklessly inflict them on everyone else. But even if you choose, for whatever reason, not to share your responses with anyone else, it is imperative that you at least let yourself in on them. This keeps you honest and clean with yourself. When you don't face yourself, you have a very difficult time looking in the mirror.

4. Once you have figured out that you are feeling and know what you feel, your job is to learn to share that feeling in a way that invites intimacy and connection with the person with whom you are attempting to share. If you care about the person with whom you want to share your feelings, it is very important that you learn to disclose your responses in as inviting a way as possible. For example, saying to a best friend, spouse, or lover, "I would love it if you called me when you are going to be late. It would make me feel very appreciated and understood. And then, I won't worry that you're hurt." This approach probably will draw the two of you closer. Contrast that with, "You never call me when you are going to be late. You are inconsiderate and thoughtless, and never think about anyone but yourself." Both contain the same basic content: You would like to be notified if the person is going to be late. But the messages are as different as night and day. Remember, part of what makes it hard for people to hear us is the way that we express it.

5. Next, learn how to tell who will be receptive to your feelings and who likely will not. For a host of reasons, most of them having to do with their own intimacy fears and with the way they were brought up, many people dislike to share feelings or to have others disclose theirs. It makes them feel too vulnerable. So that you do not repeatedly get yourself and your feelings rejected, learn to tell who is open to hearing your

feelings and who likely is not. There are several ways to learn to tell. One is to try taking a small risk, and see what the response is. For example, it is a small risk to say that you would prefer not to go to a movie when you know the other person would; it is a gargantuan risk to share that you have been sexually harassed or abused. Taking smaller risks and working up to bigger risks will help trust to grow while people gradually increase their comfort level with each other.

6. Learn how to deal with your feelings appropriately and non-defensively, even in the face of an unreceptive response. Of course, this is easier said than done; it hurts to feel rejected. It is important to keep in mind three kinds of unreceptive responses. The first is the defensive response that is an off-the-top-of-the-head reaction to a disclosure that likely will be softened when the person has some time to think about your revelation. This is a fairly normal response, even among closest intimates, to hearing something that is threatening or hurtful. Try to give that person some room to mull over your comments without getting too defensive yourself. The second kind of unreceptive response is one in which you and your emotions are invalidated. Here, the hearer implies or directly says that you shouldn't feel a certain way. But the trouble is, you do, and being told you shouldn't only compounds the pain and isolation that you experience. The third kind of unreceptive response is one in which the other person lets you know, directly or indirectly, that he or she does not care to have you sharing this—or probably any other—personal material. Although you most certainly will be disappointed at the unempathic comeback, in the end, you can be grateful that you found out that this particular person is not someone who will be trustworthy for you. Then you will not be frustrated, repeatedly hurt, and waste your energy trying to get something from and with a person who is not interested or capable, for whatever reason.

7. Remember, when you have had a lifetime of being trained away from your emotions, they are not going to come back overnight. Be patient with yourself. If it took you 20, 30, 40, 50, or 60 years for your feelings to get deadened, they are not going to come back just because you—or your therapist—want them to. It takes hard work and a commitment to feel, so that you can feel better. But it will be worth it in the end. So don't give up.

# Appendix B:
## List of Feeling Words

| **HAPPY** | | **SAD** | |
|---|---|---|---|
| Excited | Assured | Devastated | Despised |
| Elated | Determined | Hopeless | Disappointed |
| Exuberant | Grateful | Sorrowful | Upset |
| Ecstatic | Appreciated | Depressed | Inadequate |
| Terrific | Confident | Wounded | Dismal |
| Jubilant | Respected | Drained | Unappreciated |
| Energized | Admired | Defeated | Discouraged |
| Enthusiastic | Delighted | Exhausted | Ashamed |
| Loved | Alive | Helpless | Distressed |
| Thrilled | Fulfilled | Crushed | Distant |
| Marvelous | Tranquill | Worthless | Disillusioned |
| Justified | Content | Uncared for | Lonely |
| Resolved | Relaxed | Dejected | Neglected |
| Valued | Glad | Rejected | Isolated |
| Gratified | Satisfied | Humbled | Alienated |
| Encouraged | Peaceful | Empty | Regretful |
| Optimistic | Hopeful | Miserable | Islanded |
| Joyful | Fortunate | Distraught | Resigned |
| Proud | Pleased | Deserted | Drained |
| Cheerful | Flattered | Grievous | Slighted |
| | | Demoralized | Degraded |
| | | Condemned | Deprived |
| | | Terrible | Disturbed |
| | | Unwanted | Wasted |
| | | Unloved | Abandoned |
| | | Mournful | Lost |
| | | Pitiful | Disenchanted |
| | | Discarded | Deflated |
| | | Disgraced | Apathetic |
| | | Disheartened | |

## ANGRY

| | |
|---|---|
| Strangled | Disgusted |
| Furious | Smothered |
| Seething | Frustrated |
| Enraged | Stifled |
| Hostile | Offended |
| Vengeful | Displeased |
| Incensed | Controlled |
| Abused | Peeved |
| Hateful | Annoyed |
| Humiliated | Agitated |
| Sabotaged | Irritated |
| Betrayed | Exasperated |
| Repulsed | Harrassed |
| Rebellious | Anguished |
| Pissed off | Deceived |
| Outraged | Aggravated |
| Exploited | Perturbed |
| Throttled | Provoked |
| Mad | Dominated |
| Spiteful | Coerced |
| Patronized | Cheated |
| Vindictive | Uptight |
| Used | Dismayed |
| Repulsed | Tolerant |
| Ridiculed | Displeased |
| Resentfu | |

## SCARED

Fearful
Panicky
Afraid
Shocked
Overwhelmed
Intimidated
Desperate
Frantic
Terrified
Vulnerable
Horrified
Petrified
Appalled
Full of dread
Tormented
Tense
Uneasy
Defensive
Insecure
Skeptical
Apprehensive
Suspicious
Alarmed
Shaken
Swamped
Startled
Guarded
Stunned
Awed
Reluctant
Anxious
Impatient
Shy
Nervous
Unsure
Timid
Concerned
Perplexed
Doubtful

## CONFUSED

Bewildered
Trapped
Immobilized
Directionless
Stagnant
Flustered
Baffled
Constricted
Troubled
Ambivalent
Awkward
Puzzled
Disorganized
Foggy
Perplexed
Hesitant
Misunderstood
Doubtful
Bothered
Undecided
Uncomfortable
Uncertain
Surprised
Unsettled
Unloved
Unsure
Distracted

# Appendix C

The Feelings Poster. © 1989, Creative Therapy Associates, Inc., Cincinnati, Ohio. Reprinted with permission.

# Appendix D:
# Clinical Presentations That May
# Indicate Long-Term Treatment

Six factors need to be noted regarding this list:

1. Some, most, or all of these may be present.
2. When clients present with just a few of these symptoms, short-term treatment may suffice.
3. Many symptoms also indicate the likelihood of the presence of a developmental arrest to one degree or another.
4. Although many people commonly report some of these feelings in times of situational stress, candidates for long-term treatment report these states as a way of life.
5. Don't be fooled by the absence of severe pathology such as multiple personality disorder. Many of these symptoms (i.e., feelings of depersonalization) are apparent in clients with less severe diagnoses.
6. Some clinicians, agencies, and insurers only allow short-term therapy or see short-term work as preferable. Thus, they may see many of these same presentations as justifications for short-term treatment, stating that the depth and duration of many of these problems makes

them intractable. Clearly, intractability seldom has been my experience, and it does not have to be yours, if you understand the art and the process of long-term treatment.

### Age-Inappropriate Functioning

1. Manifests inability to establish and maintain intimate relationships.
2. Persistently wishes to remain a child or acts like a perpetually old person who has been robbed of a childhood.
3. Professionally underfunctions or is underutilized.
4. If a parent, assumes the role of the child while expecting the child(ren) to do the parenting of both.

### Confounding Contextual Factors

1. Unresolved problematic family of origin issues.
2. Childhood trauma (early death of parent, divorce, abuse, witnessing abuse of family member(s), etc.).
3. Sense of never belonging or not feeling wanted from childhood that carried over into adulthood.
4. Cut off from family of origin.
5. Brought himself or herself up, without the nurturing involvement of parents.
6. Received messages repeatedly that he or she was/is incompetent.
7. Moved frequently throughout his or her life, leading to a sense of rootlessness and fragile connections.

### Cognitive Underfunctioning

1. Manifests little cognitive complexity.
2. Evidences black-and-white thinking.
3. Displays intolerance for diversity, differing opinions, or alternative life-styles.
4. Has a personality style of avoidance of challenges, so that cognitive dissonance can be evaded.
5. Has few tools for or engages in little or no introspection.
6. Seeks out and settles for easy answers and quick fixes for highly complex situations.
7. Displays little tolerance for and great fear of ambiguity.
8. Splits the world into camps of good and evil, black and white (e.g., sexuality, gender, races, categories of people, etc.).

9. Has little ability to generate alternatives or interest in doing so; easily feels and gets stuck.
10. Overemphasizes rationality and emotional self-control.
11. Is the classic underachiever (either undersells, underestimates, or devalues own abilities).
12. Is the classic overachiever who succeeds because he or she is terrified of failure.

## Problematic Affective Markers

1. Feels predominant emotional states of confusion and disorientation.
2. Experiences incompetence about feelings (either rigidly shuts them out, or typically is overwhelmed by them).
3. Is fearful, intolerant, and avoidant of facing existential questions because of the painful emotions that both the questions and the resulting cognitive dissonance generate.
4. Trusts inappropriately (either too much or too little).
5. Is afraid of and avoids intimacy.
6. Is afraid of dependent feelings and denies needing help or the therapist.
7. Feels isolated, different, weird.
8. Fears change and therefore resists growth, even at the cost of frustration and stagnation.
9. Complains of and manifests low self-esteem.
10. Displays extreme emotional constriction.
11. Complains of depersonalization or dehumanization.
12. Reports a profound and pervasive sense of identity confusion and the attendant lack of directionality.

## Ineffective Functioning in Relationships

1. Reports never having had a meaningful relationship with anyone, and is stumped about how either to have one or to build one.
2. Reports not knowing how to make or have friends.
3. Is ineffective at getting needs met (either is passive and self-effacing, putting others' needs above own, or is aggressive and narcissistic, with the kind of egocentrism that a child displays).
4. Exhibits a poor sense of interpersonal boundaries (either too rigid or too penetrable).
5. Evidences poor problem-solving skills (either acts impulsively or is chronically indecisive).

6. Is overprotective of children out of own needs, not the children's.

7. Is unable appropriately to control or discipline children (either too harsh or too permissive).

8. Fears losing control either of self or situations.

9. Believes he or she needs to control every aspect of life.

10. Feels powerless and acts on that (either by deferring all power or by imposing his or her own will on others).

11. Engages in excessive triangulation rather than dealing directly with people and problems.

## General Dissatisfaction With Life

1. Manifests psychosomatic symptoms to change the subject from perplexing emotions.

2. Reports feeling directionless.

3. Feels cut off from life.

4. Reports a generalized sense of ennui or disappointment with life.

5. Evidences either a joylessness or inability to play, or is hyperplayful as a means of avoiding growing up and facing difficult issues or questions.

6. Anticipates nothing bright in the future.

7. Is either obsessional and indecisive or is impulsive and reckless in managing his or her life.

8. Experiences life cynically and believes it is inevitably a disappointment.

9. Expresses feeling like a failure or that his or her life is meaningless, despite outside appearances of having an ideal or successful life.

10. Has difficulty allowing self to be happy.

11. Allows self to stagnate in relationships, work.

# Author Index

461

# Subject Index

# About the Author

**Beth M. Erickson, Ph.D.,** founded and is Clinical Director of Family Resources Institute, a private marriage and family therapy practice in suburban Minneapolis, Minnesota. She completed her Ph.D. at the University of Minnesota where she researched adult psychological development. Then she concluded 2 years' postdoctoral training in marriage and family therapy at The Family Institute of Chicago, part of Northwestern University. Currently, she holds adjunct faculty positions at the Minnesota School of Professional Psychology and at St. Mary's College Graduate Center, both in Minneapolis. She holds memberships in the American Family Therapy Academy, American Association for Marriage and Family Therapy, American Psychological Association, American Society of Clinical Hypnosis, and American Counseling Association. She is on the Editorial Board of the *Journal of Family Psychotherapy* and is a reviewer for the *Journal of Marital and Family Therapy*. Over the past 20 years, she has lectured extensively to various professional audiences nationally and internationally. She has a stepson and lives in suburban Minneapolis with her husband and three cats.